Bound in Wedlock

Bound in Wedlock

*Slave and Free Black Marriage
in the Nineteenth Century*

TERA W. HUNTER

THE BELKNAP PRESS OF HARVARD UNIVERSITY PRESS

Cambridge, Massachusetts, and London, England

First Harvard University Press paperback edition, 2019

First printing

Library of Congress Cataloging-in-Publication Data

Names: Hunter, Tera W., author.

Title: Bound in wedlock : slave and free Black marriage in the nineteenth century /
Tera W. Hunter.

Description: Cambridge, Massachusetts : The Belknap Press of Harvard
University Press, 2017. | Includes bibliographical references and index.

Identifiers: LCCN 2016054878 | ISBN 9780674045712 (cloth : alk. paper) |
ISBN 9780674237452 (pbk.)

Subjects: LCSH: African Americans—Marriage customs and rites—19th century. |
African Americans—Social life and customs—19th century. | Slaves—United States—
Social conditions—19th century. | Slaves—United States—Social life and
customs—19th century. | Free African Americans—Social life and customs—
19th century. | Marriage—United States—History—19th century.

Classification: LCC E185.86 .H86 2017 | DDC 390/.25097309034—dc23

LC record available at https://lccn.loc.gov/2016054878

To the next generation

Anaya
Alaric III
Armand II
Avery

Contents

Bound in Wedlock

Introduction

The Marriage Certificate

The marriage certificate of Ellen Morrison and Moses Hunter has both personal and historical significance (see Fig. I.1). Moses and Ellen are my paternal great-great-grandparents. I can trace my father's clan to Virginia, the founding place of slavery in the American colonies, as far back as a year before American independence (see Fig. I.2). Ellen Morrison Hunter was a midwife and Moses Hunter was a farmer. Most of their ancestors did not have the same opportunity they did to choose their own mates and marriage partners. Moses was born free in 1835 in South Carolina, though he would become a slave by the time of the Civil War. His mother, Patsy Hunter, was born a slave in South Carolina in 1820 but was freed in childhood. Moses's father, James Hunter, born in 1804, was a white man related to the Alexander Hunter family that would eventually enslave Moses. Patsy's mother was Sally Hunter, born in Africa in 1790, and her father was Edward Garrett III, a slave-owner born in 1787. Sally had lived in Jamaica as a slave before being sent to South Carolina. Dublin Hunter, a black mechanic who had bought his freedom some years before, purchased Sally and at least two of her children, including Patsy, by 1830. Dublin and Sally began a new family together as free people, but despite this achievement she witnessed her daughter Patsy, her grandson Moses, and other grandchildren sink back into servitude by 1850. Freedom for black people was generally precarious. The privileged few who were born free or manumitted in the antebellum era were not always able to sustain their status.

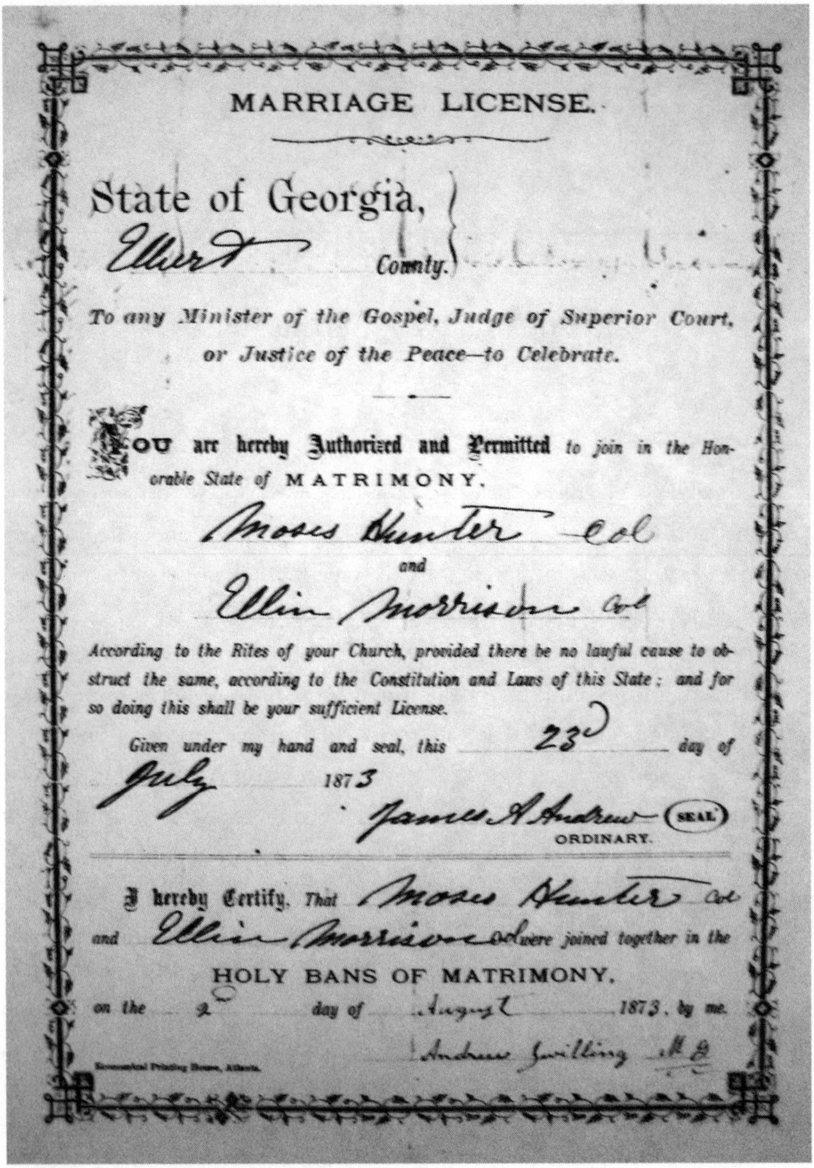

MARRIAGE LICENSE.

State of Georgia,
Elbert County.

To any Minister of the Gospel, Judge of Superior Court, or Justice of the Peace—to Celebrate.

YOU are hereby Authorized and Permitted *to join in the Honorable State of* MATRIMONY.

Moses Hunter col

and

Ellin Morrison col

According to the Rites of your Church, provided there be no lawful cause to obstruct the same, according to the Constitution and Laws of this State; and for so doing this shall be your sufficient License.

Given under my hand and seal, this 23d *day of* July 1873

James A Andrew (SEAL)
ORDINARY.

I hereby Certify, *That* Moses Hunter col *and* Ellin Morrison col *were joined together in the*

HOLY BANS OF MATRIMONY,

on the 2d *day of* August 1873, *by me.*

Andrew Swilling M G

Economical Printing House, Atlanta.

Fig. I.1 Marriage certificate of Ellen Morrison and Moses Hunter.

Peter Adams *(slave-owner)*

Melinda Morrison *(great-great-great-great-great-grandmother)*

Edward Garrett, III *(slave-owner)*

Sally Hunter* *(great-great-great-great-grandmother)*

Thomas Wheeles *(slave-owner)*

Sarah Morrison *(great-great-great-great-grandmother)*

James Hunter *(white)*

Patsy Hunter *(great-great-great-grandmother)*

John Gordon McCurry *(slave-owner)*

Louisa Morrison *(great-great-great-grandmother)*

Moses Hunter *(great-great-grandfather)*

Ellen Morrison Hunter *(great-great-grandmother)*

Elijah Hunter *(great-grandfather)*

Ella Blackwell Hunter *(great-grandmother)*

James Hunter *(grandfather)*

Anna Sadler Hunter *(grandmother)*

Willie James Hunter *(father)*

Inell Harper Hunter *(mother)*

Tera Hunter *(author)*

* *Sally Hunter married Dublin Hunter, who freed her and two of her children.*

Fig. I.2   Hunter family ancestry.

Ellen was born a slave in 1850 in Elberton, Georgia, where she met and married Moses. The two kin groups of the couple moved in and out of clusters along the edges of state borders in Abbeville and Laurens County, South Carolina, and Elbert County, Georgia. Ellen was the daughter of Louisa Morrison, born in Elberton in 1829, and John Gordon McCurry, a slaveowner born in 1821, also in Elberton. Ellen's maternal grandmother was Sarah Morrison, born in 1812 in South Carolina, and her grandfather was Thomas Wheeles, a slave-owner born in 1790. Sarah's mother was Melinda Morrison, born in Henry County, Virginia, in 1775, and her father was the slave-owner Peter Adams, born in 1762 in the same place.

This family tree puts in stark relief the preponderance of interracial pairings among my earliest known direct ascendants. It exposes the consequences of the sexual economy of slavery in my bloodline. Black women gave birth to the capital that helped forge the nation's wealth, typically under the duress of coerced sex with the very men who sired biracial progeny and turned them into commodities. They also gave birth to children by enslaved black men whom neither mother nor father possessed according to law and white society, and whom their enslavers literally capitalized. Their families constituted people of mixed racial ancestry, differing parentage, and mixed status. The character and extent of any of those relations can probably never be known. But Ellen and Moses shattered at least a century of mostly obligatory interracial pairings. Ellen was the first woman in my direct paternal line to give birth to children by a black man and marry him. They were the first intraracial couple in the family who we can say with certainty were legally married. Compared with the far more sensationalized legends of interracial sex that rivet historical narratives and popular culture, such as the relationship between Thomas Jefferson and Sally Hemings, intraracial relationships may seem more sanguine.[1] And yet they had their own complications as partners of subordinate status struggled to define and express the terms and conditions of a relationship over which they had no control.

Moses and Ellen had eleven children; the first was born in 1866, when Ellen was sixteen, and the last was born around 1887, when she was thirty-seven. We know that three children did not survive. The birth of their first child after the Civil War may have marked the start of their marriage. But the point at which marital relations began is not so easily discerned. The mar-

riage certificate identifies Ellen's last name as Morrison, but the census identified it three years earlier as Hunter. The latter could have been the name
she used and was known by in the community, or it could have been assumed
by the census-taker. The certificate indicates that the marriage was not legally formalized until 1873. Ellen may not have been Moses's first wife, given
their fifteen-year age difference, or perhaps being cast into slavery as a young
man made it difficult for Moses to form a family before meeting Ellen. Ellen
died in 1938 at age eighty-six. Moses died some time toward the end of the
nineteenth century before his grandson, my grandfather James, was born.
Relatives today remember Ellen as the midwife who assisted the birth of family
members still living. Although we think of slavery as part of the distant past,
memories of the enslaved remain alive today.[2]

Ellen and Moses's marriage certificate is typical of many such documents
issued during Reconstruction, when slaves secured their freedom, citizenship, and a host of rights including the right to marry. Their story pieced together here encapsulates many aspects of African-American marital love and
struggles in the nineteenth century. Although the process of regularizing
slave marriages began during the Civil War, tens of thousands of marriage
certificates were drawn up in a short period of time soon after. They symbol-
ized new beginnings as African Americans reconstructed their families, often
over long distances and in the face of continuing opposition from former
slave-owners. Most states passed laws between 1865 and 1866 recognizing
prewar slave marriages and legitimizing the offspring that resulted from them.
Congress passed the Civil Rights Act of 1866, which extended the right to
make contracts, including the right to marry, to all former slaves. Marriage
thus became a guaranteed civil right for African Americans for the first time in
law, though it was not easily obtainable in practice.

The Freedmen's Bureau led the federal initiative to validate black marriages,
aided by army chaplains, civil clergy, and missionary organizations. Rufus
Saxton, the assistant commissioner for South Carolina, with jurisdiction over
Florida and Georgia, sent out a set of marriage rules in August 1865 to guide
newly freed slaves. Mansfield French, a New York minister, wrote an elaborate list of rules to inform ex-slaves about the duties and obligations of married couples and to instruct them on how to gain official sanction for their
relationships. Moses and Ellen Hunter lived in Georgia and were covered by

these overlapping regulations. Despite the rules and the new laws, however, many couples in these states did not have the opportunity to formally register their relationships until later given the dire postwar conditions. Many of those who were able to marry at the time did so in local courts and churches without the help of the Freedmen's Bureau. Ellen and Moses were members of Vance Creek Baptist Church, and their newly appointed black minister married them.[3]

Biblical views of marriage, whose origins lie in the book of Genesis, have had a strong imprint on American ideals of marriage. "To have and to hold, in sickness and in health . . . till death do you part": these words have been uttered by brides and grooms privileged to enjoy Christian marriage rites since the Middle Ages. African Americans held in bondage were forced to revise the standard wedding vows to make them befit the absence of standing in civil law. As one white minister officiating at a slave ceremony frankly reminded the couple, their marriage was binding only "until death or distance do you part." A black preacher named the culprit of this caprice more bluntly: "Till death or buckra part you"—meaning the white man.[4] They were forced to reconfigure the idea that two flesh would become the proverbial one, that man and woman, like Adam and Eve, would merge in all respects. One scholar refers to this union in marriage as "an economy of scarcity," in which two distinct and opposing individuals battle for mastery within an entity that has room enough only for one arbiter—that one always being the male. If this was the case for free people, "the economy of scarcity" must shrink to nonexistence for the enslaved.[5] If there is room in a relationship for only one fully endowed person, that person was neither husband nor wife but master. Could that be a marriage at all?

As chattel, slaves were objects, not subjects. Marriage for them was not an inviolable union between two people but an institution defined and controlled by the superior relationship of master to slave. The interventions of what I call the "third flesh" did not make for a legitimate union that could be easily reconciled in the growing body of law or in Christian traditions derivative of Western Europe. These conundrums and their consequences during the nineteenth century can best be explored through relationships involving slaves, free blacks, and ex-slaves following the Civil War. The focus is the

South, given its centrality to black life in this period, but the significance of such relationships is national, owing to the expansive scope of slavery.

In this book, I define marriage as it was understood during and after slavery to encompass committed conjugal relationships, whether legal or not, monogamous, bigamous, polygamous, or serial. Black heterosexual intimacy comprised a wide range of domestic arrangements out of necessity, not all of which were described as marriage. African Americans did maintain relationships that they called marriage, however, despite the lack of support that safely scaffolded Euro-American relationships as sacrosanct. Much was at stake beyond intimacy in slaves' marital relations: marriage (and its denial) inevitably invoke questions of public status, state recognition, the exercise of personal freedom, and the enjoyment of social rights.[6] African Americans understood the importance of contesting the standing of their relationships as integral to any prospects that freedom might hold for them on the most basic level. Marriage was by no means synonymous with freedom, but slaves and free blacks knew that their future as liberated people was less certain without the guarantee of marriage—or the right to choose whether to wed or not. How far could they go in the world without beloved kin, the foundation of which was secured on the bedrock of publicly protected marriage?

As one scholar has argued, marriage designs "the architecture of private life," yet it has assumed the characteristics of a public institution regulated by local communities and the state.[7] Marriage in U.S. history has always been intertwined with a person's gender, race, and identity and place in the social order. How men and women relate to the public world has been tied to their status as married or potentially married people. As such, marriage has been linked to citizenship and civil rights. A black soldier in the aftermath of the Civil War articulated this sentiment: "The Marriage Covenant is at the foundation of all our rights."[8] Marriage was at the foundation of liberation because it had been at the foundation of racial subordination. Legalizing marriage bolstered the ability of ex-slaves to keep their families together, to make decisions about labor and education, and to stay out of the unscrupulous grasp of erstwhile masters. But at the same time that African Americans acknowledged the fundamental civil rights embedded in legal monogamous marriage, they responded in multifarious ways to the conventional matrimonial script once they legally secured the right to marry. Freedom meant not just access to social conventions but also the ability to reject them. Blacks understood the price of conformity and inclusion in a nation-state that continued to mobilize racist double standards into new disciplinary forms.

Yet even white Americans who refused to grant slaves and free blacks inviolable rights often acknowledged that what looked like marriage among blacks was marriage "de facto." The dominating role that marriage played in mainstream society made it difficult to label and account for varieties of intimacy that did not in some way get defined like the sanctioned custom. Blacks and whites alike thus referred to "slave marriage." They did not always understand or share the same ideas about what that term meant and under what circumstances it should be or could be applied to black intimacy. Slaveowners considered "marriage" only those relationships that they affirmed and sanctioned, but ultimately they could not dictate personal feelings. Sex, both inter- and intraracial, could be thrust upon slaves for the purpose of reproducing and thus increasing an owner's property. But marriage was ultimately a mutual exchange of affections and services, a chosen emotional and social bond. A person could be forced to play the roles and abide by the form, but that did not make a marriage. So what did constitute marriage for African Americans before and after emancipation? What were the complex ramifications for the limited choices they made about cherished and personal affairs?

The overarching history of marriage in slavery and emancipation undergirds the narrative of this book, from colonial times up to the end of the nineteenth century. Most of the original colonies implemented marriage laws modeled on the common laws of England within the first twenty years of organization and settlement. Colonial officials met resistance in their efforts to replicate formalized monogamous marriages, however, and they would not succeed until the mid-eighteenth century. Ordinary settlers preferred to rely on mutual consent and sexual consummation of their unions to designate marital status, without the imprimatur of clergy or civil authorities. Whatever forms marriages assumed, some of the earliest African arrivals were granted more leeway to secure their marriages before the codification of racialized laws, and some were even allowed to register their unions legally. But slaves had to obtain the permission of their masters and could still be separated against their will, which meant their marriages were never inviolable. Even a master's permission would soon diminish in value as marriage laws became deeply implicated in the system of racial subjugation that built the Anglo-American colonies.[9]

Marriage and race were closely linked as slavery was codified. The very first law defining racial difference set into motion a series of regulations that would make it difficult and eventually impossible for most African Americans to gain legal recognition and security of their marriages and families. The Virginia General Assembly passed a law in 1643 that defined African women as "tithable" labor. Tithes were taxes, revenue raised by the colony, that were usually imposed on men engaged in agricultural labor and male heads of households. The law inscribed racial difference by exempting the labor of English women whether indentured servants or free. It distinguished between African women as productive laborers capable of arduous physical fieldwork and English women as weak, dependent wives and servants unsuitable to labor under the same regimen. The tax on an African woman had to be paid by her master (if she was a slave or servant), by her husband (if she was married), or by herself (if she was single). The consequences for black marriages and families were grave. Paying the tax could be prohibitive, making it difficult for African Americans to advance economically or purchase their freedom. The law created obstacles for free blacks to marry because it burdened their households with levies, unlike white households, in which men enjoyed the fruits of the labor of their wives and daughters tax-free. It stigmatized black women's bodies as constitutionally different and amenable to super-exploitation and marked their inability to overcome all of these hurdles as a moral failure.[10]

After establishing the uniqueness of black women's productive labor in the law, colonists were faced with the potential conflict between their roles as producers of agricultural commodities and their importance as reproducers of chattel. If the master owned exclusive claims to the products of a slave woman's labor, who owned the offspring she produced? By 1638 some colonists in New England were already operating under the assumption that

Africans were uniquely situated to being treated as permanent laborers who could be forced to breed future increase on demand. Farther south, white Virginians decided to codify the concept into law by altering the rules of English family lineage and descent.[11] In 1662, the General Assembly condemned African slaves and their descendants to lifetime tenure. Unlike British laws in which paternity determined a child's birthrights, Virginia law stipulated that children of African slaves followed the condition of their mothers. The law denied the paternity of black fathers and removed any possibility that black women could resort to the law for protection against the sexual predations of white men. Fathers could not be forced to recognize, care for, or support black children or be charged with violations against their mothers.[12] Though marriage and childbirth were highly valued cultural practices in the West African nations of origin, the institutionalization of slavery as an inheritable, permanent condition would profoundly trouble the consciousness of slave men and women who contemplated either or both.

The legal foundation for racial slavery in Anglo-America was constituted in the subjugation of black women. African-American women's sexuality was a central axis of power of masters over slaves, the means by which gender, racial, and material oppression were enmeshed. The diminution of motherhood, the negation of fatherhood, the disavowal of sexual violence, and the invalidation of marriage became an interlocking system of white dominance over blacks that would be further codified in the laws and carried out in everyday practice for centuries.[13]

The most significant innovations inscribing racism into marriage laws occurred in the nineteenth century. Not coincidentally, the history of marriage and the history of slavery converged as both were newly consecrated. Whereas overlapping and contradictory jurisdictions, disparate statutes, court decisions, and ecclesiastical rules marked the colonial era, marriage laws in the early nineteenth century became modernized and more distinctly American. Governing bodies at the state level implemented their own codes to supplant many of the inherited traditions of the common laws of England. The American Revolution played a major role in stimulating this shift by calling into question all forms of hierarchy, inequality, and coercion. Both the influence of Enlightenment thought as well as changes in the economy spurred by the expansion of capitalism and market relations reconfigured the ideals attached to marriage, emphasizing individualism, mutual consent, and freedom of choice.

Slavery also changed after the Revolution. Some observers had hoped that slavery would die a natural death, and it was in fact gradually eliminated in the North in a protracted process. But it grew in the South and demarcated a portentous fault line in the new nation. More slaves entered the United States from 1787 to 1807, just before the African slave trade was permanently abolished, than in any two decades previously. Subsequently, there were more slaves in the early republic than there had been under the former colonies, despite Northern manumission and a marked rise in manumissions in the upper South. The escalating demand for slave labor and the intensified commitment to the institution were due in part to the new cotton gin and the increased profitability of chattel. With the spread of cotton plantations south and west and the subsequent removal of many slaves via the internal slave trade to those areas, slave spouses faced increased separations. The closing of the African slave trade and the predominance of slaves born on this side of the Atlantic had a profound influence on the evolution of distinctive African-American cultural practices and adaptive strategies that helped to sustain families under very harsh circumstances. But at the same time black family life was never more threatened.

Reforms in marriage and slavery collided at the interstices of regional discord in the decades leading up to the Civil War. As one historian has argued, "domesticity supplied a language for sectional conflict, and marriage a measure for the morality of opposing systems." The discourse of abolitionism focused centrally on the degradation of marriage and the family under slavery: slavery severed parental ties, brutalized the female body, and interfered with relations between husbands and wives. The integrity of family could not be sustained under such a violent system. Proslavery advocates averred that the "peculiar institution" was in itself like a marriage—a hierarchical and unequal, but benevolent and reciprocal, relationship that provided the best familial supervision and care for an inferior race.[14]

Marriage laws in both the North and the South were reformulated to reflect these divergent meanings in the antebellum years. In the North, marriage moved in constancy with the principles of a modern republic in which consent, individual freedom, and mutual contracts were critical. In the

South, marriage laws bolstered the prerogatives of the old system of patriarchy. With respect to African Americans, the slave codes that were passed,
presumably to placate antislavery opposition, did nothing to protect slave
families. Marriages for slaves were not expressly prohibited by statute, but
the lack of legal protection stood as a powerful impediment at a time when
the standard law, the church, and popular culture all championed marriage
and family as the foundation of civilized society–for whites. The ideology of
race trumped the ideology of domesticity. But the increasing winds of change
in Northern ideology would eventually push white Southerners to perceive
that the only way to defend their distinctive household order was through
secession.[15]

The language of contracts increasingly came to govern the controversy of
marriage, slavery, and freedom.[16] Marriage was a civil contract in which slaves
could not partake because they had no civil standing. Though slaves could
marry by their mutual agreement, their vows were legally null and void. A
marriage contract was considered special, unlike other contracts, in that it
was not subject to the bargaining of individuals alone. The state held stakes
in regulating it. Under the rules of other contracts, parties could agree to dissolve agreements, but consent alone was not enough to abrogate a marriage
vow, and the law recognized very few legitimate causes for separation or divorce. Above all, marriages had no legal footing between slaves because of
the primary right of the master to control his property however he saw fit.
The interests in reproducing human capital and the prerogative to sell slaves
to increase profits or cut losses mitigated the ability of slaves to secure their
unions. Slavery could not be reconciled with the pledge of exclusivity and
permanence of legal marriage.[17]

No one spoke more eloquently to the antithesis between slavery and marriage than slaves themselves. The story of the marriage of the famous fugitive
slave couple William and Ellen Craft affirms this. Both were born slaves in
Georgia and were traumatized by forced separation from their parents at an
early age. They had known each other for years before they broached the topic
of building a future together. As William described it: "our marriage was
postponed for some time simply because one of the unjust and worse than
Pagan laws under which we lived compelled all children of slave mothers to
follow their condition."[18] For Ellen, "the mere thought of her ever becoming

the mother of a child, to linger out a miserable existence under the wretched system of American slavery, appeared to fill her very soul with horror." Sensitive to Ellen's feelings, William stated: "I did not, at first, press the marriage, but agreed to assist her in trying to devise some plan by which we might escape from our unhappy condition, and then be married."[19] They pondered the prospects for escape at length, hoping to find a way to execute them. They eventually decided to take a practical route, to obtain consent to be married, "settle down in slavery, and endeavour to make ourselves as comfortable as possible under that system; but the same time ever to keep our dim eyes steadily fixed upon the glimmering hope of liberty, and earnestly pray God mercifully to assist us to escape from our unjust thraldom."[20]

Very shortly after their marriage, they pulled off one of the most daring escapes ever recorded. They traveled a thousand miles to freedom with Ellen, who had inherited the white skin of her father, dressed in drag passing as a slave-owner and William posing as her slave. For William and Ellen Craft there could be no marriage without freedom. While their method and outcome of escape were not typical, their sentiments about marriage were. Yet most slaves were forced to resign themselves to carving out the best conjugal relationships they could under circumstances they could not fully control.

The conditions of slavery made marriages distinctive, though in reality they did not look much different from the arrangements of common whites in the South. White marriages unsanctioned by either civil or religious officialdom reigned in the antebellum South.[21] The critical difference was that marriages of slaves existed only at the forbearance of masters, whereas the common-law marriages of the white majority were recognized by society and the law and were not subject to external forces of destruction. Another difference was that slave couples frequently did not cohabit the same household, because slaves who were owned by different masters had to remain on their respective plantations even after they had wed. This had the obvious disadvantages of keeping couples apart except for weekly visits, thus inhibiting intimacy on a daily basis and making it difficult for men to protect their wives and children. Marrying a person "abroad," as this arrangement was known, could expand the potential pool of partners to help ensure that slaves could practice exogamy, that is, marry nonblood relatives. This cultural preference was unique to African descendants and differed from the marriage practices of many Southern whites.[22]

The expectations and obligations of enslaved husbands and wives resembled those of free people in important ways, though the context of bondage forced significant modifications on the former. Slaves expected to marry partners of their choice, individuals they loved or at least liked. In some cases, however, masters foisted pairings on them and labeled them as married; in other cases slaves submitted to choosing spouses governed less by affection than by practical circumstance. Marriage encompassed expectations of love, devotion, affection, fidelity, and mutuality. Gender roles were defined much the same as in the dominant culture. Men typically tried to assume the role of head of the family and wives were considered their subordinates. The division of labor followed suit, with women having primary responsibilities for cooking, cleaning, and caring for children, while men provided food through hunting and fishing. Wives with abroad husbands could be held less accountable to their husbands' authority, but either spouse could prevail if disputes arose. Nonetheless, the gender arrangements were far less than patriarchal. Slave men did not have final authority over their families, and whatever influence they exerted was largely the result of internal family and community pressures and was always subordinate to the needs or desires of the planter class. Relations between husbands and wives in the slave quarters had to be nimble, though not necessarily egalitarian. The daily realities of the slave system, bent on maximizing profits, meant that neither women nor men could strictly adhere to the gender assignments of the dominant society. Survival dictated that African Americans had to endow gender values and ideals with their own particular inflections.[23]

The association between marriage and liberation long articulated by African Americans took on increasing significance as the end of slavery approached. As slaves escaped to freedom following the foot trails of Union soldiers, marriage often became the first civil right they exercised, overwhelming the capacity of the occupying forces to accommodate them. It opened up new demands on the federal government to create policies regarding the intimate relationships that had once been regarded as the purview of individual states and slave masters. In order to secure a Union victory and fully enfranchise black soldiers, the federal government had to implement policies to accommodate their families, first by offering them freedom and then by giving them the benefits due to soldiers' wives and dependents. Although the Emancipation Proclamation is often heralded as the most important landmark policy of the Civil War, other significant legislation came before it, such as the Militia Act of 1862, which began to emancipate the female relatives of soldiers owned by Confederates. Once the war ended it became even more imperative to put marriages on legal footing in the former slaveholding states, in the Confederacy and the Union. Yet the historical opposition to the legalization of black marriages was not easily dismissed. White Southerners initially resented the implication of equality inherent in solemnizing black conjugal unions. But the passage of the Civil Rights Act of 1866 opened the way for overcoming these impediments by validating black rights to make contracts of all kinds. Former slaveholding states were forced to make provisions in new laws that recognized black marriages, and they quickly discovered that they could concede to marriage while manipulating it to serve their racist aims. With the support of the federal government and Northern missionaries, they sought to enforce black conformity to the dominant social order.[24]

Marriage rights invited new forms of racial subjugation. Despite the fact that the state had colluded with slave-owners for centuries in invalidating the legitimacy of black marriages and burdening these relationships with encumbrances that wreaked havoc on a regular basis, amnesia was widespread in the wake of emancipation. Whereas under slavery blacks were not allowed to get married, they would now, under freedom, be disproportionately punished if they did not marry while cohabitating. The multiple partners that many men and women had as a result of forced separations and the unknown whereabouts of spouses would be defined as illegal bigamy. And whereas sex outside of marriage was required and expected of the enslaved, under the new system it could be condemned as criminal fornication and adultery. Former slaveholding states showed no sympathy and little awareness of the impact of the violence of slavery on black families and the entanglements produced by transforming a once forbidden right into a legal and moral requirement for full citizenship. Instead, it enforced the technicalities of the law to the harshest extent possible.[25]

Consequently, for many African Americans, the right to marry became not the source of empowerment they had yearned for but a form of punishment and containment. Many of the new state laws automatically recognized the marital relationships of ex-slave couples at war's end, which was fine if the couple intended to continue their relationship. But for those who were married under slavery and wanted to pursue other options in freedom, such as legally marrying a person other than the spouse belatedly recognized by the state, they could be and were often prosecuted. In some cases, African Americans were not aware that they were violating the law. In other cases, ex-slaves deliberately transgressed the new laws in pursuit of their own personal desires and goals, befitting their understanding of freedom. Although marriage was now a legal right for all to enjoy with a national "single standard" forged after the Civil War, in actual practice former slaves faced a different reality.[26] Blacks were singled out disproportionately and punished for failure to meet the requirements of legal, monogamous marriage, which had been denied to them for so long. The federal government, state legislatures, judicial entities, and the planter class found common cause in using marriage to demarcate racial difference and to transfer the liabilities of ex-slave livelihoods from former owners to current husbands.

Given the punitive standards of marriages applied to African Americans, it is not surprising that they responded to the institution with ambivalence after emancipation. While the majority eagerly embraced legal marriage, many preferred to maintain their conjugal relationships as they had before, unpersuaded that legalization would protect them or fearful of the coercive interventions that seemed to accompany state sanction. Yet despite the considerable constraints of getting married under this new regime, African Americans considered the formalization of their relationships an important measure of race progress. Ironically, marriage would survive as one of the few civil rights that was safe from revocation at the century's end, which heightened its eminence all the more.

In the era of "Racial Uplift," the years between the 1880s and the 1890s, middle-class and elite African Americans articulated the sentiments tying together marriage and race progress most explicitly. The discourse on domesticity, similar to that portrayed in the antebellum years defending the integrity of the black family and humanity, continued in the form of fiction, periodical literature, essays, and speeches by literate and mostly educated blacks. Marriage was identified and trumpeted as the key to the realization of full citizenship, the means by which African Americans would once and forever be accepted as capable and worthy people. Yet while marriage was valorized, it was not heralded uncritically. The unique needs of a people subjugated by racial oppression striving for uplift and progress required an institution that reflected their experience. Marriage was seen as a vehicle for advancing the interests of the group, not just a privilege to be enjoyed by individual couples.[27]

The transformation of ideas about black marriage would take yet another turn by century's end, stimulated by the dashed hopes and optimism of the post–Civil War years, which failed to live up to black expectations of freedom and democracy. The rise of Jim Crow, disfranchisement, sharecropping, convict lease, crop liens, and peonage increased the pressures on African-American families to counter the new technologies of power and repression. Marriage as the route to racial progress could not fulfill its promise but would become more consistent with the pursuit of bourgeois individualism pervasive in society. Twentieth-century marriage could be held in esteem as a personal aspiration, but it would no longer carry the weight of securing the fate of the entire race.

The state of the slave family and the meaning of marriage within it have been enduring sources of controversy in discussions of the value of black life in American society. Proslavery thinking questioned whether people of African descent regarded families as important or were capable of forming meaningful relationships in the ways that white Americans did. Such thinking has enjoyed a shelf life of centuries with no end in sight. Since the inception of research on the topic, scholars have been largely preoccupied with questions of how African Americans either conformed, or failed to conform, to dominant notions of family life. The long genealogy of scholarship dates to W. E. B. Du Bois, editor of *The Negro American Family* (1908), and E. Franklin Frazier, author of *The Negro Family in the United States* (1939).[28]

And yet European categories of kinship alone cannot fully capture the dynamic values and strategies that people of African descent used to define, create, and embrace their own notions of marriage and kinship. Africans throughout the Atlantic world expressed broader and more flexible patterns of kinship, reflecting both their cultural heritage and their conditions under enslavement in the Americas. They had already experienced traumatic disruptions in their patterns of kinship before crossing the Atlantic. Many circumstances in West Africa, despite the ethnic and national diversity of the captives, taught them to define malleable notions of family in order to survive enslavement, warfare, drought, famine, and colonization in their homelands. Those understandings served to buttress their survival and regeneration as they moved within and across European Atlantic empires. Many captives already knew what it meant to be alienated, isolated, and ruptured from biological kin and social networks. They understood the importance of incorporating strangers and newcomers into their families on reciprocal terms that might not be recognized or appreciated by outside eyes, minds, and hearts. People of African descent had, of necessity, become adept at forging kin-like networks as they were severed from communities of origin and thrust into slave ships among strangers taking them to the Americas. Black families under slavery were nothing if not practical, adaptive, and creative in combining natal and social ties to meet the needs of emotional and material sustenance from birth to death.[29]

The nimbleness of black responses to degradation has been a source of inspiration to some, but in reacting to racist charges about the absence of slaves' affections for their kin relations, others have argued that the utter brutality perpetrated by enslavers effectively destroyed black families.[30] Du Bois and Frazier made this case in their early-twentieth-century studies. These works became the seeds of mid-twentieth-century polemics regarding the state of black life in America and the role that slavery had played in retarding black marriage rates, which in turn exacerbated racial inequities.

Daniel Patrick Moynihan, then assistant secretary of labor under President Lyndon B. Johnson, wrote that the root problem, "that the Negro family in the urban ghettos is crumbling," could be laid at the doorsteps of slavery. Black family structure was warped. Slavery had produced a prevalence of female-headed "matriarchal" households, a "tangle of pathology" in which black families in the twentieth century were still ensnared. A "fundamental fact of Negro American family life is the often reversed roles of husband and wife," wrote Moynihan. Whereas white families were "equalitarian," wives dominated black families. African-American family structure existed outside the norms of white culture, which imposed a "crushing burden on the Negro male" and retarded group progress, he argued. Aberrant, antisocial behavior in inner cities, from crime to unemployment, could be traced back to this weak family structure. The 1965 "Moynihan Report" was originally intended for discussion within the president's inner circle of advisers. But once leaked to the public it took on a life of its own. It sparked controversy among scholars, policymakers, and political pundits who defended and critiqued its methods, speculations, and conclusions. Although Moynihan made faulty historical assumptions about "marital instability" among African Americans (especially the poor) based on little empirical data, the controversy has yet to dissipate.[31]

Several revisionists, either directly or indirectly, set out to challenge Moynihan and the depictions of slavery in earlier scholarship. Foremost among them were Herbert Gutman, John Blassingame, and Eugene Genovese.[32] They focused a lot of attention on questions of black family structure and the extent to which it mirrored the family structure of whites. By the early 1970s they had produced abundant research to show that the African-American family was not a tangle of pathologies of black matriarchies. Rather, they argued, slaves had created viable, productive, resilient families that closely resembled the white ideal: they were mostly nuclear, male-headed households with parents and children intact.

Pioneering scholars of slave women's history, such as Angela Davis, Deborah Gray White, and Jacqueline Jones, challenged the normative assumptions that accompanied the emphasis placed on the role of slave men as heads of households.[33] They emphasized the large numbers of slave families that were matrifocal while also rejecting the stereotype that they were "matriarchal" (emasculating) simply because many married spouses lived "abroad," some distance apart. They highlighted the mother-child dyad as the most basic family unit in slavery and demonstrated how female-centered relationships and networks were marshalled daily in the absence of men. Some attributed these predilections to a West Africa in which childbearing and -rearing took precedence for women over marriage to men.[34] Yet diminishing the status of marriage has also obscured the diverse roles that men played in their families despite the reckless ways in which they were often separated from spouses and kin. Their affection and devotion to their wives, children, stepchildren, and other relatives are abundantly clear in their own words in many extant documents. Today, we are much more attuned to looking at the social constructions and experiences of manhood as well as womanhood.

Building on and critiquing the work of revisionists has added further layers to the debates about family structure, questioning and rejecting some of the well-intentioned, but still problematic, assumptions. The current consensus view, which I share, is that slave families were much more complex in structure than the normative patriarchal, nuclear family ideal can capture. Wide-ranging research of small and large slaveholdings, different labor systems and occupations, and various subregions in the antebellum era reveals the enormous diversity of domestic arrangements: matrifocal, monogamous, bigamous, single parent, abroad spouses, multigenerational, single- and mixed-gender sibling groups, single-sex groups, and orphaned children. Slaves tended to move in and out of various kinds of family formations over the course of their lives, depending on their circumstances and constraints, because of economic and social pressures. But the most enduring family form was indeed the matrifocal unit, often created out of the remnants left behind when families were sundered or turned into saleable units put on the auction block. Some women had abroad husbands when they were stationary, but many did not. Most slave children grew up knowing their fathers and some lived with them throughout their entire childhoods, but most did not. Slave men were more likely than slave women to live apart from their families.[35]

Despite this consensus, the revisionists were not entirely wrong: many nuclear families did, in fact, exist in slavery.[36] The problem was that most of them could not be sustained through slavery, displacement, and war. With each passing year of an intact couple's marriage and their offspring's' childhood, the chances of fracture increased. Though the invalidation of black marriages had been integral to the system of racial subjugation since the colonial era and capricious disruptions made it hard to sustain monogamous marriages and nuclear families at any time, the closing of the Atlantic slave trade in 1808 and the emergence of the cotton economy severely stressed black families further. They may have fared better as they settled in new locations and reconstituted their kin by the time of the Civil War, but the outbreak of military conflict incited yet another cycle of forced migration and escape that broke up families once again.[37]

The lack of sustained treatment of black marriage over a wide temporal and geographical scope has inhibited a full understanding of the intricacies of its nature and historical evolution.[38] This book challenges claims that underestimate the importance of marriage in the family lives of slaves or that argue that it was utterly destroyed. It focuses on intraracial bonds rather than on the interracial liaisons that have disproportionately transfixed the nation's cultural memory. It challenges mistaken views about black marriage under bondage and freedom throughout the nineteenth century, which are used to make claims about the origins of late-twentieth and twenty-first-century black marital decline.[39] Slavery certainly disfigured marriage, but a far more vexed history of its harms and injuries remains to be told. The deprivation of paternal authority and the lack of conformity to gender norms can hardly suffice as an estimation of the most tragic consequence of slavery when judged by the damages that will unfold here. And yet despite all that African Americans suffered, they created meaningful bonds of wedlock.

This book is the product of research in the most extensive and diverse primary sources available, including slave narratives, ex-slave interviews, laws and court cases, church minutes, congressional debates, government agency records, missionary reports and correspondence, personal letters, pension records, newspapers, and federal and Confederate military documents. Using each of these sources incurs benefits and risks that derive from the intentions of individual and institutional authors. A personal letter may reveal more than the writer intended, given that there was little expectation that it would be made public. An appeal made in a court of law or in response to an official inquiry could be shaped by very particular interests, especially when resources were at stake, like pensions or alimony. And an autobiography written by a fugitive slave in the midst of abolitionism, in which those first-hand accounts proved crucial to gaining sympathy, could be pitched to telling tales to that end. The biggest deficit in sources is that most of the central subjects of this book were illiterate as a result of their enslavement and the laws that prohibited them from being taught to read and write. Thus those who became literate either as slaves, or shortly thereafter, are often privileged because of the paper trail they generated. But the voices of the illiterate have not been completely lost to posterity. They often enter into public and private forums and conversations and end up on the record in surprising, though sometimes indirect, ways.

These rich sources from the perspectives of all stakeholders in slave-holding societies allow us to uncover one hundred years of history. A century is required to amply assess and comprehend the distinctive twists and turns of black marriages, from those that preceded Moses and Ellen Hunter in the context of bondage, to those that their children would enter into by century's end. It is that story of the pursuit of marital union among slaves and then newly freed people that will unfold here in all of its trials and terrors, its fears and faith in family, its desire for the acknowledgment and acceptance of love between two people deemed worthy of it. This story will demonstrate the power of marriage to challenge our understanding of what slavery has wrought, the capacious promises and curbed perimeters of what freedom has rendered.

1

⧼⧽

"Until Distance Do You Part"

Henry "Box" Brown fled slavery in Richmond, Virginia, via a custom-made dry goods box sent through the U.S. mail service in 1849. The box was only big enough to hold his six-foot, two-hundred-pound frame, curled up into a fetal position, along with a flask of water and a few biscuits. He mailed himself safely to Philadelphia, Pennsylvania, where he arrived twenty-seven hours later. The tale of his innovative escape is perhaps all that current-day readers know about him. But his testimony of life as a slave was the subject of broadsides, posters, and as-told-to memoir, all mass-produced and circulated throughout Northern states and abroad during his lifetime. Brown's escape was motivated by the disruption of marital bonds and family life suffered by so many slaves in antebellum America.

From an early age Brown's mother had taught him about the forced separations common among slave families: "She would take me upon her knee and, pointing to the forest trees which were then being stripped of their foliage by the winds of autumn, would say to me, my son, as yonder leaves are stripped from off the trees of the forest, so are the children of the slaves swept away from them by the hands of cruel tyrants."[1] And yet nothing could prepare him for the trauma that he would endure firsthand. By the time he was fifteen, after the death of his master, his family members were redistributed as inheritances among the slaveholder's heirs. His sisters and brothers were sent in different directions. He was initially left with his parents on the plantation before being sent to work in a tobacco factory in Richmond.

Given his experience, what would make Henry Box Brown consider starting a family of his own as an adult? Like so many other young men, he put rationality aside when he met a woman, Nancy. He believed they could build a life together as a married couple. They obtained the consent of their masters—Christians, after all—who promised not to sell them away from each other. But within a year's time, Brown reported, his owner's "conscientious scruples vanished," and he sold Nancy to "an exceedingly cruel man" and to a "still more cruel" woman.[2] Brown's growing family was sold several more times but eventually ended up in the hands of a prospective buyer who offered Brown a deal: if he would pay a portion of her sale price, the man would keep his wife nearby and sell her back to him once he had saved enough money. The promise began to unravel as Nancy's latest master demanded increasingly more money. Still, Brown was willing to pay to maintain even a tenuous hold on a domestic life with his wife and, by then, three children. Eventually Brown, a hired-out slave, could not keep up with the owner's unreasonable demands, given that he had to turn over the greater part of his earnings to his own master.

Events took a dramatic turn when Brown discovered that his family had been sent to the auction block. They were sold and housed in a local jail in preparation for a journey out of state. Brown hurried to witness their departure, a brutally familiar but still jarring scene. "These beings were marched with ropes about their necks, and staples on their arms, and, although in that respect the scene was no very novel one to me, yet the peculiarity of my own circumstances made it assume the appearance of unusual horror," he related. Brown captured the experience of those who suffered not only social death but often, quite literally, physical death, unable to withstand the loneliness, debilitating treatment, and unhealthy conditions. Brown was able to lay eyes on his family one last time as they were held in abeyance awaiting their journey into an unforeseen world. His eldest child called out as he agonized about her fatherless future. He locked eyes with his wife and was able to catch hold of her hand for several miles as he walked along the side of the wagon carting her away. "But both our hearts were so overpowered with feeling that we could say nothing, and when at last we were obliged to part, the look of mutual love which we exchanged was all the token which we could give each other that we should yet meet in heaven," he recalled.[3] This story of love and loss prompted a dramatic escape by a man desperate to get out of bondage and to tell the world about the sufferings of his fellow slaves. It is emblematic of the forces of a changing tide that would sweep at least a million slaves in the undertow of the interstate slave trade between 1810 and 1861.

By 1800, African Americans had been enslaved on the North American mainland for nearly two hundred years. Slavery had undergone significant changes that impacted the lives of slaves and free blacks, including their ability to marry and maintain family lives. Henry Box Brown and his family were victims of a catastrophic consequence of the closing of the Atlantic slave trade in 1808; known as the "Second Middle Passage," this journey was nearly as life-changing as the first. It increased the commerce of human flesh within and across states and pushed continental expansion into Southwestern territories. It was driven by the demands of rising cotton and sugar production, the acquisition of the Louisiana Territory, the expropriation of Native Americans' land, and their violent expulsion from it.[4]

The internal slave trade was a traumatic displacement of slaves from the established Eastern seaboard states, especially Virginia, the Carolinas, Maryland, and parts of Georgia. They were sold to the Southwestern interior states, including Texas, Louisiana, Mississippi, Alabama, and southwest Georgia. These slaves came by licit and illicit means, sold by smugglers, kidnappers, and merchants of human flesh. Human contraband from Africa and the Caribbean continued through Spanish Florida and Mexican Texas before entering the Union. Free blacks, even those in the North, were susceptible to enslavement as a result of the rising prices for slave labor in the cotton fields. To be black in antebellum America meant being vulnerable to the "chattel principle," the idea that one's value actually accrued in dollars and cents, which put a price tag on the heads of any who could be captured.[5] Trading human commodities became big business in the slaveholding states, second only to plantation slavery itself. It supplied the brute labor necessary to fell trees in forests and clear the wilderness to create arable and fruitful soil and thus fuel the agricultural revolutions that would ignite wealth production of the nascent nation. Planters picking up stakes and moving east or those starting fresh out west looked for particular skills and characteristics in their bound work forces. They wanted young, fertile, healthy, strong, and pliable workers. They looked for "fancy maids," "bucks," "prime hands," "broad mares," and "breeding wenches." Black bodies were objectified, branded, and hawked by buyers to meet the nearly insatiable appetites of flourishing new markets.[6]

The interstate slave trade did not account for the slaves who were either sold or transferred to different residences as a result of new ownership. Nearly a million more slaves were bartered, auctioned, hired out on long-term contracts, or moved from one white family to the next, through estate distributions and sales. Changes in the financial circumstances of owners could prompt quick sales or redistribution of their human stock. Large planters often spread their slaves across their multiple farms and plantations, some adjoining one another, others in different states and even the Caribbean, as economic and family needs dictated. When younger relatives married, owners often sent slaves away as wedding gifts.[7]

All told, the impact on slave families was devastating. One third of first marriages were disrupted by the interstate slave trade, and many more were broken apart by temporary loans and long-term hiring out. The upheaval skewed the demographics of slavery. The southwestern frontier became a place for the very young, and slightly more male, population. The sugar plantations in Louisiana employed mostly men because of the exacting labor required to grow and process the crop. Planters who invested in sugar, one of the riskiest enterprises, requiring large amounts of capital to grow and manufacture, along with technical and managerial skills, often spent money only on male slaves. The harshness of sugar production, combined with the reluctance of owners to spend their money on female slaves, made it difficult for captives to reproduce. Cotton planters in Mississippi, by contrast, were satisfied with slaves of either sex, who would perform the same kind of field work. Traders tried to avoid purchasing entire families in order to satisfy planters' demands. Instead they looked for individuals or partial families, like women and small children, whose lower prices and evidence of procreation made them attractive to prospective buyers willing to think long-term about women's capacities for compounding returns on their investments.

Slave-owners may have preferred men, but they also needed women. Although partial families were occasionally sold out together, they did not necessarily stay that way. They were sometimes sold off en route to their new destinations as masters recalibrated their needs for labor or bargained for better deals to cut their costs.[8]

As exporting Eastern seaboard states lost their prized young male slaves, they became a site for older slaves and women, at least initially. This was especially true of areas like Virginia, where tobacco farming declined and the production of cereal crops like wheat increased. The older plantations needed fewer slaves. They sold off their excess and hired out others to farmers who were diversifying and unable to purchase them outright. Slave women in the East would gain a reputation as breeders of slaves sent West, as they were forced to seed and replicate the most profitable "crop" of all. The British colonies on mainland North America exported the lowest number of people from Africa, but by the nineteenth century they had the largest slave population in the Western hemisphere because of the rapid rate of natural reproduction there. Two-thirds of slaves in the Americas lived in the United States on the eve of the Civil War. And yet their offspring, which they reproduced in large numbers, became a burden to plantation owners in the East eager to cut the costs of their maintenance and care. African Americans' reputation in the Atlantic world for having the highest rate of natural increase was used to the advantage of their enslavers to buttress the modernization of regional and national economies reliant on their productive and reproductive labor. Nonetheless, fewer children were born as slave populations shifted to the Southwest, forcing planters to shrink their human assets to stay afloat.[9]

Long-standing slave communities in the East had lasted through generations of struggles but were threatened by deportations that fractured couples and families. But that was not the case in every area. Rice cultivation in low-country South Carolina continued to thrive, and slaveholding there was more dynamic than ever (see Fig. 1.1). Large plantations became even larger. Economies of scale, the ability of plantation owners to use their size to maximize profits, created fewer incentives to divest slaveholdings. Slaveholdings were expanded as a result of natural increase and the acquisition of more land, which required additional workers. Economic stability and the affluence that rice production generated kept most slaves off the auction block

Fig. 1.1   Five generations on Smith's Plantation, Beaufort, South Carolina. This photo
captures a family of slaves at the time of the Civil War, showing longevity of familial lines
in low country South Carolina.

and out of the arms of interstate traders. Slaves in the low country were more
isolated from absentee owners relative to those elsewhere, which also reinforced their ability to create family and community bulwarks against the
swirling forces of migration and change.[10]

The character and nature of slave marriages and families depended in
large degree on regional, demographic, and temporal shifts in slavery during
the antebellum era. The size of plantations and farms, sex ratios of enslaved
populations, the level of contact with absentee or residential slaveholders,
and masters' attitudes about honoring slave relationships were all influential.
And yet there was a great deal of consistency in the challenges slaves faced and
the strategies they used to adjust. Slaves were never passive in response to
the forces that propelled the internal slave trade, as Henry Box Brown dem-

onstrated. They fought back with their resources, their might, their wit, and whatever leverage they had managed to build up over the years. They tried to cajole masters into not selling off relatives, or selling them together, or buying off those living on different farms and plantations—whatever it took to keep them from being separated. But forced migration took its toll by making most black marital unions more fragile and shattering many bonds between parents (especially fathers) and children. Some slaves were able to maintain contact with extended kin who were moved or hired out close by. But kin networks had to be reconstituted from fractured pieces left behind or formed out of newly arriving individuals. Slaves searched for surrogates to make up for missing loved ones, giving greater emphasis to extended and adoptive familial strategies.[11]

Most slaves formed marital bonds in adulthood, despite the obstacles their peculiar condition as property created for them. But they were often circumspect and hesitant to turn to marriage. Harriet Jacobs, a former slave who hid out for seven years in the tiny garret of her grandmother's house in North Carolina before escaping to the North, wondered aloud why slaves would ever want to get attached. "Why does the slave ever love?" she asked. "Why allow the tendrils of the heart to twine around objects which may at any moment be wrenched away by the hand of violence?"[12] Slave marriage was by design an oxymoron, equivocal largely through no fault of the slaves. Not a marriage respected in the law, but a kind of marriage in the heart. Lunsford Lane, a former slave from North Carolina, described the central paradox this way: "I was bound as fast in wedlock as a slave can be. God may at any time sunder that band in a freeman; either master may do the same at pleasure in a slave."[13] The glaring disadvantages of wedlock under bondage were always evident and troubling. As Thomas Jones, also an ex-slave from North Carolina, acknowledged: "*We called* it and *we considered* it *a true marriage,* although we knew well that marriage was not permitted to the slaves as a sacred right of the loving heart."[14] Slaves believed that their marriages were as "true" as they could be, but they also knew they were encumbered by unique burdens that free couples did not face.[15]

Slaves struggled to reconcile their status as chattel with the desire to form (in)divisible unions with partners of their choosing. Marriage and slavery were both forms of property relations and bondage. Slaveholders often invoked their similarity as hierarchical relationships founded in dependency as a reason to limit a slave's right to marry. Slavery, after all, was a domestic institution very much like marriage. The enslaved (functionally children) were subsumed within the family circle of masters (functionally fathers and mothers). In effect, slave marriage was superfluous because slaves were already married, symbolically, to their masters. Slaveholding patriarchs were the leaders, providers, and protectors of their own (white) blood kin, of the slaves they owned, and of the broader plantation society. Slave marriage in its constrained form was lacking in the inviolability that distinguished marriage (for free people) from other kinds of affairs. And yet, an approximation of marriage was tolerable to masters because it helped to augment their productive and reproductive power while it marked African Americans as inferior. Marriage was a tool for soothing the souls of human property and keeping them complacent and stable. It provided masters with a veneer of humane paternalism. They could permit and even encourage their slaves to marry to satisfy certain Christian dictums and to bear more fruits of capital from the babies born of those unions.[16]

In the antebellum decades this proslavery ideology steeped in paternalistic symbolism and language rankled the ire of abolitionists who claimed the family as central to all the reasons slavery was wrong. If patriarchs governed slaveholding units, literally of biblical proportions, they were wrongheaded in their replication of unrestrained tyranny, monetary greed, incest, licentiousness, physical brutality, adultery, and violations of female chastity. The reverential imitations of Abraham from the Old Testament left no one unscathed; blacks and whites were mired in their lecherous perversions. Nothing short of radical abolition could eradicate the savagery and redirect this system of incalculable injustice to meet the normative expectations of Western civilization.[17]

Slaves understood these matters better than anyone else. Henry Bibb, a fugitive slave born in Kentucky, made this clear: "I presume there are no class of people in the United States who so highly appreciate the legality of marriage as those persons who have been held and treated as property."[18] But they were still ambivalent about whether to wed and under what circumstances. Their intimate relationships were fraught within the context of coercion, force, and violence, as the plantation economy grew. Slaves fought for and negotiated meaningful relationships, as much as they could, in a society in which masters, the third flesh, had legal rights to intervene in relationships otherwise considered sacrosanct. Conjugal relationships generated a number of problems that slaves had to contend with: the lack of bodily integrity, the public performances of carnal acts for prurient onlookers, the dispersal of kin, the lack of parental rights, and the constant threat of sexual exploitation.[19] It would take many decades even after emancipation to undo the havoc wreaked upon marriages and families sustained and formed in this era. Although African Americans struggled to nurture and uphold vibrant, genuine, intimate relationships that buffered their degradation as human beings, they did so with eyes wide open, with vigilance and with trepidation given what infringements lurked around them.

Slaves adopted a variety of responses and strategies for negotiating and reckoning with these challenges. If they chose to enter into intimate relationships they participated on a spectrum that ranged from openly acknowledging their vulnerability and defining them more informally and as short-lived, to declaring them to be as permanent as they could make them. But they developed and articulated gradations of intimacy that were quite complex and not visible to those judging them through the conventional lenses of heterosexual marriage. The categories that slaves used to define their most intimate relationships were not always easily distinguishable or understood by outsiders and even led to disagreements among slaves themselves.[20]

Some slaves chose to be "sweethearts," a short-term connection adopted by young people and those who were unable to claim any semblance of a stable life, often as a result of being sold or moved around often. They were essentially lovers and not necessarily monogamous. They might have children together, which could help to transform their relationship into a more sustained bond. Or they could simply quit and move on at any time. These were the most precarious relationships and could go undetected beyond the couples themselves. The lack of community sanction also put them in vulnerable positions when it came to protecting each other or their offspring. Fellow slaves felt less obligated to support or give community sanction to what appeared to be fleeting liaisons. Masters were less likely to know about them or acknowledge them if they did.[21]

"Taking up" was a term often applied to intimate bonds that sometimes looked like marriage and other times did not. They could be temporary or long-term. They were usually monogamous. These couples shared the same residence (or visited if they lived on different farms). Couples forced by circumstances beyond their control, such as sale, migration, mortality, or other outside interventions, might end the relationship. Slaves who were moved around from place to place might create these bonds because they were the most substantial ways they could connect with a person of another sex without making commitments they knew they could not keep. They could have children together, which sometimes prompted the use of the same surnames. Their relationships were formed by tacit or expressed agreements between the spouses, but they could also be known in their communities as having some kind of claims on each other. Masters might acknowledge these relationships, by the consent required to allow the couples to share a common residence, but there was usually no ceremony that they initiated or approved to mark the onset of the relationship.

Slaves considered marriage the most treasured heterosexual bond. They were married in the sight of fellow slaves and their masters when they gave their consent. Slaves made promises to adhere to Christian dictates of monogamy and longevity—with an asterisk, "until burkra [the white man] parted you." They shared common surnames, lived in the same cabin, or lived "abroad" on different plantations or farms and visited regularly. They had children together. They were known in their communities as "husband and wife." Wedding ceremonies certainly made a difference in distinguishing these relationships from the others. But there were slaves who "took up" and lived together in long-term relationships that were, practically speaking, no different from marriage, save the lack of legal standing. A ceremony by itself did not necessarily heighten the bond any more than cohabitation alone, given the lack of regard that could be shown in the ways that the weddings were conducted by ministers of the gospel, usually chosen by slaveholders. Couples themselves did not always agree about what to call their relationship, especially when disputes arose. Were they married or simply taking up together? It was all too easy for one spouse or the other to later say that they had only taken up with each other when admitting to marriage might cost them something after the relationship had soured. These were the sad realities of slave marriage. How could they demarcate beginnings? How could they determine endings?[22]

While some slaves were paired with partners whom masters foisted on them, they did not call these arrangements "marriages." If they did not choose one on their own, their masters took it upon themselves to decide for them. They were obliged to live with partners they had not chosen to be with, but were essentially coerced into playing the role of a spouse. Or, in other cases, masters showed little regard for their choices even if they had formed their own genuine relationships. While masters had their own ideas about what constituted marriage for their bonds people, they could dictate intimate relationships only to a certain extent. They could make couples inhabit the same living space as though they were "man and wife," but slaves bestowed their affections selectively. Of course, slaves who had spouses picked for them could over time learn to like or love them and raise a family together as amicably as any others.[23]

If left to their own devices, slaves surely found reasons to maintain or dissolve their relationships just as often as free people. Slaves did, however, engage in casual sexual relationships with no pretense of anything else. Sex ratios were one factor contributing to how often they availed themselves of this option. The greater distribution of men in places like Louisiana sugar country, for example, gave women more options for choosing and rejecting partners for sex and enjoying the full panoply of heterosexual relationships. The surplus of single men also meant that male slaves may have had their sexual needs satisfied on an informal basis but could not all find partners for more long-term relationships. Some slaves everywhere opted out of taking up or marrying altogether, choosing to snub the rules of Christian monogamy they knew were contradictory and impossible to fulfill. How could you be married and be a slave, monogamous and yet be subjected to forced separation and violation?[24]

The majority of slaves typically engaged in a succession of marriages or partnerships over the course of their lives, as involuntary (and some voluntary) separations and death intruded and their needs for companionship changed. Although there were known incidents of plural marriages in which all partners knew about and agreed to the arrangement, these were unusual. More typically, men (and sometimes women) had bigamous relationships, as they moved from one partnership to another, with unauthorized beginnings and inexact endings. As they were thrust into the internal slave trade, hired out, or moved about to different farms, plantations, and urban employment, they made love and friendship along the way, constantly reconstituting their conjugal and familial ties.[25]

Slave marriage was a product of affection, love, fear, anxiety, and practicality—any combination of which existed in a state of perpetual turmoil. Those who entered into it had to endure the third flesh of the master while living under the shackles of the individual plantation states on which they were captives. Should they or shouldn't they go ahead with marriage when there was no guarantee that it could be sustained?

Some slaves had what they called "trial marriage," meaning that they tried hard to see each other but were frequently thwarted, for various reasons, because each spouse lived in a different location.[26] Plantation size and masters' attitudes shaped the context within which slaves could marry people at home or farther away but still in close proximity. Most slaveholders owned twenty or fewer slaves, which meant it was difficult for most slaves to find spouses on smaller farms and in towns and cities. The fewer slaves on a given plantation, the more difficult it was to find a mate at home. Crossplantation or abroad marriages were thus the most common arrangements throughout the South, but increasingly so in the declining and diversifying areas of the Upper South. Couples regularly experienced at least temporary separations from each other as long as their relationships survived. Marriages were forged in the interstices of living miles apart and short-term reunions and under the ever-constant threat of separation. Men did most of the shuttling back and forth to visit their families in the common space they shared at their wives' places (though there are some cases of women visiting their husbands). Men walked several miles each way, except for the fortunate few who had access to horses they owned or could borrow. Before every trip husbands had to obtain passes from their owners or overseers certifying that they had permission to be out on the roads to avoid being captured and beaten by slave patrollers or "paddy rollers." The visits took place some weekday evenings, but typically on weekends and holidays. The challenge of commuting added more caprice to marriages as it required perpetual displays of good faith by masters to consent to regular visits and to accommodate absent husbands. If a slave requested leave to visit a spouse for urgent reasons, such as sickness, and was denied a pass but went anyway, he might well meet with swift, sometimes deadly force.[27]

Coresidential marriages were less common and were mostly found on the largest plantations, especially those with one hundred or more slaves. Slaves in the Lower South areas with thriving rice, sugar, and cotton plantations would have these options. Slaves who cohabited had the advantage of dealing with a single master, as opposed to one for each spouse, to negotiate their arrangements. Coresidential couples were assigned their own space. Homes were typically decrepit log cabins that required repairs and reinforcements to make them livable. The challenge increased for slaves who shared quarters with two or more families. To maintain a semblance of privacy in the cramped lodgings they built partitions using whatever materials were available—old boards or hanging clothing. Some slaves in those places could even engage in a variation of crossplantation marriage, with people who were owned by the same person but were separated over widespread properties.[28]

Whatever their residence, husbands and wives had no legal claims on each other's time, which was primarily devoted to satiating the needs and filling the pockets of enslavers. Slaves in some areas, usually larger plantations, won concessions over time, which allowed them the privilege of developing "internal economies," whereby they spent their nonwork hours engaging in activities to supplement the meager supplies provided by their masters. Slaves bargained for plots for gardens, small farm animals, and the time needed to tend to them so that they could better provide for themselves and sell the surplus of their labors for other personal items and products. In some cases, slaves sold their surplus products to the masters, who then had access to garden crops at considerable discounts. Many masters were thus able to shift the burden of caring for slaves on to those dispossessed of their own labor. Rarely did masters provide enough food to sustain laboring bodies, though they might increase food supplies at the height of the harvesting season to maximize productivity. Further supplementation by the slaves, es-pecially off-season, was essential to avoid malnutrition. Clothing was also insubstantial. Slaves were provided with one or two sets of clothes and one pair of shoes annually. Non–working-age children were often given less. Women spent time making and mending their clothing rations so that they could have adequate protection from the elements.[29]

Couples often adopted traditional gender roles, with men expected to provide for their wives and children, which, however earnestly pursued, were onerous burdens to bear. To do so, they might hunt, fish, and help women grow garden vegetables, or build furniture and make handicrafts for use and to sell. The more slave men earned, especially as skilled craftsmen, the more they were expected to devote to caring for their families, which allowed slave-owners to reap even more benefits and shed responsibilities for those they claimed as property. Lunsford Lane recalled: "almost every article of clothing worn either by my wife or children . . . I had to purchase; while the food he [the master] furnished the family amounted to less than a meal a day, and that of the coarser kind." So while his wife's owner claimed all the fruits of her labors, Lane had to support her and their children to make up for the owner's neglect. The hardship took its toll as Lane struggled to keep up, earning what he was required to for his master and earning what he needs for his family to eat, and yet still hoping to have something left over to save for eventual freedom.[30] More novel arrangements involved slave men actually purchasing their wives' services. What free men could expect by virtue of a marriage license, slave men could only hope to be in a position to buy from other men. Urban slaves who were hired out and allowed to keep a portion of their wages were in the best position to do this. For an annual fee, slave men bought some or all of their wives' time to be used toward housekeeping duties for their own families.[31]

Not all men were able to contribute something to their families, through no fault of their own, leaving their wives largely in the position of having to fend for themselves, materially and otherwise. As one slave woman recalled of her abroad husband, "He never did have nuthin' to give me 'cause he never got nuthin." She continued, "I had to work hard, plow . . . and split wood jus' like a man."[32] In other cases, this responsibility was picked up by other men in slave communities who would occasionally donate wild animals to help feed women whose husbands may have had multiple wives or been unavailable to contribute.[33]

One of the biggest challenges for married couples split between households was dealing with two sets of masters and the ever-present possibility that one spouse would be taken away or sold. Abroad couples could not always count on enslavers to abide by agreements for visits, which could be withdrawn at will and often were. They had to be vigilant about strategies for finding ways of uniting their families under one roof or, at the very least, keeping them from being sold farther apart. Some slaves tried to manage their living situations by negotiating with their masters to make it easier to commute. If the couple lived within easy reach, the man might be allowed to work by day on his plantation and sleep at night with his wife on her plantation.

During the first three years of William and Ellen O'Neal's marriage in Louisiana, her mistress died. Her new master made plans to move her out of town but was willing to sell her to William's master or to buy William. William's owner did not want to part with him but was willing to buy Ellen, which would keep the couple intact. Meanwhile, Ellen's owner became frustrated by her failure to reproduce and thereby add to his slaveholdings. He made continual efforts to sell her on the market. William devised a plan. He persuaded a friend to lend him the money, with interest, to buy Ellen. "She was no longer the 'goods and chattel' of a white man, but the sole property of her husband in deed and in truth," he declared. The bondage of slavery and marriage were crossed in this convoluted deal. Ellen both gained and lost her freedom as her master and her husband exchanged her as property, from slave to wife. The sale came at an even higher financial cost as the friend ultimately changed the terms of the deal at the last minute, capitalizing on a desperate slave husband. Meanwhile, William's owner had a change of heart, too. In need of cash, he offered to allow William to buy himself out. To raise the money, William needed to sell his wife—temporarily—to a trusted friend who would allow him to repurchase her at a later date. William paid for his freedom on an installment plan, with nothing in writing to confirm the deal. The master's son got involved in the negotiations toward the end of the last installment and insisted on adding nine hundred more dollars to finish the deal. Enslavement was all-encompassing in its web of oppression and injustice to its victims.[34]

Most slaves were not able to successfully negotiate or buy their way out of separations and watched their spouses being taken away, as Henry Box Brown discovered. The first few months and early years in a couple's marriage were the most critical because, being young, they were more likely to be split apart or sold off.[35] Women tended to marry in their late teens and men by their early twenties. Still strong and vital slaves were the most prized chattel on the market. Proslavery proponents tried to downplay incidents of sales, especially those that split up families, to counter abolitionist arguments. The sheer number of slaves auctioned and sold off was proof otherwise. Yet they insisted that separations were rare and even that they mattered little to people of African descent, who were unattached to their kin. Masters replied to grieving slaves by telling them to carry on. In some cases, they replaced loved ones right away with substitutes, without the slaves' consent. One slave woman was sold away and her husband greeted by another woman sent with a message from their master stating, "That is your wife." The grieving husband recalled later: "I was scared half to death, for I had one wife whom I liked, and didn't want another." He continued, "there was no ceremony about it."[36]

Involuntary separations often led to overlapping entanglements. Despite the fact that the separations were usually decided by the masters, they created emotional turmoil and conflict that slaves had to resolve. Should couples continue to honor their relationships even when separated by long distances? How long should they continue to hold out the possibility of reunion? Separations that led to subsequent relationships might also eventually lead to repair and reunion years later. Women and men were often involved in several relationships, sometimes leaving (or separated from) the same spouse and later getting back together again.[37] New partners, on either or both sides, however, could complicate reunions. One couple, both fugitives, accidentally met on the street one day. When they recognized each other, the woman's first words were, "Dear, are you married?" When the answer was returned in the affirmative, "she shrank from his embrace, hung her head, and wept," according to a witness. The man then proceeded to introduce his old and new wives to each other. Though the couple was considered divorced, according to the conventions of slavery, they each felt a moral obligation to honor a relationship they had not willingly breached. The husband decided to provide a weekly stipend to his first wife. The man essentially had two wives, although he had been satisfied with just one. Whatever vows he had spoken to the first wife he was bound and determined to keep, even if it required a bigamous arrangement to accomplish.[38]

Multiple spouses were par for the course where slavery and marriage intersected. Patty and Isaac Clement were married when the same master owned them, and they had five children together. Living on the same plantation did not protect their union. Patty was sold away. It is not clear if the couple considered this a permanent breach, but Patty then took up with another man, Isaac Snipe, at her new home. Patty and Snipe, who apparently already had a wife and children, had a child together as well. Clement searched for Patty and found her at her new home after she had begun a relationship with Snipe. When Clement arrived to visit her a fight ensued between the competing men. The owner claimed Snipe as Patty's husband and kicked Clement off the plantation. Patty also had children by at least one other man before she was even separated from Clement.[39] Although it was more typical for men to be involved in multiple relationships, Patty's situation was not unusual. Being sold away had severed her first relationship, she probably assumed, and provided an occasion for starting a new one. There was no guarantee that it would not happen again.

Slaves often disobeyed their masters' wishes, marrying other than chosen partners without their consent or even knowledge. Harriet and Charles Tisdale's marriage involved a total of five people and two other marriages aside from their own. They considered themselves married in opposition to their masters, who seemed to be unaware of this arrangement despite the open secret within the slave community. Harriet's master had paired her with Tony Jackson against her wishes. Harriet was forced to go along with this forced union up to a certain point, but she refused to recognize him as her husband, as her master wished. It was rumored that Tony contracted a "disease," after which Harriet kicked him out of the house and then took up with the man of her choice, Charles Tisdale. Tony's actions and words suggested a different version of the story; he claimed to have left Harriet after five years of marriage shortly after the birth of a son. Was the baby Charles's or his? He did not say explicitly whether this uncertainty motivated his leaving. Meanwhile, Charles was married to Clarecy with their master's approval in a ceremony officiated by a minister. But after she caught him cheating, she threw his belongings out of their cabin. Charles was probably cheating with Harriet, given that the two took up together subsequently, if not before. Clarecy was sufficiently angry with Charles after the breakup that she stopped using his name and resumed using the name of her first husband, Shawney Ford, who had died before she married Charles. Masters had the power to separate couples or force them to live together as man and wife, but they could not control their emotions. Slaves asserted their own preferences, sometimes by waiting years to reunite, though in the meantime they sometimes formed relationships of convenience with those in close proximity or with whom they were forcibly paired.[40]

The everyday social relations of marriage under bondage and its attendant contradictions were constantly at odds with slaves' efforts to carve out domestic lives they could call their own. Powerful emotions and needs prompted slaves to flirt with love, to court, and to marry despite restricted rights. Slaves' sentiments and values were articulated and acted upon in the context of their own worldviews, but the most privileged had a stake in upholding the norms of domesticity. Their literal freedom depended on it. The recognition of all black humanity rested upon it even more.

Much of what we know about the messiness of slave marriages has been made visible in the aftermath, as descendants struggled to reckon with them. The heirs of early antebellum slaves or late-era slaves themselves often presented their tangled genealogies in court to prove their relations in order to gain the benefits of inheritances. Enslaved widows of enslaved soldiers took pains to retell their convoluted relationship histories, tracing their roots back for the purposes of receiving pensions. And former slaves revealed complications of slave marriage in interviews conducted after emancipation. Taken together these sources allow us to reconstruct compelling narratives that provide insight into how these relationships worked and what they looked like, often in ways that counter conventional standards of respectability and monogamous sex.[41]

During slavery, a select group of slaves worked with the abolitionist movement to publicize their many struggles to create families. Slaves testified in the court of Northern and international public opinion about the toll that slavery took on their intimate relationships. Former slaves were recruited to speak on the lecture circuit and to publish autobiographies to explain to Northern audiences in vivid detail what precarious unions were like in order to win minds and hearts for the abolitionist cause. Their job was to explicate how slavery corrupted black and white alike by compromising Victorian sexuality. They also showed that despite these corrupting influences African Americans were capable of feeling the full range of human emotions and expressing moral scruples.[42]

Slaves like Henry Box Brown who ingeniously escaped the shackles of bondage and lived to tell the tale were able to write their way into humanity, or dictate their stories to white interlocutors. The success of this enterprise rested on proving that they already possessed the family feelings that white supremacists argued they did not, that they aspired to the kind of domestic bliss of monogamous marriage and little children under a shared hearth that the free white North idealized. Their autobiographies expound on the central trope that abolitionists said made slavery so odious: the separation of parents (especially mothers) from their children, the sundering of ties between husbands and wives, the interference of the third flesh of masters, which violated the marriage bed in its most extreme forms, and the marketing of progeny. The stories that fugitive and former slaves chose to tell and how they told them were influenced by the audience for whom they were intended. They could not be sullied by the depravity that they described within the system. Their tales were ultimately expected to depict captive Africans moving toward the full embrace of Protestant Christian conversion and its ethics of obedience, hard work, moderation, and sexual propriety. Certain stories, those that implied values and behaviors that were inconsistent with this portrait, were unwelcomed. Fugitive writers, if they controlled their own pens, sometimes managed to challenge antebellum conventions of the polite, sentimental nonfiction genre they inhabited.[43]

Fugitive slave and ex-slave writers told their audiences that black people were capable of the same aspirations for marriage and family as others starting from the age of puberty and early adulthood. They then began the proverbial search for true love through courtship rituals to which free people could easily relate. Thomas Jones described the desire he felt for a domestic retreat of his own making after facing one catastrophe after another as a young man. "I wanted a friend to whom I could tell my story of sorrows, of unsatisfied longing, of new and fondly cherished plans. I wanted a companion whom I could love with all my warm affections, who should love me in return with a true and fervent heart," he wrote in his autobiography. Enslavement made him yearn even more for marriage: "to have a wife to love me and to love. It seems to me that no one can have such fondness of love and such intensity of desire for home and home affections as the poor slave."[44]

Perhaps no slave man wore his emotions on his sleeve as well as Fields Cook, who lived a relatively privileged life as a literate slave hired out in Richmond, Virginia, and who would later rise to hold public office. What is unusual is that Cook wrote his autobiography while still in slavery, though it was not discovered for nearly a century and a half. The form of his story was quite different from the published narratives that circulated on the abolition circuit, but his sentiments were consistent with them in emphasizing aspirations of Christian conversion, chastity while single, and the normalcy of marriage and familial relations. Cook, in a manner that was self-effacing and exuberantly self-revelatory, provides a window onto the struggles, joys, and pains of a young man coming of age—a young man who also happened to be black and enslaved.[45]

Cook captures scenes of courtship among urban slaves, almost as though these rituals existed in a bubble, removed at least momentarily from slaveholders' oversight. And they probably were, as slaves in the city inhabited social worlds outside of the usual containment that rural farms and plantations induced.[46] "The female sex . . . was a great troble to me in the first part of my manhood," he admitted. The trouble was that, like many men in such circumstances, he simply could not figure out how to approach and attract a woman—any woman—which led to self-doubt and awkwardness in their presence. He seemed to "fall in love" with "pretty women" repeatedly, though he never gave himself a real shot at getting to know if his feelings were true. He paced in front of these women on the street, discreetly, to see if he could muster the courage to speak or if they would say anything to him. He failed to make eye contact, to show the right gesture of interest, or to find any kind of opening. In repeated frustration he noted: "And I were still standing single." He tried a different strategy at a neighborhood dance on a Sunday afternoon. He decided he would set his eyes on two women who he knew in advance would attend the event. He showed up early dressed smartly for the part. As the girls arrived, he recalled, "I would jump up and make my obesionce to them in the most polite manner and walk a cross the flooer 2 or 3 times after which I would take my chair and set it down by the side of one of the girls just as close as I could get it after which I would set myself down and throw one leg a cross the other." He heightened the tension further as he decided to "look in to her face as much as if to say to her do you see me?" See him? She had no choice. But hear anything, in the form of words, coming from his direction? She did not. Cook was so struck with fear of saying the wrong thing that he could not say a word. He watched in silence and frustration as other men gracefully moved from one woman to the next, carrying on conversations. "I was stuck as tight as a man could be against his will," he sighed. It would take years of trial and error before Cook could find the love he dreamed of. But his status as a slave, of course, would interfere once he did. His first engagement to marry a fellow slave was cut short, probably by her master. He did not specify the reason, but they both were aggrieved by the split. "I were most deranged about her and she poor creature was the same for me but we were not to marrie although I never shall for get that love," he wrote. He would eventually recover and find another woman to marry.[47]

The process of courtship was mutual. Like Cook, women and men alike sought mates in the context of everyday work and leisure activities. But the options and the context were not the same or equal. Men had more mobility, whether they were urban slaves like Cook or lived in rural areas. They had official reasons to be out and about in the process of their daily work, more so than women, whose range of occupations was confined mostly to working in the fields or in the homes of white families. Women in cities had the most flexibility as they moved from running errands to working in more diverse settings, from factories to homes. The process of courtship appeared to follow conventional gender scripts, with men taking the lead. But at weekend frolics, women and men checked each other out and decided whether to make a move or bide their time. Men like Cook were clearly afraid to make the first step. Others deliberately held back, wanting to be chosen ones, hoping that the right woman would make them the object of desire rather than the reverse. Women could capitalize when men competed with each other for their attentions. When Reba turned fifteen she appeared uninterested in the attention of young men, despite the apparent games they played together, drawing straws to determine who would win her affection. She decided to assess the qualities of the men she found most appealing. Buck was one whom she liked best. She admired his independence and willfulness, though these attributes had caused him to be beaten. She began to contact Buck on her own, in secret, and learned more about him that endeared her to him, and vice versa. He eventually proposed marriage and she agreed.[48]

Women, more than men, were restricted in their options of whether or not to pursue or respond to the affections of men. Getting their masters to consent to their wishes was the biggest hurdle. Masters were concerned about the influence a visiting male slave might have on others, especially if he was literate. They had not only the woman to consider but also her future increase. When Harriet Jacobs entertained thoughts of love her mind was set on a free black carpenter whom she had known since childhood. His integrity and character made her fall in love with him. Jacobs's carpenter lover wanted to purchase her from her owner and marry her. But her master refused to allow the pair to unite. The difference in their status was a huge obstacle, and she knew her master, "Mr. Flint," would object, as he did. Most important, Flint wanted Jacobs for himself.[49]

Owners of slave men had less vested interest in their slaves' mates, but they still had some. Isabella Van Wagenen, nee Baumfree (later known as Sojourner Truth), became attached to a slave named Robert in upstate New York. But Robert's master forbade him to visit her, "anxious that no one's property but his own should be enhanced by the increase of his slaves." He ordered Robert to find a wife among the local slaves. But Robert refused to obey and continued to sneak to see Isabella, until he was finally beaten so severely for doing so that he gave up.[50]

Some masters refused to allow any courting because they simply disapproved of married couples on the plantation, which led slaves to make surreptitious cabin visits. Sometimes the success or failure of courtship between plantations could rest on whether or not neighboring planters got along well. Slaves caught in the middle might downplay their interests in each other to avoid the possibility of becoming casualties of their enslavers' mutual dislike. Some masters played a role by using either positive incentives to encourage slaves to mate and marry or negative punishments if they seemed to be reluctant to do so on their own. In many instances, spouses were foisted upon slaves who refused to comply.[51]

For all the love and affection that fugitive writers emphasized in their narratives, some slaves looked past sentiment and went straight to the pragmatism of living in a hard-edged world. They dispensed with the niceties, the "foolishness," of courtship rituals—the chase, the strategic games, the gifting of small tokens of affection (like candy), and the role playing. Be over and done with, was the attitude. If they agreed to marriage, it was for them merely instrumental, a practical surrender to the need for companionship, domestic help, or a way of escaping from frustrating isolation. "My idea was to have a wife to prevent me running around—to have somebody to do for me and to keep me," admitted Robert Smalls, who became famous during the Civil War for piloting a Confederate boat to the Union Navy and later served in Congress. He bluntly stated that his priority was the "service the women will render." Love had nothing to do with it.[52]

The casualness and lack of seriousness with which slaveholders and other whites treated the marriages of slaves influenced the meaning that blacks assigned to these relationships. The devaluation made some slaves feel like there were "no marriage[s] at all," leading to cynicism and rejection of the institution altogether.[53] Still others saw marriage and slavery in opposition; they could not conceptualize how they could inhabit both at the same time. This is what motivated Ellen and William Craft to initially postpone getting married, but then to marry as slaves and immediately embark on an elaborate plan to run away to freedom in order to have the greatest security for their bond and future offspring.[54] This was a common tension that slaves wrestled with and one of the biggest emotional hurdles they had to get over before they would agree to marriage.

Slaves also sought the approval of their parent(s) despite the absence of parental powers under slavery. Parents sometimes tried to impose their choice of suitor and even ally with him to pressure a reluctant daughter. Parental support was an important part of the community of slaves and free people of color, and it often surrounded the couple as their relationship grew.[55] To the extent that they could, parents helped couples gather resources to start their joint household. Preparation for marriage by a betrothed couple involved the pooling of goods and labor. Men might collect wood to build a cabin or furniture or put in extra hours to make money for a new family. Spouses would save money for gifts for each other, such as cloth and handkerchiefs, as well as other goods and supplies.[56]

Ceremonies often followed quickly after couples secured the requisite permissions. The most privileged slaves could have elaborate weddings, replete with borrowed or gifted bridal and groom attire, followed by big feasts. Most slaves, however, could expect no more than light refreshments to mark the occasion. Most simply began or continued their cohabitation with their new status as husband and wife. Those who did have some kind of ceremony participated in a range of officiated rituals. Many slaves had masters or mistresses (or anyone else drafted for the purpose) say a few words to pronounce them united. Christian marriage was not the norm for most, despite its dominant influence on how the institution was defined and used to judge slave relations. The majority of slaves had not converted to the religion in the antebellum era, and even among those who had they were not guaranteed a wedding in keeping with their faith. They preferred to be married "according to the gospel," though only a select few, typically elite slaves, had "scripture weddings," led mostly by black, but sometimes white, preachers. Individuals might be deputized on the spur of the moment to serve the function. When Bethany Veney, a house slave in Virginia, was given permission to marry, she requested a Christian ceremony, but her master enlisted a black peddler who just happened to be passing by.[57] But even those undergoing Christian rites were not always allowed authentic ceremonies. Enslavers were ambivalent about fully embracing the edicts of Christian marriage that infringed on their own rights or could cause them to face rebuke from church peers if they later decided to separate couples. They often made mocking gestures to the Bible by substituting random books as though they contained some kind of ecclesiastical authority to appease the illiterate slaves who could not tell the difference. Some slaves assumed they had a Bible ceremony but could not say for sure. "I guess it was the Scriptures," one slave reported about the book read at a ceremony she observed. "Then he'd tell 'em they was married but to be ready for work in the mornin'."[58]

The most common wedding ritual was jumping the broom (see Fig. 1.2). Some slaves noted that they jumped forward for nuptials and backward for divorce (though there would have been few occasions where they had the opportunity to do the latter). Others reported jumping backward or jumping both ways to get married. The tradition most likely originated in Europe and, like many others, was adapted for African-American slaves. Slave masters were less than earnest in exploiting the tradition given its association with premodern paganism. But many slaves used it to mark new beginnings in their lives when few other commonly observed rites were available to them.[59] Usually the master or other slaves held a broom or pole while the couple held hands and tried to jump over it and land on both feet, to sym-

THE BROOMSTICK WEDDING.

"Look squar' at de broomstick ! All ready now ! one-two-three-jump ! "

Fig. 1.2   The broomstick wedding. Jumping the broom was a folk practice used to unite slave couples in marriage. The ceremony, which had its roots in pagan traditions in Europe, was adapted in the context of American slavery in lieu of weddings marking legal marriage.

bolize good luck. The broom was sometimes placed on the ground or held at the threshold of the couple's cabin so they could symbolically jump into their new life together. It was said that if one person did not touch the handle or landed first, this was a sign either that that person would be the boss of the other or that there would be trouble in the marriage. Slips on the broom were moments of comic relief, especially when it was the man who fell down or touched the broom.[60] But the folk ritual was not universally embraced. As one former slave declared derisively: "We didn't jump over no broom neither. We was married like white folks wid flowers an cake and everything."[61]

Those who did jump the broom did not necessarily embrace it as special: "I didn't have no sho' 'nough weddin'," another former slave recalled. "Me and Julie jus' jumped de broom in front of Marster." Slaves knew what a proper wedding looked like and they understood that masters might try to denigrate the sanctity of their unions.[62] There is little indication that slaves elected to jump the broom and little evidence of sentiment attached to the act. But the tradition did signal to families and communities that the marital knot was being tied. (See Fig. 1.3.)

Wedding vows were scripted and selectively edited for the particular condition of slave marriage. Slaves could not determine what the minister or other persons officiating would say or require them to recite. When the Bible was invoked it was used to reinforce not just the bond between the couple but also their subservience to their enslaver. Francis Terry Leak, a slave-owner in Tippah County, Mississippi, recorded a ceremony verbatim in his plantation diary in the 1850s. Leak owned a large cotton plantation with more than one hundred slaves by midcentury. He may have presided over the ceremony himself, since that person was apparently white but not identified. As Moses and Pol stood hand in hand, they were administered these rites of matrimony:

Moses,—Do you agree, before me and these witnesses, *to take Pol as your wife,* and do you *solemnly pledge yourself* to discharge towards her all the duties of an *affectionate, & faithful husband?*

Pol,—Do you agree, before me and these witnesses *to take Moses as your husband,* & Do you solemnly *pledge yourself* to discharge towards him all the duties of an *affectionate, & faithful* wife?

As the parties have thus publicly agreed *to enter into the marriage relation with each other,* and have *solemnly pledged themselves* to a faithful discharge of all its duties, it only remains for me to pronounce them, & accordingly, in the presence of these witnesses, *I do pronounce them, man & wife.*

Salute your bride.[63]

GIVING THE BRIDAL COUPLE A GOOD SEND-OFF.
The company filed in, followed by the black musicians with their banjos and fiddles.

Fig. 1.3   Giving the bridal couple a good send-off. This artistic rendition of the post-broomstick ceremony appears in the memoir of Mary Livermore, who was born in Massachusetts and worked as a tutor on a Virginia plantation before the war. Her memoir describes her experiences living in the South, including observations of African-American life, which inspired her to become an abolitionist.

Some striking aspects of this ceremony are the symmetry of the vows between "man and wife" and the absence of references to God or duration or permanence of "the marriage relation." Nor did the slave-owner remind the couple of their devalued worth, as did many others, including the former governor of Georgia and slaveholder Charles J. McDonald, when he stated frankly: "I have a Negro preacher who marries them for the union to last as long as they live or until it is the pleasure of their owner to separate them."[64]

Slave weddings were bittersweet moments suffused with irony. Slaves knew that what came next might rend their hearts. Many vows mixed references to the commitment of the couple to each other, to their respective families, to their masters, and to a higher power. Some masters openly mocked what they perceived as contrivances, imitative performances and false hopes. Others took pride in their own perceived magnanimity in allowing their chattel to go forth in holy wedlock. Yet slaves always knew that masters' self-interests were at stake in the marriage ceremony, God or no God. They welcomed their participation to heighten the symbolism of the moment and, they hoped, to give masters greater pause before breaking their bonds. The celebrations summoned extended family and communities to witness their pledges and to do their part in helping couples sustain their unions.[65]

Aside from concerns about involuntary separation, slaves worried most about sexual intrusions of the master or his family. In anticipation of this perpetual threat, Bethany Veney insisted that the peddler cum minister take this into account when she said: "I did not want him to make us promise that we would always be true to each other forsaking all others, as the white people do in their marriage service, because I knew that at any time our masters could compel us to break such a promise." Henry Bibb captured the problem this way: "The strongest reasons why southerners stick with such tenacity to their 'peculiar institution,' is because licentious white men could not carry out their wicked purposes among the defenceless colored population as they now do, without being exposed and punished by law." He continued: "If slavery was abolished, Female virtue could not be trampled under foot with impunity, and marriage among the people of color kept in utter obscurity.[66]

Slave women were often forced to engage in sex against their will with masters, overseers, and other white men. A slave-owner might force a slave husband to exit the marital bed as the slave-owner took his place with the slave's wife. Moments like these diminished the advantages of couples' living together, given the fact that men were told to provide for their wives but could not exercise the prerogatives of free men to protect them. While slave men did not have the power to protect their wives and daughters from sexual exploitation, this does not mean that they stood by passively despite the threat of violent retaliation; their presence could, in fact, discourage lecherous masters. Nonetheless, the representation of mixed-race people within the slave population provides one indicator of the frequency of interracial sex resulting in births. There is no way to distinguish voluntary from coerced procreation in these figures, but the correlation of higher numbers of biracial slaves with the prevalence of abroad marriages on plantations is striking in some locations. And as abolitionists argued, the disrespect of the marriage vows of slaves by Southern slaveholders redounded to their own relationships. Contrary to the idea that opening marriage to an excluded group would sully the institution for the privileged, the reverse was true. In denying legal rights to slave marriages the marriages of whites were also open to violation. Slaveholders desecrated their own vows by engaging in sex with women whose bodies they owned and whose progeny they produced, capitalizing their wealth with impunity.[67]

Sexual abuse extended to forced couplings between slave women and men. Henry Watson, a slave transplanted from Virginia to Mississippi, explained the practice on the plantation on which he grew up: "Whenever a vacancy occurred in any of the cabins of either sex, of marriageable age, it was immediately filled up by my master purchasing another slave." The master would stand before the cabin and announce to the man and the woman what he expected of each of them as a married couple. Even when slaves were not purchased specifically as spouses to other slaves, unwilling parties were often paired. The master's will did not end with the initial coupling. On one plantation where the planter exclusively made the pairings, William Ward, a former slave from Georgia, recalled that "these married couples were not permitted to sleep together except when the husband received permission to spend the night with his wife."[68] In other situations, masters refused to recognize existing relations between slaves, even when they themselves had paired them up. Slaves did not disregard those they considered their spouses when separated against their will, which often made them reluctant to remarry; some even refused outright. Silvia King was part of the last generation of slaves with fresh memories of Africa, though she arrived by an unconventional, circuitous route, from Morocco, to France, to New Orleans, and then to Texas. She told her master: "I got a man and three chillen back in de old country, but he don't understand my talk and I has a man give to me." King expressed her displeasure by barely calling the man by his name: "He's just Bob to me," she stated. She tried to fight him off physically but failed. The overseer forced the consummation by shaking a blacksnake whip over her. We do not know how Bob felt about the compulsory coupling, but it could have been traumatic for him, too.[69]

Forced couplings were often done to encourage procreation. Masters often redirected courtships to prevent pairings that did not meet their expectations for future progeny. Young women would be watched to see if the young men they liked measured up; if not, the women were told to make different choices or be forced to marry others against their will. Couples who were allowed to select their mates were given time limits to reproduce or face separation and reassignment to new, more fertile mates. The couplings could be crude and violent. One former slave described what happened to his grandmother. She told him that "several different men were put to her just about the same as if she had been a cow or sow." Some masters would allow only select, hearty slaves to marry for the purpose of breeding healthy slaves, and others would force breeding but not marriage. One particularly cruel master forced married slaves to have sex with others who were not their spouses. If they showed any sign of reluctance he would punish them by forcing them to engage in sex acts in his presence.[70]

Some of the gender dynamics of slave marriage are revealed in the tensions between couples that surfaced in the private spaces that were breached. If slaves were able to achieve any relief and normalcy for any length of time, they settled into the highs and lows typical of marital relationships. Negotiating their own differences and conflicts and appeasing or evading meddlesome in-laws were among the common stresses and strains on couples. Slave couples did not exist as isolated pairs but were part of broader communities of other slaves, and sometimes free blacks, who had an interest in the functioning of their relationships. Extended kin and community members often played a direct role in shaping their marriage. Kinfolk interceded when they thought it necessary to help adjudicate disputes or set errant spouses back on the right path, thus interjecting yet more people into the relationship.[71]

Extramarital affairs in particular caused great strife, not only between the couple, but also in the wider community. Moses, a slave man on the Sea Islands of South Carolina, was put on trial for killing Juno, the alleged lover of his wife. He apparently beat the man to death with a club. The fight was a culmination of a long-simmering dispute between the two men over Moses's wife, Maria. Juno was himself married to Jemima. Several witnesses testified that they had seen Moses and Maria in compromising positions, kissing on the beach and hiding out in the woods. Moses and Juno had nearly come to blows over Maria on other occasions, several witnesses testified. Moses was overheard saying that he knew that Juno had impregnated his wife, but that he forgave him. Juno apparently admitted it, promising that he would stay away from Maria in the future. Other witnesses said that they had warned Maria to leave Juno alone.[72]

The major source of conflict between Maria and Moses, however, was over who ground her corn, literally and figuratively. Maria claimed that Juno was her cousin, not her lover: "I never slept with Juno—never done anything with Juno—know I should be punished if I did." Maria said that her husband had beaten her just because he was a "bad man." She did admit that they had argued over her carrying corn to Juno. The fight resulted in Moses's kicking Maria out of their cabin and putting her belongings on the road, forcing her to retreat to her mother's house for safety. Others witnessed the beating that preceded this ejection and overheard the verbal quarrel between the two as well. Maria reportedly was defiant even while Moses beat her, saying that "this thing [her private parts] is my own and I will do with it as I please." Another witness repeated a variation of this line also: "I heard Maria tell Moses that she would do as she pleased with her thing." Clearly, Moses felt he was exercising his prerogative as a husband to chastise his wife for improper behavior. She acknowledged his authority to some degree when she testified officially that she knew right from wrong and that she deserved to be punished had she in fact been guilty of what she was accused. But in the heat of the argument she refused her husband's authority over her body and asserted her right to do as she pleased with her sexuality. This was a bold statement by a slave woman who literally did not own herself, and it put her in a double bind—as slave and wife—with all the negative repercussions and few of the privileges of her status.[73]

Moses, for his part, treated her as his property to do with as he pleased. Far from being the upstanding husband harmed by an errant wife's peccadilloes, he himself had been brought up on charges for having extramarital affairs. Charles, Maria's uncle and a slave-driver, depicted Moses as a violent man. He had whipped Moses three times for "being caught with another man's wife." Moses may have been extra angry with Juno because Juno had also been accused of having an affair with his sister. Whereas free men were allowed to mildly chastise their wives to avenge their honor, Moses, as a slave, had no formal right over his wife or her body. He did not own himself. The impotence of such a role might help explain the need to seek favor among other women outside marriage. Slave husbands were expected to assume what often amounted to ceremonial roles, to give the appearance of power that ultimately they did not have. Slave women suffered as a result of these frustrated masculine aspirations, bound in wedlock to disenfranchised men and bound in slavery to enfranchised men.[74]

It is difficult to overstate how significantly the unique predicament of slave marriages exacerbated the more universal challenges of merging the proverbial twoness into one. Extramarital affairs may have been common problems in marriage, but for slave couples, the third flesh in all of its guises was ever-present, threatening the integrity of their union. There could be no such thing as a normal marriage as experienced by free people. Slavery added encumbrances and burdens that led to marital practices forbidden by church doctrine and frowned upon by a state that precluded legitimacy for slaves' monogamous relationships. The ironies and the double standards led to untold injustices and violations.

Christianity had an outsized influence on slave marriages because it reinforced the authority of the master class as arbiters of slave unions as sanctioned by God. In the antebellum era slave masters began to take more interest in slaves' religious beliefs and practices and how they affected their sexual conduct and familial relations. Various denominations urged masters to serve as moral guides and enforcers of Christian doctrine.[75]

Charles Colcock Jones, an influential Presbyterian minister and slaveholder from coastal Georgia, devoted his energies to evangelizing among slave communities and published an instruction manual for slave-owners. On marriage, he wrote: "The Negroes receive no instruction on the nature, sacredness, and perpetuity of the institution; at any rate they are far from being duly impressed with these things." He chastised owners for not enforcing any "particular form" of marriage, for not assigning appropriate persons to conduct ceremonies, or for not requiring ceremonies at all.[76] There was "no special disgrace nor punishment visited upon those who criminally violate their marriage vows," he wrote, except for what the Christian churches imposed by way of suspensions and excommunication. But he was most critical of slaves' failure to show reverence for marriage. They treated it as a "contract of convenience, profit, or pleasure, that may be entered into and dissolved at the will of the parties, and that without heinous sin." Despite the fact that slaves could not make "contracts" of any kind, he questioned their ability to commit to their spouses. Although it was masters who were driven by economic concerns that put couples in danger of separation, he accused slaves of marrying for "profit," as though their financial fortunes were changed by submitting to marriages that he or others of his race respected. He resorted to the common excuses that slave couples could be split apart because of "improper conduct" or "by necessity, as in the case of the death of owners, division of estates, debt, sale, or removals." But he claimed that these instances were rare: they were "carefully guarded against and prevented as far as possible, by owners, on the score of interest, as well as of religion and humanity."[77] Jones seemed unaware of the long-term fidelity among slave couples who were left alone, arguing that infidelity and voluntary dissolution were the greater problems. The disabilities of slave marriage rested with their own immorality, according to this logic. It was up to Christian ministers to correct them.

"Why not gratify the home feeling of the servant?" Rev. H. N. McTyeire, a Baptist minister from New Orleans, asked. He urged masters to cultivate "family feelings" among slaves, to keep order on their farms, plantations, and households. "It is the duty of Christian masters to promote virtuous and fixed attachments between the sexes, and while encouraging marriage to guard it with all the forms, of consent, postponement, preparation and solemn consummation," wrote McTyeire. He believed that inattention to sexual morality opened the door to "bigamy, polygamy, with all their corruptions and evils." Jones expressed similar worries, but he also sympathized with exasperated slave-owners who he believed faced recalcitrant pupils and incessant moral infractions that disrupted order on their plantations.[78]

Christian educators and ministers wrote and distributed catechisms to aid masters in the religious instruction of their slaves.[79] Slaves were taught to know God, the ten commandments, the purpose of the Lord's Supper, and obligations of their various human relationships (as church members, slaves, parents, and spouses). They were given scriptures to recite and short, simple lessons drawn from the Bible to illustrate each precept. Wives, as the "weaker vessels," were told to love, honor, and obey their husbands. Husbands were told to love their wives as Christ loved the church and to assume the role of "the head" of their families, which meant that they were responsible for the material provisions of their families as the Bible instructed: "But if any provide not for his own, and specially for those of his own house, he hath denied the faith, and is worse than an infidel."[80] Some catechisms even acknowledged that marriage was sacred in its permanency and no human authority should interfere with it. This meant that divorce was forbidden except in the case of adultery. But it also meant that masters should not separate their slaves. As one such catechism called for slaves to recite:

Q. How long must they cleave to each other?
A. Until they are parted by death.
Q. May we separate two married persons?
A. No; we must not take one from the other.[81]

But all were told to be subservient to their masters as well and to obey them unconditionally. If slaves were willing to "suffer for it" when met with "unkind" masters, they would be considered more acceptable in God's eyes.[82] It was made patently clear which precept should take precedence, which relationship was most holy in the eyes of God's delegates on earth.

The contradictions of Christianity in slave marriage were rife. McTyeire called for the institution of marriage to be "magnified" by masters, with "all the mutual rights it confers," and also to be "protected by his authority." And yet he seemed little bothered by the way even Christian slave-owners approached the marriage ceremonies they conducted with slaves, without even the pretense of religion involved. McTyeire noted in passing having witnessed one such master pick up "a book" and go down to the slave quarters to marry a couple: "Opening his book he pronounced a ceremony. The writer though he heard them, would not vouch that the words used were in any book, but believes the one used was an old copy of the English Reader." Instead of being bothered by the master's reading not sacred words from the Bible but nonsensical words from a grammar book, the Rev. McTyeire was impressed. "The effect was magical," he noted. "They twain became one flesh."[83] The moral of the story for him was that the master had succeeded in converting a "hard case" of a "young and good looking, but not very amiable," woman who had already had multiple husbands without any ceremony at all into a serious and well-intentioned bride.[84]

The church showed its ambivalence toward slave marriage in other institutional practices. It is striking how infrequently marriages were actually recorded in the extant records of biracial Southern churches, even when the names of black members were noted. Infant and adult baptisms were often listed for both races. But when it came time to note marriages, only those of white members were recorded. It was as though writing down the marriages of black couples in the same way as white marriages would confer on blacks the same standing and privileges. Marriage ceremonies could be performed, whether with sincere or farcical scripts, but the act of recording them in church books would have given them more power than most ministers and church leaders were willing to allow. The fewer formalities attached to them the easier it was for masters to escape the rebuke of their peers if they later decided to separate Christian slaves. By contrast, some clergy did report slave marriages in public records. Catholic priests in Saint Louis denoted the slave marriages at which they officiated, along with white marriages, but this did not protect the slave marriages from breach.[85]

The church's sanction of slave marriages served to compensate for the denial of legal legitimacy in the eyes of white Christians. The church provided the mechanism for managing these relationships, enforcing the rules and beliefs of the faith. Proslavery advocates used arguments harking back to ancient history to justify the disjuncture between legal and religious prescription. Slaves, they argued, were married in the sight of God, even if they could not gain the highest recognition of man. The exchange of personal vows, without witnesses or priests, had been the norm of Christendom up until the mid-eighteenth century. According to this logic, slaves were married in the eyes of the one to whom it mattered most, making legal marriage extraneous.[86]

Slaves were subjected to close scrutiny once they converted to Christianity by churches governed mostly by white clergy and elders, though in some cases they were also supervised by black watchmen and ministers. An estimated 22 percent of African Americans in the South identified as Christian by 1860.[87] Slaves were far more likely than white members to be indicted before disciplinary boards and punished for moral crimes and marital infractions: adultery, cohabitation, bigamy, polygamy, quarreling, desertion, abuse, illegitimate births, and (re)marrying or separating without church permission. These procedures were often very intrusive and punitive. The "Committee on Colored Members" of the First Baptist Church of Charleston in 1851 indicted two slaves for having an adulterous relationship. The committee called witnesses, gathered information, and questioned the errant couple. The affair had started seven years earlier, when the man "was in the constant habit of visiting" the woman. "They were on remarkably intimate terms," one witness noted. They were often seen together in her room when her husband was absent. The man's wife heard about the affair and then discovered her husband in the other woman's room with her seated on his lap. On another occasion she saw them in the room and then turned off the light, after which she forced open the door and heard them jump out of the bed. Others claimed to witness the adulterous pair in the act of "illicit intercourse" in bed. The couple was found guilty after their own testimonies were filled with contradictions, giving credence to the accusations. The committee recommended that they be excommunicated from the church.[88]

The church openly struggled with the problems it created being at once proslavery and promarriage. Clergy were especially befuddled about the problem of remarriage, specifically, whether to sanction this practice when couples were involuntarily separated. They were forced to be more lenient in ways that ran counter to both biblical principles and civil law. Churches in states that forbade divorce except by legislative enactment more readily granted divorces to slaves.[89] But proslavery advocates put the onus on slaves to live up to the values demanded by strict Christian principles at the same time that they were required to obey their earthly masters. White Christians treated slaves as though they were able to freely make the choices that the faith dictated while their own interventions were the grossest violations married couples faced. Permanent sale or separation were the fate that all slave couples were threatened with and large numbers actually suffered. Sexual violations perpetrated by the third flesh were also a reality in many slave marriages. The greater irony was that slaves were judged by and blamed for their own predicament. Christian defenders underwrote this stubborn fiction: "forsaking all others" was a choice that slaves could freely make. Failure to do so merely reflected their sullied racial ancestry, not the transgressions of exemplary slaveholders—chaste and benevolent mothers and fathers all. White Christians sanctioned a tarnished system by dishonestly claiming that it was superior, that slave marriages were formed in the eyes of heaven, not man. Slaves knew the contradictions that Christian marriage offered them. Still for many, there were benefits. Membership in the Christian church affirmed community recognition of their bonds, provided a forum for airing and resolving disputes, and could potentially lead masters to think twice about spousal separations that were neither honorable nor obedient to the Christian spirit.

Slave marriages ebbed and flowed in response to the structural changes of bound labor that affected their daily lives during the antebellum era. The story of Henry Box Brown and so many others underscores how the Second Middle Passage wreaked havoc by the continual threat of removal that it provoked. But differences in demography, plantation size, and urban and agricultural systems produced very similar consequences. Slaves created and adhered to marriages, making them as binding as they could be. But they were perpetually haunted by fears of separation and sexual violation. Departures generated confusion and uncertainty about how to regard one's current spouse and when it was safe to think the breach sufficiently severed to start a new relationship. This situation created serial marriages and overlapping entanglements, often with multiple spouses and partners. Slaves struggled to reconstitute new relationships and social networks out of fragments of existing kinfolk and strangers lumped together. Stasis could never be taken for granted. They had to be nimble and creative in order to respond effectively to the caprice of change. The pursuit of basic human needs for companionship, affirmation, affection, solace, and love won their hearts and guided their feet, despite their caution. They managed to create many deep and meaningful relationships.

And yet the harms done were monumental. The absence of state recognition and protection of marital rights for the enslaved distorted their unions and cast aspersions on their meaning. "A bond that is not real anyway, a bond that does not 'exist,' that never had a chance to exist, that was never meant to exist," as one scholar has argued, can trigger insecurity for those whose kinship rights are denied. "If you've actually lost the lover who was never recognized to be your lover, then did you really lose that person? Is this a loss, and can it be publicly grieved?"[90] Slaves struggled to reconcile these existential questions within the context of coercion and a system of violence. Slave couples were tolerated to the extent that they served as central pods in the production and reproduction of units of labor, to reinforce the social order of the profit-making regime dictated by enslavers. The master class was the lawgiver and slaves lived within its domestic domains, not as independent householders able to protect and sustain the integrity of their intimate and familial relationships. The church sanctioned the desecration of these relations while holding slaves to impossible standards of idyllic domesticity. Slaves were expected to play the roles of the dominant gender script as husbands and wives but were stripped of the powers and privileges that underwrote them. They were flogged by the rhetoric of paternalism, which shifted the blame for their failures away from the beneficiaries of their degradation. The slave states (and the nation-state) recognized only those marriages produced by virtue of one's citizenship, one's freedom, one's ability to freely give consent and act as a sovereign person joining in union with another sovereign person. The question remains, why and how did proslavery forces actually justify their refusal to grant legal standing to slave marriages?

2

2

"God Made Marriage, but the White Man Made the Law"

Harriet Robinson and Dred Scott were united in holy matrimony by Major Lawrence Taliaferro, a justice of the peace, in 1836 or 1837 in a public ceremony in Wisconsin Territory. Several considerations make this event remarkable. Harriet and Dred were both slaves, though at the time they resided at Fort Snelling, a federal post in a free territory, present-day Minnesota. Taliaferro was the bride's master, who acted in his official capacity to sanctify what he considered to be a bona fide legal marriage of the couple, with the consent of Dred's master, Dr. John Emerson. Taliaferro would later clarify his intentions in performing the wedding in his autobiography, stating that he "gave" Harriet to Dred, and thus freed her. He relinquished his property rights to her as he may have assumed Emerson had likewise done for his slave, to grant them the liberty to fully embrace their status as "Mr. and Mrs. Dred Scott."[1]

After years of living as de facto free people and raising a family, the Scotts individually filed suits in 1846 to obtain de jure recognition of their freedom on the grounds that they had lived in a territory where Congress had "forever prohibited" slavery, had legally married as free people were entitled to do there, and thus should be considered free regardless of having relocated to the slave state of Missouri. The two cases were merged into one that eventually made its way to the U.S. Supreme Court in *Dred Scott v. Sandford* in 1857, which resulted in the most important decision in the antebellum era concerning the rights of African Americans.

The couple's marriage figured prominently in the case made by the defense, forcing the court to reconsider the relationship between marriage, freedom, and citizenship. Could one be truly married and be a slave? Does marriage in itself imply certain rights of citizenship and confer social belonging? As Justice Benjamin R. Curtis of Massachusetts, among the minority on the Court who did not come from a slaveholding background, stated in his dissenting opinion: "There can be no more effectual abandonment of the legal rights of a master over his slave, than by the consent of the master that the slave should enter into a contract of marriage, in a free state."[2] Both the intention of the masters in freeing their slaves for the purpose of marriage and the conduct of the wedding by a public official signaled that the marriage was legal and should be so regarded no matter the place of subsequent residence. (See Fig. 2.1.)

This argument was rejected by the majority of the Court. These five justices, led by Chief Justice Roger B. Taney, came from slaveholding families. Taney, of Maryland, and James Wayne, of Georgia, had divested their personal slaveholdings at the time. But proslavery beliefs were nothing if not transparent in Taney's opinion written on behalf of his colleagues. The infamous ruling that blacks had "no rights which the white man was bound to respect" has overshadowed the dissent, which only a few scholars have explored. Harriet, as wife and mother, and the couple's marriage have been sidelined in the historical memory of the case, best known for its sweeping implications for regional and national politics of racism, slavery, and constitutional rights. Yet the family saga at the eye of the storm is a compelling one.[3]

The case symbolizes the legal quandary inherent in slave marriage. The legal standing (or lack thereof) of slave marriages would have significant ramifications for freedom suits, like the one that the Scotts had initiated in the lower courts of Missouri before reaching the United States Supreme Court. The Scotts were unusual in that they were able to take their appeal to the highest court in the land, but the controversial issues at stake went beyond them. The laws did not ban them from marrying, but neither did they protect them. Slavery and legal marriage were considered antithetical. Legally recognizing the latter in the context of the former could undermine critical components of permanent servitude, as the argument by Justice Curtis

Fig. 2.1 "Visit to Dred Scott, his family, incidents of his life, decision of the Supreme Court." The front-page spread in a leading weekly magazine shows how much the Dred Scott case captured the attention of the nation after it reached the United States Supreme Court. The depiction of the entire family in the photo series acknowledges an important dimension of the case that is often lost in the focus on Dred and citizenship rights.

made clear. Thus in the minds of most legal theorists, judges, lawyers, legislators, and slave-owners, slave marriages could not be made legal. But why
not? What were the barriers to legal recognition and why were they considered
essential to the preservation of the system?

Many answers to these questions can be found in a variety of legal treatises, court cases, and statutory laws throughout the slaveholding states.
Reading and interpreting these legal sources may not tell us all we would like
to know about how they affected the daily lives of the subjects and objects of
their regulations. We cannot say for sure how strictly any given law was enforced in specific localities. But the ideas and doctrines articulated in this
body of legislation represent the aspirations of lawmakers, the vision of the
kind of society they wanted to create, the social order they wished to enforce,
the broader conscience of the people they represented, and the tensions they
stirred between ranks.[4] And as we have already seen, the law is a powerful
instrument, yet it could not fully eschew contestation. African Americans
and their allies did everything they could to undermine the law's refusal to
protect and recognize their families. Proslavery authorities created roadblocks
to forestall African Americans' rights. They were remarkably consistent in
crafting legal precepts that denied civil standing to slave marriages. In the
South slave marriages were not legal, yet they were not explicitly prohibited
by statute. In the North, slaves were given explicit rights to marry in some
states. But even in those situations the respect for such rights was always at-
tenuated, resulting, in the waning years of slavery, in more similarities than
differences between the North and the South.

The legal principles used to justify the denial of marriage rights for slaves
were established in the colonial era. Not coincidentally, they emerged along
with the codification of slavery to ensure that they would be inextricably
linked to the institution they were designed to buttress. When the Virginia
General Assembly in 1643 passed a law categorizing African women as "tithable" labor, thereby taxing their agricultural work, it imposed economic constraints on black couples. The tax, ironically, encouraged African men in some
counties of Virginia to marry European women to avoid the extra burden
they would bear by intraracial marriage. This was a few decades before the
tide would begin to turn against interracial relationships. Being married was
important to men's ability to prosper and to become masters of their own

domains. The domestic and reproductive labors a wife provided helped them safeguard their status and invest in their futures in a patriarchal society. Marriage provided a route to extending their lineage with multiple offspring, stretching their ties through extended kinship, and expanding the creation of wealth—as had also been true in West Africa. The tithe against black women's labor made it that much more difficult for men to achieve these goals with their countrywomen. Black families were burdened with raising funds to purchase members out of slavery and to buy land if they hoped to prosper in colonial America. Racial difference was written on the backs of black women as they were denied the privileges of white womanhood and their men were thus denied the rights of white manhood.[5]

The 1643 law marked only the beginning of the construction of the sexual economy of slavery in mainland North America. The status of black women would devolve over twenty years, foreshadowing a predicament from which they would not recover for quite some time. In 1662 the Assembly ensured permanent servitude for slave families by passing a law that recognized *partus sequitur ventrem,* meaning that the offspring follows the mother in her condition as slave or free. The law was unprecedented in English common law. It grew out of the Roman or civil law tradition, which determined the lineage of slaves by their matrilineal ancestry. Anglo-Americans found it expedient because it had been applied to cattle since ancient times. When animals reproduced, the brood belonged to the owner of the mother. Not all the American colonies passed similar laws—in fact, nearly half did not. But eventually they would all follow this law de facto. It became an article of faith of American slavery that masters held the rights to the increase of slave women. The law was a powerful tool for both assigning degradation on the basis of racial status and amplifying the property rights of slaveholders.[6] This profound alteration of the paternal-descent rule would trouble black marriages from that point on.

African slaves became legally kinless by the mother-descent rule, which gave priority to the rights of slave-owners above the familial rights of slaves. Neither mother nor father was recognized. Neither could pass on an inheritance to their heirs. The mother served as the vessel for the replication of capitalism's most valuable commodity, capable of transferring only her own ceaseless subjugation. As one scholar has argued, this put the children of slaves in worse positions than children born out of wedlock, whose mothers were at least given the prerogative to claim them.[7] The role of father was divested as well, though functionally it was reinvested in the position of the master. By making African women uniquely distinguishable for both their productive and their reproductive labor and stripping all rights of fatherhood from African men, the combination of these two laws would be foundational to negating the marital rights of slaves. If slaves could be denied the right to kin they could not possibly be allowed to have any legal rights to marriage, as the latter would empower slaves to topple the fortress (and the guaranteed profits) that the rules of descent and permanent servitude erected.[8] Thus denying legal recognition to slave marriage was absolutely essential to making slavery inheritable, perpetuating a bound species of property attached strictly to one race.

And yet despite these principles calculated to undermine the legitimacy of black marriages, some colonies implemented procedures and passed laws to explicitly uphold slaves' right to marry. Puritans in New England insisted that slaves publish banns and appear before magistrates or clergy, the same requirements they had for whites. Slave marriages differed from free marriages in that they required masters' permission, however, and Puritans conceded to desecrating slaves' vows by splitting couples and families apart as their pockets induced them.[9] Such customary practices permissive of slave marriages did not suffice for some colonies. Massachusetts felt it necessary to pass a law sanctioning them, again with masters' consent, in 1707.[10]

African Americans pushed for greater recognition of their marriages during the American revolutionary era. A group of slaves in Boston petitioned lawmakers to prevail against masters who mocked their nuptials in 1774: "The endearing ties of husband and wife we are strangers to for we are no longer man and wife than our masters or mestesses [mistresses] thinks proper. How can a husband leave master and work and cleave to his wife? How can the wife submit themselves to there [their] husbands in all things?" Appeals like this one fell on the deaf ears of church and state. British authorities had often complained before independence that colonists were lax in their Christian duties to baptize slaves and too permissive in allowing slaves to marry outside Christian norms. Masters feared that conversion to Christianity would inspire emancipation. African slaves themselves often resisted Western precepts, preferring to continue their traditional marital rites. But even those slaves who did adopt Christian rites, as the petitioners showed, were rebuffed. Progress was made farther south in Maryland in 1777, where a law was implemented conceding slave couples the right to marry with their masters' consent, though without giving them any civil standing. Pennsylvanians passed a law in 1788 against the separation of slave families. But this law could not pass the legislature without an additional proviso that permitted separations of up to ten miles, so as to minimize interference with the property rights of slave-owners. The fact that these statutes were enacted in this era testifies to the problems that slaves faced in gaining legitimacy for their unions.[11]

The rationale foreclosing the legal standing of slave marriage was articulated mostly by judges, lawyers, and legal theorists rather than by legislators, however. Daniel Dulany, a distinguished lawyer, political leader, and slaveholder in Maryland, wrote one of the most influential early opinions in 1767. Dulany wrote his verdict in the context of explaining an inheritance case involving manumitted slaves. He looked to British laws in search of precedents, but since slavery was not legal in England, he cited villeinage, a form of serfdom that seemed approximate to slavery in Anglo America. Villeins were allowed certain rights, including the right to marry. If a neif, a female serf, married a freeman she would become free by virtue of her new status as a wife. Marriage was equated with freedom, and although her lord could not stand in the way to disallow it, he could demand compensation for the injury caused by the withdrawal of her labor. But slaves, Dulany argued, were "incapable of marriage by the civil law, because incapable of the *civil rights annexed to it.*"[12] He insisted that slaves and villeins operated under different systems because of the chattel principle. Slave-owners had property rights in the bodies and the harvests of their chattel that lords did not obtain in serfs. The "essence" of the system of slavery depended on this, he noted. Dulany invoked *partus sequitur ventrem* to equate slave women with cows and mares; the principle granted masters' rights according to "the law of England" and "the law of nations." Marriage and slavery were entirely incompatible: "either the master's property must give way for the support of the marriage of a female slave, or her marriage must be deemed invalid in order to preserve her master's property." The property of the master could not be contravened by the contract between slaves.[13]

Dulany argued that slave marriages were amoral because they existed beyond the pale of the standards established for Western man. Slaves were treated like animals as the precepts behind the mother-descent rule indicated. Animals were not bound by expectations of sentiment or morality. Although the undeniable human character of slave misdeeds made them subject to criminal laws, slaves were otherwise not constrained by civil laws or "objects of such laws as relate to the commerce between the sexes." Slave marriages were not regulated, nor were infractions deriving from them punished, so long as sovereign people were not hurt by the slaves' actions or affairs. A slave man could not expect to gain relief "against the violator of his bed." Slaves were not scorned for promiscuity, punished for fornication or adultery, or prosecuted for bigamy. The absence of civil recognition in no way interfered with the main priority of the master's interests in sex between slaves: "There is no danger that the consideration of their progeny's condition will stop propagation." The need to enforce conformity to the morality of the dominant society was thus suspended. Dulany's opinion underscored the major arguments that jurists and proslavery ideologues would use over the next century to justify the absence of legal marital rights for slaves. Slaves were chattel. Their marital acts could not supersede their masters' rights. They had no "civil rights" or civil standing in the law that allowed them to make contracts of any kind. And they were amoral at best.[14]

Proslavery spokespersons amplified and expanded these rationales as they broadened the scope of slave law in response to the growth of slavery in the antebellum era. Lawmakers felt compelled to shore up their "peculiar institution" to defend against growing attacks from the North. A flurry of legislation was enacted in the slaveholding states. Although these slave codes differed in many ways, they contained commonalities based on shared values, ideas, and fears. Separate judicial systems were established in some places for the purpose of dealing with felony cases involving slaves. Other states tried them within the dominant judicial system but formulated separate rules for convictions, trials, and juries.[15] Slave codes authorized masters' dominance and at the same time provided a measure of public regulation. Masters were told that they had the right to manage their property however they deemed appropriate, but neither their beneficence nor their malfeasance could be tolerated if it infringed upon the rights of other white citizens or on the well-being of society in general. The laws governed the market relations of commercial transactions involving slaves, spelled out guidelines for the provision of basic sustenance and care of the enslaved, set limits on a master's brutality and on his or her acts of kindness, and called for the absolute submission of slaves in return for improved provisions.[16]

Slave law allowed for the subjectivity of slaves in a constricted way. Their humanity was largely defined negatively in the law; the most robust recognition of slaves' will and intelligence was when they were marked as criminals, for which they could be prosecuted and punished more severely than free persons.[17] This demonstrates a central distinction of slavery from other areas of the law: the dual nature of the slave as person and as property. When it was expedient to do so, the law recognized that slaves were people with volition, will, and the ability to think, not animals or inanimate objects. But it otherwise defined them as commodities, fungible parts of the credit and finance system. This dual recognition was at odds with itself and could never escape the circular logic that always returned to the bottom line: slaves were chattel, even if they were not literal things.[18]

The lack of autonomous legal standing made even the few positive protections difficult to enforce since slaves could not file suit on their own or testify against whites. Laws against cruelty to slaves were designed to curtail unprovoked and excessive viciousness that had previously gone unchecked. They were also enacted to prevent masters and their surrogates from engaging in cruel behavior that might cause slaves to rebel, steal, run away, or otherwise create turmoil that would disturb the peace. But prosecution had to be initiated by white persons offended by the infliction of extreme bodily harm on a slave, and the punishment, if the perpetrator was convicted, was almost always less severe than if the victim had been white. In the crude calculus of dual recognition of slaves as persons and property, punishment was doled out disproportionately to slaves for infractions against whites while redress accrued mainly to slave masters to allow them to recoup the loss or damages to their investments. Even in extreme cases where slaves were executed for crimes committed, many Southern states reimbursed slave-owners for a portion of the value of the deceased property.[19]

While some slave codes aimed to better protect the enslaved physically, they disadvantaged blacks in other ways, especially in the aftermath of slave rebellions like those of Denmark Vesey (1822) and Nat Turner (1831). Slaves faced harsher reprisals for acts of defiance after such incidents. They were more closely watched and their movements carefully contained. Free blacks also suffered because of their involvement in slave revolts and simply because of guilt by association. Whites feared the contradictions that the mere presence of free blacks in a slave society posed for the rationale of the institution. Southern states put restrictions on manumissions, usually requiring special legislative acts to grant individual owners the privilege of freeing their slaves. They forced those allowed to go free to leave the state promptly or face re-enslavement.

Despite the flurry of slave laws passed in the early decades of the nineteenth century, very few were designed to mitigate the negative repercussions that slavery imposed on the integrity of families.[20] Proslavery leaders did not broach the subject of reforming laws in favor of slave families until late in the secession crisis running up to the Civil War. Yet even then, while there was much talk about protection of slave families from separation and even talk of legalizing slave marriage, few actual changes were made. Louisiana was the only Southern state before the antebellum era to pass a law against the separation of mothers and children under age ten, though it did not apply to slaves seized for debt or used in the settlement of estates. Georgia and Alabama were the only other states to pass similar prohibitions for children under five, in the 1850s, though loopholes allowed administrators to separate them if deemed necessary. And there is no evidence to ascertain how often any of these laws were enforced. No such laws were ever implemented anywhere to preempt the splitting up of spouses.[21]

Southern law was not a neutral instrument but a powerful force that contributed much to the destruction of slave marriages and little to their protection, as abolitionists were fond of broadcasting.[22] Court-ordered slave sales provide a clear example of how the law could be used to protect the interests of slaveholders's profits. The image of slave trading typically brings to mind the much maligned figure, and convenient scapegoat, of the individual trader selling his human wares in an untoward manner from slave pens or commercial houses that even slaveholders shrank from. But many slaves were bought and sold on the steps of county court houses, where human property was disposed of on behalf of debtors suffering financial crises or divided for the benefit of descendants awaiting distributions of estates. Black families were split apart and sold away for the security of white patrimony and the consolidation of wealth. These sales were conducted by agents of the law, which resulted in frequent separations of slave families. Buyers and sellers moved with efficiency and ease in condoning these acts because of what was at stake financially. The law authorized profit-making as the highest priority. The selling of slaves as fungible assets was not a by-product of blind market forces or the application of rules with unintended pernicious results external to human intervention or control. Public officials were empowered to sell slaves with regard only for maximizing the profits entitled to the beneficiaries. They were required to break apart slave families as necessary in light of the fact that "slaves sell best singly." Officials who refused to abide by this dictum could be held personally liable for failing their clients.[23]

No one was more aware of the role of the law as a negative force in slave marriages than slaves themselves. They were most vocal in speaking out against these injustices in slave narratives, interviews, and speeches on the abolitionist circuit. As one ex-slave from Virginia stated: "God made marriage, but the white man made the law." Slaves fully understood the forces they were up against in man-made laws that gave little recognition to their most intimate relationships.[24] Fugitive slaves recited a litany of harms that resulted from the absence of legal protection: the forced sexual violations, the coerced breeding, the lack of parental privileges, and the dispersal of kin—all for the amusement and benefit of masters. Recall the exclamation from the fugitive slave Henry Bibb that no one held the legal protections of marriage in greater esteem than those who were deprived of them. This consciousness haunted slaves terrified to embrace what would likely be breached, absent the protective arm of the law.[25]

The law's refusal to condone slave marriage reveals clearly how slaves' rights were made null and void. No state explicitly banned slave marriages in statutes. Southern legislatures passed more laws on slavery than on any other issue, but they left it to the courts to explain why slave marriages could not be legalized. Some scholars have argued that states were less interested in the private law aspects of slavery and chose to leave it to individual masters to decide.[26] Yet the lack of marriage laws, either pro or con, does not reflect an absence of governmental concern or influences. In the tradition of common law, lawyers and judges played the dominant role in constructing tenets relevant to slave marriages. And they were by no means neutral bystanders. Many lawyers had a direct interest in how their cases were decided. The legal issues surrounding slavery kept most of them in business, allowing them to build law practices, translate their earnings into buying slaves and land, and eventually enter the planter class. From there it was only one stop to the judiciary for the most privileged, who were also the most influential legal minds and political leaders in the South. Thus slavery had a broad and direct influence on Southern law and lawmaking.[27]

Slave marriages entered the antebellum courts at the state level in criminal and civil cases. As common law, these powerful rulings shaped and determined public policy, obliging lower courts to follow their decisions, and they were used as precedents at the discretion of courts in other localities. Slave cases were the "core material" for educating lawyers in training about the nature of Southern law, and they formed the body of thought for judges and lawyers to consider in litigation and adjudication.[28] Such cases make clear how the law and the broader society regarded slavery and African Americans more generally. The cases that made their way up through state courts show not only the variety of issues that slavery generated for judicial consideration but also the repetition of key concerns across time and geographical space.[29]

Slaves could only be named as individual subjects as defendants in criminal cases, under charges that ranged from theft of property to murder, and such cases often involved spousal or family affairs. Most of the criminal cases to reach appellate or state supreme courts involved murder of one slave by another slave, often stemming from disputes between a slave husband and his wife's lover, in which the latter ended up dead. In other cases, free blacks could be culpable for crimes committed while protecting their relationships with enslaved people. Marriage itself was classified as a crime, as for example when a free black man was convicted of marrying a slave woman in 1846, contrary to the laws of the state of North Carolina, which prohibited these mixed-status relationships.[30] Or, in another example, a free black husband was convicted of stealing his slave wife from her owner in Delaware in 1834.[31] The extant record of the case is brief, but the judge's ruling indicates that he believed that the master's capital invested in the slave trumped whatever claims the husband made for his wife in a marriage not deemed legal or legitimate.

Civil cases were more common, and slaves could not formally initiate them. Rather, they arose after slaves were manumitted or in the process of gaining their freedom, and they involved slave marriages. Most were cases of inheritance in which surviving relatives, usually offspring, made claims on the estates of parents, and the outcomes turned on the legitimacy of the marriages of the elders, sometimes with inquiries going back generations. Similar cases also involved ex-slave widows seeking to claim estates against the interests claimed by their husbands' alleged creditors. In fewer cases, the issue arose when slave masters left wills to free their slaves and pass on property that was contested by their executors and heirs. Cases of indentured servitude were significant as well, usually involving fights over the custody of children or the service terms of adults. Marriage issues were raised in transactions involving free spouses purchasing their enslaved loved ones, in cases where widows became town paupers, and in rare cases of divorce between free people of color.[32]

These cases were adjudicated up to the Civil War, but the most decisive ones were concentrated between the 1810s and the 1830s, as indicated by how frequently they would be referred to in later decades. Many of the early cases originated in Northern and border states, which manumitted more slaves and thus handled more legal cases pertaining to ex-slaves and their early marital histories. Louisiana was the only Deep South state that bucked the trend, but it too had a more forgiving tradition of manumission than most Southern states. Nonetheless, the number of legal cases brought before the courts is testament to how protracted the process of emancipation actually was and how former slaves continued to be entangled by their prior identity even once freed. The legacy of slavery would not be erased simply by virtue of a new status. Heirs would have to deal with it for many generations. The cases also call into question the sharp divide between North and South regarding the treatment of slaves. In reality, there are striking similarities in the

challenges that slaves faced in gaining recognition of their unions from jurists
determined to deny them rights. Most slaveholding jurisdictions would not
reckon with the legal implications of slave marriage until after 1865, however.

Judges wrestled with how to delineate the distinguishing features of slave
marriage compared with marriage between free people, and to rationalize
them within pertinent legal traditions. Early colonial laws, which defined racial status and permanent servitude in the bodies of black women, were taken
for granted as indispensable edicts. The proslavery judge James A. Clark of
the Kentucky Court of Appeals stated it bluntly in 1811: "the father of a slave
is unknown to our law."[33] The conflict between this rule of descent and marriage laws was dramatized by a case in New York in 1822. In that state slave
marriages were legalized and the children of those unions defined as legitimate in 1809. But this statute did not alter the slave law of maternal descent.
This case is particularly curious because it places the rights of a free woman
in opposition to marital and parental rights. In 1817, Francisca, a former slave
woman, married a slave man. The man continued to live with his master,
though the records say that they had "cohabited" from the time of their
marriage until her death in Kingston. They had a child, Dinah, in 1821, and
Francisca died shortly after childbirth. Upon the mother's death the child
was taken away from her father, grandmother, and great-grandmother. The
guardians of the poor in the town of Kingston sent Dinah to be a ward of
Marbletown, claiming that that town was responsible for her because it was
the place her mother, Francisca, had been born a slave, whereas Kingston
had merely been the place she'd last resided after her master abandoned
her. The two towns ended up in court, with each trying to make the child the
pauper of the other without any consideration given to the fact that Dinah
had a father and other family.[34]

The court took pains to articulate Francisca's rights as a free woman, even
in a mixed-status marriage. According to Judge Jonas Platt, delivering the
opinion of the court: "I cannot admit, that by such a marriage a free wife
subjects herself to the custody and control of the slave husband. The general
law of *baron and femme,* the legal relation between husband and wife, cannot
apply to such a case."[35] In other words, Francisca was not legally subordinate to her husband, as was the case with free women married to free men.
The court went on to reiterate that the status of the child should follow the

status of her mother, and the mother had exclusive custody of her children. It also made sure to clarify that the slave husband was not emancipated as a result of marrying a free woman. Yet the case did not take into account the central fact that Francisca, the mother, was dead. The court ruled "as though their father were dead." If the law refused to recognize the father, regardless of the flesh-and-blood man prepared to care for her, the child belonged to Marbletown, where her mother was born, not Kingston, where her family resided. So although the couple's marriage was legal, the wife's status as a free woman was used against her husband, the father of her child, despite what we would presume to have been her wishes after her death.[36]

In addition to precepts stemming from colonial laws, the imprint of Daniel Dulany's 1676 opinion is also evident in the most foundational arguments articulated by antebellum jurists. The principal legal objection to slave marriage was that it interfered with masters' property. In a society in which those rights reigned supreme, slavery could not be reconciled with the pledge of exclusivity and permanence that characterized legal marriage. One of the most explicit statements coming from the bench on this issue originated in Pennsylvania in *Commonwealth v. Clements,* 1814. In that case Chief Justice William Tilghman argued that a slave could not "acquire any rights by marriage in derogation of the rights of her master, who retained the absolute control over her person and her services."[37] Tilghman owned a plantation with slaves in Maryland before he moved to Pennsylvania. He maintained his property while serving on the state's supreme court until he ran (unsuccessfully) for governor, a few years before the *Clements* decision was decreed.[38]

The judiciary in slaveholding states shared Dulany's belief that slaves could not make contracts to marry. One of the most influential judicial decisions to articulate this dictum was *Girod v. Lewis,* in the Louisiana supreme court in 1819. According to presiding Justice George Mathews, a second-generation planter and slave-owner, "slaves have no legal capacity to assent to any contract. With the consent of their masters they may marry, and their moral power to agree to such a contract or connection as that of marriage, cannot be doubted; but whilst in a state of slavery it cannot produce any civil effect, because slaves are deprived of all civil rights."[39] Judge Mathews introduced an unconventional twist, however. He argued that the lack of civil standing for slaves could be reversed upon emancipation, which meant their

marital rights were merely dormant. Louisiana still operated under the influence of a Spanish civil law tradition more forgiving than the evolving American common-law system. Other jurisdictions mocked and rejected the
ruling out of fear that the influential Catholic Church would push to make
marriage a religious sacrament rather than a civil contract.[40]

The ruling also conceded the curious point that slave marriages had
"moral power." It acknowledged the reality of conjugal connections between
slaves that could not be outlawed. This recognition of slave morality marked a
decisive shift from earlier thinking. At least since Thomas Jefferson's *Notes on
the State of Virginia* (1787), Anglo-American slaveholders had argued that
slaves were incapable of moral feelings or actions: "love seems with them to
be more an eager desire, than a tender mixture of sentiment and sensation.
Their griefs are transient." Thomas R. R. Cobb, one of the most influential
proslavery legal theorists, had a similar argument: A "striking trait of negro
character is lasciviousness. Lust is his strongest passion; and hence, rape is
an offence of too frequent occurrence. Fidelity to the marriage relation they
do not understand and do not expect, neither in their native country nor in
the state of bondage." Like-minded ideologues would continue to promote
these ideas into the next century.[41] And so it seems odd that judges would
make a different kind of argument, moving away from both the amoral claims
of Dulany and the immoral claims of Jefferson and Cobbs. Some of the leading
jurists distinguished between "natural law" and "civil law." Natural law recognized that slaves were compelled by human impulses, as old as Adam and
Eve, to mate, to procreate, and to form marital bonds. Natural law advocates
believed that God governed the universe and set in motion unalterable tenets. Civil law, by contrast, was devised by man.[42] Court officials may have
been motivated to give these ideas credence to counteract abolitionist claims
of the inhumanity of slavery and their awareness that abolitionists mined
their rulings for evidence to support the cause. Justice Pearson, for example,
argued that slaves did not have indiscriminate intercourse and that "as a
general rule, they respect the exclusive rights of fellow slaves who are married." But because of their informal relationships, slaves were considered
moral in a different way from whites. They had their own system.[43]

That judges typically used the word "marriage" to refer to slave relationships as they rendered their opinions is significant as well. In many cases,

this language was difficult to avoid, though it was sometimes qualified, as in "quasi marriage" or "marriage de facto."[44] But in describing how slave unions might fit within existing laws, different legal or extralegal terms were applied more in keeping with their subordinate status. Slave couples existed in a state of "cohabitation" because "society has impliedly permitted certain conventional arrangements to be entered into between slaves for the purpose of propagating their species."[45] The problem with cohabitation as a basis for adjudicating the legitimacy of slave marriages was described this way by the planter and slave-owner Chief Justice Thomas Ruffin of North Carolina in 1836, in *State v. Samuel:* "For at what period of an illicit cohabitation shall the incompetency begin? Or how long after the cohabitation terminates, before the competency shall be restored?" In other words, slave marriages differed from legal marriages in that they were slippery slopes with promiscuous beginnings and endings. Yet it was the "illicit" nature of these relationships that also made them ambiguous with regard to their standing. In some instances, "this connection between slaves" was called "concubinage."[46] In other cases it was called "contubernium," which grew out of a Roman slave law tradition that allowed slave marriages to be recognized retroactively after emancipation, as was the case in Louisiana.[47]

But no matter what terminology was used, it was repeatedly stated that married slave couples had no civil protections. The use of terminology to demarcate slave marriages as different and even the recognition of slaves' own moral system worked together in the end to rationalize why slave conjugal relations existed outside of the law. The tautology can be summarized as follows: They could not be prohibited, but neither could they be given legal endowment. They were illegal because they could not be made legal within the existing strictures of property rights and the demands of civil society.[48]

Antebellum judges went beyond the foundational precepts outlined in Dulany's opinion to elaborate other reasons for denying slaves marital protections. They took up the charge to explain whether or not certain concepts that governed the relationships of free people could be fruitfully applied to slaves. Coverture was an ancient legal doctrine that gave men the power to control their wives under the twoness blended into oneness construct, in which the husband controlled all matters of the law on behalf of the couple.

Women's legal identities disappeared as they moved from being *feme sole* to *feme covert,* from an unmarried state to a married state, in which they gave up many civil privileges, including property rights. Many states reformed these strictures in this period, though not to promote women's equality in this first wave of legislation. Married Women's Property Acts were especially useful in slaveholding states to help shelter investments in bond labor by shifting ownership to wives, which kept husbands' creditors from being able to collect damages on human chattel and seize them. Coverture also affected women's labor, allowing men to control their productive work and their earnings. The concept was used against Francisca's family in the New York State case, in which her enslaved husband was denied custody of their child after the free mother's death. Although the law said their marriage was legal, the court said Francisca was legally single, not subject to the power of her husband because he was not a free man.[49]

Judges also scrutinized the relevance of the concept of spousal recusal. In *State v. Samuel* in North Carolina in 1836, Justice Ruffin explained the legal principles behind the usual common-law prohibition against spousal testimony and why it could not be applied to slave couples. He called the precept a "civil institution" designed to keep peace in families. Courts used it to avoid causing dissension or severing ties between married couples so as not to "deprive their union of all cordiality, separate them in feeling, and make their connexion intolerable." He emphasized that this privilege accrued only to legally obligated couples: "Hence a marriage de facto will not, but only a marriage de jure, will exclude one of the parties from giving evidence for or against the other." Marriages between slaves were not legally inviolable; there was no public interest in the impact that spousal testimony could have on their relationships.[50]

But here is another irony. While slaves were denied most marital rights, some courts did acknowledge the authority of slave husbands over their wives, even if abridged and inferior to masters' property rights. A slave man who killed his wife's lover after catching the two engaging in adultery was understandably outraged, according to some officers of the law. The slave man could be declared guilty of a lesser charge of manslaughter rather than murder because of the "legal provocation" of his wife's betrayal. In one such case Judge Pearson argued that it was not a civil law issue; rather "it has its

origin in nature; and a violation of the right which is peculiar to it, in that respect, excites the *furor brevis."* Defense attorneys invented a medical condition to describe men who committed passion killing: "laboring under mental
alienation" or "manomania."[51] The court rejected this defense, and slave men
did not get off scot-free, but it affirmed the logic of the appeal. Some judges
espoused the legal theory that slave men were indeed men, even if inferior
and powerless.[52] Their prerogatives could be violated by an errant wife's
extramarital affairs. Killing may have taken that privilege to an extreme that
could not be entirely excused, but it might be mitigated with a lesser penalty.
The invocation of natural rights thinking in these instances shows how those
in power marshalled gender norms, for or against the interests of slaves,
whenever it was expedient to do so.

Such rulings were consistent with the trend in Southern courts toward
showing less concern for "crimes of passion" than for crimes of property.[53]
But when such passions provoked crimes against whites, slaves were unam-
biguously reviled. Killing a fellow slave was not acceptable, but in some circumstances it was tolerated. By contrast, stepping in to protect one's wife or
one's own honor when the wife was abused by a white man was punished to
the full extent of the law—if the case made it to court before informal "justice"
was meted out. In a Mississippi case in 1859, Alfred, a slave, was sentenced to
death for killing an overseer who raped his wife. The court would not allow
the jury to consider motivation as part of Alfred's defense. Raping a slave
woman was not a crime, and avenging her honor by killing a white man was
not defensible. Alfred appealed on the grounds that the jury should have
been allowed to hear the evidence and decide if it justified a sentence of manslaughter rather than murder and thus a death sentence. Alfred's lawyer
argued that while slave marriages had no recognized civil rights, "still, the
humanity of our law regards them as human beings, with lively emotions and
social instincts, and regards with as much tenderness the excesses of outraged
conjugal affections in the negro as in the white man." This was the same logic
that lawyers used to defend clients for murder when the victims were black,
but it did not elicit sympathy here. No leniency would be shown to the mur-
derer of a white man.[54] Albert was put to death.

Another important legal doctrine was pertinent to the status of slave marriage but not taken up directly by the courts or subsequent scholars. Slaves

were allowed a host of customary rights, most of which they won on the basis of both individual and collective contests in hard-fought battles over time with their masters. They were allowed free time on Sundays, certain holidays off, and, in many instances, time and space to grow vegetable gardens. Masters acknowledged these rights and knew that they would provoke the ire of discontented workers if they refused to abide them. But slaves could not claim a legal right to the time amassed or to the products they made. While slave marriage was among the many customs that were allowed and recognized without official sanction, to what end? It was never treated as a right, a privilege, or an obligation—nothing that could be attached to entitlement. And unlike other kinds of benefits that slaves won, customary traditions of marriage were burdened with much more weight. The stakes were clearly higher for slaves if masters revoked their promises to permit wedlock as the costs were excruciating. Custom did not offer slaves the protection that ultimately made marriages sacred relationships, as they did for free (especially white) people who married informally.

Slave marriages did not have comity, a concept that obligated mutual recognition of marriages across state lines. Couples who were married on one farm or plantation in any given location could not move elsewhere and have their marriages protected. There could be no secure slave marriage without broader social recognition that gave priority to slaves' relationships over masters' property interests. If the couple could not step beyond the bounds of their own farm, plantation, or households and have safety and recognition across state lines, they could not have secure marriages. Masters were the law-givers. Their plantations were like mini-states. Their informal recognition of slave unions was time-limited (the lifetime of the master at best) and subject to economic and emotional impulses. Whatever effect, whatever relief, whatever customary privileges that slaves enjoyed at any given moment were always subject to change. Their marriages lacked the durability of the norms of inviolable marriage that free people took for granted.[55]

Judges adjudicating cases related to slave marriage perceived legal marriage and slavery as dueling polar opposites. Granting sovereignty to slave couples would encroach on the fundamental meanings and objectives of enslavement. As one scholar defined the institution: "Slavery regimes established the means by which that category of humans named as slaves might be placed uniquely and absolutely at the disposition of that category named masters (or mistresses or owners)."[56] The two were so at odds that some legal theorists posed the idea that they could not be mutually constituted and one could cancel out the other. Connecticut jurist Tapping Reeve stated that while slaves could not make contracts, slave men who married free women were emancipated, "for his master had suffered him to contract a relation inconsistent with the state of slavery. . . . The master, by his consent, had agreed to abandon his right to him as a slave."[57] Reeve reasoned that slave women could not be emancipated by marriage, however. He implied that the *partus sequitur ventrem* rule made this impossible, and he referred to the *Marbletown v. Kingston* case to substantiate his argument. But his reasoning based on legal theory does not mean that it translated into actual interpretations of the laws.

Slave-owners feared they would be forced into the scenario that Reeve described, that granting legal rights to couples in violation of their property rights could call those rights into question. How could the civil effects of marriage not spill over into an acknowledgment of freedom? This was a critical question raised in the Dred Scott case. Major Taliaferro had married the Scotts the same as he had other couples at the federal fort. In addition to being a justice of the peace, he was also a devout Presbyterian and a member of a federal mission to "civilize" the frontier. Many white couples from the fur-trading community (though Catholic) sought out his services. But he was especially interested in using Christian marriage to domesticate Native Americans and normalize their families according to Western values. He identified the Scotts' marriage as a "gift of freedom" by giving Harriet to Dred, a concept that the U.S. Supreme Court had favorably ruled on in 1829 in *Le Grand v. Darnell* and which Justice Curtis cited in his dissent.[58] Taliaferro showed no interest thereafter in treating Harriet as his slave. In fact, he would eventually manumit all of his holdings, probably influenced by his religious faith. Dred Scott was listed in the territorial census in 1836 as the head of his household, which affirmed that they conducted themselves as a married couple and as free people. The death of Emerson, Dred's master, probably triggered their motivation to secure their freedom formally. They had no reason to think that their marriage and family were insecure until then. Emerson's death created anxiety about how they would be treated by his heirs and whether or not they would be sold and split apart. That vulnerability, not an abstract desire to gain legal freedom, led them to take extraordinary measures to achieve justice through the courts.[59]

Justice Curtis, a conservative jurist and no abolitionist, understood the terms under which the Scotts had married and the implications for their freedom. He reasoned that "there can be no doubt these parties were capable of contracting a lawful marriage, attended with all the usual civil rights and obligations of that condition. In that Territory they were absolutely free persons, having full capacity to enter into the civil contract of marriage." He called it a principle of "international law" that marriage in one place should be considered valid in another. He argued further that Missouri had violated the U.S. Constitution in effectively nullifying the Scotts' marriage by denying their freedom.[60]

Though the Scotts ultimately lost their case, the court that initially ruled in Scott's favor was in Saint Louis, which had an unusual practice of recording some slave marriages at the city hall between 1813 and 1846. This despite the practice of warning slaves that the state of Missouri did not recognize their marriages and that those who did marry could be separated and sold without notice. This ambiguity or liberality, however it may be interpreted, may have been the result of French and Spanish legal influences in the state, previously a part of the Louisiana Territory, as well as the influence of the Catholic Church. Catholic priests conducted the ceremonies of the slaves entered in public records, which elsewhere would have been consigned to church archives. A record by Father Joseph A. Lutz in 1832 stated: "I hereby certify to have joined together in the holy bands of matrimony Ignatius, slave belonging to Buchoquite(?) and Hyacintha, slave of Mr. Renurd(?)"[61] It is difficult to determine how widespread this practice may have been. Saint Louis did not keep consistent records of any marriages. Couples were not required by law to obtain licenses or register their marriages until 1881. Before then, marriages were recorded depending upon clergy or the court recorder's decisions to do so, sometimes long after the actual ceremony. Sometimes they were recorded not in the county where the ceremony was performed but at courthouses that were convenient. Thus, although only a relatively small number of these slave marriages are on record, it may be due in part to the inconsistency of record keeping. Still, the key question is what do these records actually mean? Even if they looked like the marriages of whites on paper, this did not mean that the slave couples had any enforceable civil rights. The requirement of the master's consent effectively diminished the inviolability of slave marriages. The fact that Catholic priests recorded them meant they did so primarily to instantiate a religious sacrament.[62] This was different from what the Scotts had experienced, however. Theirs was a bona fide legal marriage conducted by a civil official while they lived in a free territory, which to their minds, their masters, and their community emancipated them.

All of these issues raise curious questions about the nature of slavery and marriage in the United States and whether the two institutions were inherently inimical or whether it was possible to have a genuine, legally enforceable slave marriage anywhere. In most slave societies in the Western Hemisphere, particularly those colonized by the Spanish, Portuguese, and French, slave marriages were protected, at least theoretically, mainly as a result of the influence of the Catholic Church. This does not mean that slavery was milder or slave families under less duress, as many scholars of Latin America have made clear. But in Protestant-controlled British colonies in the Caribbean, such provisions were implemented less frequently and late in the slavery era. But the place where slaves had the most sustained legal support for their marriages was in colonial Mexico. Both the Spanish Crown and the Catholic Church insisted that slaves under their domain should be allowed to marry legally, regardless of their masters' consent and even in direct opposition to it. Neither the Crown nor the Catholic Church was opposed to slavery, but they considered monogamous marriage to be the most visible sign of a person's submission to the Christian faith. The requirements of the religion superseded other interests. Slaves gained unprecedented subjectivity and agency as persons with souls, independent of their status as property. Not surprisingly, they used their consciousness of their legal rights to marry in unintended ways, to advance their freedom.[63]

This example highlights the distinctiveness and the primacy of property rights, the significance of marriage as a civil institution (as opposed to a religious one), and the narrowly constricted legal subjectivity of slaves in the

United States. Despite Protestant churches' increased efforts to promote slave marriages in the antebellum era, they always conceded superior authority to slaveholders and civil laws that contradicted Christian marital norms. While historians have viewed the repression of black marriage as primarily a sign of degradation, the control over black sexuality and access to marriage meant much more. It was essential to sustaining the peculiarity of slavery as an inheritable, permanent condition, which could not have existed in the form that it did in the United States without the legal constraints on slave marriage. The Dred and Harriet Scott case, which reached the Supreme Court, and the multitude of other cases that were adjudicated in state supreme courts provided the raw materials for the most influential lawyers, judges, and theorists to enunciate all the reasons slave marriages could not be legal.

The law governing slave marriages was based on long-standing statutes dating back to the colonial era and to judicial law constructed through criminal and civil cases during the antebellum era. Many of the most influential cases originated in the North, even as it was moving in the opposite direction to the South, as the traces of slavery's legacy would not disappear overnight. Both regions granted limited recognition to slave marriages, always with caveats. Slave couples were precluded from a bundle of privileges: inviolability of their unions, sexual exclusivity, control over their children, the right to spousal recusal before bench and bar, coverture, and comity. Yet judges, in their own way, acknowledged the human dimensions of these relationships. They knew they were real relationships, even moral, and that they existed of their own accord, no matter how they were regarded by white society. They considered them to be a product of "natural law," the undeniably human compunction to form emotional and personal bonds to mate and procreate. But the civil law could not sanction them and maintain a system of slavery simultaneously. Legal thinkers turned to laws that were rooted in the treatment of animals to substantiate slaves' status as chattel and permanent servants. And they used race to divine the perpetuity of bound labor that could not be severed from the superior rights of ownership of sovereigns. Race was used to resolve the seeming conflict between two institutions considered highly incompatible. Not making marriage legal was essential to making slavery sustainable. The legal quandaries that the two ignited simultaneously could never be fully resolved.

Yet the problem of slave marriage did not adhere to slaves alone, as the case of Francisca has already indicated. The taint of slavery on race was so powerful that the integrity of all African-American marriages was threatened as long as slavery existed anywhere in the nation. To be sure, those who were slaves and lived in the South faced the most dire, life-altering consequences. But slaves and free blacks were typically intertwined through bloodlines and marriage ties. Mixed-status marriages were granted the same lack of legal regard as those of slaves married to each other. In some states they were expressly outlawed by statute. The struggles of quasi-free and mixed-status couples derived from the same legal neglect and want of protection that plagued marriages of the enslaved.

3

More Than Manumission

The *status* of the African in Georgia, whether [bound] or free, is such that he has no civil, social or political rights or capacity, whatever, except such as are bestowed on him by Statute," wrote Joseph Henry Lumpkin, the slaveholding chief supreme court justice of the state, in 1853. He argued that "the act of manumission confers no other right but that of freedom from the dominion of the master, and the limited liberty of locomotion." Manumitted slaves did not have masters, but they did need white guardians to protect their interests and watch over them. They were expected to live in a "state of perpetual pupilage or wardship," which they could not escape of their own volition, he wrote. In reality, even their "liberty of locomotion" was of a limited kind, encumbered as it was by a state increasingly restricting where black people could live upon emancipation in the antebellum decades. Justice Lumpkin's sweeping opinion went well beyond the conventional boundaries of a case adjudicating the property rights of free blacks. He argued that "to become a citizen of the body politic, capable of contracting, of marrying, of voting, requires something more than the mere act of enfranchisement." Free blacks should never expect "to be the peer and equal of the white man," he opined. The free black "resides among us, and yet is a stranger. A *native* even, and yet not a citizen."[1]

Lumpkin's opinion could not be more clear about the lack of legal protection for the intimate relationships of blacks, regardless of their status as slave or free. Slaveholding states provided free African Americans few of the positive rights in the statutes he identified. The right to marriage was not guaranteed. Lumpkin's sweeping condemnation reflected what free blacks were up against in slave societies in the South and even societies in the North where the number of slaves was dwindling. Georgia was one of the states most hostile to the rights of free blacks, but Lumpkin's views were neither extreme nor singular. His words anticipated the Dred Scott decision, and his sentiments were widely shared by like-minded peers in positions of power. In the first half of the nineteenth century, freedom and slavery were not polar opposites for African Americans but points along a continuum. The protracted process of emancipation in the North and the uneven process of individual and episodic manumission in the (mostly upper) South meant that many African-American families were part-slave and part-free for years and even decades on end.

Free African Americans encountered an avalanche of restrictive legislation, psychological assaults, and physical threats and violations that diminished their status in the antebellum era. Mixed-status marriages, unions between slaves and free blacks, were treated no better than slave marriages and sometimes even worse, since some states expressly forbade them by statute As the South increased its commitment to slavery, white elites minimized the distance between slavery and freedom by dividing society into two distinct groups: enslaved (black people) and white (free people). Free blacks were increasingly forced to take extreme measures that were incongruent with their presumed status in order to protect their most viable assets—their marriages and families. They understood their ability to form intimate ties as essential to their individual and group survival, and, as we will see, they sometimes were forced to sacrifice their freedom to sustain them. Black couples were the least privileged and most fragile among the free married people in their communities. And yet surprisingly little has been written about their relationships, despite attention to nearly every other aspect of their experiences, including political activism, labor, property ownership, housing, education, and religion. Interracial relationships rather than relationships between blacks have attracted the historical spotlight.[2]

The family matters of free people of color are most visible in the historical records in legal proceedings, some of which they initiated themselves, and others that targeted them for various infractions that threatened both their status as free people and their relationships. Even as their rights became ever more limited and increasing numbers of free people were denied citizenship, they used the legal system, especially in their local communities through petitions to counties and state legislatures, and civil and criminal court cases, including divorce proceedings. Extant documents not only tell us about their official status but also allow us to peer into their intimate affairs. They offer a rich repository of narratives about the daily domestic lives of a diverse group of free people of color. Together their stories illustrate the range of experiences and challenges they faced. Most strikingly they reveal that freedom, at best, was a process, not an achievement that could be taken for granted. "The mere act of enfranchisement" did not guarantee marital or any other rights.

The process of emancipation had been protracted in the Northern states, and manumission of individuals in the Border States, begun following the American Revolution, was still under way after 1800. Many blacks remained caught somewhere between slavery and freedom. The end of slavery in the North was propelled more by atrophy of the slave population (through mortality, low fertility, runaways, and the decline of the Atlantic slave trade) than by the efforts of abolitionists. Vermont was the first state to outlaw slavery in its constitution, in 1777, but the ban applied only to men over twenty-one and women over eighteen, not to children. All other states passed variations on legislation that promised freedom to children born of slave women after a certain date and then prescribed indentureships for them. In effect, this meant that adult slaves would by law live out their natural lives in the same condition, and their unborn children would suffer the fate of involuntary servitude to their mothers' masters until they reached the prescribed age of maturity, later for men than for women. In all cases, the initial laws and constitutional provisions were ineffective enough to require the passage of subsequent legislation that took decades to complete. Northern states with the most slaves were the most resistant to laws proscribing enslavement, such as New York and New Jersey. New York began a gradual program in 1799 and then ended slavery completely in 1827. New Jersey began its gradual plan in 1804. The number of slaves declined there significantly by the 1840s, but a few slaves still remained in the state when the Civil War began. The Thirteenth Amendment to the Constitution, ratified in December 1865, freed the rest.[3]

The gradual emancipation plans implemented in Northern states were particularly difficult for the offspring of slaves, who were remanded to indentured servitude until well into adulthood. Masters, not parents, retained final authority over the children of slaves. They were birthed into a system that crippled their ability to advance economically or socially. Masters had few obligations to teach black children skills or educate them, as they had done with white servants. Thus there were few distinctions between being a slave for life or a servant for a term. Indentured servants were especially vulnerable to abuses in the system, even to the real threat of being sold to the South. Some slaves were able to negotiate to end their indentureships before their terms expired, and others ran away. Manumission could also come with strings attached, forcing those who violated agreements with former masters back into bondage. The arrival of refugees from the Haitian Revolution—foreign slave-owners with slaves in tow—also boosted indentured servitude in places like Philadelphia, where the judicial system upheld the right of masters to subject their slaves to terms of servitude. The situation was worse in New York, where the law permitted masters to prolong their authority over formally enslaved chattel through indentures as late as 1848. Ironically, some abolitionists inadvertently prolonged indentured servitude in the North in their attempts to rescue Southern slaves and place them in positions of term service rather than outright freedom. Marriage was typically illegal for indentured servants, and when it was allowed, the permission of the master was required, just as in slave marriages. These restrictions negatively affected the family lives of free blacks in communities where they served terms until late in their twenties, pushing their marriages much later in their life-cycles than was the case for whites.[4]

Most free blacks lived in the South. Their numbers grew in the Upper South following the Revolution as changes in the economies allowed masters to sell off excess slaves or let them purchase their freedom. But the window that had opened at the turn of the nineteenth century quickly closed by 1820, as slave-owners feared that the growing numbers of free blacks were a threat to slavery. After 1820 masters tended to manumit only their most privileged slaves, especially their mulatto offspring, on an individual basis. The number of free blacks in the Lower South stagnated and then declined. Typically, only the most elite slaves were able to purchase their freedom or gain access to it as a stipulation included in their masters' wills. Yet despite the limits imposed on free blacks in the South, they were better off economically than their counterparts in the North because they faced less competition for certain skilled jobs. Nonetheless, their physical and social mobility was far more limited by the constant fear that their color made them vulnerable to re-enslavement.[5]

Free blacks were increasingly perceived as a menace to Southern slave society as it became more reliant on bound labor. The absolute subjection of people of color, no matter their status, became an imperative because freedom contradicted the rationale for the enslavement of blacks, and ties between the enslaved and the free made it difficult to distinguish one from the other. As one group of whites in Virginia wrote in a petition to the state legislature in 1831, "Standing thus in a middle position between the two extremes of our society, and despairing of ever attaining an equality with the higher grade, it is natural that they should connect themselves in feeling & interest, with the slaves among whom many of their domestic ties are formed, and to whom they are bound by the sympathies scarcely less strong, which spring from their common complexion."[6]

Southern states passed laws over the course of the antebellum era making it harder for blacks to gain and retain any meaningful free status. Many states forced manumitted slaves to leave or prevented free people of color from migrating there. In 1806, Virginia was one of the first states to force manumitted slaves to leave the state within one year of their freedom. Mississippi lumped all African Americans together—"slaves, free negroes and mulattoes"—in one consolidated law in 1822 that contained eighty-six parts. Among the requirements of the law, free people were forced to pay security of five hundred dollars "to keep the peace" and ensure their good behavior. If they failed to pay the security or violated its terms they could face jail or be sold into slavery to the highest bidder. The state passed more laws in 1845 that were part of a restrictive campaign referred to as "the inquisition" as violators were rounded up and deported from the state. Manumissions by last wills were outlawed. Georgia required all free people of color to pay an annual tax of five dollars starting in 1851. Within a few years it permitted those who could not afford to pay to be fined or hired out. Those who were considered "idle immoral profligate" or were caught "strolling about" could be convicted for vagrancy, with the severe punishment of sale into slavery for two years for the first offense and permanently after the third offense.[7]

The process of manumitting slaves individually in the South significantly disadvantaged blacks when choosing marriage partners. The uneven achievement of freedom meant that many blacks found themselves related to or married to unfree people. These mixed-status marriages were part of a larger pattern of irregular marriages in European colonies in the Americas among slaves, quasi-free people, and poor populations across the color line. Formal marriage was initially a privilege that people in the (mostly white) upper echelons could attain, though it was becoming more accessible within the lower ranks, at least in the North in the eighteenth century. Mixed-status marriages were common throughout slave societies, although their legal status and white society's level of tolerance toward them changed over time.[8]

In the colonial period, mixed-status intraracial marriages had some legal standing in the North and even in some places in the South—though in all cases the unions fell short of inviolability because masters could interfere at any time. At first states tolerated such couples, in some places, like Virginia, allowing them to register their unions legally and legitimize their children. By the end of the eighteenth century, however, legislatures begin to pass laws restricting slaves and free blacks from socializing. Eventually, they increased the constraints, prohibiting marriage without a master's consent or in some places outlawing it altogether. In North Carolina, if the master of the enslaved granted permission to marry, couples could expect to pay him a fee. Louisiana, which outlawed mixed-status marriages, punished the slave-owner and the free spouse when the law was violated. But it also allowed an unusual exemption. Free men of color could marry their own slave women (if they had no legitimate wives) "according to the forms prescribed by the church"—sacramental ceremonies officiated by Catholic priests. Their wives would then be declared free and their children legitimate. This practice ended, however, after the Louisiana Purchase and the implementation of American civil laws in the state in 1808. This was consistent with the general antebellum trend toward more policing and prohibitions of mixed-status coupling.

Mississippi, for example, included restrictions in its 1822 omnibus law, but they were designed to give masters' optimal control over enslaved women by empowering owners to sue free black men who took their property away.[9]

Regardless of statutory laws, mixed-status relationships could hardly be avoided or eliminated. States struggled to enforce the laws and prosecute violations, which meant that many couples found ways of evading the laws or disobeying them with impunity. There is no way to estimate how many mixed-status couples existed or what proportion of black marriages they constituted at any given time. There is substantial evidence of the presence of such marriages everywhere, however.[10] Because women were manumitted more often than men, they made up a greater percentage of free black populations and were forced to seek spouses outside their cohort, including among the enslaved. Mixed-marriages in general were the product of several converging forces. Slaves and free blacks lived, worked, and played in close proximity to one another, forming various kinds of allegiances on the basis of blood and social connections. The staggered nature of manumission meant that though some couples began their marriages while both were slaves, at some point one spouse became free and the other either followed at a later date or was never manumitted. Slaves able to hire themselves out and live independent of their masters were most likely to be in positions to marry or engage in intimate arrangements with free blacks. Many of them were thus able to share the same households, though some, as was the case with enslaved couples, lived abroad. Still others lived full time in the household of the master of the enslaved spouse. In some cases in order to get masters to agree to such an arrangement, the free person became an indentured servant for a time, sacrificing their own freedom and risking subordination beyond the agreed-upon terms. These deals could be attractive because they sometimes entailed the freedom of the enslaved spouse at the end of the specified term. This was especially crucial for slave women as prospective mothers as it meant their children would be free at birth.[11]

These couples remained at the mercy of the master of the enslaved spouse. A decision to move slaves into the master's household or to sell them off could create havoc. Theoretically, at least, the free person could potentially move or follow behind a beloved one if they were to be separated. Doing so, however, meant incurring the financial costs of relocating and potentially violating laws that impeded free people's migration across state lines. Laws forcing migration on manumitted slaves sometimes meant that the free spouse was the one to leave the state. Returning legally to visit or to reclaim kin left behind required dispensation from legislatures, which was not often granted.[12]

Mixed-status couples had big incentives to free their enslaved loved ones, given their divided family status. They depended on masters, legal guardians, and surrogates to keep their word when they made arrangements to buy out kin. Slaves in positions of relative privilege often worked overtime to earn enough money to buy their own freedom. Once the agreed-upon sums were accumulated and paid, they might assume that the deal was complete. But it was not necessarily legally binding. Most slaves could not read or write, furthering their disadvantage and dependence on the goodwill of outsiders. Southern laws that required former slaves to leave their homes upon manumission meant that freedom could come with a price. Any hope of staying in place often meant raising extra money as security to be paid for their good behavior and also special commendation from state legislatures granting them exemptions from forced-exile laws. One former slave, for example, petitioned the Tennessee legislature in desperation after being told that he was not legally free, despite the deal he had made and fulfilled with his former master. He was concerned about his own status but even more worried about his wife and child. As his sponsors explained, as "dear as liberty is to him, and galling as are the chains of bondage, he would prefer remaining a slave." That is, if he could not be free and keep his family intact, along with his land, freedom did not amount to much. With the assistance of many white friends who vouched for his character, industry, and honesty, the state legislature granted him a reprieve.[13]

Many slaves tried to purchase themselves and other family members to protect their interests. The birth of a new child might spark the desire to emancipate family members, especially if the mother was a slave.[14] When one spouse was free and the other a slave they worried about the fate of the enslaved spouse upon the death of the freedperson. Buying family members and holding on to them as nominal slaves could be a strategy for protecting them. But it could backfire if the free spouse died first, leaving the enslaved spouse in abeyance or at the mercy of executors. As couples advanced in age freedom became more imperative. One elderly free person argued that he feared "the tyranick grasp and relentless cupidity of some unfeeling wretch, [to] be deprived of that portion of liberty, which the sweat of [his] humble brow has purchased for them."[15] Unfortunately, not all free people were able to get their fiscal affairs in order before they died, even if they may have been in the process of trying to do so. Drawing up wills could be protracted affairs for free people reliant on others to carry out their wishes for their estates, putting enslaved family members at risk while the details were worked out. If they died intestate their enslaved loved ones had to rely on the good graces of white guardians to carry out their wishes and do right in freeing their wives and children.[16] Free spouses might also deliberately choose not to free their enslaved spouses whom they nominally owned before they died to avoid automatic ejection from the state, instead devising other creative maneuvers to safeguard them. One husband thought his enslaved wife was better off if he left her property in his will, which he presumed would in itself make her free. Sometimes these arrangements were made in consultation with lawyers who helped free blacks find loopholes within tenuous laws. Such risks paid off for some, though by no means all.[17]

Enslaved men with sufficiently accumulated resources for self-purchase sometimes preferred to free their wives even before freeing themselves. One couple had endured years, if not decades, in an abroad marriage living at a considerable distance of twenty-five to thirty miles. But despite their years together, they still felt their relationship was not secure from a separation that would make it harder to care for each other as they grew older. The desire to emancipate one to make it easier for the couple to live in closer proximity was further complicated by forced-migration laws for manumitted slaves, however. The slave man was required to get a white guardian to go before the legislature of his state to seek a special exemption that would allow him to purchase his wife and also allow her to stay in the state. The absence of such a guarantee would defeat the entire purpose of her emancipation.[18]

Couples in mixed-status marriages could feel especially vulnerable when they had property owned by either spouse or both. Imagine this predicament for slave men married to free women. They were helpless and dependent, beholden to women who would otherwise be their subordinates, if not for their own enslaved status. Whatever property a slave man owned he could not legally claim, but he could vest it in his wife. A slave man in North

Carolina petitioned the legislature (through a guardian) with care and trepidation for his freedom. The couple had accumulated significant wealth,
which consisted of land, livestock, cash, and even slaves—none of which a
slave could legally claim. His wife had purchased him from the executor of
his master's estate, but the transaction appeared to be incomplete. He was in
limbo, which put him at the mercy of his wife. He acknowledged that he was
concerned that either her death or change of heart could wipe out his share
of their treasure. He had no reason to believe the latter would happen, but he
clearly did not want to see his hard work wiped away under either circumstance. Unfortunately for him, the legislature did not agree to pass an act on
his behalf.[19]

Some free people tried to prevent the problems that mixed-status couples
faced by removing their beloved from the grips of slavery even before they
married. A free man in Virginia designed such a plan when he became "fas-
cinated by a lovely female of his own Color who happened to be a slave."
They agreed, however, that she should be emancipated so that they could
marry legally. He had to borrow money to make the purchase and entrust a
white guardian for help. He succeeded in buying her on an installment plan,
and they began to build their family, welcoming two children within a short
time. But they had to face another bind: the laws of the state required his wife
to leave upon being granted her freedom. Even as the husband continued to
pay off the debt of purchasing his wife, he pleaded with the legislature to
allow them to remain in the state and keep their freedom, which it refused
to do.[20]

Legislators were not always amenable even to the wishes of slave-owners.
In some cases, masters were willing not only to permit mixed-status couples
to wed but also to do everything in their own power to protect them from the
caprice that could threaten or dissolve their union. This required extra vigilance, expert legal counsel in estate planning, and faith that their heirs and
executors would follow through with their wishes post mortem. Slaves as
valued property were frequently entwined in legal cases that could drag on
for years, as the estates of decedents were settled, partially or entirely on the
basis of redistributing, exchanging, or selling bound labor in ways that broke
up black families, leaving the free spouses unable to do much if anything
to intervene.[21] Masters using the greatest forethought tried to avoid these

predicaments, but they were also limited by laws designed to prevent them from having unfettered reign over the disposal of assets without due consideration of other fiduciary and social stakeholders. Others died intestate with all the best intentions never being formalized in their wills, leaving mixed-status families stranded. A slave-owner could give a plot of land to a special slave and her free husband and allow the slave to hire out her time to him, effectively allowing them to live as quasi-free. But in the absence of a will, others could easily question the legitimacy of those decisions and accuse the deceased of breaking rules against illegal trusts or skirting the laws that prevented masters from manumitting their slaves without legislative approval.[22]

The gender configurations of mixed-status coupling could make a difference in how spouses were considered by slave-owners. Free men married to enslaved women were often looked on favorably by masters of the women, as the addition of the man's labor and economic contributions could be financially beneficial. But free men could also raise competing interests between the rights of husbands and the rights of slave-owners, a conflict over coverture. The rights of husbands to have unencumbered dominion over their wives and children were considered so foundational that they could not be easily reconciled in the face of challenges of property rights. Even in jurisdictions that tried to make clear that recognition of marital rights of people in bondage did not contravene the preeminence of property rights, mixed-status couples' ambiguous status could call these into question. But there was no such right safe from revocation even in the North or Border States, where legal marriage was sometimes protected.[23]

Free men who had slaves as wives faced further complications, especially if they tried to purchase their freedom. In the process of obtaining ownership of a spouse, did the slave become a wife or was she merely the property of a man who could not be her legal husband? The perverse contradiction of the laws of slavery and freedom is exposed in a scenario in Kentucky. The laws in that state made it clear that African Americans could not participate in the slave trade for commercial purposes. They were allowed to purchase only certain slaves who were relatives for the purpose of protecting them and keeping families from being split apart. This was further buttressed by the fact that a master's consent to sell his slave woman, effectively "giving" her (for a fee) to a man to be her husband, sealed the objective of solidifying marriage. And yet creditors were legally entitled to challenge these very facts when they inconveniently disrupted their own fiduciary interests in the marketability of slaves. They could assert their superior rights to make claims on slave property regardless of the relationship between chattel and owner. Creditors could claim that a free man's purchase of his wife was a "pretended sale" designed to exempt his property (wife or no wife) from execution for the purpose of paying his debts. A free black man could purchase a slave (wife) only for the purposes of rescuing her from the normal rules of the slave market. And yet the same slave was legally liable to being subjected to creditors demanding that she be sold off to pay her husband's debts. Free black men had few enforceable legal rights that white men were bound to respect.[24]

Free women who married slave men, by contrast, were in the unique position of being considered heads of household because their husbands had no legal standing. In one sense they were regarded as *feme sole,* single women who had legal rights that women customarily relinquished when they married. They had to play out reversed gender roles and perform the duties as providers and protectors of hearth and home that their enslaved husbands could not. But in other respects they were treated as inferior forms of *feme covert,* married women who were more like dependent children or slaves in the eyes of the law.

A case from Massachusetts illustrates these dilemmas. Whatever concessions Northern states made with one hand to support slave and mixed-status marriages, they took away with the other. Harriet, a pauper in the state of Maine in 1820 and the mother of an infant, was the subject of a battle between two towns, neither of which wanted to be deemed her official place of settlement and thus responsible for her care. The determination rested in large part on whether her grandfather Isaac Hazzard Stockbridge, a slave, and her grandmother Cooper Loring, his free wife, had a legal marriage. Hazzard (as he was called in the documents) died in in the colony of Massachusetts in 1780, before Maine became a separate state and before his granddaughter Harriet was born. Harriet's mother, Lucy, was eleven years old when he died. The plaintiff in the case, the town of Hallowell, argued that Hazzard was effectively abandoned by his master and thus was emancipated, which established his residence, and that of his family, in the town of Pittston, later incorporated into Gardiner, where he and his family had last lived. Thus the marriage to Cooper Loring was legal. But if he was still a slave, then his marriage was void and his wife's settlement would have been assigned to the other town. If the marriage was legal and Hazzard was still a slave, then neither he nor his wife could be legal residents. In short, Hallowell argued that no matter what his condition or the legality of the marriage, Hazzard did not belong as a resident there, and thus, neither did his wife nor children and grandchildren.[25]

The defendant in the case, the town of Gardiner, argued that his master did not emancipate Hazzard. But regardless of his status, slaves had the right to marry under the laws of Massachusetts colony since 1707. As a slave, he could not establish a settlement of his own for himself or his family. Nor could his wife, a free woman, establish residency because to give her such recognition would violate the norms of marriage by treating husband and wife as separate entities rather than as one. If the wife was allowed to establish residency on her own, her children could not, unless they were illegitimate. So if the marriage was legal the children were legitimate and their settlement rested with their father, who was a slave without rights. Like Hallowell, Gardiner tried to pass along responsibility for taking care of the family at the center of the case. It worried about the limited services that Harriet, a *feme covert* with an infant, could render and the taxes that she could not afford to pay. The plaintiff's rebuttal summed up how the logic of the arguments on both sides left Harriet in a bind: "she has no settlement by the father he being a slave;—none by the mother, she being lawfully married;—and none in her own right;—and yet she is a native of this State."[26]

The judge ruled that Hazzard was indeed a slave, not manumitted by his master, and that the slave marriage was valid, though in the same way that minors had the right to marry. He also ruled that Hazzard's wife, Cooper Loring, could not obtain a separate settlement from her husband, as the defense had argued it would contravene the relationship of the couple. In effect, the wife's rights to establish residency was overruled by the determination to protect the mixed-status couple's abstract marriage, albeit not one that accrued all the civil rights of fully endowed adults. Thus she could not be a resident of Gardiner. Neither could Lucy, the daughter of the couple, as a child, ten years old at the time the town of Pittston was incorporated by Gardiner. Legal marriage came to naught for Hazzard, who suffered the disadvantages of being a slave and Loring, who suffered the disadvantages of being a free woman of color married to a slave man. The plaintiffs lost. Harriet lost more.[27]

The gender implications of mixed-status marriages were highly consequential for children and other descendants of the couples. Fathers were given great latitude in the law for the care and custody of their natural-born children, but not if they were enslaved. In some localities free children of color could be bound out for paid service terms for a set period of time, typically until they reached a specified age of adulthood. Parents were required to consent to these arrangements, unless it could be determined that the child was an orphan. If the parents were deemed unfit to raise them properly, the law empowered county courts or overseers of the poor to bind them out and collect the payments. But when disputes arose about the status of free children, their freedom and their parents' rights over them could rest on marital status. If a father was a slave and a mother was free, the children could be deemed "bastards" because the parents were unable to marry legally. Free children could be treated as having both no father, because he was a slave, and no mother, because, though free, she was married to a slave man. In one such case in Virginia, a local judge ruled in favor of allowing an indenture of daughters to stand against the wishes of mixed-status parents in *Brewer v. Harris* in 1848. He argued that even the marriages of free people of color (married to others of their same status) were not legally binding, since, similar to Justice Lumpkin's argument, there were no statutory laws in the state expressly designed to uphold them. Mixed-status couples could expect even less respect.[28]

At other times, de facto marriage of mixed-status couples was regarded as legally binding when it served the interests of the state, especially when criminal prosecutions were involved. The extension of limited recognition was malleable and contradictory, though free people could sometimes use this to their advantage. In a Missouri case, a free woman married to a slave man was charged with running a brothel. She wanted her enslaved husband to be able to testify on her behalf at trial but was denied on the basis of spousal recusal. She appealed because their marriage was not recognized by the state. Her lawyers argued against the hypocrisy of the laws: "the objection insisted upon the State is suicidal for it is admitted there can be no marriage in contemplation of law between a slave and a free person of color, and yet insist that the relation of marriage can subsist so far as to exclude them from testi-mony for or against each other."[29]

The state made a different argument: "It may be true that formally he is not her husband, but substantially he is. The law does not refuse to allow the husband or wife to testify for each other because of the mere technicality of the relationship they bear to each other, but because of solid reasons founded in wise policy." The state waxed eloquently about the love they were pre-sumed to have for each other. It wished not to endanger this domestic rela-tion by subjecting it to such potentially fractious proceedings: "It cannot be doubted that such a relation may exist between slaves and free persons of color as to bring them within the scope of the reasons above mentioned, al-though not technically man and wife." For slaves and free blacks married to each other these were not mere "technicalities." In most other cases, these de-tails were held firmly against African Americans. Ultimately, the free woman in this case prevailed on appeal to the state supreme court on the matter of the spousal recusal issue, though she still faced charges for keeping a brothel. The court stated: "We know that marriages *de facto* exist among this class of persons," but it also said that it was up to the legislature to make them legal. The higher court's ruling against mixed-status marriages in this instance worked to the advantage of the free woman charged with a crime.[30]

The standing of mixed-status marriages had wide-ranging implications for broader familial relationships, as well as for the future of their children and grandchildren even after they were manumitted. African Americans were often held to the highest standard or burden of proof in documenting their marriages. Upon manumission, mixed-status couples did not always formalize their informal relations—at their peril. Perhaps they felt that doing so was un-necessary, given their own feelings about the meaning of their intimate relationships. For example, couples in Louisiana married by Catholic priests abided by the notion that marriage was a sacrament. In a state that provided retroactive sanction to the marriages of manumitted slaves, such couples might have had little reason to suspect that their relationships would be con-sidered illegitimate in the eyes of antebellum laws. And yet those strictures could creep in and be used against them. Couples who failed to register their children after manumission could have the legitimacy of their marriages ques-tioned in proceedings determining the rights of inheritance of their heirs.[31]

This situation contrasted sharply with the forbearance shown by the same Missouri court to white couples equally lax in following the letter of the law to formalize their relationships. In *Holmes v. Holmes* in 1834, the court argued that "marriage is regarded by our law in no other light than as civil contract, highly favored, and depending essentially on the free consent of the parties capable by law of contracting. Our code does not declare null a marriage not preceded by a license, and not evidenced by an act signed by a certain number of witnesses and the parties; nor does it make such an act exclusive evidence of a marriage." The ruling made clear that the requirements for witnesses, ceremonies, and registries were "directory only" and not compulsory. White couples were encouraged to abide by the law, but their failure or refusal to do so would not be used to nullify their marriages. The judiciary was eager to preserve social order by recognizing informal marriages when white couples cohabited and behaved like "man and wife." A different, more stringent standard was applied to free people of color, however.[32] The state was more likely to call into question the legitimacy of their marriages formed under slavery, to rule against the legitimacy of their children, and to deny their capacity to inherit property from their forbears on the grounds that they were the issue of formerly enslaved parents who were not legally married.

If the marriages of mixed-status couples were insecure in the first half of the nineteenth century, the marriages of free people of color married to other free people were often subjected to scrutiny as well. Free blacks were confronted with laws that ranged from supporting aspects of their relationships to those that challenged their legal standing. Mississippi had perhaps the harshest written law. In 1822 the state recognized only marriages "between any free white persons in the state." This law has been interpreted primarily as a statute against interracial marriage, but it also left vulnerable free black marriages. The law did not prohibit them, but it clearly denied them recognition and legitimacy.[33]

The state of Georgia was a close second when it came to severity of laws, but it could be deemed first in cruelty shown toward free people of color.

Justice Lumpkin articulated this most painfully in *Bryan v. Walton* in 1853. He wrote passionately and extensively beyond the pertinent matters of an inheritance dispute that even he admitted was unusual: "I confess, to give my sentiments pretty fully upon this subject—to go beyond the usual limits of an opinion; and to speak in the style of argument rather than of authority." He made his "subject" free black rights more generally. Free people of color were entitled to nothing but their freedom. They suffered from "the social and civil degradation, resulting from the taint of blood, [that] adheres to the descendants of Ham in this country, like the poisoned tunic of Nessus; that nothing but an Act of the Assembly can purify, by the salt of its grace, the bitter fountain—the '*darkling sea.*'" He compared American slaves to those of "ancient republics" to show that they could not marry or be charged with adultery. But he amplified American exceptionalism, which made racial inequities permanent. Free blacks could never escape the original caste to which they belonged. They were perpetual minors, he argued: "he never ceases to be a ward, though he attaint to the age of Methuselah. His legal existence is forever merged in that of his guardian." Free people had nowhere to hide, no place of safety to escape to anywhere in the country: "To him there is but little in prospect, but a life of property, of depression, of ignorance, and of decay. He lives amongst us without motive and without hope. His fancied freedom is all a delusion." More than that, manumission was a grave mistake: "generally, society suffers, and the negro suffers."[34]

No judiciary ruling could be more demeaning of free blacks, unless, of course, it was rendered by the U.S. Supreme Court. But not all lower court judges fully agreed with Judge Lumpkin's sweeping nullification. In 1855, Judge William Bennett Fleming of the Chatham County Superior Court (who came from a slave-owning family) stated that marriage rights could be inferred from the Act of 1819, "so far as may be necessary to determine the question of descent." An 1818 state law revoked free black rights to purchase, acquire, or transfer property, including slaves, and called for existing property to be confiscated and sold with proceeds distributed between the relevant counties and the state. But the Act of 1819 modified this by sparing free blacks' property from seizure and allowing them to pass it on to their descendants after death. The case before him questioned whether slaves could pass on property to heirs without state recognition of marriage. A property dispute between a widow and her sister-in-law was at issue. When the husband died, the sister-in-law claimed her right to the whole of the property that her enslaved parents had left to her and her brother, above the rights of his surviving widow. The legal question boiled down to whether the law could recognize sibling relationships of free people of color if it did not sanction marriage or recognize parent and child relationships. The judge decided that both women should share the land in question, since they lived on it. But the sister-in-law wanted the whole lot and appealed. In order to win, her lawyers argued against the rights of free black marriage. This presented a legal conundrum that could not be resolved in the sister-in-law's favor. If a free black man could not have a wife, neither could he have a sister. There were no special laws stipulating that free people of color could have any legitimate familial relationships. Marriage was the relationship from which all others legally derived.[35]

When the case, *Ranghill v. Anderson,* reached the state's supreme court in 1855, the staunch proslavery advocate Justice Henry Lewis Benning wrote the opinion for the majority. He affirmed the lower court's decision that the lot in question should be shared. But Benning stated that if a free man could not have a wife, he could not have a sister or any next of kin. But he did believe, as the 1819 law stated, that an exception was made by the legislature to recognize direct descendants, allowing free people to pass on inheritances to their offspring. He did not believe, as Fleming did, that this law gave implicit recognition to husbands and wives. The majority affirmed Justice Lumpkin's opinion that free black marriages could not stand the legal test without special legislation.[36]

The slight divergence between the lower court and the superior court may have left room for some couples to register their unions. The application of punitive laws against free blacks varied greatly and was inconsistent throughout the South. It is impossible to quantify how many Georgia couples were impeded from marrying in light of the state's supreme court rulings, but it certainly had an impact. Some free people of color lived together as husband and wife and complained that they were not allowed to marry in the state. This put them in the odd position of both being denied the right to marry legally and in violation of the state's laws against extramarital sex.[37]

Regardless of these laws, most couples would have been allowed to form de facto common-law marriages recognized by their local communities. Their marriages stood unless they were either prosecuted for violating a law or chose to file suits in which their relations came under attack. Many free people tried to use the courts to the best of their advantage, but others avoided public institutions (or even being counted by the census) for fear they could be held accountable for exorbitant bonds and taxes or otherwise imposed upon. Couples did their best to work around the lack of guarantees that Justice Lumpkins declared necessary. Louisiana couples felt the sting of the 1808 law, although it restricted mixed-status relationships. Many rushed to the altar of the Catholic churches to legalize their marriages out of anxiety that the law could be used against them as well. Members of the elite, such as leaders in the free black militia, openly campaigned for their comrades and others to adopt marriage to prove they were fit and respectable citizens of the state, to impress the new governors when incorporated into the American republic.[38] The best they could hope for was partial rights, as in Texas, where couples who "live together as man and wife" were acknowledged if they entered the state by 1840. They were categorized like common-law spouses, with some, though not all, privileges of whites.[39] Virginia also offered limited rights, though not necessarily marriage. A justice in the *Brewer v. Harris* case echoed Lumpkin: "There is no form of marriage, as regards them, pointed out by our statutes. It is true they are permitted to inherit the real property of parents, not as being legitimate, but because the law has made no other provision for it; and where that is the case, as property is the creature of the law, it is permitted to pass according to our act of descents." Free black Virginians could pass on property to their heirs, but their marriages still had no legal standing.[40]

Some Border State judges explicitly made clear that the marriages of free blacks were legal even without the statutory provisions Lumpkin dictated. Kentucky affirmed this in *Free Frank and Lucy v. Denham* in 1824. This case became a landmark for subsequent litigation. Lucy owed a debt to the estate of William Denham and argued that at the time of the debt she was married to Frank, which meant that she should not be held accountable as a married woman. Denham's estate argued that as free people of color they could not be married legally and so Lucy should be treated as a single woman capable of paying her own debts. Denham initially won the case, but Lucy and Frank appealed. The upper court ruled in their favor, arguing that the incapacities of slavery were removed once slaves were emancipated, similar to the situation in Louisiana. This meant they could make contracts, including marriage: "for to marry, is a right common to all the human species, and whenever in fact contracted by persons able and willing to contract, the *femme* becomes subject to the disabilities of coverture."[41] The supreme court of Kentucky continued to affirm the Denham ruling and even went further by invoking racial equality as a reason to affirm informal marriages of free blacks the same way that common-law marriages of whites were routinely legitimized.[42]

Free black couples in the North fared the best. But a person did not have to live in the South to have his relationship questioned or even annulled, as a man in Indiana discovered. Arthur Barkshire violated a law against "encouraging Negro immigration" by marrying a woman from Ohio and bringing her into the state, eight years after establishing his own residence. The state's new constitution was amended with an antiemigration law in 1852. They married that year, and two years later he was charged with violating the law, which stated that "all contracts made with those coming in, contrary to such prohibition, shall be void" and punishable by a fine. He was convicted in the Ohio County Court of Common Pleas and appealed the decision in the Indiana supreme court, which affirmed the lower court's ruling. The marriage was voided and the husband was fined. The state's highest court also argued that the wife could have been prosecuted under the law, but it failed to take action. Free and semi-free blacks could not take for granted that their marriages would not be further encumbered by the law.[43]

The Indiana case may have been an unusually harsh application of the antiemigration law, but the marriages of free blacks were frequently threatened in local Northern jurisdictions eager to discourage the growth of black populations. Free people of color were questioned publicly and punished disproportionately for failure to provide proof of legal marriages, legitimacy of children, and legal residency as gradual laws increasingly manumitted slaves. Women were most closely scrutinized and were "warned out" (notified of ejection or the refusal of services) from towns if they could not produce marriage certificates or the names of the officiants at their weddings. The same expectations were not typically imposed on white families who lacked documentation. Requiring official papers was a method towns could use to weed out poor black women and children and to avoid responsibility for their care.[44]

And yet despite all the challenges that free blacks faced in gaining their independence and forming and sustaining families, the majority of their households were headed by married (whether legal or informal) couples with children living under one roof. This was true in the North and the South, despite the gender disparities in cities where free blacks were dispro-portionately represented. Of course, the unions were fractured at a higher rate compared with those of whites. In 1850, for example, women headed 25 percent of free black households, compared with 9 percent of white households. Female heads of household tended on average to be older women, often widows, not young women living alone with children as would be the case in the late twentieth century. Some of the female heads had white spouses who lived apart from them. Some had enslaved husbands who would not have been counted by census-takers. In other cases, adult spouses lived elsewhere, usually as servants in white households. Many children also lived apart from their parents because they were either servants or farm la-borers living in the households of whites. To be sure, these figures provide only a glimpse of family upheaval resulting from legal constraints. Free black families tended to be more complicated than census representations could capture, relying as they did on cooperation with extended kin and adopted kin across multiple households, not just among those who shared a single dwelling.[45]

The ambiguity and outright hostility of the law amplified the unique chal-lenges that free black couples faced as a result of their race and status. They compounded the universal pressures and internal dynamics that all couples had to manage. Maintaining the proverbial twoness and sustaining lifetime bonds were a fraught process that couples had to negotiate along their shared life journeys. Conflicts were inevitable and not easily contained within the boundaries of bed and board of individual households. Though many of these struggles were kept private or close to local circles, they could spill over into yards, neighborhoods, social gatherings, and ultimately end up in the county court when all else failed. When they reached the boiling point and required a wider public, if not the law, to settle matters, they left behind a paper trail. The documentation of couples working out their issues, or in the process of severing their ties for good, provides a rich repository to witness, oddly, the normality of marriage, albeit under crisis.

Gossip was generally local, but it could explode on a national scale for celebrities of the day. This was the case with the public spat between the former slave and abolitionist William Wells Brown and his wife, Elizabeth Schooner Brown. They married in 1834, after he had successfully evaded his slave mistress's entreaties to marry a woman she had purchased just for that purpose. He ran away to freedom then met and married Elizabeth in his first year as a fugitive in Ohio. They had two daughters within a few years, but William spent much of his time on the road engaged in political activities while his family lived in Buffalo, New York. Husband and wife finally separated in 1847. The marriage became a fatality of the higher cause of abolition.

William left for England in 1849 to speak on the abolition circuit. While he was abroad the couple's problems spilled over in public. Elizabeth wrote a letter to the editors of the *New York Daily Tribune* in March 1850 appealing for help. According to the paper, Mrs. Brown "sends us a long statement of her conjugal difficulties, the upshot of which is that notwithstanding she is a very respectable woman and exemplary wife (which she proves by 'no end' of certificates) her husband has deserted her and her youngest child, does nothing for their support, but on the contrary repudiates them both." She reportedly included a line insinuating that he may have found favor with women of another race as his fame soared: "Mr. Brown has become so popular that he did not wish his sable wife any longer." The newspaper editors, allies of William in the movement, labeled Elizabeth "malicious."[46]

William responded with a detailed letter addressed "to the public," which was published in the *Liberator* a few months later. He painstakingly spelled out his marital history and the years of strife soon after his escape from slavery. He acknowledged that he married Elizabeth after a short courtship without knowing anything about her family background. He discovered that her mother had married a second time without dissolving the first marriage. A brother-in-law had died in state prison, while a sister-in-law had a child out of wedlock. William claimed moral superiority over his wife's compromised lineage. But he also claimed that he was willing to keep his vows despite what he felt was his wife's deception about her family's history. When he returned from an antislavery speaking tour, he found one of his best friends in his home with his wife, which filled him with "the most painful suspicion." This pattern would repeat itself on other occasions, despite the mutual agreement that the friend would stay away in his absence. The marriage broke down further as the alleged affair persisted and William said that Elizabeth asked him to come get their children so she could pursue the extramarital relationship. He charged his estranged wife with besmirching his character by alleging his misconduct as a husband and father. He noted that he was reluctant to make his feelings public but felt compelled after a long period of silence to defend himself and repair any damage to his reputation that his wife had caused.[47] Although William Wells Brown tried his marriage in the court of public opinion rather than the law, his confessional style and form were consistent with the kinds of divorce petitions that judges encountered on the bench, where defendants had to get down and dirty if they had any hope of winning. He engaged in a very open campaign to save his own reputation and impugn his wife's. To bolster his claims he took his in-laws to task for the sullied branches in the family tree. He dragged his wife and their marriage through the muck of anger, hurt, and bitterness in a painful retelling of love gone awry and betrayed by either or both parties.

The letter had the desired result of quelling the controversy, at least among William's abolitionist allies. It would be difficult for any woman to survive the accusations hurled at her, but especially so when it came from a man of such standing as William. In the same issue of the newspaper the editors responded that they had conducted their own investigation and determined that William and not Elizabeth had been mistreated. "There was nothing in his conduct toward his wife worthy of censure; but that, on the contrary, he had shown her great forbearance," they argued. They found every reason to reject Mrs. Brown's accusations. The couple's marriage ended in separation.[48]

The Browns' dispute was magnified in the media far beyond what was usual for most couples. But separations and divorces were difficult when couples played out their differences even on smaller stages in county courts, being judged by officials and involving at times family members and friends called to testify for or against one or the other spouse. Legal divorce was a rare occurrence in the antebellum era. Most couples could not afford the fees for lawyers, and most seeking to dissolve their marriages did so informally, abandoning their spouses or agreeing mutually to part ways without official sanction. The social opprobrium against it gave few people incentives to bring disgrace and dishonor to their families unless they felt they had reached the end of their ropes with little recourse or great stakes that required them to seek judiciary interventions. Before the American Revolution absolute divorce, the ability to remarry after separation, was rarely granted and usually for limited reasons when it was allowed, such as when the marriage at its inception was questionable as in cases of incest, impotency, insanity, or underage. It was usually up to legislatures to grant separation from bed and board on an individual basis. After 1800, states began to expand the possibilities to obtain divorce, though still limiting complete divorce and the right to remarry. Adultery, desertion, excessive cruelty, and the infliction of gross indignities were specified in laws as legitimate reasons for legal alienation of couples. South Carolina was an outlier, however, and granted no divorces at all. Over the course of the antebellum decades, states passed laws that gave local chancery and equity court judges, and sometimes juries, control over divorce. Most slaveholding states had made this transition by early 1840.[49]

Divorce laws forced aggrieved parties to be adversarial. One spouse had to initiate a complaint against the other. Couples were not allowed to collude in making cases, though it was possible to do so behind the scenes if they felt the urgency of separating from their spouses for reasons that did not fit the law or would not satisfy judiciary review. Couples had to show that the conditions leading them to seek separation from those to whom they had vowed to be permanently bound rose to the highest level of disregard and violation. This forced individuals filing divorce petitions to offer great detail about their intimate lives gone awry in ways that polite society often chafed at revealing or exposing publicly. The petitioning spouse tended to paint a picture of a marriage that started off with the best of intentions but was interrupted by a change of heart or objectionable behavior. Such spouses presented themselves as entering into marriage with good faith and good humor, expecting lifelong bliss. They were dutiful, affectionate, and faithful spouses who had become long-suffering victims. They were the fit parents of their offspring. They had tried to repair their marriages, coaxed deserting spouses to return, or tolerated the worst abuses in the name of keeping the marriage together, and ultimately turned to divorce because they had no other recourse. As a result of this candor, or the compulsion to write a narrative to fit the requirements of stringent divorce laws, extant divorce suits provide a rare opportunity to see the inner workings and breakdown of marriage in ways that other documents, such as diaries and journals, are often too guarded to reveal.[50]

Divorce seekers in the slaveholding states in the antebellum era were overwhelmingly female slave-owners and other white women. (This is in contrast to the dominance of men before the Revolution.) Their most prevalent complaint was domestic violence, which had to be extreme, beyond the normal moderate spousal corporal punishment that husbands were allowed to impose on their wives, in order to be persuasive in courts of law. Charges of adultery were also common, with accusations of husbands having outside relations with slaves and free blacks as well as with white women. White men, by contrast, most often charged their wives with adultery or desertion. Plaintiffs who filed charges against their spouses won the majority of cases, but women's suits tended to have more success than men's. Men, however, were at an advantage when making charges of adultery. A single incident of a woman's infidelity could suffice in substantiating a man's claim, unlike the higher bar set for women's complaints of their husbands' infidelities. Double standards gave men more leeway in exercising their prerogatives to have sex outside of marriage. Most of the non–slave-owning white men who filed suit and claimed adultery accused their wives of having sex with black men, in which cases judges and juries ruled harshly. Courts were much more tolerant when white men were accused of having sex with black women.[51]

Free people of color who filed divorce petitions were even more rare, making it harder to draw generalizations that could be considered representative. Few of their extant records are available. Still, they, too, were mostly filed by women and were usually successful. According to one scholar, they had a slightly higher success rate than petitions filed by whites. This was likely because courts were reluctant to intervene in the domestic affairs of white men, especially elite slaveholders. Free people of color who filed for divorce were exceptional because most had limited financial resources to hire lawyers. Those who did file were likely among the most well-off, with property at stake in postdivorce distributions. The modesty of their economic circumstances, especially relative to whites', is most striking. Although the monetary stakes brought up in the complaints were often small, women of color were vulnerable given the narrow opportunities available for them to earn a living and support their children without the help of spouses.[52]

The divorce petitions of free people of color reveal how they were affected by the problems of all married couples and also how they faced additional stresses and strains because of racial subjugation. The universal and the particular often overlapped and merged in ways that make them hard to disaggregate, however. Their most frequent complaints were adultery and desertion, though they tended to express their grievances in gendered terms. Women, not men, reported domestic violence from their spouses.

Jane Davis Mount Edmunds, a free woman of color from Louisiana, married her second husband, William Edmunds, in 1835 and they "lived together happily and contentedly" for about twelve years. They probably met in Philadelphia, where she had lived with her mother and worked as a washer, ironer, and servant. At some point in the early years of their courtship or marriage they may have lived apart, as William owned a drugstore in New Orleans and would send her money while she was up North. She argued that William broke their marriage vows by abandoning, deceiving, and mistreating her. She discovered that he was in "the embraces" of another woman. When these troubles surfaced, William, she said, added insult to injury by "defaming and blackening" her character by publicly claiming that they had never legally wed. Petitioners like Jane, especially women, took the risk that they could indeed incur countercharges from their former loved ones that called their own reputations into question. In this case, Jane was forced to bring in witnesses locally but also from her previous residence to vouch for her good name. Her husband, for his part, brought in witnesses not to testify to his goodness but to besmirch his wife. At least one (white) man was brought in to insinuate that Jane had been a prostitute on steamboats in Philadelphia before she moved to Louisiana. But Jane endured these tactics, however reluctantly, given the considerable property they had jointly acquired, including land and horses worth more than five thousand dollars. She wanted a fair share and for her husband to bear the monetary costs of filing for the divorce.

It took a while, as several years passed from the time of her initial filing, but Jane won in the end. Other women similarly fought hard to secure their property, especially for what they had brought into their marriages by inheritance or by their own exertions. They fought to secure future property they expected to inherit to safeguard it against later encroachments after their divorce was granted.[53]

Material support for themselves and their children, and child custody, figured prominently in most women's divorce petitions. Sometimes they specified amounts for alimony, but usually they just asked for whatever support they could get. Even when women worked outside the home for wages they still expected their husbands to take care of them and their children. Failure to do so was perceived as a sign of a disavowal of their marital commitment. They discussed how they were left to live in destitution, especially with young children to feed and clothe. But even those who were childless struggled to support themselves on their own earnings.

One wife revealed that she had experienced one of the worst nightmares that free black people in the South could imagine, though with an unusual twist. Her husband had sold three of their four children to support his drinking habit, she claimed. The irony is difficult to fathom, that a black father would disown his offspring, putting them on the infamous slave market to satisfy his appetite for alcohol. If true, this was an egregious offense, but it was one among a series of troubles. He cheated on her with other women and would desert her periodically for months at a time. When he was around, she said that he provided "but little & often nothing at all. Not even Bread for herself & children." She was forced to work to take care of their family and even forced to provide for him, which upturned the norms of marriage. She claimed that though she did everything to please him, his idleness, intemperance, and violence only grew worse, making it impossible for the family to live in peace and safety. After one particularly brutal episode she displayed her injuries to her neighbors and then filed for divorce.[54]

In some cases abandoned wives wanted judges to force their husbands to return to resume their financial obligations.[55] In most cases desertions were accepted as a fait accompli, but wives struggled for access to their husbands' economic resources. Women were sometimes driven away from home by domestic violence. They were sometimes physically kicked out of their homes or chose to flee in search of safety with parents or friends, but it was hard to survive in these circumstances without continued help from their errant spouses.[56]

Free black husbands' expectations of the obligations of their wives were manifest in their divorce petitions as well. They expected women to live up to the same vows that they expressed, but especially in the roles consistent with their gender. George Conley complained of the defiance of his young wife, Josephine, especially her refusal to cook his dinner. He claimed that she no longer loved him. There were other men "whose little fingers she cared more for than she did for complainant[']s whole body," and they would buy her whatever her heart desired so that she did not have to work. She abandoned him and kept company with other men, single and married, "in a most wanton and disgraceful manner," he alleged. He emphasized that his parents had taught him "the art of farming and the habits of industry," which he had pursued in taking care of an ungrateful wife. For her part, Josephine denied some though not all of the charges. She disputed refusing to cook dinner for him and never said he should get dinner himself. She never claimed that she had men to buy her whatever she wanted or to enable her not to work. Josephine countered George's charge of adultery with the same against him. He had an affair with a slave woman, Ester, "who is old enough to be the mother of complainant." She admitted that she left him, for good reasons. It all came down to the in-laws. The couple lived with George's parents, whom she accused, especially his mother, of verbal intimidation that verged on physical violence, which made her feel unsafe. Her husband was abusive as well, locking her up and being mean and vile toward her. His "exceeding jealous disposition" and his interfering mother, she argued, were the primary causes of their dissension.[57]

Meddling parents often got marriages off on the wrong foot when they denied their sons or daughters the right to marry spouses of their own choosing. One husband claimed that he found his wife in bed with another man and abandoned her for that reason. He wanted to annul their marriage, as though it had never come to pass. A friend of the wife testified on the husband's behalf, saying that the man the wife was having an affair with was the one she loved, but her parents would not allow her to marry him. The man himself was called as a witness and, surprisingly, testified against the errant wife. He admitted that he had paid for her housing and lived with her after she separated from her husband, but things soured after a year. He then accused her of being a prostitute.[58]

Husbands had legal rights to their children, but they did not always seek physical custody. When they did they accused women of moral turpitude, of "forgetting" their wedding vows. If they were unfit wives, that made them unfit mothers, especially when they abandoned their homes, leaving not only husbands but also children to fend without them. Some men had very little patience for infidelities when they suspected their wives. Others endured violations patiently, waiting for years before filing complaints. One husband discovered that his wife had committed adultery just a few years after their marriage. They separated for nine years before he made a formal effort to end their marriage. They had children together, but she also had children with other men during this period. He confided that he should have filed for divorce long before, "but he disliked to do so, but now feels it a duty to himself and his children to be separated from one who has so improperly and illegally Sinned." He wanted not a divorce but an annulment of the marriage. Witnesses who testified on the wife's behalf, however, challenged his narrative, claiming he was abusive toward his wife and had a mistress before she abandoned him.[59] It is difficult to ascertain who had affairs first, since one bad act by one party often led to affairs by the other, though the first to err was not necessarily the one to file for divorce. Charges and countercharges of adultery often included confessions by both spouses, each blaming the other for having sex outside of the marriage because the other one did so.[60]

Marriage always posed the possibility that couples would encounter irreconcilable differences that would lead to extreme measures to dissolve their unions. Free people of color were no more exempt from those tensions than others and experienced the full range of highs and lows of coupledom. They had hopes and heartaches; they were committed and unfaithful; they were jealous and generous. They craved and hungered for love and affirmation and searched for the safety of emotional shelter that only intimate companions could provide. But their quasi-free status put them in unique positions that nonblack free people did not face. In order to preserve their unions and shield their families, they were sometimes forced to take even more extreme measures such as a return to slavery.

~~◆~~

No matter the internal challenges of sustaining viable marriages, free people of color would always be most disadvantaged by external constraints. The severity of those limits was revealed in the intensification of laws passed in the 1850s to expel free blacks and laws to encourage them to submit to so-called voluntary slavery, in which freed people petitioned states to be re-enslaved to white masters to avoid expulsion or other dire circumstances. Virginia led the way again by creating a law in 1856 to formalize this process. Seven states created voluntary slavery laws over the next five years: Alabama, Florida, Louisiana, Maryland, Tennessee, Texas, and Virginia. South Carolina and Georgia approved voluntary slavery by special acts of the legislature in individual cases. Georgia also passed other laws to force free people into bondage. It mandated that they pay an annual tax of five dollars beginning in 1851. A few years later it added the proviso that failure to pay could result in fines or being hired out. But free persons of color could simply be charged with the nebulous crimes of being "idle" or "immoral" and sold into slavery for two years or permanently after a third offense. Voluntary laws were debated in the other states that did not pass them. All slaveholding states in one way or another moved decidedly in that direction. Arkansas was the harshest, however, as it expelled nearly all free blacks from within its borders with the passage of the Expulsion Act of 1859. The naked contempt of lawmakers was demonstrated by the way they referred to free blacks as imposters, as "acting free."[61]

Mixed-status families were the ones most deeply affected as they were more often put in the position of having to choose between keeping their families together or having one or more members submit to enslavement. Some of them had already tried and failed to get exemptions from laws that forced them to leave the state. Acquiescence to legal slavery was the last resort. Their families were already circumscribed by the lower status of their enslaved kin, since they were likely to live and work alongside them on the same plantations under the same constraints. The privileges that free people in this context experienced were more often abstract than real. Still, the gravity of their sacrifice was no less daunting. Even some freeborn men submitted petitions to "elevate" themselves into slavery in order to remain with their wives and children and to avoid separation from them or expulsion from the state.[62] Free spouses were put in a bind when their owners moved their enslaved partners. In some cases, they were able to follow them, but doing so usually violated antiemigration laws. A slave-owner who submitted a petition on behalf of a free person wishing to become his slave explained the circumstances this way: "The said Boy, had taken up with my negro girl and lived with me several years in South Carolina unmolested." He moved the household to North Carolina in 1856 and "the said free negro came with me not knowing it was contrary to law." The slave-owner sent him back to South Carolina, "but the Said boy preferring a life of slavery with the master of his choice & with the woman he had taken up with & his children," returned, "giving himself to me."[63]

Others faced problems when the enslaved spouse was sold away and the new owner was less than generous in supporting their marriage. In North Carolina, for example, one owner was willing to allow Percy Ann Martin, a free woman, to live with her enslaved husband on his property, but when her husband was sold, the new owner pulled out the 1830 law and threatened to break up their illegal marriage. Her petition noted that "she was attached to her husband and does not wish to be separated from him—that she is poor—has no property and in these times of scarcity of provisions and high prices, she does not know how she is to support herself and is fearfull she shall come to want."[64]

The willingness to submit to "voluntary" slavery signified that some free blacks were prepared to prioritize their marital and family ties at any costs. Even families already separated by manumission often reconsidered the relative costs of being free. One man left the state of Virginia and moved to Ohio upon manumission, forced out by law, but grew to regret it more and more. After "not being reconciled to live without his wife," he "has lately returned to Virginia and is anxious to remain," several white men writing on his behalf stated in their petition. Though a free man, he "would prefer returning to slavery to losing the society of his wife." The petitioners requested a law "permitting him to live out the balance of his days here where he was born and where he hopes to die."[65]

Free African Americans did not experience freedom as an absolute condition or right they could take for granted. The increasingly oppressive tactics used by Southern states pushed more free people to weigh the costs of being forced apart from family members or remaining intact, even if in the context of bondage. Slaveholding states had become quite adept at diminishing the status of free people of color over the decades leading up to the Civil War. Their ambitions to bifurcate free status on the basis of race was largely brought to fruition. The free black population peaked in 1830 and began to decline every decade thereafter.[66]

Whites used "voluntary" slavery to further their own proslavery aims. It fit the ideology that defined slavery as a societal good. The laws reinforced the idea that blacks were simply better off as slaves and were unable to cope as free people. What could be better evidence of black people's unfitness than their apparent failures that required their (re)subjection? Voluntary slavery advanced the goal of building a biracial South, in which blackness and slavery, freedom and whiteness were inextricably linked dyads. White people benefited by exploiting black romantic love that propelled most free people's desperate moves to petition to be enslaved for the sake of their families, all the while denying those relationship legitimacy and standing when they did not serve white interests.[67]

Voluntary slavery offered significant benefits to less wealthy whites unable to buy slaves outright or those with limited assets. Free people of color were sometimes appraised at absurdly low rates. Owners often only had to pay half the fee, plus court costs, even when rates were higher. They were allowed to take out bonds, a system of credit, for the person's value. Southern lawmakers used voluntary slavery not only as a way to extend slavery but also to subsidize slave ownership for a broader cohort of whites, further sharpening the racial dichotomy. In some cases, free people proposed to submit themselves to white owners (who also owned their family members) even when those persons had no resources to buy them. As one petitioner made plain in a petition to become a slave to her husband's owner, she (along with her children) though free, already had a "master and servant" relationship with him. "It only requires the authority of your honorable body to make that relationship a legal one," she wrote to the Mississippi legislature in 1860.[68]

Ironically, the legislatures rejected many petitions for re-enslavement. The fact that African Americans themselves used the courts displayed self-assertion, which made lawmakers ambivalent about honoring their appeals. Petitioners not only risked losing their cases; they also invited scrutiny of their circumstances that could lead to penalties and countercharges. Cases were dismissed, costs assessed, and free people remanded to jail to stand trial for violating laws that imposed expulsion on those who overstayed their residency requirements, for example.[69]

In many cases, legislatures simply refused to act, no matter how resilient and determined the petitioner. Lucy Andrews, a freeborn woman (the daughter of a white woman and a slave man), submitted her first petition to the South Carolina legislature at the age of sixteen in 1858, with a long list of endorsements from white men. At the time she had lived on a slave plantation since 1856, was the mother of an infant, and had a hard time finding steady work, probably as a domestic, going from place to place in temporary stints that did not pan out into permanency. According to her petition: "she sees, and knows, to her own sorrow, and regret, that Slaves are far more happy, and enjoy themselves far better, than she does, in her present isolated condition of freedom." She preferred to select her own master and give up her freedom. The petition was referred to committee, but no act was passed. In 1861, months after the Civil War had begun, she tried again; as a woman of a mixed-status marriage, she emphasized that "she has no one of her status who can take care of her and provide for her. She therefore voluntarily desires to go into slavery." Her words fell on deaf ears. Undaunted, with two children (her firstborn child had died) and an enslaved husband on the plantation, she still felt desperate enough to request to be enslaved two years later. She was turned down again. But Andrews had no way of knowing how close to the end of slavery she would be. Sherman's army would occupy the town close to the plantation where she lived a year and a half later.[70]

Marriages and families present a complex picture that troubles the fictive sharp demarcations of geography between slave and free territories in the North and South and the fraught conditions of freedom African Americans increasingly faced during the antebellum era. Justice Lumpkin's opinion was harsh but representative of dominant white sentiment. Free blacks could expect nothing beyond mere manumission, which did not guarantee marriage or any other civil or human right. As slavery declined in the North free blacks faced decades of a protracted process of removing the shackles of servitude and bound labor from each family member. As the South expanded slavery, free blacks faced an avalanche of restrictions designed to expel them from the region, to criminalize them with fines and incarceration for innocuous infractions, and to confine them to quasi if not real bondage. Free blacks were literally and figuratively akin to slaves. They were often related to slaves by blood and marriage, which tied them in perpetual knots of abjection.

Mixed-status families were at the mercy not only of the owners of their enslaved spouses, who determined how much to tolerate their relationships, but also of state laws and judicial opinions that typically ranged from ambivalent to hostile. Their unequal relationships challenged many conventions of heterosexuality with respect to gender hierarchies. Free wives had more theoretical power than their enslaved husbands, but the couples in reality often faced a double bind in which neither wives nor husbands had enforceable rights. Free husbands were in a better position as heads of households to protect their families, but they, too, faced dreadful situations. They were the nominal owners of enslaved wives who could be treated as ordinary chattel subject to being sold to pay debts owed to creditors. And when their loved ones remained in the hands of white owners, they could be recalled back to those white households or sold away at any time.

Free people of color devised many different strategies to work around the dilemmas posed by their race and status and the institutional roadblocks that interfered with their most intimate relationships. They bought loved ones, they freed them, they willed them property, and they appointed friendly white surrogates to act on their behalf. They used informal marriage, sacramental marriage, and civil marriage to give their relationships the best protection available to them. They combined forces across many households to maximize kin and near-kin networks to enable their daily survival. They petitioned lawmakers for their freedom, to stay in the South to keep their families intact, to return home after periods of forced exile, and even to divorce errant spouses when their own internal mechanisms for emotional sustenance and protection failed. They won some. They lost most. And when all else failed in preserving their families they resorted with utmost desperation to offer themselves up for re-enslavement. What could be more attractive to proslavery advocates than admissions of defeat that proved black people were unfit to be free? And what could be more appalling to abolitionists than free people who would relinquish their self-ownership? Neither side acknowledged or understood what was most at stake. African-American dreams of freedom were primarily perceived not to be individualistic but collective. Free blacks could not be truly free if they left their spouses, their children, other relatives, and community members behind. Freedom and family were inextricably linked.

That free people of color continued to submit petitions for voluntary slavery as the Civil War progressed and even after the promulgation of the Emancipation Proclamation speaks volumes about the slender degree of difference between bondage and liberty for all African Americans. And yet the Civil War would offer an unprecedented moment for slaves to put their marriages on legal grounds for the first time. They would seize the moment to use the presence of the Union Army's invading forces to reconstitute their families under the new authority of the United States flag.

4

❧

Marriage "under the Flag"

Lucinda and Solomon Sibley were both slaves in Hinds County, Mississippi, on the same plantation. They were married at the home of their master, Hamilton Sibley, around 1849. Solomon ran away to join the Union Army in December 1863, and his regiment was posted in Helena, Arkansas. Lucinda and their children followed him and lived in a nearby contraband camp, a settlement of fugitive slaves and their families who had joined Union forces. On May 14, 1864, the couple was married again by an army chaplain, Reverend J. R. Locke, an event their son Hannibal recalled witnessing. As Lucinda explained it, "there was a general impression that our old slave marriages were not valid and we were advised to marry again under the United States regulations."[1]

Similar scenes took place across the slaveholding states as the Union Army advanced its troops. Civilians and soldiers were given opportunities to formalize slave marriages under a new authority. The federal government embarked into mostly unknown territory, assuming functions that had been previously considered the prerogative of the states. Former slaves adopted the phrase marriage "under the flag" to refer to these ceremonies of remarriage (and first marriage), capturing a multiplicity of meanings about the transitional nature of their former relationships and of their status as dispossessed chattel. In some cases ceremonies were officiated by military officers and army chaplains literally below flags flying above or nearby. The United States flag emblazoned many of the certificates that served as concrete proof of their sanctification and became a powerful symbol redefining former

slaves' intimate relationships. Such marriages suggest a civic quality, reinforced by the military institution most closely associated with their valida-
tion. To stand before an officer or chaplain and be married under the flag
was like taking an oath of allegiance or being inducted into the service. The
symbolism invoked was appropriate to the moment of United States recognition and the reconfiguration of marriage as a hierarchical relationship in
which former slaves could legally take part.[2]

The flag represented far more than military authority as untold numbers
of antebellum slave couples remarried or married for the first time during
the war years. The army played a central role in bringing newly freed slave
couples into the national family and sanctioning their unions as a federal
act. The flag represented the nation-state, the throwing off the shackles of
Southern plantation states, the restoration of U.S. law above white law. It
represented the hope of citizenship by offering a key proving ground for
developing the kind of respectability that would be essential to being fully
welcomed into the land of the free. Yet standing beneath the flag meant new
encumbrances, marked by forms of supplication and subordination that
complicated the unique challenges of sanctifying intimate relationships under
the duress of war and the transition from slavery to freedom.

The Civil War marked another watershed moment in the history of African-
American marriage, following the colonial era, the expansion of the cotton
kingdom and the internal slave trade, and the retrenchment of rights for the
quasi-free. It was a moment in which events were not just a "rehearsal" for a
postwar order but were themselves a new and shifting universe. Four years of
internecine turmoil offer a distinct window onto how slaves negotiated their
relationships as the government and its civilian agents came to inspect and
comment on their efficacy and attempt to reshape them. The conduct of the
war produced mixed outcomes. It brought couples and families under a new
authority, diminishing the power of masters. But it also tore them apart as a
result of mayhem caused by displacement and the deaths of civilians and
soldiers. It would take time to assess the full measure of the sacrifices.

Contraband camps were the first sites that fugitive slaves seeking safety
and refuge found to be amenable for resacrilizing their bonds; then too,
the abandoned plantations that the Union Army occupied also provided
places for slaves to marry under federal authority. The evolution of marriage-

making, especially in locations such as Tidewater Virginia and coastal South Carolina, where these events unfolded first, reveals how the interests of marriage dovetailed and diverged between ex-slaves and agents of the Union. Ex-slaves often believed that their relationships should be renewed "under the flag" in order to obtain the imprimatur of the nation-state. Remarriage in the context of the Civil War became one of the first "rites" of freedom exercised by the newly freed. It not only opened the way for the consideration of other rights but also moved toward fulfilling an important social prerequisite for citizenship by initiating a family.

Yet some slaves were not as eager as others thought they should be to embrace this new rite of civil standing or to conform to it in the ways that their tutors prescribed for them. Their interests collided with those of outsiders eager to use marriage instrumentally to extract labor to resurrect the plantation economy as slavery was being destroyed. As the Union Army advanced, plantations across the South were seized and run by government agents, entrepreneurs, and erstwhile Confederates. Marriage was treated as the infrastructure that would build self-sufficient labor units among the newly freed to perform the agricultural work so important to these new enterprises. Men were to assume the roles of heads of households and women their subordinates. The implementation of modified male-dominated families within a nascent agricultural system ran up against the realities of uneven sex ratios as men were siphoned off to fight in the army, leaving behind an "excess" of women and children. These were not the ideal workers that plantation managers had in mind, and yet they formed the backbone of wartime free-labor experiments.

Black male enlistment opened up another avenue for federal intervention into the intimate relationships of former slaves as the army embraced the dictum that neophyte soldiers should marry "under the flag." This did not mesh easily with the complicated and irregular intimate entanglements that resulted from slavery, some of which could be corralled under the rubric of legal marriage, and some not. Still, soldiers saw military service as a guarantee that their marriages would be secure and their families taken care of by the Union Army. Wartime marriages came with many benefits, but also with inherent danger in places where slavery was under attack but not yet fully destroyed. Black soldiers risked their lives for the freedom of their families, not for an abstract nation that had come belatedly and haltingly to embrace them. And yet they found themselves under fire, from Confederate slave-owners who took every opportunity to retaliate and even from some of their own allies, insufficiently moved by the gravity of their sacrifices and their indispensable contributions.

So what did marriage under the flag really mean for soldiers or civilians? The full measure of this privilege and obligation could not be reckoned in its inchoate form. Both military officials and volunteer missionaries, those most directly involved in facilitating, encouraging, coercing, and instituting marriage, insisted that it gave legitimacy and legal recognition to the irregular and inferior relationships of former slaves. But the status of fugitive slaves who joined the Union Army was still uncertain, especially during the first years of the war. Until the war ended, the permanence of marriage could be no more guaranteed than the level of freedom each slave couple achieved. Ultimately, marriage under the flag would reach certain limits without further codification that only national lawmakers could provide and successful Union victory could ensure.

The slaves' first hope of marrying under the flag began, symbolically, in Virginia. The birthplace of slavery was the birthplace of wartime freedom, too. The onset of wartime freedom was, moreover, inextricably tied to rebuilding families. Shepard Mallory, Frank Baker, and James Townsend, all field hands, seized the chance to escape across the James River in Virginia by boat under the cover of darkness on the night of May 23, 1861. They fled to Hampton Roads, in the Tidewater, the site of the enslavement of the first twenty Africans in 1619 taken ashore from a Dutch ship, which had captured them from Portuguese enslavers. Their master, Charles Mallory, a rebel officer, had pressed them to labor on behalf of the Confederacy. Worse yet, he was planning to take them with him to North Carolina to work. They did not want to go. Nor did they want to be separated from their wives, families, and community. Baker and Townsend were both married to women who lived in Hampton, one slave and one free, and both had children in the area. By forcing the Union Army at Hampton Roads to decide how to treat their arrival, they set in motion profound changes in federal government policies regarding slaves and their emancipation throughout the conduct of war.[3]

Major General Benjamin F. Butler, a newcomer to the military, had barely arrived at the fort just a day earlier. The fugitive slaves forced him to decide what to do with them and whether to send them back to Charles Mallory. He interviewed the three fugitives and also their master. In light of Mallory's disloyalty as a Confederate officer, his refusal to denounce this allegiance, and his use of the slaves to build military batteries, Butler, a lawyer, decided to use the principles of "international law" and seize the men as "contrabands of war." Rather than releasing the slaves to the rebels to make use of their labor, he reasoned that the Union could use them instead. Two months earlier, while stationed in Maryland, Butler had offered to help quell a slave rebellion. But Maryland had been a Union state, and Virginia had ties to the Confederacy. That fact, as well as the gifts of espionage from the fugitive slaves, influenced the general's decision.

Butler came to believe that by receiving and protecting escaped slaves behind Union lines the army was ending their enslavement: "If property, do they not become the property of salvors? But we, their salvors, do not need and will not hold such property." Their status as slaves had thus been transformed back to "the normal one, of those made in God's image." He believed that, no longer property, they were now persons. More than that, they were newly gendered and aged persons: "Have they not become, thereupon, men and women, and children?" he queried. The full meaning of this change in condition would become apparent in the policies that would follow from Butler and other federal agents: "If not free born, yet free, manumitted, sent forth from the hand that held them, never to be reclaimed."[4] Another observer at Fort Monroe put it this way: "Wherever the Stars and Stripes float in the advancing march of our armies, they float over *freemen*."[5]

Butler's "(Fort) Monroe Doctrine" opened the floodgates for slaves seeking refuge in Union-controlled areas.[6] The legal status would need to be determined, but de facto freedom for fugitives had now become Union policy. First by drips and then in full force fugitives began arriving at what they renamed "Freedom Fort." By July, there were nine hundred fugitives at Fort Monroe. "Such is the mysterious spiritual telegraph which runs through the slave population," noted Edward L. Pierce, the young attorney Butler selected to supervise black labor.[7] The creation of the first critical mass of freedpeople living and working to maintain the fortification and to provide casual labor for the army in these conditions would also instantiate federal engagement in marriage-making. Fugitive slaves who gained status as "contrabands" of war

Fig. 4.1   Group of contrabands at Cumberland Landing, Virginia. This photograph was taken from the main eastern theater of war, the Peninsular Campaign, May–August 1862. Diverse ages are represented in the group, from babies to older adults, some related and others not. This particular photo is more representative of what contrabands would eventually look like, with fewer men than women, as the men eventually left to join the Union Army.

became the first beneficiaries of the joint venture involving military officers, army chaplains, and missionaries eager to marry couples "under the flag."

While fugitive slaves and abolitionists in the North had publicized stories about how families suffered under slavery, many missionaries and federal officials were able to see these families up close for the first time in contraband camps (see Fig. 4.1). Some were skeptical and others scornful of the irregularity they perceived in how these families looked and functioned. This brought intense scrutiny to black relationships and resulted in concerns about sexual propriety among women and sexual fidelity between husbands and wives. One report from a contraband camp claimed: "Their idea of the marriage relations and obligations is very low." But some Northerners were sensitive to the constraints imposed on slaves and impressed by what they witnessed. Another report stated: "The greater number have lived together as husband and wife by mutual consent. In many cases, strongly attached and faithful, though having no legal marriage. Generally, I believe the men to be faithful to the women with whom they live, and the women to reward their faith with like truth. Free and married they will maintain the marital relations as sacredly as any other race."[8]

Reverend Lewis C. Lockwood was sent by the American Missionary Association (AMA), founded in Albany, New York, to work with the newly freed people and was immediately struck by the marriage issue upon his arrival in September. In one of his first letters back to the main office of the AMA, he could barely contain his enthusiasm: "I must now open a subject as thrilling as it is novel. I have ascertained that a very large portion, probably, at least, more than half of the 'married' contrabands have been married only in slave fashion, by 'taking up together,' or living together by mutual agreement, without the least marriage ceremony. This state of things has not only been encouraged, but demanded by slavery." By putting "married" under slavery in quotes, Lockwood shared the view of many abolitionists (and others) that the institution did not live up to its name in black communities. He pointed to the desecration of the sacredness of monogamy by slavery, which "even under the Christian name, teaches, aye, often forces, its victims to live in concubinage." This explained the "laxity in morals" among slaves who could be separated by their masters at any time. "And hence," he concluded, "the temptation to cohabit and separate at pleasure, and, as a next step, to indulge in promiscuous concubinage."[9] And yet by labeling the arrangement marriage, Lockwood was affording slave unions a level of recognition. The ambiguity of this status could be rectified only by resacrilizing marital bonds, Lockwood believed, and he identified marriage under the flag as his most pressing concern.

Granting legitimacy to slave marriages by remarrying freed couples appeared to be a mutually agreed upon objective among fugitives, missionaries, and federal officials. Lockwood consulted with General John Wool, the commanding officer, who advised "the administration of marriage in due form." Church, state, and civic volunteers moved arm in arm toward establishing new policies and dicta formalizing the marriages of former slaves. Lockwood spoke with unnamed African-American leaders who agreed with the plan, likely including his coteacher Mary S. Peake, a free woman who arrived shortly after him. But fugitives themselves, who were most aware of the limitations of antebellum marriage, came forward at their own behest requesting missionaries and officials to marry them under the new terms of freedom.[10]

For his fellow Christians, and specifically his Baptist audience, who he hoped would help the freedpeople, he explained the logic of remarrying couples by using the ritual of baptism and rebirth as an analogy: "You as Baptists would not be satisfied with sprinkling, either in infancy or adult age. And I, myself, was immersed after I entered the ministry." True, he noted, though this may appear to have "reversed the proper order of things; yet I felt that I was doing right in acting up to increased knowledge and conviction of duty." And so too for slaves, many of whom had been married for years and even had grown children, but needed to undertake this ritual retroactively. Lockwood recognized that many of the ex-slaves he encountered were actually already quite familiar with long-term intimate relationships. But by participating in a proper marriage ceremony he believed they would not only inspire other ex-slaves to elevate their view of formal marriage but also "convince white observers that, as soon as the bondsman emerges from slavery, he acquires higher ideas of things, and wishes to do whatever is lawful and right."[11]

Lockwood is the first known agent working under federal auspices to officiate at the marriages of former slaves, starting on September 22, 1861. Several couples voluntarily came forth, and he published their names in the long-standing Western tradition of making wedding banns public prior to ceremonies. He married five couples in the morning and six that evening, with the help of Chaplain Arthur B. Fuller of the Sixteenth Massachusetts Regiment. The first couples' names recorded were Moses and Mary McIntosh; Isaac and Sarah Eli; James and Rachel White; Henry and Rachel Holloway; Paul and Leah Patrick; Morris and Caroline Colyer; Cyrus and Nellie Brown; Richard and Nancy Jones; James and Emma Townsend; George and Lavinia Marrow; and William and Charlotte Johnson. Whereas under slavery couples did not always share surnames, as freedpeople they would adopt this convention. The two clergy took turns performing the ceremonies, which included remarks and prayers for each couple, one at a time. Both occasions were well attended. Their sermons focused on the mutual responsibilities of spouses and obligations of parenthood. By the end of these initial ceremonies, even more couples came forth to follow suit.[12]

In Sabbath day exercises the next week, Lockwood continued to pay special attention to the importance of marriage, preaching on "God's household covenant, and family religion." He focused on an aspect of the conventional Christian marriage rite that masters had taken pains to deny to slaves: "What God hath joined together let no man put asunder," he recited. This more than anything else signaled a key difference in their new marital status as freedpeople. Even if the circumstances of the war could not guarantee their relationships for all eternity, for the first time they were no longer expected to cosign third-party interventions in holy wedlock. Lockwood's marriage sermons increasingly elaborated on Christian principles drawing from many different biblical stories: the "disorders" of Jacob's family, Christ's sanction of marriage at Cana. Lockwood recorded the marriage of thirty-one couples, identifying the names of brides and grooms, that he married between September 22 and 29 in the vicinity of Fort Monroe. Within weeks of the first rites administered he requested that the AMA headquarters send him one hundred engraved marriage certificates, which would serve as physical mementos and written authorizations of their martially sanctioned bonds.[13]

After the invasion by federal forces in other parts of the South, missionaries were eager to engage in the kind of work under way at Fort Monroe. Like Lockwood, they found inspiration in the first marriage ceremonies that were undertaken under the flag. Marriages were performed in makeshift schoolhouses, modest churches, dining rooms, and parlors. Chaplain T. W. Conway on Roanoke Island, Virginia, noted that as large numbers of fugitive slaves found themselves in the contraband camps there, they "soon begin to learn the ways and customs of civilization. Some of them, on inquiring about the institution of marriage, ascertained that they were not properly married." Conway said that many had lived happily according to customary practices but that others "think themselves to have begun wrong, and accordingly make up their minds to begin over again." They wanted to be "married from the book" and were willing "to pay a right good price for the job." Harriet Jacobs, the ex-slave and author of a narrative about her travails, worked with freedpeople in Alexandria, Virginia. There she witnessed many first marriages, after having to fight opposition from naysayers. "At length I carried my point," she wrote. "The first wedding took place in the school-house; the building was so densely crowded, the rafters above gave way; the excitement was intense for a few moments, the poor creatures thought the rebels were upon them." The minister of the local black Baptist church married four couples.[14] Susan Walker, a teacher for the New England Freedmen's Aid Society in Port Royal, South Carolina, witnessed her first ex-slave marriage ceremony performed by Edward L. Pierce, who she said "conducted ceremonies in very solemn and impressive manner." The couple, Archie Pope and Madeline Wallace, was feted with "grand entertainment and fine dressing, probably finery left by *sesh* ladies in their flight, and appropriated by servants." She described the bridal attire as a "tulle tunic finished with ruche over while silk, headdresses of flowers and ribbons and *bouquet de corsage* in profusion."[15] Men, too, were known to take special care with their wedding outfits. In one case a groom, after watching his bride being outfitted with fresh attire gifted by local missionaries, asked for comparable treatment: "I don't want to be a laughing stock, and I don't look fit to stand up along uh her," he said. "We agreed with him in opinion," Lucy Chase, a teacher from Massachusetts stationed in a Virginia camp, wrote, "and made his *outside* worthy of his *brides*."[16]

Group weddings, with multiple couples being married at once, were a common scene at many camps. Lucinda Humphrey, an AMA teacher, witnessed one such event at Camp Fiske, Tennessee, where couples living together at the camp were required to marry "legally"—under the flag. The camp's namesake, Chaplain Asa S. Fiske, officiated at the ceremony. At the close of a religious service, in the presence of a crowd filled to overflowing, forty couples came forth to remarry or marry for the first time. Fiske, first turning to the men, proclaimed: "You, Africa Baily, you, Wilson Polk, you, Dennis Richardson, & c., here, in the presence of God and all these witnesses, do each take the woman whose right hand you hold, to be your only, your lawful wife. You promise to love and cherish her; to maintain her honorably, by a manly industry and energy; to nurse her in sickness; to bear with her faults; to be true to the thought of her in all the separations through which Providence may lead you, carefully avoiding improper intimacy with any other, till God shall separate you by death. Do you thus solemnly promise?"[17]

The vow was similar to those that free Christians would take, in tone and message. But Fiske tailored the vows to meet the particular conditions of people who were freed from slavery but still in transition and not yet fully free. The phrase "to be true to the thought of her in all the separations through which Providence may lead you" reflected the sobering reality that couples could still be separated against their will. Even after the federal government passed a law in March 1862 prohibiting the return of fugitive slaves, many were still vulnerable to being taken away by masters or being kidnapped by roving Confederate patrols. Even those presumably safe in Union hands were not always under the care of sympathetic officers or soldiers, who sometimes turned them back to erstwhile owners.[18]

When Fiske turned to the women, to repeat similar, though not identical, vows, he made other concessions. They, too, were to be devoted and faithful to their spouses, to love and care for them, to aid them in sickness and health, to "be true to him in prosperity or adversity." But he added a phrase that other free women would not have been accustomed to reciting. Newly freed ex-slave women were told "to aid him, diligently, in gaining an honorable livelihood." By aiding, he meant engaging in remunerative labor outside of their homes. As missionaries and federal agents had preached at every occasion, black women were told to see free labor as part of their wifely and familial duty. Then Fiske, as a minister, chaplain of the army, and supervisor of the freedpeople at the camp, pronounced each couple to be "lawful husband and wife." He added a phrase that had not been heard at marital ceremonies in the antebellum era: "whom God has here and thus joined together, let not man put asunder." No man—white or otherwise—could stand between husband and wife in the federally sanctioned marriage. The day ended with each couple receiving "marriage certificates, neatly printed, bearing a picture of the 'old flag,'" followed by dinners with friends and families at their cabins.[19]

As missionaries set about marrying couples, they discovered complicating circumstances of the intimate relationships that had been constructed within the context of servitude over many generations. As Northern, mostly white outsiders, they encountered conjugal arrangements that were anathema to Christian monogamy but were always practical adaptations to circumstances beyond slaves' control. The missionaries wrote of many heartwarming scenes in the contraband camps of loved ones' finding each other and re-uniting. The camps themselves, however, could be places where families were broken up rather than brought together. Craney Island, six miles outside of Norfolk, Virginia, for example, was set up as a holding pen for fugitives being sent away from the city for resettlement. It was heavily popu-lated with women and children whose husbands were off fighting the war or simply lost and with whom they would likely never be reunited.[20]

But they were also places where family members might re-encounter each other unexpectedly. As Harriet Jacobs reported from Alexandria, Virginia: "here mothers find their long-lost children. Husbands and wives, brothers and sisters, meet after long separation. One good old mother here found six of her children in one group." If actual relatives did not reappear, news of them, sometimes dreadful, did. As Jacobs reported, "One poor mother with seven children, was inquiring for her husband; the answer was, 'he is dead!'"[21] But even among those lucky enough to reunite, there were unique complications. Lucy Chase described an older woman "wise and faithful in her home relations, and conscientious and loving in her business relations with the whites," who encountered her first husband, from whom she had been forcibly separated. The woman recalled her reaction: "'Twas like a stroke of death to me,' she said. 'We threw ourselves into each others arms and cried.'" Both of them had remarried. The second wife looked on at the embrace of the reunited couple, jealously, it appeared. The older woman was clearly torn between her two husbands: "My [second] husband is so kind, I shouldn't leave him if he hadn't had another wife, and of course I shouldn't now. Yes, my husband's very kind, but I ain't happy." Her happiness was still tied to her first marriage, cut short when they were young. Thinking about the culprits who cast slaves in such unenviable positions, she bluntly told Chase: "White folk's got a heap to answer for the way they've done to col-ored folks! So much they wont never *pray* it away!"[22]

Contraband camps could be sites for couples not only to meet but also to part. An anxious wife stranded on Craney Island without knowledge of her husband's whereabouts might look for another. One woman who had not seen her husband in five months longed to go to Norfolk to look for a new partner. Another wife admitted that if she met a man and fell in love she would marry again, given that she did not know whether her first husband was dead or alive. His departure did not sit well with her: "I've only got *one* man, and he's away; left me here like a rotton stick to drop down and die."[23] Orlando Brown, a surgeon stationed on Craney Island as the superintendent of Negro affairs, was taken aback by what he witnessed. He did not know what to make of the seemingly casual way that some parted and started new relationships. As Chase reported his sentiment: "The negro marriage-question puzzles the Dr." In one example, a man who had a wife whom he had happily claimed for over a year took up with another woman on the is-land. He did not separate from his first wife, at least not with her consent, but accused her of being ill-tempered and impossible to live with. Brown's solu-tion was "to invite some clergyman to visit the Island to marry all who wish to be married, and to make legal the relation between those who have already married themselves. He wishes to impress the Negroes with the sacredness of the relation." In a moment of candor about how marriage by clergy in itself did not resolve the "puzzle," Chase acknowledged: "A few nights ago, we had a wedding in our dining-room; perhaps not a 'sure enough' wedding. Indeed, the doctor doubting its legality, pronounced them man and wife 'By virtue of the authority *assumed* by me.'"[24]

Christian helpers, by whatever authority was vested in them, adopted marriage as a mandate that former slaves should follow, like it or not. In Sa-bletown, a camp near Yorktown, Virginia, "energetic teachers" and the su-perintendent of contrabands "compelled" freedpeople living together as husband and wife to either remarry or separate. In one instance forty couples came forward at a church ceremony. "Many unwillingly assented to marriage, while others indicate a full appreciation of the necessity, propriety, and dig-nity of the ceremony," Lucy Chase noted. "It was a strangely picturesque and impressive sight to see, in the twilight, the neatly dressed couples, moving from their various quarters and drawing near our doorway." She continued: "Everyone had an air of serious modest reserve. Some were young enough to blush, and all seemed to say, 'This is our marriage day.'" After the wedding, the newlyweds were invited to have cake at the home of the missionaries:

"Our good friends anticipate immediate and wholesome results from the occasion. The colored people easily assume the responsibilities, proprieties,
and graces of civilized life." Eighty more couples came forward to tie or retie
the knot in ceremonies planned for the next week.[25]

The federal government would increasingly give its approval to scenes like
the one in Virginia. Agents were directed to encourage and coerce marriage
among newly freed slaves in contraband camps, freedmen's villages, and on
plantations run by private and public interests. General Rufus Saxton issued
an order in August 1862 that freedmen in South Carolina Sea Islands with
more than one wife must become monogamous husbands. He appointed a
missionary, Mansfield French, a "foremost advocate of matrimony," to supervise the implementation of this order.[26] Commanding officers, following the
example of Saxton, spelled out more rules to regularize marriage among ex-
slaves under their auspices. General Ulysses S. Grant set up contraband
camps in Tennessee and northern Mississippi and stated that "all entering
our camps who have been living or desire to live together as husband and
wife are required to be married in the proper manner."[27] Other officers made
it a rule on leased plantations in the Mississippi Valley by early 1864 that "all
persons living together as husband and wife shall be legally married; they
shall assume a family name." Registers would be kept of such marriages, as
well as births and deaths. Agents announced that these rules were intended
not only to correct the disabilities of family life under slavery but also to
respond to the urgency of creating order out of the chaos that war had produced. As one officer noted: "A rational idea of marriage was urged, so that
all the family instincts, which so largely constitute the foundations of society,
might come to our aid."[28] Marriage polices were designed as much to benefit
the establishment of martial order in all the places over which the flag flew as
to legitimize couples' relationships.

Rules and regulations were implemented haphazardly throughout occupied areas over the course of the war, and it took a while for them to be
adopted in some places. Many ex-slaves, though eager to take advantage of
legalized marriage, worried about repercussions from Confederates. This
was especially true in locations where getting married was an incendiary act
and put fugitives in danger of retaliation from enemies. Nonetheless, A. B.
Randall, a chaplain in Little Rock, Arkansas, reported that "weddings, just

now, are very popular, and abundant among the Colored People," once they learned they were legal in early 1865. Lawful marriage entitled the couples to certificates and registration in "a book furnished by the Government." This proved to be not only important to couples but also provoking to obstinate planters. Randall noted that "people were constantly loosing their certificates," usually because they carried them on their persons as a sign of how precious this new right was to them. But they did so at the risk of confrontation by Confederates who took them away and destroyed them. Those victimized were "roundly cursed, for having such papers in their possession." Chaplain C. W. Buckley asserted that the opportunities to regularize relationships had produced a "revolution" in attitudes about the "sacred nature and binding obligations of marriage." He worried, however, that the government should also complement legal marriage with legal divorce so that "evil consequences may be avoided."[29] Having just embarked on the business of marriage, the government was ill-prepared to provide analogous legal structures to undo the same. Such matters would have to wait for family policies to return to the states.

Although missionaries worried about marriage among the freedpeople, their first priority was even more fundamental: to provide food, shelter, and clothing to the destitute. Most former slaves arrived at Union lines in dire circumstances. But as much as missionaries wanted to provide rations, they were just as concerned not to encourage dependency. Abolitionist rhetoric had long suggested that slavery was a crime because it deprived captives of their ability to meet their own needs. The underlying assumption of this thinking was that slaves were "given" adequate food and supplies by their masters and so were not compelled to take care of themselves and had no skills for doing so. The accuracy of these beliefs did not withstand scrutiny as Northerners discovered that their ideas about slaves and slavery did not always match their firsthand experiences. But their prejudices deeply informed their thinking and shaped their plans for reversing centuries of degradation by teaching ex-bondsmen how to become productive, self-sufficient, free laborers, as well as neophyte citizens.

Marriage was directly correlated with fulfilling these objectives. It was the civilizing instrument that would re-create meaningful family units and communities out of former slaves by inculcating bourgeois family values. It would orient their everyday lives toward fulfilling a work ethic consistent with laissez-faire economics and restoration of the plantation system. But federal agents had one view of what they meant by a self-sufficient free-labor force and freedpeople quite another. The tensions inherent in overlapping but conflicting priorities became readily apparent as contraband camps were created and plantations were seized and run by the government and entrepreneurs. This conflict was first noted at Fort Monroe. Acceptance of fugitive slaves there was premised on their working on behalf of the labor-starved army. Butler employed them as officers' servants and as common laborers used to enhance temporary fortifications, dig trenches and ditches, and cut down trees. The First Confiscation Act, passed by Congress in August 1861, had granted freedom only to former slaves used in the Confederate war effort, but Butler accepted all who arrived without distinction into his ranks. But he needed to get approval from Secretary of War Simon Cameron, who concurred with his practices. Ex-slaves were initially promised a "full soldier's ration" (salt, beef or pork, hard bread, beans, rice, coffee, sugar, soap, and candles) but not wages. They would soon become the mainstay of workers in the quartermaster, engineer, and subsistence departments.[30]

Work took a variety of forms in and around Fort Monroe and Hampton Roads under Union occupation, much of it initiated by fugitives and beyond federal control. Many slaves in the area were already accustomed to hiring out their own labor and engaging in a variety of activities to contribute to their own subsistence. When Confederates evacuated ex-slaves, they continued to carry on these activities on their own. They survived on odd jobs selling goods and services to military personnel nearby. Women washed, sewed, and cooked. Men and women sold produce and other goods, including illicit items like alcohol. A small number squatted on abandoned farms and raised crops.[31]

Black workers demonstrated their readiness to be of service to the government in different capacities. Many missionaries were often surprised and delighted by the readiness of former slaves to work in the contraband camp, despite their initial misgivings. Very soon after his arrival in Fort Monroe, Lockwood pointed out: "Those who are able are engaged in labor of some kind, and seem to work as industriously as white laborers, and more so than many. They now work with a will, because they work in hope of liberty, and with a consciousness that they can do much to help or hinder their cause."[32] Other missionaries elsewhere seized upon how quickly former slaves became successful military workers to mark the beginning of a new era for emancipation. Private Edward L. Pierce, of the Massachusetts Third Regiment, supervised fugitive workers in July and wrote effusively about this novel move by the army and its larger implications; taking a narrow, practical military step and giving it the most expansive vision that warmed abolitionists' hearts. "I felt assured that from that hour whatsoever the fortunes of the war every one of those enrolled defenders of the Union had vindicated beyond all future question, for himself, his wife, and their issue, a title to American citizenship, and become heir to all the immunities of Magna Carta, the Declaration of Independence, and the Constitution of the United States."[33] Pierce associated these privileges with marriage as though it were now a matter of fact for former slaves. He especially related them to empowering men as husbands and fathers, which foretold how federal officials would use gender to distinguish the routes to emancipation and citizenship.

Gender would shape how the government handled its workforce and how it paid them. Those deemed to be dependents would be treated as secondary in matters bearing on how the labor market would function. By October 1861, there were hundreds of ex-slaves working for the government and nearly an equal number who found their own work by fishing, huckstering, and hiring their time to private individuals and soldiers.[34] Compensation for work for the military was assigned on a sliding scale. General John Wool, who took over Butler's post in August, initially ordered that all military and private employers allocate eight dollars per month for men and four dollars for women, plus subsistence. Escaped slaves would not get actual cash, however; their earnings were directed to a fund for taking care of all fugitive slaves. Blacks who had been free before the war received their payments directly. The scale was modified by the end of the calendar year, with small increases. Women were always at the bottom, even below sick and disabled men and boys. The logic of unequal pay was based on the idea that men were the heads of households. Women were considered their dependents, whether married or single, and thus were paid less.[35]

But regardless of the official pay scale, actual government compensation made it difficult for men to live up to that model of heads of households, able to make ends meet for their families. Many fugitives never received a dime, which Lockwood called "government slavery." Some received only rations in exchange for their work. Freedpeople objected to this treatment, however much many Northerners believed that they were ignorant of market economics. Lockwood had learned otherwise; he wrote that they "naturally think that they are entitled to as much compensation as other laborers, or as enlisted soldiers, and not have merely 'rations and clothing.' Like other men, they wish to have the means of buying many little necessaries and comforts for their families, of which they are greatly in need." In addition, they faced unique risks and dangers. "They are also often filled with apprehension that they may be remanded in to slavery," he added.[36] Former slaves who were accustomed to earning money from additional work or from being hired out were especially aggrieved by the injustices they experienced from their presumed allies. "Bro Blake says that he saw a colored man to-day who said that he had worked for govt since the first of July—has received no money—only rations, a pair of shoes & a coat. When in slavery he was accustomed to make $6 a month over what he paid his master. (I suppose he paid his Master about $10 a month, as that was the ordinary amount demanded.)"[37] That man was still waiting to receive his pay six months later. General Wool eventually approved back pay, but many of the inaugural workers at Fort Monroe were still fighting for their wages at the end of the war.[38]

Some men working for the army protested by refusing to work when their families faced starvation because the government failed to meet its minimal obligations and promises of feeding them, but they were punished with whippings and jail time for speaking up. Missionaries like Lockwood were highly critical of exploitative federal government practices: "Quite a number of families receive no rations, and only a few of the women about the Fort are supplied with clothing," he wrote. Some received blankets and straw mattresses, but too many got little or nothing from the government. He complained to officials in Washington that men who were working for the government deserved to be able to take care of their families. "Why is it withheld?" he asked.[39] An investigation by General Wool revealed that many government workers were being defrauded by their employers.

A contraband fund was established to make up for these lapses in pay, presumably to help aid the wives, children, and family members of male military workers, so that they would not become dependent on the government for help. The earnings of all black workers, regardless of whether they were slave or free before the war, were assessed with a tax deducted and deposited into the fund. The underlying presumption was that all black people should take care of one another by giving up a portion of their wages to prevent the twin evils of dependency and starvation. To add insult to injury, most of the funds never reached their intended beneficiaries. By January 1862, the contraband fund had accumulated thousands of dollars, but rations for black workers' families were cut. A group of male workers in the Quartermaster's Department in Alexandria, Virginia, wrote a letter of complaint about the burdens the tax imposed on their already limited resources. "There are some things touching our relations and obligations to the Government, which we do not understand," they wrote. They were not being paid in a timely matter, which required them to get credit just to feed their families. When paid, they did not receive all of their earnings, because it was garnished for taxes to cover the unemployed and deductions to maintain a hospital. They felt especially aggrieved as persons "in our transition state" without property, paying exorbitant rents and having large families to care for. They understood the injustice of the excise fees and questioned whether or not they were assessed on "all persons similarly situated at the various military posts."[40]

The tax did not bear on all "similarly situated" persons. No white workers were expected to provide for the infirm, the aged, or any dependents of their race. On the contrary, the care of white laborers—Confederates and Unionists alike—was taken for granted by the federal government. The racialist logic prompting fears of black dependency could have easily been reversed. The American Freedmen's Inquiry Commission, appointed by the secretary of war to investigate the condition of ex-slaves, made this clear: "it is a mistake to suppose that assistance has been needed or obtained exclusively by persons of color in consequence of such disturbance [of the war]." The commission found evidence throughout Union-occupied territories that poor whites were applying for and successfully receiving more rations and other military resources than poor blacks.[41] African Americans got relief only when they were in the most dire conditions (too young, too old, or too sick to work) and then only temporarily.[42] General Rufus Saxton, military governor of the Department of the South (encompassing South Carolina, Georgia, and Florida), testified: "all things considered, they have been no expense to the government." Ex-slaves received some charitable goods from Northern mission societies, he noted, but on balance they earned more on their own. Their contributions of labor to the military essentially paid for "the full equivalent of the rations and the wages which they and their wives and children receive."[43] The question of whether ex-slaves were capable of self-support should have been moot to any astute observer of this mounting evidence. But black workers continued to be deprived of the fruits of their labor, redirected from slave-owners to the pockets of private investors and the coffers of the U.S. Treasury, which subsidized (white) public relief. By the time the war ended virtually all freedpeople were earning enough in wages to take care of themselves.[44]

Most federal agents had difficulty recognizing self-sufficiency among former slaves and had little interest in rewarding it. They did all they could to discourage the kind of self-governance and self-employment primarily aimed at benefiting black families. In some areas freedpeople had to receive a "special permit" to hire their own time to earn a living independently. At Fort Monroe, military officials made it impossible for ex-slaves to take jobs that competed with military jobs. They were taken away from places where they could fish and catch oysters and were placed instead in tents in the woods. Lockwood was accused of "negro stealing" for his efforts to save fugitives from being dislodged from the camp. The ostensible reason given for the measure was to get them out of the way and protect them from enemy forces. But Lockwood recognized it as a ruse: "they would be full as much or more exposed there," he argued in their defense. He denounced the move as a "pro-slavery scheme under the cover of alleged military reason." He believed that some officers had duped General Wool into approving the removal under false pretenses.[45]

Federal agents did not know in advance of occupation that many ex-slaves were already experienced with exchanging work for some form of compensation, including cash. Many also were accustomed to hiring their own time, as the government worker Bro. Blake encountered. There was abundant evidence of hired slave labor hiding in plain sight all along the routes the Union Army initially invaded in Tidewater Virginia, coastal Georgia, South Carolina, North Carolina, and the Mississippi Valley. The evidence of this was on full display to soldiers in blue and gray who frequently took advantage of the perishable and durable property that the slaves relied on for their self-care. The accumulation and distribution of these resources within their extended families, neighborhoods, and communities made all the difference between malnutrition and adequate food, insufficient shelter and decent housing, modest garments and nudity.[46] Tensions over the character of work were motivated by the different priorities of ex-slaves and the army of occupation.

Northern agents were far less interested in advancing real self-sufficiency than in establishing families of "peasant cultivators" to reinvigorate commercial agriculture. Ex-slaves on the Sea Islands were among the first to experience the imposition of a free-labor regime designed to prove its superiority over slave labor and to recoup the profits literally left sprouting from the scorched earth by evacuating planters. The program shifted into high gear within six months after the initial November 1861 federal invasion of Port Royal, South Carolina, when venture capital evangelicals took charge of running abandoned cotton plantations. Their vision was driven by faith in the laws of the market to govern staple-crop production. The men judged the value and worth of ex-slave laborers on how much they contributed and how well they obeyed the rules of that enterprise and little else. Ex-slave workers acclimated to exploitation were to be paid below subsistence wages based on the perverse logic that, as one philanthropic entrepreneur, William Gannett, said, "nothing will rouse and maintain their energy but suffering." Suffering meant that any work ex-slaves pursued outside of cotton production, like growing food to eat, was scoffed at. With little regard for recompensing vested tenants, wartime plantation managers would redistribute the proceeds outward and upward to the federal treasury and private lessees privileged to buy up the largest tracts of the best land. The incommensurate rewards of unencumbered capitalism were hard to miss after two years of management. Private lessees, like Gannett and Edward Philbrick, made phenomenal profits, which ex-slaves and sensitive allies protested.[47]

Ex-slaves' priorities were to advance the interests of their families, not to line the pockets of entrepreneurs. They fought for and won certain concessions under the new system, despite what looked very much like slavery by another name. When Philbrick tried to introduce the much reviled gang system of labor, in which groups would be randomly assigned tasks, they successfully rejected it in favor of family organization. This gave workers more control over the division of their labor in the fields and within their domestic units. They regained access to garden plots to grow produce to supplement their diets and to sell to eager buyers in Hilton Head. They preferred self-employment activities to cotton cultivation, not just because the latter was associated with slavery, but also because it enabled further exploitation under the guise of a new system.[48]

Ex-slaves could not preempt the implementation of a peasant, family-based labor system, which was rigged by derogatory views of the race and gender of the workers, imposed throughout Union-occupied areas. Judging by the characteristics of classic peasant classes, the achievement of wartime free labor was more aspirational than real. The antebellum rallying cry "free soil, free labor, free men" did not stand a chance to take root during wartime occupation. The exigencies of the war and the needs of commercial agriculture resulted in a system of wage slavery not unlike chattel slavery. Federal agents and entrepreneurs positioned to benefit from this system strongly objected to ex-slaves' gaining access to land as a few families did in South Carolina and the Mississippi Valley. Gannett, the proponent of enforced suffering, claimed it would be "unwise and injurious."[49] Others thought ex-slaves could be trained to become smallholders—in due time. But until they could prove themselves worthy of landownership they would be peasants of a lesser sort, with women, men, and children all required to do their part.

Marriage was the infrastructure for building these self-sufficient units. As the American Freedmen's Commission reported, marriage should be required for the newly freed as it "imposes upon the husband and father the legal obligation to support his family."[50] Married men were told to assume roles as heads of households, with wives and children as their subordinates and charges. Marriage encouraged an orderly sex ethic that countered the promiscuity associated with female slaves and produced stable domestic lives and the will to work. Marriage also tied together the creation of a market society and civil society. Field labor would be supplemented with missionary-run schools and churches to cultivate morality, good housekeeping, health, hygiene, and consumerism. Keeping up with these habits and appearances would encourage an appetite for goods manufactured in Northern factories and grains grown out West, conveniently supplied by plantation stores.[51]

But an agricultural system built on the model of adult male heads of households posed problems, both practical and ideological. Ex-slave men were sought-after workers in every arena of the Union war effort. Federal agents most often associated the word "contraband" with men. Only men were considered military workers and, of course, soldiers. The triptych paintings by Thomas Waterman Wood, *A Bit of War History,* capture these popular representations. (See Figs. 4.2, 4.3, and 4.4.) The paintings show the progression of slavery to freedom via the construction of masculinity: "The Contraband," "The Recruit," and "The Soldier." It is especially note-worthy that Wood depicted "The Contraband" in 1865 as a man, by which time the prototype figure in reality was a woman.[52] But women, perceived as nuisances as soon as they began arriving within Union lines, had no official category to fill. A mismatch between the demand and the supply of labor in-creased as men were siphoned off from the camps and women kept pouring in. After the initial surge of men running to Union Army lines, family groups began to appear more regularly, led by women along with their children and elderly kin. They poured into contraband camps or set up makeshift shanty-towns close to federal lines when they were not welcomed within them. They faced hostile Union soldiers who defied orders by sending them back to slave-owners. They encountered slave patrols and rebel soldiers who sought to re-enslave them just as they did fugitive slave men.[53]

At Fort Monroe, General Butler was far more pleased by the prospects of using adult men than having to deal with women, the young, and the elderly. Men would bear special responsibilities and obtain privileges for what they could offer the Union. Fugitive women were simply wives. Single women were easily mistaken for prostitutes, although in reality all women were vul-nerable to being marginalized regardless of their marital status. Butler was overwhelmed by the female population. "I am in the utmost doubt what to do with this species of property," he wrote to his superiors in Washington.[54] President Lincoln, too, was exasperated. When advising an officer who

Fig. 4.2 *A Bit of War History: The Contraband.* The first painting in a triptych inspired by the Civil War. It shows the progression of a black man as he served the Union in different capacities and was transformed into a citizen of the nation. Notice the posts on the wall and the rifle in the background, suggesting that the man was offering himself up for the military. He is humble, as shown by the tipping of his hat, but earnest and prepared to fight.

Fig. 4.3 *A Bit of War History: The Recruit.* The second painting in the triptych shows the man outfitted in the full regalia of a Union soldier. He is erect, dignified, and armed and ready to carry out orders on the battlefield to make his family and his nation proud.

Fig. 4.4   *A Bit of War History: The Veteran.* The last painting in the triptych depicts the results of war. The man has returned but is now disabled. His sacrifice proved his valor and his worthiness to partake in the privileges to come from a Union victory.

complained about fugitive women being a "weight and encumbrance," Lincoln made a clear distinction between "able bodied male contrabands [who] are already employed by the Army" and "the rest [who] are in confusion and destitution." To the president, women, children, and the elderly fell into the latter category. "They better be set to digging their subsistence out of the ground," he noted. He had little patience for or interest in these women, whom he perceived to be nonessential dependents and consumers of precious resources.[55]

Sometimes women were cordoned off in places, warehoused to get them out of the way. Harriet Jacobs called one of these makeshift camps set up in an old school house in Alexandria, Virginia, "the most wretched of all the places." As she described it: "Any one who can find an apology for slavery should visit this place, and learn its curse." Women and girls from infancy to old age were sheltered there, along with some elderly men too sick to be of service. "In this house are scores of women and children, with nothing to do, and nothing to do with," Jacobs reported. "Their husbands are at work for the Government. Here they have food and shelter, but they cannot get work." Slaves fleeing from Maryland and Washington were sent there "to protect them from the Fugitive Slave Law."[56]

Women were often in a peculiar predicament. They were not the prized laborers federal officials valued. In every sector where black labor was thought to be useful, federal agents complained about the shortage of adult men and the overly abundant supply of women and children. And yet women were still expected, coerced, and forced to work—sometimes with the same violent compulsion that slave masters had employed. Lockwood wrote irately about a particularly egregious example of this at Fort Monroe: "Dr. McKay will have to be taken in hand with a firm grasp. For yesterday sent the guard from house to house with gun in hand, & ordered dozens women to clean the Seminary promising 12 ½ cents pay, but at night gave none." Lockwood reiterated his outrage: "Force work at 12 ½ cents a day, & paid themselves & not paid at that!" Yet women's work, whether ostensibly paid or volunteered, was essential to the Union effort. Women cooked, cleaned, washed, nursed the sick, grew crops for subsistence and for the market, sewed, knitted, served as hospital attendants, and worked as informants and spies for federal forces.[57]

Susie King Taylor, a fugitive slave who worked as a cook, nurse, teacher, and laundress for a South Carolina regiment during the war, wrote in her postwar memoir: "There were 'loyal women' as well as men, in those days, who did not fear shell or shot, who cared for the sick and dying: women who camped and fared as the boys did." She noted their unsung heroism: "They were hundreds of them who assisted the Union soldiers by hiding them and helping them to escape. Many were punished for taking food to prison stockades for the prisoners." Taylor informed her readers that "many lives were lost—not men alone but noble women as well." And yet she knew that their nobility was often denied and ignored. Presciently, she insisted that the memory of black women's wartime deeds be preserved—"these things should be kept in history before the people."[58]

Women's work was integral to free-labor experiments and imprinted into the DNA of marriage that federal agents propagated. Recall the wedding vows recited by women at Camp Fiske: "to aid him, diligently, in gaining an honorable livelihood." Wage work was the handmaiden of wifely duty. As Gen. James A. Wadsworth said before the American Freedmen's Commission about the prototypical wife and mother of the peasant cultivators: "she must go to work on the plantation for wages."[59] Edward Pierce made clear the labor policy that should be implemented at Port Royal and the Sea Islands: "a certain just measure of work, with reference to the ability to perform it, if not willingly rendered, is to be required of all"—and that work should be given a fair wage. Pierce noted that the treatment of women under slavery had created an impression of abuse, but he remained agnostic as to its severity and unpersuaded that it should modify the new regime's expectations of them: "Whatever may have been the case with women or partially disabled persons, my observations not yet sufficient to decide the point, have not impressed me with the conviction that healthy persons if they have been provided with an adequate amount of food, and that animal in due proportion, could be said to have been overworked heretofore on these islands." In return for their dutiful attention to wage labor, all former slaves would be assured that "parental and conjugal relations among them are to be protected and enforced," and that children (and adults who wished) should be educated.[60] The protection of family ties was treated as both reward for obedience and compulsory responsibility. Marriage benefits were the quid pro quo for wage labor.

As the free-labor experiment at Port Royal proceeded, Pierce articulated a more elaborated view of women's work. He had ample opportunity to observe women engaged in staple-crop production as they quickly became the primary workforce, along with children and elderly men. By the fall of 1862, the entire operation of the U.S. military was dependent on the work of former slaves. On plantations, this meant there were far more women than men, an imbalance that only increased with time.[61] "It has been suggested that field-work, as an occupation, may not be consistent with the finest feminine culture or the most complete womanliness; but it in no way conflicts with virtue, self-respect, and social development," he wrote. But he added a qualification to his justification that was peculiar to race: "Better a woman with the hoe than without it, when she is not yet fitted for the needle or the book."[62]

Ex-slave women should not expect the full benefits of womanhood while still being tutored in the ways of freedom. Ladyhood was still a privilege a long way off. This was in marked contrast to what Pierce thought about black men. At the very moment they began to offer their service as military laborers at Fort Monroe for the Union Army, he asserted that they deserved "the title of citizenship."[63] The recognition of black manhood fit the interests of the federals, as it put more bodies in the service of the military, as civilian workers and eventually soldiers. The recognition of black ladyhood, by contrast, would do the reverse. It would remove and exempt the labor of prime workers who were just as indispensable to the military as male workers and even more so in agricultural production. Like it or not, ex-slave women were the primary workforce planting and harvesting crops on the land confiscated by the army, under production by government and private hands.

Ex-slave women themselves often expressed very different views about their work and its value. There were reports throughout Union-occupied territory of growing labor unrest on the part of women and men on government farms and privately leased plantations, run by erstwhile Confederates and Northerners alike. Women made clear delineations between work performed on behalf of their families and work performed on behalf of outside interests running the plantations. In Plaquemines Parish in Southern Louisiana,

George T. Converse, a Treasury Department inspector for plantations, was
called upon to help quell labor unrest and punish defiant laborers unwilling
to work on the plantations as instructed by overseers. In one case, thirteen
women refused to work "except on the patches of ground given to their husbands by the overseer."[64] In return, Converse ordered that their husbands'
pay be withheld until the women returned to the fields as directed, hoping to
pressure men to exert control over unruly wives. In a similar case, in La-
fourche Parish, women had started to make it a regular practice to avoid sug-
arcane fields, "stating that they are ladies as good as any white trash." The
common complaint coming from this government plantation was that "the
negroes do as they please and what work they please." The men found better
wages by working for private planters during the grinding season. Those
who worked in the fields did so for only five days a week. What they preferred to do, as was the case with the women in Plaquemines, was to tend to
their own gardens. Doing as they pleased was their idea of free labor.[65]

Austa French, a female missionary on the Sea Islands, took a stance that
was more sympathetic than Pierce's views to the plight of black women in
Louisiana and South Carolina. Pierce must have had French in mind when
he wrote his piece, which reads like a rebuttal to what she wrote. French argued: "If our government cannot afford to let women confine their labors
mostly to the house and garden, at least, it condemns four millions, still to
live in a half-civilized manner; it condemns them whether it frees them or
not, since it has THE POWER to free them." She believed it was unfair to
expect women to "work equally with the men" and then afterward do the
work that should have occupied the entire day in the domestic sphere.
French found it especially unconscionable that the same expectations held
for elderly women. "Is it to be expected," she asked, "that so noble a government, can, all at once, abolish field-labor in aged women?" To wit: "No, it is
not the woman, but the color of her face, the accidents of her birth, training,
education, and the tinselry thrown around her, that this noble government
considers." Addressing these women directly, she wrote, with sarcasm: "Patience! noble, pious ex-slave women! the government is in debt! It needs
aged women to toil upon burning sands, and under fiery skies, to help it out!
It will free you when it will cost nothing." No wonder the home lives of ex-
slaves did not live up to Northern standards of homemaking, she pointed

out. Who would have time to care for children, set kitchen tables, prepare
family meals, and observe genteel etiquette under these circumstances?

French did not flinch from analyzing the racial ideals that colored how
such poor workingwomen were regarded compared with white women.
"Other women under government's care, must have many personal servants,
so you must pay for it, by doing all your week's work in half-a-day, and then
you, and yours, are expected to be as clean at preaching as any one," she said
rhetorically to black women. Northern men, she argued, rationalized this arrangement further by claiming that black men would be jealous if their wives
did not work as hard as they did in the fields. In truth black men, when given
the chance, spoke differently, more in tune with the views of their female kin.
French called on the government to do better, naming male leaders. "Have
not the noble Saxton, Dupont, Sherman, Benham, Stevens, Hunter?" she
asked. She called out Pierce and her own husband, Mansfield French, a
comissionary. But she believed it was ultimately up to "the people" to hold
federal officials accountable so that "we will have no woman-driving under
our government"—by this she meant a corollary with slave driving.[66] Still,
however compassionate, Austa French's critique was grounded in Northern
attitudes about domesticity.[67] Her desires for re-creating black families was
based on that model, which former slaves themselves did not entirely share.
Their vision of freedom, free labor, and family life was rooted in their own
values and conditions as former chattel, denied rights to the benefits of their
productive and reproductive increase. The problem of a female-dominated
workforce was exacerbated after January 1863 when the Emancipation Proclamation authorized the enlistment of African-American men in the army.
Enlistment took even more men away from contraband camps, military
jobs, and plantation agriculture. Complaints about the mismatch between
supply and demand in agriculture mounted. John Eaton referred to the disproportionate number of adult women and children on the plantations as a
"crippled body of workers." Edward Philbrick decried not having "the best
field hands" under his charge. One group of Wisconsin lessees in Mississippi arrived in December but left by the following January, dismayed that
the "proportion of able bodied men to women, children and infirm persons"
was insufficient for the work that needed to be accomplished. Many agents
and investors who complained that women workers were inferior to men

often later acknowledged, if only indirectly, that their assumptions were wrong. Eaton noted that the "crippled" workers "could be compared not unfavorably with slave labor," by which he meant they produced as much as male-dominated workforces. Philbrick took home a pretty profit by all estimates from his inferior female workforce and even admitted that their cotton output was greater than the men's. The American Freedmen's Commission noted that women workers should be appreciated because they raised food for the army and released men for military service. It underscored that they were an important part of the calculus of refugee slaves' material contributions to the war.[68]

The centrality of black women's wage work to the Union war effort exposes the contradictions in federal objectives to simultaneously enforce legal marriage and institute free labor. Legal marriage subjected ex-slave couples to a deformed version of coverture. In the classic interpretation of this principle, husbands were heads of households invested with the rights and obligations to control and benefit from the labor of their wives. Women's unwaged labor within the household economy was supposed to take precedence over the market. But marriage for ex-slaves was conceptualized in accordance with the reigning racial logic, which reversed these priorities and directed the proceeds outside family circles. Freedwomen had to work for wages in the wartime plantation economy, just as they did under slavery. While men were designated as heads of households and women as their dependents, they were denied access to the family wage ascribed to the breadwinner ideal. Wage rates were set to ensure that suffering drove all the able-bodied into the labor market, as Gannett argued. And yet the strictures and privileges of coverture were ambiguous. Men gained property rights in their own labor power and social standing as representatives of their families. Women were "civilly dead" as subordinates "covered" by their husbands, and yet that covering was still a limited power. Women who were married, widowed, engaged, and single proved their muster as able workers, despite the prejudices and complaints of male-thirsty plantation owners and federal agents. Individual freedoms, however, were not necessarily their sole or most important goals. Women and men expressed kin-based views of freedom that put the needs of their families' subsistence, safety, and autonomy first. Most government agents and plantation managers rebuffed their efforts to reorder their domestic lives to meet these fundamental human needs at every turn.[69]

Military enlistment among black males proved another arena for federal officials to mediate ex-slaves' most intimate relationships.[70] The government exercised more control over soldiers than over civilians working either for the armed forces or on plantations. And yet enforcing the dictum to marry (or remarry) "under the flag" was far more difficult than officials with only rudimentary knowledge of antebellum relationships could have anticipated. The complicated romantic liaisons, long-distant entanglements, overlapping intimacies, coerced and fraught arrangements that characterized slave relationships came to light as the war progressed. The most straightforward scenario involved soldiers and their wives capitalizing on the husband's enlistment to remarry or to marry for the first time under the new authority of the federal government. When Roger Young enlisted in December 1862, he had already been married to his slave wife, Ellen, for about seven years, and they had three children together. They were both owned by a local lawyer in Jacksonville, Florida, until Roger ran away to join the army. He was mustered off to Beaufort, South Carolina, where Ellen followed him. They were told by General Saxton to marry again to make their union legitimate, since they were now free. Col. Higginson performed the ceremony at a dress parade at camp in front of the entire regiment.[71] Many if not most couples followed this pattern. But things were not always so simple. The war turned people's lives upside down. And yet the normal conduct of daily activities continued apace for many living in slaveholding states under attack. Couples continued to meet, mate, and marry despite the duress of violent battles being fought, homes destroyed, and families and communities "refugeed" by owners and once again split apart. Black enlistment opened up opportunities to meet new partners, to depart from old ones, or to claim those who were forbidden by their masters. African Americans seized the chance to formalize existing intimate relationships, initiate new ones, and reconstruct households under new terms. Both women and men used the occasion to make choices that may not have otherwise been available to them, though men were more mobile and in the best position to make the most of these opportunities. Men en route to joining the army and newly initiated soldiers were especially well positioned to make and unmake their conjugal bonds. But women were not so isolated that they could not exercise similar choices. The mating and marriage stories of soldiers and their partners in this era expose the ways they negotiated this new terrain. They reveal how complicated slave relationships were in the antebellum period, which authorities making simple declarations to "marry under the flag" did not understand.

The Civil War, like all wars, offered soldiers opportunities for informal dalliances. Soldiers met up with women near their camps on their time off or sometimes took unofficial leave to pursue affairs. Some of these were temporary attachments or "sweethearting" which neither person intended to be a lasting relationship. But feelings could change as men moved around to different stations, sometimes expecting the same women to be available to them if and when they returned. A soldier could choose to sever ties with his old wife and acquire a new one, leaving the first woman behind to figure out how to interpret the signs of possible infidelity unless he confronted her directly. Most soldiers were illiterate when they joined the army, though many found literate men in their units, officers, or others willing to write to family on their behalf. Communication lines were damaged by the war, making it difficult for correspondence to reach the intended recipient. In the space of that silence, a wife might ask, Is he dead? If alive, has he moved on to another relationship?[72]

Soldiering gave black men the opportunity to try on new identities. They often changed their names or used aliases to mark their departures from their former status. A new name might appear to be randomly chosen, but it often marked a way to honor family members, like the names of lost (as in dead or separated) fathers or grandfathers. It could also mean taking on a new wife, in a legal ceremony, performed by civil or religious authorities. Perhaps they did not think they would make it back home to their former beloved. Perhaps they used the occasion to strike out in a new direction and start life afresh. But soldiers' intentions were sometimes ambivalent as they formed new relationships while they were out in the field. It was not always clear if they were attempting to juggle two wives in different locations or giving up one for the other. None of this would be easy to sort out for the women involved, who often discovered that their husbands had had other wives or sweethearts after their deaths. In some situations they had heard rumors, but the truth would come to light after the war when they applied for government pensions as widows, only to discover a "competing widow" claiming the same man.[73]

Anyone involved in intimate relationships with a soldier had to face the very likely scenario that she might lose a loved one. Fatalities from disease and battle wounds among black soldiers were extremely high.[74] Both soldiers and the women they partnered with dealt with this vulnerability in very complex ways. This situation helps explain the pattern of short-term, seemingly committed but serial relationships. We have already seen how forced separations, living abroad, or being hired out encouraged slaves in the antebellum period to pursue multiple spouses. Soldiers' wives faced similar burdens. By any measure Rebecca Smith Gathen had experienced the trauma of being sold and resold multiple times in the years before the war. James Roane in King William County, Virginia, her first owner, sold her to Bob Lumkins, a trader in Richmond, Virginia, who took her to New Orleans and sold her to Bob Campbell. A man named Smith bought her in Mississippi, where she would settle for a little while. Smith, the last name she would be known by, also purchased Henry at the same time, who would become the father of Rebecca's first four children. They may have been partnered against their will, as Rebecca did not identify him as a love interest, only as the father of her children. Henry died on the plantation some time during the war, and Rebecca ended up in Nashville, Tennessee, living in a house with Margaret Webster, a friend. There she met Allen Gathen, a soldier who enlisted in January 1864, and his regiment's chaplain married them. She followed him to camps in other parts of the state. But their marriage was quickly terminated by his death on September 10, 1865, after he was hospitalized in London, Tennessee, for chronic dysentery. Rebecca remained with Gathen's comrades, washed for the men, lived in the tent with Sergeant Allen Williams and his wife, Cynthia, for a while and moved along with them to Huntsville, Alabama. By the time the war ended she had married again. The war had created conditions that encouraged serial relationships, as death could bring marriages to a screeching halt, leaving behind survivors who continually renewed their efforts to find companions who worked best for them.[75]

Perhaps more tragically, many couples married as young people for the first time during the war, only to have their marriages cut short by military service. Elisabeth Turner and Rufus Wright were joined together in marriage in December 1863. (See Fig. 4.5.) The Reverend Henry McNeil Turner, a minister of the African Methodist Episcopal Church and chaplain of the U.S. Colored In-

Fig. 4.5 Marriage certificate of Rufus Wright and Elisabeth Turner, December 3, 1863. The couple had the privilege of being married by Rev. Henry McNeal Turner, a prominent minister in the African Methodist Episcopal Church. He organized one of the first regiments of black troops and became its chaplain. The couple's marriage was short-lived, however. Rufus died as a result of war wounds in 1864 in Petersburg, Virginia. The certificate is filed with an affidavit from Elisabeth Wright on August 21, 1865, when she applied for a widow's pension.

fantry, officiated at the ceremony, which was held at the home of a friend, Harriet Hudson, in Portsmouth, Virginia. Those attending the wedding included other soldiers and young women. The couple rented a room in Hudson's house and began to build their lives together while Wright was still actively serving in the Union Army. The couple kept in touch by letter as Wright moved from camp to camp, and he occasionally came home for visits or she went to see him. But Wright died as a result of combat wounds in 1864 in Petersburg, Virginia.[76]

Marriage under the flag remained one option added to the mix of several complex intimate relationships. Slaves still located in areas under Confederate control did not have access to this new right. Many couples continued to marry according to slave custom without federal recognition. The practical difficulties of two people being in the same place at the same time behind Union lines meant that not all qualified couples could take advantage of this new privilege.[77] Some wives ran away to be near their husbands but missed seeing them before they moved on, frequently to untimely deaths. These were missed opportunities that prevented couples from renewing their marriages. And yet slave marriages during wartime were still in transition, despite the ways that missionaries and federal officials characterized the formalization of these relationships. They remained subject to the whims of fortune and fate that former slaves could not control. African Americans were still not completely sure that their relationships were more secure than before the war began.

Black military couples faced additional obstacles. Marriage was not unanimously embraced among officers. The decision to discourage or reject it grew out of the same motivations, though expressed in opposite ways. Unenthusiastic officers denied their soldiers the right to marry when it was perceived as interfering with control over their troops. Other officers took to making selective decisions about who should and should not marry. "I discourage all the young men's marrying while they are in the army and urge marriage upon all those who, already, have families," James Peet, the chaplain of a black regiment in Mississippi, admitted.[78] Other white officers disparaged and denigrated black wives as whores and prostitutes and refused to treat them with the same respect they gave to white wives. They did all they could to keep the men apart from these women living on the outskirts of army camps. In some cases, when military officials disapproved of the choices black soldiers made they could exact harsh punishments. John G. Hudson, a

commander of a Missouri regiment in Helena, Arkansas, passed an order an-
nulling any marriages that took place without his written permission. The
soldiers were "in the habit of marrying Common place women of the town,"
which he pledged to stop. No married women were allowed to have contact
with their husbands if they did not meet this prior approval.[79] Clearly,
federal control over marriage was not always consistent with the priorities
of making men most available to the demands of fighting a war, rather than
serving the needs of their families.

For couples able to marry under the flag, it was just one step in the long
process of re-creating familial relationships. Protecting those bonds was
quite another feat. Military enlistment gave black men, as soldiers, the power
to assert new rights to protect their families. While some families followed
their husbands, fathers, and male relatives and camped nearby, most slaves
were stuck back on their home plantations, at great risk. The conflicting
claims between the newfound freedom that accompanied military service for
African-American men and the masters' right to exercise control over their
property came to the fore as ex-slaves joined Union ranks.

Once men enlisted, the problems began immediately for their wives and
children. Marriage placed a convenient target on the backs of wives. Masters
unveiled just how much they understood the worth of these couples and
their families by leveling reprisals they knew would be especially agonizing
for men given the choice to join the army or stay home to protect their loved
ones. Confederate owners fought proxy wars against black soldiers by tor-
turing their wives and children. Masters drove families out of their homes,
forcing them to seek refuge in Union camps. In some cases, women were not
able to escape with all of their children and arrived with only the youngest,
since the older ones were more capable of fending for themselves. A popular
tactic of retaliation, both threatened and carried out, was to send the wives
and children of black soldiers to Kentucky, where the interstate slave trade
had been revived, to sell them, virtually guaranteeing that their husbands and
fathers would never recover them. Wives left behind were given heavier
workloads. Some masters enhanced this punishment by assigning the women
to do the work that their husbands had left behind. Wives were beaten when
their husbands escaped and joined the army. George Johnson, a soldier in the
Louisiana Native Guards, learned that his wife, Arana, had been taken from

their home in New Orleans to be abused on a plantation eleven miles away. The overseer "beat her unmercifully with a Stick. He afterward turned her clothes over her head, and Struck fifty two lashes," refusing to heed the warnings of the driver that he could kill her. Cases like this one were difficult to prosecute because the provost marshal in the area had the reputation of being "in league with the planters and [tells] them to treat the negroes as they please."[80] Aaron Oates, a soldier from Kentucky, went to the top and asked the secretary of war to intervene on his behalf after his wife's master cut off communication by intercepting letters between the couple. Jerry Smith, the owner, wrote to Oates: "Lucretia don't belong to you I only gave her to you for wife dureing good behavior and you have violated your plede." But Oates offered a different rationale to the secretary of war for why his wife and children should be liberated from "a man claiming to be my Wifs master." His family should be free, he stated, "as I am a *Soldier,* willing to loose my life for my Country and the liberty of my fellow man."[81]

Enslaved wives and families of soldiers who suffered reprisals at the hands of Confederates surprised no one in the context of a war in which the very institution of slavery was at stake. But some of the most egregious bodily harm and vicious violations came from the hands of black soldiers' titular allies in the Union Army. Incidents in Camp Nelson, Kentucky, from mid-to-late 1864 exemplify the problems of federal policies regarding marriage and family that came into conflict with other interests and priorities of the military and the federal government. The camp became a major depot for recruiting Union soldiers in the spring of 1864 and had also become an attractive meeting point for families of soldiers escaping plantations. Soldiers built huts and cabins for their families, and women themselves paid for their dwellings, often using discarded material from the military for their shelter.[82]

In the summer of 1864, Brigadier General Speed S. Fry, himself a loyal slave-owner and the commander of the camp, wrote to the commander of the Kentucky district about the problems of dealing with destitute women, children, and elderly people, the families of both military laborers and soldiers. They were "a burden to themselves as well as to ourselves," Fry wrote. General Lorenzo Thomas gave Fry permission to remove them from camp and permitted their masters to retrieve them, even if the masters were disloyal to the United States. All those men who were fit for serving in the army were to be enlisted. All other men, women, and children were to be "delivered up" to those masters who made applications for them. But none of the fugitive slaves wanted to leave; most of them feared retribution from their erstwhile masters. This made the order to evict and exclude women much more difficult to implement than camp leaders expected. They continued to pour in, despite efforts to discourage them. They returned again even if they were turned out. Fry gave orders to pickets to keep them from entering the camp. He told officers and military labor supervisors to turn over all women in their charge except those working as laundresses and cooks. He threatened to punish guards who accepted bribes or otherwise admitted women seeking entry. He openly colluded with slave-owners to retrieve their human property.[83]

In late November 1864, Fry escalated the expulsion orders by a wholesale eviction of all freedwomen and children in the camp. More than four hundred were forced out into the dead of winter, with thin clothing and no shoes for most. They were taken by wagon and disposed of outside the Union lines with nowhere safe to go for refuge. Some starved and others froze to death as a result. At least one woman went into labor, giving birth while suffering in the woods. Their homes were destroyed, in some cases before they could evacuate. Others were beaten, some fatally, by masters when they returned to their old homes. More than one hundred people died as a result of the expulsion.

John Higgins, an enlisted soldier, gave an affidavit about how this expulsion affected his family. When he came to the camp to enlist in the army, his wife and two children came with him. He was told they would be taken care of, after having been driven out by their master. He built a small hut for them to live in at the camp during his service. About a month later the family was given a notice of eviction to move the next day. His wife was sick at the time and asked not to be removed. She was turned out anyway and told if she did not leave voluntarily her house would be burned to the ground. When the soldier received the news he went in search of his family; he found them about six miles away in Nicholasville in an old building with insufficient shelter from the elements. This was a woman who had supported herself and her children by washing. "They never eat a mouthfull off the Government" while in camp, Higgins exclaimed.[84]

John Burnside gave an affidavit regarding the treatment of his family at Camp Nelson that same winter. "I am a soldier," he wrote. "I am a married man." This succinctly captured his license to speak and expect results. His family had been in conflict with their rebel slave-owner, William Royster, who had a son fighting for the Confederacy. Burnside's wife provided some key information that helped the provost marshal make a case against the Confederate son. Royster responded by telling Burnside that his wife "had been trying to ruin him for the last two years," and if he found that she had passed on vital information about his son, "he would scatter them to the four winds of heaven." Because of this threat Burnside sought shelter for them at Camp Nelson and was initially assured that they would be safe there. "While my wife and family were in Camp they never received any money or provision from the government but earned their living with hard work," Burnside pleaded. And yet his family was among the masses ordered out into the woods, seven miles away.[85]

The Northern media bristled at such stories of the wives and children of soldiers being treated with grave disregard. Missionaries and concerned military officers, especially those involved in recruiting black soldiers, were also disturbed. Many of them filed complaints. The quartermaster officer, Captain Theron E. Hall, arrived at the camp the day after the evictions. He did what he could to find temporary help for victims and appealed to Fry to cease and desist. Direct pleas to Fry went nowhere. But Hall did eventually reach General Thomas, whom he persuaded to revoke the order of eviction.[86] Abisha Scofield, a missionary and clergyman on site, spoke with sixteen women and children who had walked from Nicholasville to try to get back into the camp after the order of eviction was reversed. But a guard refused to allow them to enter, despite Scofield's intervention. A day or two later they were allowed back in, but much damage had been done. "Their condition has been most abject and miserable, whereas they were pretty comfortable before they were driven out," Scofield reported. "While out of camp they incurred disease and are now suffering the effects of this exposure."[87]

This incident clearly marred the reputation of the U.S. military in the eyes of African Americans and dampened their enthusiasm to enlist or continue fighting. "The recruit has no desire to bring miseries upon his family which might be averted by his remaining in slavery," Hall wrote. "Indeed I have the authority of distinguished officers for saying, that in some instances soldiers have actually laid down their arms, when their families were driven from their sight without protection and a home." Soldiers drew a clear line around the values they held dearest and their motivations for fighting. Serving in the Union Army would be for naught if their families could not be saved. Hall offered a plan for building a home for the protection of black soldiers' families at Camp Nelson, which became the inspiration of the Colored Refugee Home eventually built by the spring of 1865. The incidents at Camp Nelson would become a major motivation for congressional action in February 1865, when they freed the wives and children of slave men enlisted in the armed forces.

Former slaves had to prove themselves worthy of freedom and citizenship by offering unselfish service to the nation as military laborers, agricultural producers, and soldiers. The federal government had taken an unprecedented interest in reconfiguring the intimate affairs of a people it began to claim as an essential constituency to help preserve the Union. Missionaries and army officials faced conflicting goals in their efforts to stabilize fugitives that came under federal auspices. Regularizing marriages, along the lines of the patriarchal traditions idealized in the dominant society, was tied to the military goal of revamping the commercial agricultural system under the guise of free labor. Marriage was used instrumentally to shift responsibilities to black male breadwinners, to prevent dependency on federal resources, and to inculcate the values that were considered commensurate with Christian civilization and an orderly republic. Northern free-labor precepts embodied in these efforts did not reverse the unjust antebellum practices of unrequited toil. Ex-slaves continued to work without commensurate rewards. Free-labor experiments proved to be more financially beneficial to the U.S. Treasury and private investors, insensitive to the needs and priorities of ex-slaves as individuals, as families, and as self-governing entities.

Gender and sexuality constituted a terrain of struggle for standing in the republic and touched on some of the most private human concerns in pursuit of freedom and citizenship. Northern bourgeois norms undergirded the assumptions about why marriages were necessary to initiate ex-slaves as free people, with little regard for the complex arrangements and entanglements that antebellum slavery had wrought. Former slaves defined freedom in terms of family most of all. They sought to protect the integrity of those bonds by what they did on the battlefield and off. Gender shaped routes to freedom and to the rewards for service to the military and the nation. "Through a baptism of blood," black men would earn the highest honor, the right to be recognized as citizen-soldiers.[88] They used their new rights as soldiers (and government workers) to claim prerogatives of husbands and fathers that were long denied them. They fought to remove their families from the clutches of sadistic slaveholders, and they pressured the Union Army to use its considerable muscle to protect their families when that failed. Women could enter into the covenant of the new nation as wives. And yet while not capable of earning citizenship as their men did, neither would they be granted the privileges that free wives could claim, which ultimately meant that their men's standing as free husbands would be derogated too. While women asserted claims of "citizen wife" or "soldier's wife," they were not readily granted either. And yet their carefully chosen self-descriptions defied how they were at once vital to and undervalued by the Union. They spoke about their contributions and sacrifices as though they had, like their husbands, "entered the army." They inserted themselves to help win the war for liberation.[89]

African Americans made trade-offs for marriage under the flag. They fulfilled an essential prerequisite of citizenship. The imprimatur of the nation-state on their relationships gave them new legitimacy, paved with promise of the universal recognition that they lacked when slave marriage could only be sanctioned within the small world of the plantation. They began "to vacate the lonely particularity of the nonratified relation" that had long ensnared their lives.[90] Suddenly slave bonds that were previously questionable were now made "real" in the eyes of federal law. Parents were granted rights and obligations to care for their children. Men and women had more control over choosing spouses to their liking, without masters having the last word.

As black marriages were welcomed into the national body politic they were still scripted by race, however. The rubric of "legal marriage" brought on unprecedented scrutiny of conjugal ties. It created new hierarchies, outlawing certain practices and arrangements in exchange for the legibility of monogamous, nuclear family forms. Kinship was yoked to marriages, unlike before, when familial forms were diverse by necessity to cope with the vicissitudes of bondage.[91] While most former slaves seemed eager to avail themselves of at least the nominal legal standing of marriage under the flag, others were coerced against their better judgment. They could not fully grasp the benefits of being governed by a still-evolving regime that could not fully protect their relationships. Marriage provided no guarantees or foolproof protections that couples would be truly free from external impositions infringing on their rights and obligations to each other and their kin.

Matters on the ground drove federal policy to respond to the contingencies that compelled the promotion of marriage as a matter of national interest. The federal government had overturned prior thinking of leaving family policy to the states to decide. But the exigent conditions of war led them to see marriage as a military solution, even as much as they trumpeted it as a permanent benefit for former slaves. Agents throughout occupied areas established a tapestry of regulations enforcing monogamous marriage. There were strong consistencies among these policies, though they emerged in a haphazard manner as edicts from commanding officers and civilian authorities throughout slaveholding states. All agreed that marriage should be compulsory for couples already cohabitating, and most wanted to encourage new relationships to be formally consummated. Most agreed that marriage would need to be strictly enforced to counteract the legacies of slavery, and that it would be the template for ushering ex-slaves into a postwar, postslavery world. Christian-inflected marriage was so deeply ingrained in the fabric of American culture that it was nearly impossible for elites to fathom any other social structure to accommodate newly freed people. Emancipation policies and marriage-making were deeply entwined. But ultimately marriage under the flag was still provisional until the war could be won. It would take time for Congress to catch up.

5

A Civil War over Marriage

The federal government would take its role in marriage-making to new heights, beyond collaborating with missionaries and entrepreneurs in contraband camps, freedmen's villages, and confiscated plantations. Everywhere, federal officials had to contend with masses of ex-slaves who presented themselves as families and wanted to be recognized and included in a war they were advancing for their own liberation. Families had to be taken into account in nearly every issue that military officials and those working with freedpeople confronted: the provision of food, housing, clothing, work, and military service. Agents in the field and army officials had quickly learned to implement policies and approve practices to capitalize on the ex-slaves' eagerness to serve. But events on the ground spiraled in unanticipated directions, requiring leaders to introduce more comprehensive measures to recognize and to protect black wives and families of soldiers and government workers.

The Union Army had made a big push to end the war in the spring of 1862. General George B. McClellan led an offensive known as the Peninsular Campaign, stretching from Washington, D.C., toward Richmond, Virginia, in hopes of capturing the Confederate capital. But Union troops suffered a bruising defeat by the end of June. A malaise set over the nation as it became increasingly clear that the slaveholding republic was a far more formidable foe than initially assumed. Even beyond the defeat suffered by McClellan's army, the Union seemed stuck in a logjam at best. Moreover, the Northern public was frustrated that the Union was not doing more to punish secessionists and to use their ex-slaves against them. There were growing concerns that the war needed to be associated with a higher calling than just military success and political expediency. Both Congress and the president realized that they needed to shift strategies and steer the war in significantly new directions.[1]

Emancipation became the grounds on which manpower needs could be met and a higher moral objective could be fulfilled as events progressed on and off the battlefields and the number of fugitives crossing Union lines mushroomed. Slave and free black men had offered themselves up to fight for the military since the first day of the war. In a climate in which a seismic shift seemed imperative, Congress finally decided to consider their enlistment in the army and to push the president to do the same. Near the end of the second session of the Thirty-Seventh Congress, in July 1862, lawmakers began to debate changing the Militia Act of 1792, which restricted enlistment to the "free able-bodied white male citizen." The Militia Act of 1862 would empower the president "to receive into the service of the United States, for the purpose of constructing intrenchments, or performing camp service or any other labor, or any military or naval service for which they may be found competent, persons of African descent." The act would reinforce the military's ongoing confiscation of slave labor. Lawmakers hoped that it would also push Lincoln to allow black men to enlist as soldiers, too, but this would not happen until he signed the Emancipation Proclamation in January 1863.

Starting in the summer of 1862, the Senate discussed black enlistment and opened a sustained and protracted debate about black marriages, families, and the character of gender relations, which lasted right up to the end of the war. The Militia Act of 1862, a bill to encourage the enlistment of black soldiers, equalize their pay, and change the pension laws to give benefits to widows of African-American soldiers, preoccupied lawmakers. All of these policies touched on the importance of marriage as an instrument of war. Congress realized that the surest way to inspire more black men to put their lives on the line was to protect their wives and children and give them freedom. This action was necessary for the Union to secure a margin of victory.

Meanwhile, the Confederate States of America, despite its plucky efforts and often effective attacks on more powerful armed forces, faced a crisis of its own. The Emancipation Proclamation marked a spectacular turning point that even the slaveholding nation-state had to acknowledge. The actions it had most dreaded had occurred and could no longer be denied. The United States of America had become an avid agent of the destruction of slavery. And the slaves that Confederates had assumed would be loyal to them were passionate weapons of war—on the other side. Reform-minded Confederates began to offer proposals, out of desperation, to turn the tide and win back men and women in bondage. They debated the legalization of slave marriages, the enlistment of black soldiers, as well as emancipation of the men who fought and of their wives and children.

The debates on both sides of the war illuminate how important the denial of legal marriage was to sustaining slavery and how integral the promulgation of marital rights was to emancipation. The intimate arrangements of African Americans took center stage in this debate as both sides considered how to win the war. They both proposed taking away nominal control of ex-slaves' marital relations from slave-owners and putting them under the auspices of the state—the United States and the Confederate states. This undoing of a fundamental authority, without which inheritable servitude could not survive, would mark a significant reversal that would move these relationships and their guarantors into new territory. Black marriage and family were now unmistakably national problems, a crisis that each side would need to rectify if it wanted to advance its own interests. Black relationships had previously been defined as inferior versions of the same white relations, but now both combatants would have to decide whether to bring them in line with the dominant race.

As the idea of marriage as the undoing of slavery and as a way to preserve the nation-state took hold it also meant the further inscription of masculine conceptions of freedom and citizenship. If the nation-states were to formally recognize slave marriages they would need to enfranchise black soldiers and government workers as husbands and heads of households, making them miniature sovereigns on par with whites. Lawmakers had trouble conceptualizing a role for black women other than as wives, however. And even this category was still fraught by race as the legacy of slavery weighed heavily on black women's reputations, and whites in power could not imagine them occupying a position equal to white women. Despite their diverse contributions to the war effort, black women would continue to be perceived as expendable compared with their men. African Americans themselves, however, insisted otherwise as they continued to press forward to secure the integrity of their families, believing that the roles that women and men played were essential to their own conceptions of freedom.

When Congress began to debate the Militia Act of 1862, the main question was what the just rewards for African-American military service should be. Section 13 of the act stated that "when any man or boy of African descent" offered services to the U.S. military, "he, his mother and his wife and children, shall forever thereafter be free."[2] The bill did not offer unrestricted emancipation, however. Slave men who served would be freed regardless of whether their owners were loyal or disloyal. But their enslaved families would be freed only if their owners had "borne arms against the United States." Emancipation of soldiers and their families was thus at the heart of the bill. For some lawmakers, mostly Republicans, the bill did not go far enough, since it limited emancipation of families to those enslaved by Confederates. For others, mostly Democrats, the bill went too far because it used federal power to offer emancipation to any slaves.

Those for and against the Militia Act of 1862 engaged the debate in blunt gender terms. The question asked repeatedly was, does the slave have a wife? Clearly, "the slave" was defined as a man, a metonym standing in for the whole race that would structure how lawmakers addressed the problems before them. By this point in the conflagration, the federal government had already gathered enormous amounts of data on the state of black families during slavery and under the duress of war. The answer to the question was empirically knowable, although still quite complicated, as the opinions of the lawmakers would reveal. The question would dominate the jousting over this bill as well as the other legislation, including the bill to encourage enlistment, provide equal pay, and guarantee pensions. Congressmen assessed black marriage and families for themselves, drawing on both wartime knowledge and long-standing perceptions informed by Border State slaveownership among those in the body, and the writings of slaveholders and abolitionists, which contained deeply held views about race, gender, and sexuality.

Supporters of the bill grounded their responses in the assumption that slaves had ties to family that were discernible and vital. They emphasized the importance of justice and Christianity informing their perspectives and challenged their colleagues to be empathetic, to put themselves in the position of slave men. "What would freedom be worth to you if your mother, your wife, and your children were slaves?" asked James H. Lane, a Republican from Kansas. "I say that the Government that would restore that mother, that wife, and those children to slavery after that father and husband has been covered with wounds in defense of the country, deserves to be damned," he continued. Proponents knew that they needed African-American men's zealous participation in the military in order to win the war. And they understood what motivated their fighting. They knew what it would mean if the United States did not guarantee them, at a minimum, emancipation as a reward for service, not just for themselves, but also for their families. They also understood what the moral repercussions would be of expecting so much and giving so little to African Americans who served the Union. Denying black men basic manhood rights would reflect poorly on the manhood of whites and their purported Christian beliefs. The almighty would not be pleased. Their own self-worth would be diminished. How could they look themselves in the mirror after willingly accepting men to risk their lives entirely for the benefit of other men?[3]

Opponents, by contrast, harbored no such existential fears about the shadow of providence haunting them. They spoke with the ease of those convinced of their unequivocal white supremacy. Democrat Willard Saulsbury of Maryland claimed that the bill was designed to "elevate the miserable nigger." He cried foul that the bill was effectively a "wholesale scheme of emancipation" in disguise. As a Border State representative, he was especially concerned about how the bill could violate the rights of loyal slave-owners who held fast to slavery while staying committed to the Union. Others expressed outrage that the reward for service seemed incommensurate with the exertion. By serving in the army for a "single hour," or worse, "one half hour," black men would earn the right to freedom for themselves and their families, an honor disproportionate to their efforts.[4]

The naysayers were bold in their declarations of the catastrophe awaiting civilized life if the bill was approved. They played on the fears generated by those who predicted savage behavior by slaves left behind on plantations run by slaveholding women after their men left for the battlefield. Lazarus W. Powell, a Democrat from Kentucky, unabashedly provided his slaveholding bonafides to buttress his arguments. He knew the Negro well, he asserted; he was a subspecies capable of "brutal ferocities." Giving black men arms and freeing their families would provoke rapists and create mayhem. He continued: "the torch of the incendiary, the assassin's dagger, the violation of female chastity, and the putting of the innocent women and children of the South to death by the most cruel tortures will follow." He ended his speechifying by piling on the specter of the violent overthrow of slavery in the Haitian Revolution.[5]

The debate bogged down less on whether black soldiers should be emancipated as a result of their enlistment and more on whether their families deserved manumission. Some congressmen tried to strike the provisions for families from the bill to allow it to pass. Several senators, even some Republicans, worried that the bill was flawed in presuming that slave men had wives and children. Jacob Collamer, a Republican from Vermont, offered: "I am constrained to say, whether it is to the honor or dishonor of my country, that, in the land of slavery, no male slave has a child; none is known as father to a child; no slave has a wife, marriage being repudiated in the slave system." His comments were the opposite of constrained. He invoked the long-standing precept of *partus sequitur ventrem* and simply declared that the slave had no wife, no children, and that the bill was "a dead letter" from the start. Other congressmen worried not that slave families could not be ascertained but that they could be. Calling up other kinds of stereotypes of profligacy among slaves, they were concerned that "multitudes" would come forward, that the progeny of one man and many women would claim kinship to a single soldier. They imagined scenarios that could not be reasonably interpreted from what the bill actually stated, among the most alarming that siblings, not just wives, children, and mothers, would find ways to seek liberation as well.[6]

Other issues that were bounced around included the financial costs of emancipating so many slaves. At the time Congress was still seriously considering the idea of compensating slaveholders for the loss of their property, as it had done only recently when it approved emancipation in Washington, D.C. But others chimed in that if costs were considered too great to justify emancipation, the government should not allow blacks to serve in the first place. Jacob M. Howard, a Republican from Michigan, stated it this way: "I do not care how lowly, how humble, how degraded a negro may be, if he takes his musket or any other implement of war and risks his life to defend me, my countrymen, my family, my Government, my property, my liberties, my rights, against any foe, foreign or domestic, it is my duty under God, it is my duty as a man, as a lover of justice, to see to it that he Shall be free."[7]

Inevitably, congressmen seemed to stall around the issue that puzzled the most skeptical among them: "Who are the children of the slaves; who is the wife of the slave?" It would take several months, but in the end, the urgent need for manpower settled the debate. The Union needed the service of black men in order to sustain the war, however unthinkable it may have been for the fiercest opponents of their enlistment. The Militia Act of 1862 was passed on July 17, the last day of the session. It emancipated black male military workers and future soldiers, regardless of who owned them. It effectively granted black men who served, in either capacity, citizenship, which was a criterion in the original Militia Act of 1795, and which Congress did not change. The 1862 amendment meant that their citizenship preceded their enlistment instead of being a reward for service. The revised act cleared the way for the entry of black men into the military with the Emancipation Proclamation.[8] It freed the women and children in their families if their owners were disloyal. It gave no benefit to the fathers of slave men, however. They would have to earn freedom on their own. The law was a remarkable achievement for recognizing that slaves did in fact have families and that those families should be rewarded and protected. The recognition of the mothers of the men is noteworthy. Union Army officials and missionaries in occupied areas were focusing their attention on the formation of ex-slave nuclear family units—husbands, wives, and children—to the exclusion of other kin. But in Congress, at least for a while, extended families that hewed closer to slave ideals were acknowledged.

The Militia Act was signed into law the same day as the Second Confiscation Act. The latter widened the scope of emancipation beyond the First Confiscation Act, which had formalized Butler's contraband policy. Together the two policies provided the clearest declaration that thenceforth, fugitive slaves and others seized were to be used unconditionally as weapons of war. Black men would serve as military workers, on the basis of the abolitionist calculus that every slave working for the Union was double the sum of the single soldier. For every slave seized by the Union, one white soldier would be freed from manual labor to fight on the front lines, and one less slave would be available for the Confederates to use against the Union.[9]

The law also instantiated gender inequities, which would have grave consequences not only for women, who would be treated as second-class citizens, but for all former slaves. It privileged freedmen over freedwomen. Congress made a clear distinction between the emancipation and citizenship rights of women and men. Men would gain the right to freedom and citizenship by virtue of their service to the Union Army and Navy, in whatever capacity the president determined. Radicals in Congress were disappointed that Lincoln did not immediately endorse enlisting black soldiers. He did announce to his cabinet in the aftermath of the bill that he would issue general emancipation plans by year's end, however. His preliminary proclamation in September did not include black male soldiers, but by the time he issued the final decree the following January, he had come around. But the Militia Act granted women their freedom only through marriage and motherhood. An unequal two-tiered system of emancipation was effectively erected, further burdened by the fact that the wives, mothers, and children of loyal masters would not be considered free, unlike their men. It denied public recognition of the service that women actually rendered to the army every day, in the form of wage and unwaged labor. It put women who were owned by loyal owners in harm's way by making it easier to retaliate against slaves still on the plantations when their husbands were away working on behalf of the U.S. forces. Problems related to this disparity would escalate, especially in the Border States, after President Lincoln authorized black men to take up arms. They grew worse as black men were impressed by the Union as laborers and soldiers, forcing them to leave their families behind.[10]

President Abraham Lincoln's issuance of the Emancipation Proclamation, in January 1863, moved federal regulations in the direction of encouraging monogamous marriage and privileging the position of black men. Nothing in the act defined the terms of emancipation according to gender. The implications, however, would soon become clear in how the act was perceived and the influence it would have on other federal policies and initiatives. It sanctioned the official enlistment of black men in the military as soldiers, which dramatically transformed the war, the men, and their families. The mere sight of black men in blue uniforms broadcast the humiliation of Confederates who had failed to win their loyalty. Black men who took up arms against former masters proved their valor and manliness in combat. They were rewarded with reverence in the eyes of their families, communities, and the nation at large. In the process a new path to citizenship was opened—but only to men. While it empowered slave men by offering federal protection, it would leave women to fend for themselves.[11]

Lincoln and other officials failed to acknowledge that black men were not the only ones fighting for full recognition of their rights. Women led themselves, their children, and their elderly kin out of bondage as men's enlistment accelerated. They poured into contraband camps or set up makeshift shantytowns close to federal lines when they were not welcomed within them. They faced hostile Union soldiers who defied orders by sending them back to slave-owners. They encountered slave patrols and rebel soldiers who sought to re-enslave them. Women were disproportionately represented as plantation laborers keeping the Southern economy afloat.[12]

If the Militia Act or the Emancipation Proclamation left any room for doubt about the federal agenda to use marriage as a military tool, the issue of gender roles among ex-slaves would continue to percolate as Congress contended with other policies related to military service and government work. In the early months of 1864, congressmen resumed the debate about the character of slave families. Their conversation revealed a clear disconnect between many of their preconceptions and the actual conditions and experiences of African Americans coming under the auspices of the federal government. Military officials were forced to face the contradictions of antebellum thinking about the state of black families under slavery and adopt policies that dealt with their material reality and complex needs during the war. Many in Congress, by contrast, continued to view the status of black families under slavery and in the context of war as uncertain abstractions, unconvinced by revelations that challenged their racial prejudices. Some held on to old canards because they served their political interests, no matter how much growing empirical evidence may have challenged them.[13]

In January and February 1864, the Senate picked up the conversation where it had left off two years before. Two acts came before Congress: one to encourage enlistment by freeing the slave wives and children of soldiers, regardless of the status of their owners; the other to provide equal pay regardless of race. It was as though the lawmakers did not believe their own findings and affirmations of slave families specified in the Militia Act. But now the stakes were higher and the implications broader. Some congressmen looked back searchingly to antebellum slavery to ascertain how slave families were regarded in the law and on the plantations in former times, to answer the question that persisted: Did the slave have a wife? No, some insisted emphatically. Slave marriage was not legal. It was a horrible "misfortune" of the institution of slavery that marriages were not sanctioned. Slaves were made "forgetful or ignorant of the relation." As a result, vices were rampant. The worst was the prevalence of polygamy, some inferred. This raised the issue, similar to one broached previously, about how a slave "wife" would be discerned from multiple wives. As Reverdy Johnson, a Maryland Unionist, put it, hordes of women would claim, "'I am the wife' and 'I am the wife,' and 'I am the wife,' and each will be able to prove it by precisely the same evidence." The chamber erupted in laughter. But Johnson did not see the humor. He considered it a grave matter that nonmonogamous marriage could be a basis for military privileges.

Some congressmen tried to shift the debate in a different direction, by focusing less on de jure legitimacy and more on de facto relationships. But this cut both ways. They acknowledged that slave couples lived as though they were married, which was not the same as real "marriage." Instead, they harked back to definitions of cohabitation, conternubium, and natural law. "They lived together but were never man and wife except in the eye of Heaven," Reverdy Johnson stated, which disturbed him. This "loose association," he believed, devalued the institution and made those who inhabited this kind of relationship unworthy of federal recognition.[14] The lack of a genuine marriage then called into question the progeny these relationships produced. Congressmen worried that since slave fathers had no legal standing their children did not exist in the eyes of the law either. The bill did not help to clarify matters on this point, some argued, as it made no effort to define how to discern the children of soldiers for the purpose of providing them with benefits, like emancipation.[15]

Other congressmen perceived that de facto marriage among slaves was adequate affirmation of the value of these relationships. They pointed out precedents for recognizing similar relationships among free people. Common-law traditions among whites were widely known and practiced, they noted. They could have also referred back to retroactive recognition of slave marriage, as the supreme court in Louisiana validated for manumitted slaves, but they did not make the connection. Discerning the wife (and husband) of the slave was as simple as according respect to those relationships that slaves defined for themselves. Whatever the form of solemnization they used should be worthy of federal rights. Evidence of marriage would be based on mutual consent, association, and cohabitation. If couples identified and were known as married and lived together as a couple, that should suffice.[16] Acting married was an acceptable standard used within white society, why not apply it to slaves? The intimate relationships of slaves were not so peculiar or irregular as presumed when judged by these standards. It was up to Congress merely to concede this.

As Congress fretted over the character of slave marriage and family, events in the field continued to spiral out of control, and the need to act became more serious. When another month passed in the spring and Congress had still not proceeded precipitously, the families of black soldiers suffered, though not in silence. The strongest allies of black soldiers took a different tact by bringing in African Americans to testify on their own behalf. For perhaps the first time, the voices of ordinary slaves and ex-slaves were allowed to resound on the Senate floor by proxy through their dictated letters. Black men were called out by name, as soldiers writing up the chain of command in order to gain protection for their families facing retaliation from angry slave masters as a result of their enlistment.

In one case, Captain A. J. Hubbard, a white officer of a black regiment in Missouri, wrote a letter to Brigadier General William A. Pile on behalf of several of his men on February 6, 1864. Simon Williamson and Richard Beasley had asked him for help as their ex-master beat their wives in retaliation for their military service. The master refused to allow the women to go to the post office to get letters from their husbands and beat them when they disobeyed. Henry Wilson, Republican from Massachusetts, brought their names and stories before Congress to provide evidence of how real families of soldiers were put in peril. Other black soldiers mentioned by name included Martin Patterson, William Brooks, and Marshall Taylor, who complained that their wives were forced to do the physical labor that they had previously done, such as chopping wood and splitting rails. In some instances, they worked in conditions in which they nearly froze to death.[17]

For those who doubted whether there was any such thing as a "slave wife," the women's letters spoke powerfully and plainly to the nature of that relationship. Excerpts from the letter of Ann Valentine, written to her husband, Andrew, were read out loud by Henry Wilson. Ann, who dictated the letter to a neighbor, described the escalating abuses from her master that she and her children suffered. Writing in January, in the dead of winter, she requested that he send money for food and clothing, but she directed him not to send it directly to her or her master would intercept it. More interesting are the small details Wilson did not read, which would have conveyed a level of intimacy and tenderness within slave families that challenged some congressmen's denials and skepticism. "Our child cries for you," Ann wrote to her husband. She closed with a postscript: "Sind our little girl a string of beads in your next letter to remember you by."[18] Little did Valentine and others know that their personal stories would have profound significance for the nation grappling with the nexus between slavery, marriage, family, and emancipation in the middle of a civil war. The stories were printed in the *Congressional Globe,* and the actual letters have been preserved in the National Archives for future generations to discover.[19]

But if lawmakers could not be moved by the words of slave women, perhaps they would listen to Union military officers in the trenches as they dealt with the consequences of leaders slow to act. An officer who recruited black soldiers pleaded with Congress "in behalf of these suffering patriots," asking them to get the president to issue an order of emancipation or for lawmakers to issue their own solution. Still waiting weeks later, another officer wrote emphasizing the urgency of the matter: "We cannot wait for the routine of amendment to the Constitution; we want an immediate remedy." The Thirteenth Amendment to abolish slavery was under deliberation as well, but it would require state-by-state ratification once it passed Congress. This would not help the families of soldiers who faced imminent danger, like those being sold away to markets in Kentucky.[20]

Lawmakers dragged their feet and continued to debate the same contentious issues. In addition to concerns about the cost of the bill, opponents raised the question of the efficacy of the government's becoming slave buyers, which some argued would be the consequence of emancipating slaves and then compensating owners for their property. This, of course, was a disingenuous argument coming from those who wanted to protect the rights of slaveholders. They looked skeptically at the hard evidence of retribution exacted against black soldiers, claiming that even if it was true, buying slaves from their masters would be for the good of slave families, who would be "happy" to be relieved of "miscreant" owners. Others still could not find an affirmative answer to the question of whether the slave had a wife. As Waitman Wiley, an Unconditional Unionist from West Virginia, reiterated: the category of "slave wife" was "truly *nullius filius.*"[21]

If a "slave wife" was a vacant term, that meant she was also valueless, unlike her enlisted husband. Men's worth resided in their manhood, women's worthlessness in their womanhood. Garrett Davis, Democrat from Kentucky, argued that Congress had the power to conscript all men regardless of race, but it could not appropriate legitimate private property if it was not intended for "public use." Women were not being emancipated for the purpose of making them soldiers, but in the hopes that their freedom would encourage their husbands to enlist. To his mind, this was not a legitimate use of federal power, and it was unwarranted. And since the bill applied to men who were already in the army, it could not be rationalized for the purpose of encouraging enlistment. This was just a blatant attempt by some Republicans to advance their emancipation agenda and deprive loyal owners of their property. Davis argued further about the grave consequences of freeing wives and thus alleviating their owners of the obligations of their care. "What, then, is to become of the negro wife for whom this mock sympathy is expressed? What, then, is to become of the helpless children who are too young and altogether unable to support themselves?"[22]

The most liberal lawmakers were already quite familiar with the charge that former slaves left to their own devices would not be able to take care of themselves, and they were quick to rebut it. The same objection had been raised in the debate about emancipation in the Federal City. The assumption that freedpeople would become paupers requiring vast expenditures for poor houses proved to be false. Ex-slaves had shown "a wonderful facility for taking care of themselves and adapting themselves to any condition." The federal government had already accumulated a vast data pool throughout the theater of war to support this perspective, and most Republicans were already persuaded on this point.[23]

As the Senate dragged on the debate over the bill to emancipate the families of black soldiers to encourage further enlistment, they were also called upon to address their inequitable pay. Certainly, one way to ensure that soldiers' families would be able to take care of themselves would be to pay the men fair and equitable wages. Black soldiers were paid less than white soldiers and civilian workers and even some black military workers, which discouraged enlistment. Black soldiers were paid ten dollars per month, minus three dollars for clothing. White soldiers received thirteen dollars, plus clothing. Even black officers received the same wage as black soldiers, which meant they earned less than whites at the lowest rank. Black soldiers protested. Several army regiments refused to accept any pay rather than take the lesser amount, which they considered insulting to their service rendered. The Massachusetts 54th and 55th regiments refused to accept a compromise from John A. Andrew, the governor of their state, who had promised from the start that they would be treated equally. After going to Washington to appeal on behalf of his troops and getting nowhere, Andrew offered to make up the racial differential using state funds. But black troops still refused to accept anything less than equal treatment from the federal government. Protesting soldiers from a South Carolina regiment were dealt harsh punishments in return. William Walker, a sergeant, led his men to put down their weapons and refuse to conduct their normal duties. He was charged with mutiny and executed. Congress felt the pressure to step in and resolve the situation, though they did not act precipitously enough.[24]

The debate about equal pay for black soldiers in Congress, from February through June 1864, turned on what lawmakers thought about whether black soldiers deserved a fair wage, whether former slaves were capable of taking care of themselves, and how an increase in pay would affect their families.

Some lawmakers made explicit white supremacist arguments, creating no distinction between (mostly Northern) free black men and (Southern) former slaves. Black men did not deserve equal pay, as it would degrade white soldiers. It would be "unwise and unjust" because black men did not have family responsibilities, in light of the lack of legal standing of their marriages. They could not be held responsible for taking care of kin, and there was no reason to assume that they would. If black men were paid more they would spend it frivolously, leaving their wives and children to flock to the stores of the federal government in search of food and clothing, they argued. One paternalistic solution was for Congress to act as "the agent of these negroes," taking a portion of their wages and distributing it as they saw fit to their family members. Of course, no one mentioned the fact that a tax was already imposed on government workers, the Contraband Fund, set up for a similar purpose, which went mostly to the federal treasury and not the intended beneficiaries.[25]

Some lawmakers did point out the hypocrisy of members of the body depicting images of freeloading black people while not acknowledging how white people, even among the Confederates, drew on federal largesse. Henry Wilson noted: "We are dealing out rations to white people, some of them the wives and children of rebel soldiers, by the tens of thousands." He cited a report from an army officer in Norfolk, Virginia, that thousands of rations per day were given to white people "who do nothing at all." He explained that rations were given even to professed enemies "as a matter of humanity to keep them from starving." Others chimed in to buttress this argument by indicating that destitution among white soldiers' families was a common sight, in every state of the Union. Yet they received additional support from their respective state governments, unlike African Americans. It was up to the federal government to step in and help those yet-to-be-confirmed citizens who had abandoned the Confederate states.[26] There was evidence throughout the theater of war that former slaves were more than capable of taking care of themselves. Black soldiers, as well as their wives and children, deserved more.[27]

In a rare acknowledgment of the contributions of African-American women, Samuel C. Pomeroy, Republican from Kansas, made bold assertions. "The laboring class at the South is not confined to the men at all," he noted.

Unfortunately, what he gave with one hand, he took away with the other. The recognition of women's labor came at the expense of their men in the zero-sum game of racial and gender politics. He invoked the principle of *partus sequitur ventrem* to explain that slave men did not have any legal responsibilities for their families and were motivated by little sentiment to support them materially. It was up to the women, the wives and mothers, to take care of themselves and their children, which they did by their own labor. He noted the exception of some men's contributions through earning extra money from additional work or other activities outside of their master's supervision, but he categorized these as inconsequential. Henry Wilson amplified the positive recognition of women's labor that not only allowed for self-sufficiency but also helped the government. He acknowledged that the federal government actually owed money to black women along the Atlantic coast, especially in South Carolina, because they were not paid for work on government-seized cotton plantations. These women and children were a far cry from loafers; they "earn more than they cost to the Government," he concluded.[28]

It would take a few more months before Congress would act on the issue of equal pay. It was not until a tragedy occurred at Fort Pillow in Henning, Tennessee, in April that Congress finally understood the emergency pleas for support and protections of black soldiers. Confederates summarily executed black men who surrendered at defeat at the Fort Pillow battle. Congress passed the provision for equalizing the pay for black soldiers in June, stipulating retroactive pay going back to January of that year. Soldiers who were free as of April 19, 1861, could claim back pay from the start of their enlistment.

The Fort Pillow massacre also pushed Congress to rectify racial inequalities in the pension laws. Mary Elizabeth Wayt Booth, the widow of Lionel, a white officer who was killed at Fort Pillow, traveled to Tennessee to identify her husband's remains for burial, which she insisted be interred along with the black troops. But she realized that despite equality in the grave sites, the widows of the black troops would not receive the same recognition and support that she would because of their slave background. In July 1862, Congress had passed a law to award pension benefits to the dependents of soldiers who died of war-related injuries or diseases. Widows had to prove they were legally married to the deceased, which meant ex-slave women married in the antebellum period could not qualify. Booth visited the president in May 1864 to urge him to change this law. Lincoln responded quickly by sending a note to Charles Sumner, Republican from Massachusetts, saying, "She makes a point, which I think very worthy of consideration." He urged that "widows and children *in fact,* of colored soldiers who fall in our service, be placed in law, the same as if their marriages were legal, so that they can have the benefit of the provisions made the widows & orphans of white soldiers."[29] Lincoln made the same argument that Grimes and other Republicans in the Senate had made, that slave men did have wives, de facto, even if they were not recognized in the law. Sumner directed the matter to the Committee on Pensions for further consideration.

Lafayette S. Foster, Republican from Connecticut, picked up the baton from there. On June 2, Foster submitted a resolution to the Senate urging that his committee be allowed to investigate "whether any further legislation is necessary to provide suitable relief for the widows and children of the colored soldiers in the service of the United States who were lately massacred at Fort Pillow." Foster's committee produced an amendment to the pension law, section 13, which stated that the widows and children of black men should be entitled to pensions "without other proof of marriage than that the parties had habitually recognized each other as man and wife, and lived together as such for a definite period, not less than two years, to be shown by the affidavits of credible witnesses." The Senate passed the bill with the amendment on June 24, but the House did not fully agree. A conference committee struck a compromise, adding language to section 13: "Provided, however, that such widows and children are free persons." This proviso left standing the existing terms of the Militia Act of 1862, which recognized formerly enslaved wives only if their owners were disloyal. The concession, however, allowed the bill to pass the House on July 2, 1864.[30]

The Senate came close to paving the route to freedom for women regardless of their owners' status, but pulled back from the brink. The expedited change to the pension law effectively settled many of the questions that Congress had debated about the legitimacy of black marriage over many months. It pushed lawmakers to deepen the federal role in the business of adjudicating marriage issues, formerly an exclusive prerogative of states and local communities.[31] But the Senate proceeded with the same unease about these questions as before, and the enlistment bill still meandered along. Legislators remained reluctant and unwilling to emancipate the slaves of loyal owners. They thereby allowed enslaved family members of enlisted soldiers to continue to suffer and discouraged other black men from joining the army.

Incidents at Camp Nelson, Kentucky, in December 1864, when army officials evicted the wives and children of military laborers and soldiers alike, generated a sense of urgency for black allies for emancipating soldiers' wives and children. But opponents did not let this incident challenge their racist views. They blamed black women in the camp for their own misfortune. They had fallen into destitution because they lacked "discipline" and moral character, which is why they were evicted.[32] To use the incident at the camp to advance the bill encouraging black enlistment would show favoritism toward African Americans and thus betrayal of whites. As Garrett Davis stated: "I have more sympathy for my own race than I have for any other, for my own people, and for my own household, and for the household of my neighbor."[33] Benjamin G. Harris, a Democrat from Maryland, went a step further in the final hours of a debate that had been taken up off and on for over a year. As issues such as Reconstruction were being debated, along with the enlistment bill, he accused his colleagues of "getting perfectly wild on the subject of the Negro." To the laughter of the House he stated that they had all contracted the obsessive disease "nigger on the brain."[34]

The bill to encourage enlistment finally passed the Senate in January 1865 and the House in February. It was signed by Lincoln in March, more than a year after it had been introduced. This was the first time uncompensated emancipation for loyal owners was not stipulated—despite an early draft in March 1864 and the constant chatter that called for it. It assumed the right of slaves to marry and have families. It went further than Confiscation Acts, contraband policy, the Militia Act, and the Emancipation Proclamation. By the time the act had passed, slavery had been abolished in several Border States such as Maryland and Missouri. The law became especially important in Kentucky, which held more than the number of slaves in both states combined. After the Union officially ended the ban on recruiting slaves there in June 1864, and as a result of the additional boost from the March law, 60 percent of eligible black men enlisted, the largest proportion of any state. About seventy-five thousand slaves, two-thirds of the slave population, were eligible for emancipation as families of the enlisted men under the March law. But they suffered the greatest reprisals and the most difficulties claiming their new rights.[35]

The federal government used marriage as a direct tool to forestall the violent resistance from loyal owners who refused to free their slaves. Thomas James, a free black missionary, was sent to Kentucky by the American Missionary Association during the war to work with ex-slaves near the army encampments in Louisville. After the law passed he wrote: "I was ordered by General [John M.] Palmer to marry every colored woman that came into camp to a soldier unless she objected to such proceeding. The ceremony was a mere form to secure the freedom of the female colored refugees." Since Kentucky had been exempted from the Emancipation Proclamation, being a soldier or his wife and child were the only routes to freedom. James added: "we were obliged to resort to this ruse to escape the necessity of giving up to their masters many of the runaway slave women and children who flocked to our camp." Still, James, Palmer, and other officials continued to contend with loyal slave-owners' violent efforts to maintain slavery and a judgment from a state court declaring the federal law unconstitutional. In some cases, soldiers' wives had to be physically transported to Northern states to escape further retribution. Palmer ordered the closing of local "slave pens" where "saucy" wives of soldiers were among those held in captivity en route to being resold to individual buyers and brokers.

Palmer later offered a different perspective on the emancipation law, claiming that it was "abused by the colored people of Kentucky." He argued that "there is no reason to doubt that polygamous alliances were very often formed for the sake of freedom under this act of congress." While some men may have entered into unions with multiple wives to take advantage of the new law, some single women claimed they were free outside of marriage. W. H. Churchill, a lawyer and slave-owner in Louisville, complained to the assistant provost marshal that his house servants, "all women and unmarried and therefore not free under any law or regulation, still believe themselves free." They claimed that "General Palmer had told them so."[36] These women refused to accept the pretext of the measure that only advanced the freedom of women with husbands. Still, the violation of slave women by abusive owners had been a large impetus for the act. And Congress ultimately assented to the idea that a slave (man) did have a wife, and that a wife as such was entitled to government protection on his behalf. She gained her freedom and he gained the rights in her person that free husbands customarily possessed. Though some in Congress had urged the passage of the bill before passage of the Thirteenth Amendment abolishing slavery, they ultimately were signed into law around the same time. The constitutional amendment would require a longer ratification process state by state. It would stretch out months after the war was over, to the end of the calendar year.[37]

As Congress was debating an amendment to the Constitution to end slavery and approve emancipation policies for the wives and children of black soldiers, reform-minded Confederates and military strategists considered a different plan. Even Confederates had to begrudgingly acknowledge that the war had reached a pivotal turning point following the Emancipation Proclamation. Proposals to legalize slave marriage were broached in this environment, some emphasizing it as a way of saving slavery and others as a way of saving the white Southern nation-state—or both. All drew on age-old proslavery and Christian arguments to rationalize their positions.

White Southern clergy led the first of these initiatives. A group of bishops of the Protestant Episcopal Church gathered in Augusta, Georgia, in late 1862 and wrote a letter urging churches to hold masters accountable for preserving "those sacred relations which God has created and which man cannot, consistently with Christian duty, annul."[38] That went nowhere. The urgency of acting still seemed far removed at that stage of the war. James Adair Lyon, a Presbyterian minister from Mississippi, lodged an extended missive on the topic after the tide had clearly shifted away from white Southern favor. Lyon gave an address to the General Assembly of the Presbyterian Church in the Confederate States of America, which met at Columbia, South Carolina, in April 1863. "Slavery and the Duties Growing out of the Relation" evoked controversy when it was delivered and continued do so after it was published a few months later, in the *Southern Presbyterian Review*.[39] Lyon called for a variety of reforms to improve slavery and save it from the destruction under way. He proposed reversing antiliteracy laws, allowing slave testimony in courts, and legalizing marriage. The first two ideas seemed mild by comparison with the third, which generated a firestorm of naysayers.

Lyon laid out the rationale for his proposal by trying to spin long-standing proslavery thinking that had been used to justify the lack of legal recognition for slave marriage and family in new ways. To Lyon, the worst "dereliction connected with negro slavery" was that Southern laws did not recognize marriage. The holy institution was wholly ignored. Marriage was not recognized as a positive right for slaves, nor were marital infractions acknowledged. This meant that slaveholders ignored bigamy, incest, fornication, adultery, or rape between slaves, which violated biblical precepts, natural law, and human decency. It put white Christians in an unfortunate predicament because they could not "civilize, elevate, and Christianize a savage people, in the absence of the conjugal and domestic ties." Refusals in manmade law to uphold biblical principles had both spiritual and earthly consequences. Slaves could not reach their full capacity as moral beings because they had no incentives to nurture kinship bonds, including parental ties. The lack of legal marriage, he argued, "ignores wedded virtue; it opens the way for wandering desire; in short, it brutalizes the slave." It also made slaves more likely to run away. Slaves left to function outside the norms of marriage would likely "engage in insubordinate schemes and insurrectionary enterprises, which would devastate his home, and sunder the dearest ties of nature."[40]

Lyon parted ways with the conventional proslavery playbook by demonstrating that white souls were also at stake in their refusal to give slave marriages greater recognition. If slave-owners were not concerned about their slaves' salvation, they should take their own potential entry into heaven more seriously. He criticized the long-standing prerogative of slaveholders to exert sexual control over black women, which, to be sure, circulated a decidedly damaging image of the morally unscrupulous slave-owner. But he put the onus primarily on slave women to maintain or neglect their own virtue, which made the men less culpable. Slave marriage would give the women a tool to defend themselves, to be "shielded against the contaminating influence of beastly white men," he believed.

Lyon offered this critique of fellow white Southerners, not to diminish the value of slavery or its centrality to the Confederate nation, but in hopes that it could improve the institution and save it from what looked like imminent demise. His was a call to arms of Christian soldiers to apply the principles of their faith to shine the greatest glory on slavery's divine sanction. Proslavery advocates had been on the defensive too long, he believed. The best way to make a strong case for the positive good of slavery was to correct the abuses that he outlined. "Elevate slavery up to the Gospel standard, and then the prejudice now arrayed against it, in the minds of Christians abroad, and of great and good men every where will subside," he insisted.[41]

The Southern religious press, fellow Presbyterians, and others rebuked Lyon's proposals almost immediately, digging deep into the archives of white supremacy to construct their replies.[42] The most sustained rebuttal came from anonymous authors in the *Southern Presbyterian Review*. They agreed that slave codes required a fresh perspective to expose abuses in the system and reform the institution to be in sync with the Bible. But on one key issue they demurred. "We deem the propositions to regulate the marriage of slaves by law, as fraught with imminent danger to that very feature of our slavery which really determines the character and destiny of the whole system." Maintaining marriage as an informal system, not a legal one, was integral to the maintenance of slavery as an inheritable status in perpetuity. They could not imagine how Lyon could advocate changing that and still expect slavery to survive. They repeated the metaphor that proslavery thinkers typically invoked to rationalize the contradiction between marriage and slavery. Slavery was a domestic institution, which constituted a kind of marriage between slaves and their owners. Making marriage legal among slaves was in effect redundant. "The [slaveholding] family is his State. The master is his law-giver. He is in no sense a member of municipal society, but of the household estate," they argued.

They added other metaphors to the mix to explain the familial relation between slaves and white patriarchs by depicting bondspeople as perpetual children in the law. Slaves' childlike condition gave them no rights and no duties. They had no positive legal personhood, except when they were deemed criminals. In that position alone did they stand outside the protective cover of the slaveholding estate and confront the rule of civil law. Making marriage legal would topple this carefully built system. It "would be the first and decisive step towards a total inversion of the relation of that class to the State and to the family." Slaves would be extracted from their natural position as permanent dependents in their masters' households and given new independent identities by virtue of their ability to make contracts. It would be equal to "a revolution in the status of the slave, as great as a transfer of allegiance from one prince or state to another." It would in effect constitute "virtual emancipation."[43] Never mind that actual emancipation was already unfolding throughout the South, which was why Lyon felt compelled to put forward the proposal in the first place.

The absence of legal marriage was not the singular evil of slavery, they insisted. Slavery was designed to correct the innate immorality of people of African descent, which was the true crime against the standards of the civilized world. Slaves were not capable of living up to the precepts of Christian monogamous marriage and would surely be neglectful of the new right, if granted. Masters would still have to monitor whether slaves abided by their vows and would be liable for the repercussions of failed relationships and extramarital affairs. This would require more litigation to "suit the hardness of their hearts," as contractual marriage would lead to the profuse need for legal dissolution. The wandering predilections of slaves would suggest that reformers would need to create a mechanism to mediate tensions and dissolve their relationships, which Lyon or others did not specify. Divorce would be left for masters to adjudicate, meaning they would still have control over their property. In effect, the evil that reformers like Lyon wanted to remove in theory would not translate in practice. It would be counterproductive by making it harder for masters to regulate the intimate affairs of their chattel, which only white people as overseers of perpetual children could be entrusted to do.[44]

The writers rebutted the Lyon article by arguing against the notion that there was anything wrong with the current status and condition of slave relationships. They refused to accept the idea that masters unduly separated spouses. The claim was "greatly overrated," they stated flatly. They made an absurd argument that "many things which look theoretically wrong work practically right." Masters had nearly unlimited power to theoretically do as they desired with their property, but they were kind men and women of goodwill, which meant they always did what was "practically right."[45] It was a mark of honor and Christian sentiment to protect slave families and not split them apart. In those rare cases in which they were separated, slaves themselves were to blame, not masters, who sold slaves regularly to preserve and advance their financial interests. Masters separated couples who were "unequally yoked, as it is to encourage and instruct them to form proper connexions."[46] These rare cases prove that masters were in fact not sinful but prudent. Of course, the record shows that separations were not only common but predictable for slaves during their prime productive and reproductive years. The critics of reform had nothing to say about the profit-motive driving masters to the slave market. It was better to blame errant slave behavior for the breakup of families than to acknowledge the exploitation that fed the system of bondage.

One of the cruelest strategies that critics used to diminish Lyon's reform proposal was to turn the devotion and affection that slaves shared with their families against them. Slaves did not need legal recognition because their relationships were already expressions of the highest form of love, they said. The critics contradicted their own assertions that slaves were immoral and incapable of handling the prerequisites of Christian marriage, however. When it served their interests, they waxed eloquently about how slaves formed meaningful conjugal bonds witnessed by and affirmed before God. Theirs reflected the most ancient form of romantic love and marriage, dating back to biblical figures like Moses and the Apostles. Slaves engaged in this ancient tradition were by no means sinners. They asked: "Who has failed to witness frequently in the cabins of the slave as beautiful instances of conjugal love and helpfulness as ever adorned the goodly mansions of the free-born?"[47] The rhetorical reversal was breathtaking. Slaves were both innately immoral as a result of their ancestry and super moral as a product of the actual bonds they formed in the context of enslavement. Slaves were free to practice: "consensus facit nuptias"—a Roman tradition of marriage by consent. They could cohabit faithfully as man and wife without legal recognition, rejecting "promiscuous sexual intercourse," and still be consistent with "the word of God."[48]

The authors of the article attacked Lyon's proposal to legalize slave marriage most vociferously using the same arguments that had always been held as the most important defense. White property rights took precedence over black conjugal rights, which could not be altered without breaching a purposeful and essential boundary between civilization and savagery. But they took that idea even further. The desire to marry was natural, they admitted, but the right to property was "even more deeply imbedded in human nature." The anonymous writers took the property rights of whites in the

United States and not only universalized them but also set them above other human values, making them more important to the natural instincts of mankind than love and procreation.[49] They refused to abide the notion that marriage should trump slavery, asserting that the contradiction between slavery and legal marriage meant that they could not coexist. One institution would need to give way to the other for it to survive. They described their "capital objection" this way: legal marriage "would snap at once the tie that binds the slave to the family, and place him, as the subject of civil legislation, under the dominion of the State. From that unlucky moment we may date the decay of domestic slavery, until the whole fabric would totter to its base." It would reconfigure the master-slave relation into one in which the slave would ultimately only be accountable to the (Confederate) state. The proper state of the domestic relation of slavery could not abide this transformation and obliteration of property rights of white patriarchs. How could slaves be chattel, be capable of making contracts, and become subjects under civil law all at once? The familiar image of slaves as animals was invoked to punctuate the claim. It would be just as irrational to "encumber the statute-book with a marriage law for cattle than for slaves, who are equally without civil capacity."[50] Just as some congressmen in the United States feared, these authors could not abide the recognition of slave marriage because it would put those relationships under the domain of the nation-state, which would give it undue powers to displace white supremacy.

But if there was any doubt about the impact that legalization of marriage would portend for slaves, Lyon's critics urged reformers to look to the less than exemplary behaviors and character of free blacks, whose marriages were fully enfranchised, they assumed: "The law of marriage extends to him in its full breadth. With what result? He is filthy still—miserably below the average of slave intelligence and morality."[51] Pushing the case further for innate racial inferiority, they claimed: "a slave marriage law can do no more towards changing the morals of the lustful Ethiopian than towards changing his skin." There is no legal remedy for either. Nor was there any hesitancy to amplify virulent racism toward all African Americans, regardless of status.

In the end, reformers like Lyon were outnumbered overwhelmingly by critics of reform, like the anonymous authors. Nothing changed. The defenders of the status quo assembled a comprehensive, if often contradictory, mix of conventional proslavery thought. The perverse tone of Southern clergy harking backward while trying to move forward seemed especially archaic in light of the changes under way that could not be reversed. The rhetoric of proslavery Christianity that had been central to buttressing the system of slavery before the war was demonstrably inadequate for the current times. The Emancipation Proclamation and the enlistment of black soldiers in the Union Army provided clear evidence that slavery was crumbling toward expiration.

Although it was difficult to admit in a public debate, some Confederate leaders were far more honest and forthright in conversations among themselves that slavery could not be saved. By the end of 1863, they intensified the debate over the enlistment of black men, to counter Union efforts and address dire manpower needs. The legalization of slave marriage could be put to a related if different use than some clergy had proposed. As a reward for service it could inspire slave allegiance to their masters and help save the independent Southern nation-state. Or it could do both, preserve slavery and safeguard independence.[52]

Major-General Patrick Cleburne's position conceding the disastrous state of affairs that secessionists faced and the need for drastic measures is now well-known, though at the time it was surreptitious and controversial. In a letter submitted to fellow generals in January 1864, he said, in the frankest language imaginable for a Confederate officer: "We have now been fighting for nearly three years, have spilled much of our best blood, and lost, consumed, or thrown to the flames an amount of property equal in value to the specie currency of the world." He stated bluntly that Confederates were losing, in part because of "some lack in our system," and all their sacrifices and struggles had been insufficient, leaving "nothing but long lists of dead and mangled." Cleburne admitted that the troops were demoralized and deserting in droves, overcome as they were by superior numbers in the Union Army, buttressed by increasing numbers of ex-slave laborers and soldiers. There was a growing anxiety throughout the region that "some black catastrophe is not far ahead of us" unless extraordinary measures were taken. Cleburne warned that if things continued, white Southerners should expect an upside-down world. "Every man should endeavor to understand the meaning of subjugation before it is too late," he stated bluntly. By this he meant the loss of "all we hold most sacred—slaves and all other personal property, lands, homesteads, liberty, justice, safety, pride, manhood."[53]

Cleburne reminded his fellows that at the start of the war slavery was one of their chief strengths, but it had become "one of our chief sources of weakness." He elaborated further that as slavery was being destroyed, "the fear of their slaves [was] continually haunting them," leading slave-owners to the point that many wanted to end the war immediately, no matter what the terms of surrender might be. Confederates were driven to renounce their allegiance by swearing oaths to the Union to have any hope of salvaging their property, but at great costs. Slaves "become dead to us, if not open enemies," he declared. As slaves became "valueless to us for labor," they had become more valuable to the enemy. They operated "an omnipresent spy system, pointing out our valuable men to the enemy, revealing our positions, purposes, and resources, and yet acting so safely and secretly that there is no means to guard against it."[54]

What should "our country" do to avert further disaster, Cleburne asked? Black enlistment held the key, a subject that had already been broached in Southern newspapers early in the war and had picked up again late summer of the previous year.[55] He outlined plans for the immediate training of "the most courageous of our slaves" as troops and guaranteed freedom "within a reasonable time" to all who served loyally. He knew this would be a controversial Faustian bargain but prudent to consider. "As between the loss of independence and the loss of slavery, we assume that every patriot will freely give up the latter—give up negro slave rather than be a slave himself," he stated. This would deprive the North of "moral and material aid," eliminate slaves' motivations for fighting for the Union, and lead them back within the fold of their original nation.

The idea of arming slaves was one thing, but Cleburne was under no illusion about what slaves would expect in return. Confederates could not anticipate slave loyalty without conceding the very thing that drove them to the Union—freedom.[56] He admitted that slave men willing to fight had to be rewarded justly: "It is a first principle with mankind that he who offers his life in defense of the State should receive from her in return his freedom and his happiness." The South could do this better than the North, he argued, by guaranteeing the freedom not just of slave soldiers but also of their wives and children. The U.S. Congress had already made such a provision for the families of soldiers of disloyal owners, and at that moment it was debating whether to extend emancipation to those of loyal owners. To attract black men to fight for the Confederacy, he believed, "we must immediately make his marriage and parental relations sacred in the eyes of the law and forbid their sale." While Lyon's idea of legalizing marriage had failed to persuade fellow Confederates as a general policy, Cleburne introduced it as a military measure, not unlike similar policies followed by the United States. The South could respond to the exigencies of slavery's decline by reclaiming at least some Negroes as a source of strength. No consideration should outweigh the value of Southern independence, Cleburne urged. But "there is danger that this concession to common sense may come too late."[57]

President Jefferson Davis shot back that the ideas put forward by Cleburne were too perilous to be discussed openly. "Deeming it to be injurious to the public service that such a subject should be mooted, or even known to be entertained," he wrote, "I have concluded that the best policy" would be to "avoid all publicity."[58] One of the officers who attended the meeting where Cleburne spoke about emancipation was more outraged. Patton Anderson wrote: "this plain but, in my view, monstrous proposition" should not be taken to the rank and file. He found it "revolting to Southern sentiment, Southern pride, and Southern honor," and yet more painful still was that it was met with favor by some in the upper echelon. He pondered whether the South would "now listen to the voices of those who would ask her to stultify herself by entertaining a proposition which heretofore our insolent foes themselves have not even dared to make in terms so bold and undisguised?"[59] Anderson, like Davis, wished to suppress the conversation. Davis ordered the burial of Cleburne's proposal, but the ideas would soon come back to haunt him.

The press and a wider public revived the debate over arming slaves, forcing the way for consideration in the Confederate capital in the fall. Others did not see the choices as starkly as Cleburne had previously. Many still held out hope that they could keep slavery intact and preserve the Confederate nation. By the end of the calendar year, Davis and others had come around to seeing the benefits of slave enlistment and emancipation as compensation. It would still take more months of arm-twisting for the Confederate Congress to agree. Finally, in March 1865, it voted to make soldiers of slaves, with the permission of slave-owners, but without emancipation. Both General Robert E. Lee and Davis overruled the Congress with General Order No. 14, which allowed slaves to be enrolled only with their consent and as free men. But the war would be virtually over by the time the order was enforced, effectively nullifying the arming of black men by the Confederacy.[60]

Emancipation policies and marriage-making among ex-slaves were deeply entwined on both sides of the Civil War. Slaves had made their presence known and felt within Union lines as kinfolk, not simply as indiscriminate individuals seeking protection and relief. Securing and consolidating families drove their ambitions for freedom from the very start of the war and continued to press on the federal government as they offered their services and demanded treatment commensurate with the sacrifices they made, for citizenship, equality, and justice. Family matters touched every aspect of federal interactions with fugitive slaves, freed blacks, military workers, and soldiers. Military officials were forced to deal with these matters on the ground and to pass policies as circumstances dictated before Congress took them up for formal debate. By the time Congress considered modifying the Militia Act to free the mothers, wives, and children of military workers and future soldiers, it had already gathered an enormous amount of data about the state of the black family and would continue to do so throughout the war. Some representatives took that evidence to heart and others rejected it as they debated whether "the slave" had a "wife" and what to do about it. While Congress engaged in robust and protracted deliberations, black families felt the burdens of service to a nation still ambivalent about their humanity and their evolving status as freedpeople. Radical Republicans took the lead in affirming the legitimacy of black families, regardless of the forms they assumed or whether they had been formally recognized in laws written by their enslavers. A minority, mostly Democrats and Border State lawmakers, continued to reprise arguments made in the antebellum era of a degraded subspecies undeserving of recognition that would contravene the privileges of white property rights and racial supremacy. Despite the delays en route to action, Radicals won the day and passed several pieces of legislation to benefit African-American families: The Militia Act of 1862, an amendment to the pension law in July 1864, and the joint resolution to encourage enlistment and equal pay law in March 1865. Congress came to the resounding conclusion that slave men, both soldiers and civilians, did have wives and children just as free and white men did. Benefits were at stake that could encourage or discourage a constituency recognized as crucial not only to Union victory but also to higher principles of fairness, justice, the souls of white men, and ultimately the core beliefs of the nation. At the same time, the gendered terms of the debates reinforced the two-tiered system of emancipation. If the slave wife was not a null-and-void category, the ex-slave wife could expect her freedom to be tied to and achieved through her husband's. Her second-class status put her in harm's way as she became a convenient target of retribution by Confederates and unfriendly Unionists who resented black soldiers' presence and demands.

Meanwhile, Confederates engaged in similar debates about the prudence of reforming slave marriage to save slavery and white Southern independence, first reluctantly and then more openly as times called for drastic measures to forestall ultimate defeat. Christian reformers looked to legalizing slave marriage to align slavery more closely with biblical principles and to improve the efficiency of forced labor and the moral scruples of its managers. Once again, Christianity was at the center of proslavery advocacy. Opponents argued against proposed changes to the status quo on the same grounds that slaves' marriages had been long denied legal recognition in the first place. Blacks were a subspecies not deserving of rights due to human beings, according to this logic. Slavery itself was a domestic institution that incorporated slaves into the families of owners, but legal marriage would not simply be redundant, it would subvert slavery itself. Legal marriage constituted liberation. Thus extending it to the enslaved ran counter to the very purpose of the Confederate nation. And yet finally, leading Confederate commanders felt forced to consider the unthinkable, that the only way to save the Southern nation-state and possibly slavery was to compromise on certain keystone principles. Taking a page out of the Union playbook, the enlistment of black soldiers and freedom of their families, might be their last hope of salvation.

The two nation-states had shared a similar ambivalence about the larger ramifications of recognizing slave marriage. They each acknowledged that this would undo slavery as it had always been known and practiced. It would give slaves sufficient legal recognition that it would contravene the most sacred and fundamental rights of property that sustained the institution and formed an important cornerstone of the nation itself. It would put their intimate relationships under the rubric of the impersonal state and civil authority. Preventing marriage from becoming legal had been essential to creating and maintaining a system of perpetual, inherited status, grounded in racial supremacy. The United States Congress came to understand over the course of the war that recognizing slave marriages and families was important both to slaves and to the Union's own ability to eke out a victory against enemy combatants. The Confederate South could not abide this, even if doing so may have salvaged enslavement, until the war was nearly over. As James Adair Lyon had feared and predicted, it had come to the realization too late.

6

Reconstructing Intimacies

W hen the war ended, Philip Grey, a freedman from Virginia, looked for his long-lost wife, Willie Ann Grey, and their daughter, Maria. He eventually found them in Kentucky, where they had been sold away. Willie Ann had re-married in the interim and given birth to three more children, but her second husband was killed in combat during the war. Meanwhile, her love and affec-tion for her first husband, Philip, had endured despite the years of separation and a new family. As the prospect of reuniting with Philip emerged, Willie Ann became anxious. She heard a rumor that Philip was planning to retrieve their daughter and not her. She wrote to reassure him of her continuing feel-ings: "I know that I have lived with you and loved you then and I love you still every time I hear from you my love grows." But she wanted to make one thing very clear: "you must not think my family to[o] large and get out of heart for if you love me you will love my children." She continued, "and you will have to promise me that you will provide for them al[l] as well as if they were your own." Philip was presented with what amounted to an ultimatum: embrace a blended family or give up hopes of reuniting with his spouse.[1] And he did. Philip asked the Freedmen's Bureau for help paying for trans-portation to bring his wife and all of their children back to Richmond, Virginia.

Finding lost loved ones was the most urgent concern of African Ameri-cans as the Civil War ended and slavery took its last breath. Couples who were split apart against their will had no idea if long-lost spouses might turn up again (see Fig. 6.1 for a family that managed to stay together despite the

Fig. 6.1   African-American soldier in a Union uniform with his wife and two daughters. This is a well-dressed family (the girls in matching hats) posing for a studio portrait. The photo was originally discovered in Cecil County, Maryland. The family was anonymous until recently. The soldier has been identified as Sergeant Samuel Smith of the United States Colored Infantry 119, Company D, a Kentucky regiment mustered at Camp Nelson. His wife is Mollie and the daughters are Mary and Maggie. The discovery was made in the monthly magazine *Kentucky Explorer,* November 2012.

odds). Happy endings occurred more often than might seem possible in a war-torn region with rudimentary transportation, but for many couples and families, insurmountable obstacles kept them apart. Families separated in the context of the war had the best hopes of reconnecting, given the relatively short time that had passed since they had last set eyes on one another (see Fig. 6.2). But the war itself could change things. It exposed people to new situations and environments. It put them in harm's way. If they survived, they

Fig. 6.2 Soldier and companion. Not much is known about this photograph, but the format is close to that of the twentieth-century Polaroid. It was not an instant photo, though it could be developed in minutes. Its small size allowed a soldier to put it in his pocket, a popular practice during the war. Perhaps the couple posed together before the soldier left so that he could carry their likeness with him as he served in the army.

might reexamine their sense of self, their relationships, and their place in the world. The war sparked new ways of thinking, especially for those exercising freedom for the first time. One husband who left his wife, Chery Williams, and their children in Robertson County, Tennessee, during the war parted with words of assurance that he hoped his family would cling to, promising that he would move mountains if need be to return home after the war. But when the war ended, he did not return. His wife feared he was dead. He was not, she discovered; he had been spotted living nearby. Yet he did not come home. Something had changed. Chery had to imagine a living husband within reach yet out of her grasp.

Chery Williams struggled to make sense of this new world in which she found herself. Her beloved husband and the father of her children had not returned, seemingly of his own accord. She wrote a letter pleading with him not to forget her, their children, and the promise he had made before his departure. Chery had a clear sense of their mutual obligations as a married couple, despite the fact that they began their relationship as slaves. As far as she was concerned, nothing had changed since they had gained their freedom: "you was mine when you left and you are yet mine I shall always claim you and love you and if you will come now I will always treat you as kin as I can and I can do more for you and wait on you better now than ever." She still wanted to be his lifelong spouse, but she was willing to settle for at least a moment of reckoning about what they once shared. She pleaded with him to return, even if he did not want to stay. She sought his protection and guidance, the kind expected of a husband. Their growing son, in the difficult stages of youth, was acting "very wild" and needed the kind of tutoring only a father could provide. But Chery also understood her new rights. Although she had likely not married under the flag during the war, the end of hostilities brought new privileges and responsibilities for the marriages of all ex-slaves. Alternating her language between affection and threats, she wrote: "I have the rite to your love and protection and if you don't come I will compel you to come." She asked him politely if he had taken up with another woman, whether or not he had a "housekeeper." She implored him to come back, even if "just for an hour." She wanted closure if nothing else. But she stubbornly refused to settle for that alone: "I love you too well to be harsh with you or treat you a mis and I do not want to see you punished but if you do not come I will have you confined."[2]

The renegotiations of marital relationships among ex-slaves took center stage in the wake of freedom at war's end. The internal dynamics would be forever changed and revealed to interested parties in unprecedented ways. We do not know what happened after the Grey family reunited, despite the happy ending to their search. They had a marriage under the "old constitution" that was interrupted and then a chance for another try under the new one. Now that the third flesh in the form of the master had been legally removed, how would couples like Philip and Willie Ann Grey reshape, redefine, and renegotiate their two selves merged into the proverbial one? As the letters of both indicate, Willie Ann and Chery (and implicitly their husbands) had expectations about what their marriages meant in the context of slavery, despite the lack of legal recognition. But freedom gave them new rights, as Williams duly noted in cajoling her estranged husband to return home.

Wartime measures had set the stage for marriage-making and remaking on the part of the federal government and their agents during the Reconstruction era (see Fig. 6.3). Marriage under the flag was now generalized across the former slaveholding states. Marriage became an institution for inculcating Northern notions of domesticity, freedom, and free labor. But new rulings, new laws, new dictates from federal agents, missionaries, and restored erstwhile Confederate states and the planter class presented far more complicating factors to negotiate. Legal recognition presented opportunities and privileges, as well as constraints and dilemmas. Most former slaves eagerly embraced the opportunities to legally recognize deep and lasting attachments. But others balked at the implication that their previous relationships were inferior and required renewal or remaking. If they loved each other all the same, whether slave or free, why did they need to make it lawful? Some ex-slaves saw freedom as an opportunity to break away from partners to whom they had never been attached in the first place or reject spouses from whom they had grown apart over the years. Spouses did not always agree about whether to stay together or, if they did, how to consolidate households and negotiate their cohabitation and intimacies. As black couples transitioned into freedom under the newly constituted regime, they continued to practice resourceful and creative conjugal traditions rooted in their slave past. These

Fig. 6.3   Edward V. Richardson and Fanny Sturgis. Most likely on the occasion of their wedding, a Union soldier and his bride, both former slaves from Maryland, posed for a studio photograph. This was another rare photo in which the subjects can be identified by name.

were still tumultuous times for black couples to reconstruct their intimate relationships and reconstitute their families as the uncertainties of the post-slavery era unfolded.

The primary order of business once the war ended was basic survival. The South was devastated. Normal life had long ceased to exist, especially for those in the paths of armies. Finding food, shelter, and clothing was difficult even for the affluent. Those who had always had little had even less. Diseases like smallpox presented even more challenges that were hard to escape. Surviving fighting in the war was no guarantee of escaping epidemics engulfing rich and poor alike. Malnourishment, illness, and death were ever-present threats in the occupied South.

Many ex-slaves who had been scattered, whether taken against their will by masters fleeing the Union Army or having run away on their own, had the additional burden of finding their way back home to reunite with their families. Many more had been separated from family members for a much longer period as a result of the internal slave trade. Thousands struggled to locate relatives as best they could, often with assistance wherever they could find it. Black newspapers were filled with "information wanted" advertisements placed by those desperate to find any leads on kin who had been sold away. Steamers providing transportation between Atlantic coast cities for freed-people in search of loved ones were still popular in the 1870s.[3]

Persistence and clever maneuvering were required to bring kin together again because in some cases former masters refused to acknowledge their freedom. Fresh battles broke out over who could claim the labor and the ownership of African Americans. Former masters decided that their interests and needs as plantation owners should take precedence, even if it meant continued separation of wives and children from their husbands and fathers. Some were bold enough to try to manipulate the laws to do so. When men showed up to collect their families, they could not be charged with "stealing" chattel as in the old days of antikidnapping laws, but they could be charged with others kinds of theft, as they took away farm animals along with their wives and children. Many former masters did not resort to the law, however, choosing violence (or the threat of it) instead. Black men leaving the army often sent advance word to former owners that they were coming back to get their families, only to be met with harsh physical reprisals when they turned up.[4]

Black soldiers attempting to get their families back and protect them faced special risks that stemmed from their military service. Former masters continued to retaliate against black men who joined the Union fight, many of whom were still enlisted in the army during this period of transition to freedom. These soldiers faced a unique predicament: as soldiers, they were still serving the Union, but by doing so they were not able to protect their families. This led some men to desperate measures, such as seeking to be discharged to go home. As one soldier, who had served officially and unofficially as a spy, recruiter, artillery man, and company sergeant for three years, wrote in November 1865 from his post in Kentucky: "I dont think My country needs me anay Longer." Months later he was still serving and being moved around to different posts, though he continued to write up the chain of command asking to be released. His family was destitute, suffering from smallpox, and had faced down former Confederates desecrating their property, including a farm he owned in Iowa. "I think if the gov'ment will do anay thing for a colerd man it should be me for I have stood By it in the darkest our when the Conflict was Raggen," he wrote.[5] To no avail, he continued to write letters, including to Edwin Stanton, secretary of the war, a year after his first one.

As black families remained scattered about in wartime camps and villages, former soldiers continued to struggle against unjust treatment of their wives and children when they were supposed to be taken care of by the federal government. Rations were promised by the army but not provided or cut back, leaving ex-slaves stranded without sufficient food. Soldiers accused Union officers of mistreating their families when they tried to gain access to the commissary or demanded to be paid for their work. In some cases, veterans who were wounded and living in these camps could not get help for themselves or their families. As a last resort, some of these men collectively asked to be discharged because of their "dishonorable" treatment. They were shocked that though they had served with dignity and honor, they had not received the same respect in return: "Wee are said to be U S Soldiers and behold wee are U S Slaves." They offered a desperate proposal to get out of the army: "Wee had rather pay for our next years serviss and be turned out then to stay in and no pertection granted to our wife."[6] Black soldiers were more emboldened by Union victory to fight for their kin-based visions of freedom after the war officially ended. They had proven that they were exemplars of manhood deserving all the rights of fully endowed husbands and fathers. They fought for the lives and livelihoods of their families, not for abstract ideals. This was the foundation upon which they had stood armed in alliance with the nation-state in the rebellion to destroy slavery, and it would continue to propel their visions for the future.

Ex-slave couples entered a world of love, romance, and marital relationships that were undergoing significant changes (see Fig. 6.4). Region, class, race, gender, and former status would profoundly shape the contours of what intimate relationships would look like, how they would be remade in meaningful ways for newly sovereign individuals, couples, families, and communities. Marriage based on mutual consent and romantic love, built on ideals of personal liberties consistent with postrevolutionary republican government was

MARRIAGE OF A COLORED SOLDIER AT VICKSBURG BY CHAPLAIN WARREN OF THE FREEDMEN'S BUREAU.

Fig. 6.4 "Marriage of a colored soldier at Vicksburg by Chaplain Warren of the Freedmen's Bureau." The scene of this wedding was the front of the Washington Hotel. The officiant of the wedding was Chaplain Joseph Warren, the superintendent for education for the bureau in Mississippi.

a Northern ideal. Slavery had sullied the relationships of the free, even if not as much as it had marred the relationships of the unfree in the South. White men openly violated their own monogamous marriages by assuming the right to sexually exploit black women. The security of slavery required orderly household government to be strictly guarded under the heavy hand of white male ownership and control over all dependents. This left little room for liberalizing notions to be embraced in white marriages. Ex-slaves entered marital regimes that were shifting, however, as patriarchal governance was losing its grip. They would find themselves caught in the bind that some of these changes presented, complicated by their unique circumstances of having been expressly denied legal conjugal rights for centuries and then faced with the imposition of new rules after emancipation.[7]

Letter writing was an essential part of nineteenth-century romance. At least, that is, for the literate middle class, with the skills and leisure time to exchange letters during courtship and marriage. Letters of all kinds were an important part of the culture more generally, but those exchanged between couples were more precious and cherished as intimate, private conversations. Lovers and prospective lovers wrote to each other with the understanding that the sentiments they expressed in print would not be shared with others. Letters became proxies for the beloved, to be touched, kissed, caressed, and spoken to. Letters were the next best thing to face-to-face interactions, perhaps even better at times, as they could be kept and reread over and over again.[8]

The extant letters from Willie Ann Grey and Chery Williams fit squarely in that tradition in terms of the form and the range of emotions that they communicated, but with some distinctions. Most ex-slaves were illiterate because antebellum laws prohibited them from learning to read and write. Service in the military gave some men their first opportunities to learn to read and write, and they used these skills to keep in contact with their loved ones back home. But they knew full well that letters they wrote to their wives might be intercepted by their owners. The risks had to be carefully weighed of passing along vital information and what could be final expressions of love against the possibility of retaliatory punishment. Writing letters about wives was often more significant than writing to them. Black soldiers were the leading advocates of protection for their wives and children in seeking redress from the federal government on their behalf, as we have already seen.

After slavery ended, illiteracy hampered but did not completely foreclose written communication. Many ex-slaves who were able marshaled their literacy skills to write letters in search of lost loved ones and to express their affection for those separated by many miles and circumstances. But many others dictated their letters to friends, government agents, missionaries, and others. These letters were preceded by detective work to retrace the steps of the missing family and to tie them to locations where communication could reach them. These letters marked a signal difference from the typical epistles exchanged between middle-class couples. They could not always be private. Surrogate writers transcribed the sentiments of those asking their assistance and then passed them on to other parties, via the postal service or the bureaucracy set up by the federal government, such as Freedmen's Bureau, as well as charitable agencies.

Imagine the conflict of interests when the amanuensis was a former master. Fanny Smart's master wrote a letter on her behalf to her husband, Adam. She wrote in response to a letter she received from Adam, a Union soldier, though she had heard that he was dead. It is hard to decipher from the letter what sentiments were hers alone and how much the former master rendered his own ill feelings toward Adam. The letter, dated February 1866, stated that she was glad to hear from him, but that she found it strange that he had not written before: "You could not think much of your children, as for me, I dont expect you to think much of as I have been confined, just got up." She had apparently not been waiting for him with much anticipation, for she reported, I "have a *daughter* four weeks old, and a little *brighter,* than you would like to see." Was this her dig or the ex-master's? The letter chided Adam further for not sending support for the children, but noted that they were all doing well, despite her sole support, and wished to see him. The ex-master wrote his own postscript at the bottom of the letter, which Fanny would not have been able to read. He attacked Adam because he "trid to make the Yanks destroy ever thing I had." He warned him not to step foot on his place, but said he could come fetch his family after the year was over (when Fanny's work contract with him expired), if they wished to leave. The

still-simmering conflict had likely contributed to Adam's reluctance to return home to his wife.[9]

Whereas middle-class couples would have been appalled by such breaches
of propriety, the willingness of ex-slaves to put their relationships within a
semipublic purview would prove critical to their ability to reconnect with
their beloved. There was no time for faint-of-heart expressions when so much
could ride on exposing one's true feelings so that others might be moved to
help them and be armed with all the pertinent information to do so. Willie
Ann Grey had to expose her vulnerability to make a case for why her first
husband should return home and reconstitute their family. Chery Williams
opened up quite differently, displaying her mixed feelings and longings for a
man who appeared not to reciprocate. But the stakes were too great to put
propriety above all else.

The irony, however, is that we now know a good deal about middle-class
courtship because individuals wrote so prolifically at this time and preserved
for posterity what they assumed would be private correspondence. The
breach of that privacy by scholars a century or more later opens their internal
thoughts and feelings to scrutiny in ways impossible to have anticipated.
The letters are very revealing as they seek to explain one person's true self to
another. Self-disclosure was a sign of true affection and willingness to be vulnerable in finding the right match for a lifetime mate. The veil of propriety so
pivotal to Victorian public culture was cast aside for both women and men in
the search for unconditional and mutual love.[10] Mostly the middle and upper
classes had the time and resources to learn to read or put ink to paper, expressing their innermost thoughts and decoding replies back and forth ad
infinitum, however.

The documentation of marriages among ex-slaves was quite remarkable
for a time, despite their high illiteracy rates. This abundance of written information resulted from the level of scrutiny that these relationships experienced under the new postwar legal regimes. Privacy was harder to sustain
when a variety of external forces took on the role of examining and disciplining these relationships. Ex-slaves were often required to talk about their
intimate connections in ways that middle-class people would rarely have
been. Privacy was a privilege that freedpeople could hardly ever expect. They

were often required to document the history of their intimate relationships in order to access new rights and resources.

In addition to the letters generated through the activities of the Freedmen's Bureau, ex-slaves discussed their personal relationships in the process of applying to receive an earned entitlement as widows of Civil War soldiers, in the wake of the law passed in 1862. As a result, documents from tens of thousands of widows and veterans, both successful and unsuccessful applicants, shed light on black marital relationships during slavery and into the twentieth century. In 1864, Congress required ex-slave widows who applied for pensions to show proof that they had cohabitated as married couples for two years. In 1866, the law was modified to require only proof that they recognized each other as a married couple and lived together as such. Congress conceded the impossibility of ex-slaves' providing legal marriage documents but asked for substitute proof in the form of testimony from those who knew the couple. Owing to the absence of documentation, the authorities scrutinized black claims for pensions far more often than white claims, and subjected them to special examinations by the U.S. Pension Bureau, encouraged by the profuse reports of intimate details of marriages and family histories.[11]

A law passed in 1882 encouraged further inquiry by prohibiting all widows from living in "open and notorious adulterous cohabitation." Sworn affidavits from applicants and witnesses were taken to decide whether widows were eligible and whether they remained in good standing to receive benefits. Widows walked a careful line of revealing as much relevant information as they could to obtain a pension without in any way endangering their eligibility. As we read and interpret these letters we must be mindful of what was at stake for women in their petitions for pensions and the careful ways they had to craft their applications in order to be successful. They had to play on the politics of respectability to win over agents reviewing and determining their eligibility. Pension officials often treated them as suspect by virtue of their race, which makes it even harder to determine in retrospect the lines between truth, embellishment, and outright fiction.[12]

Only a small group of ex-slaves had to contend with the ordeal of seeking pensions, and they did so voluntarily to the extent that they wanted to receive the entitlement. But many more former slaves were subject to the continuing oversight of the federal bureaucracy intimately involved in their lives during Reconstruction, before the last troops were pulled out of the South. The Freedmen's Bureau played a unique role as mediators, facilitators, and enforcers of marital relations of ex-slaves immediately after the war. Many freedpeople willingly took their marital aspirations and disputes to the agency for assistance in fulfilling and adjudicating them. They looked to the bureau to find loved ones, to enforce promises of engagement, to end domestic violence, to enforce fidelity to their vows, to reform errant behavior, to help separate, or to gain child custody after separation. The testimony that these incidents generated exposed some of the internal dynamics of former slaves' struggling to reconstitute antebellum bonds or form new ones. The documents reveal the values and expectations of couples renegotiating their relationships in semipublic ways, as federal and missionary onlookers engaged them in those processes. They show ex-slaves expressing sentiments that were typical of what any couple would contend with: figuring out how to find love and keep it, deciding how to manage the rules of the dominant society and family expectations with their personal desires and ambitions as individuals and couples. Dealing with matters of the heart, along with economic considerations, practical concerns, and all the factors that influence intimacy, was not easy for any couple.[13]

All former slave couples came to a crossroads where they had to decide whether to move forward with the same spouse after slavery ended and, if so, how. But their situation was complicated by the continuing legacy of slavery, which could not simply be forgotten or overridden by new rules and declarations. Those whose masters had forcibly mated them against their will were now able to part ways, but should they? Sometimes, regardless of the circumstances, forced partners learned to adapt and adjust to their situation and could even develop genuine feelings of affection. In some cases one person in the couple wanted to stick it out while the other did not. The latter predicament occurred often when the ability to connect with their true love interests had been foiled by their masters' interference under slavery. Longings that had been breached or denied could now possibly be fulfilled.

Ellen and Charley Carter and Walker and Alice Wade offer a revealing example of the messiness that was created by unfulfilled love. Ellen and Charley were thrust together as slaves, but without any formalities of a marriage ceremony. Ellen had been courting Walker Wade, but her master, and possibly his, objected to their marriage. Walker got another woman, Alice, pregnant, and "as he had gotten her into this fix, he married her to save her." Alice's owner threatened to sell her if she became pregnant (again?) without marriage. They did marry in a ceremony and had other children together. Walker left to join the army and returned home to Alice, but their relationship began to fall apart. Alice "was a drinking woman." Walker said that he "stood it as long as he could." He left her without formalizing their marriage under the flag.

Meanwhile, the other couple, Ellen and Charley, also had children. When Charley left to join the army they had one child; when he returned to Ellen at the end of his service they had another. But the two would soon part. Ellen never forgot Walker Wade. She said, "Walker waited on me when we were young & my owners made me take up with Charley Carter, but I never loved Charley & I did love Walker Wade as a girl & on up to today & I never cared for any other man." According to Alice, Walker and Ellen resumed an affair after the war when they were each still married to their respective spouses. Alice wanted to legalize her marriage to Walker because she wanted to be baptized, and the minister insisted that she must be married first. She claimed that Walker refused her because of Ellen, and this drove her to drink. "They led me a dogs life for 6 or 7 years," Alice claimed in distress. Alice and Walker finally split, but not before they had another child together in 1878. Ellen and Walker reunited and legally married less than a year after the child's birth. Alice tried to prevent the nuptials but was told there was nothing she could do. She was not Walker's legal wife. This story dramatizes the dilemma of former slaves who chose to pursue love that had been unsatisfied through no fault of either party; the turmoil that resulted when they were forced to form involuntary unions; and the determination they often felt to follow their hearts, clearly divided by practical circumstances and unfulfilled love.[14]

Freedom offered even voluntary partners in marriage new opportunities to determine whether they should remain together. This new ability to choose provided an escape hatch for some problem-filled relationships. Unions that had gone sour under slavery could seem worse in the context of freedom, when masters no longer dictated the terms of marriage. The consequences of quitting, however, could be grave if the spouse being left chose to exact vengeance by calling for community sanctions even if the departing spouse had been the victim during the relationship. Churches, for example, could ex-communicate the departing spouse, regardless of the situation, since they could be blamed for the breach.[15] But even when couples were in agreement about continuing their relationship after slavery ended, disagreements about other matters influenced whether they were able to move forward as a couple living under the same roof. Couples could not afford the luxury of marrying for love alone, and economics was an important factor in sustaining their relationships. Finding sufficient and appropriate work was an issue that could keep families apart. While most former slaves were willing to take extraordinary measures to reunite their families, at least a few felt it was better to stay separated and maintain their visiting practices, while still hoping to remain married. One wife, for example, had no interest in returning to the countryside and being subjected to the "old secesh"—Confederates. Her husband, by contrast, felt it was better to remain in the country, where the economic prospects seemed brighter for him to take care of his family. The impasse was not easily resolved, and the marriage fell apart. The war had likely caused the separation of the couple and now, out of practicality, they would remain that way, as their visions of freedom did not sufficiently align.[16]

Making the decision to separate, regardless of the source of tension, was not always easy; nor was it a matter of concern for couples alone. Other family members had opinions and made them known. Maggie was a slave purchased by William C. Hebener to be his wife. According to Maggie, he promised that "he would never forsake me to marrie no other on earth," but this changed. The two were estranged and living apart, and she claimed that he did not provide support for her and their son. She accused him of disowning the child, which he denied. He wrote her a letter in which he stated: "you can show this is an evidence of the fact I do own him he is bone of my bone and flesh of my flesh." He claimed that times had been hard, and that he hoped for the day when he could give them everything they needed. He wanted her to stay in the country until he could raise enough money to support them.[17]

William appealed to his grandmother to prove that he had good intentions to do right by his family. He wrote a letter to explain the decline of the relationship to make sure that she would not think ill of him. "I love Maggy and my Child as I love my life," he contended, "and there is nothing that I would not sacrifice for their benefit." He wanted them to get back together now that he was successful enough in his business to take care of her. He contradicted Maggie's claim by saying that he had sent her plenty of money at different times to cover her expenses in Virginia. "Doe not entertain any hard feelings toward me Grandma for my motives have been pure," he insisted.[18]

Maggie accused him of taking up with another woman, though he claimed that he had not done so during their marriage. He wrote her a breakup letter: "I am sorrow to inform you that the tie that has heretofore bound us together is broken you have cause me by the cool treatment you tendered me when we last parted to give you up for ever so far as treating you as I would my wife I am theirfore free to act in that respect as I pleas." But he promised that his honor bound him to take care of his family regardless. "But do not understand me to infer," he wrote, "that I am not entitled to a wife for if I ever meet with a lady whom I can place confidance in and love her and have the ashuranse of her love I will not hesitate a moment to become her Husband I consider you have forfeited your claim so far as that is conserned." Maggie received the news by post and felt abandoned, without a home and without protection. "I have never given him no reason for such treatment & he can not say that I have," she responded. She claimed that he did not keep his promise to care for her and their child. She went to the Freedmen's Bureau to file a complaint, which by the laws of the day may have led to his arrest.[19]

The tensions between Maggie and William indicate that when the promise of monogamy was breached spouses were especially unnerved. But other common complaints among couples often led to breakups as well: ill treatment, bad tempers, or failure to provide support among them. Some couples tried to get past the disappointments and persevere in their relationships for years past the onset of their problems, but their grievances often devolved into other areas as well, making it difficult to disentangle them. Children were also important factors in their parents' marital relationships even as they grew into adulthood. Each spouse expected the other to continue to do their part in helping provide food and even education for older children still living at home. Spousal conflict could also take a toll on the children's relationship with their parents, especially if they sided with one parent over the other. Two sons were so displeased by their father's leaving their mother that they changed their surname.[20]

One of the biggest decisions for couples renegotiating existing marriages formed under the rules of slavery was whether to legally register their relationships. Some states required them to do so, but others did not. Couples might choose to do so voluntarily or to ignore the laws. For those who decided to legalize their relationships, their wedding ceremonies were not always easy to distinguish from first weddings. In general, first-time couples tended to marry with a bit more festivity than those affirming older relationships. Brides wore borrowed dresses from their former mistresses, handmade clothes given to them by mothers and grandmothers, and store-bought frocks. The dresses were made of a rich array of materials, from homespun to silks, satin stripes, wool, and velvet. The colors of the dresses were white, gray, green, and black, and they were adorned with puffed sleeves, princess necklines, scalloped edging, overskirts, bows, and lace in pink, blue, and purple. Accessories included red stockings, "Moroccan" shoes, and all kinds of hats. Men also dressed in special attire. Some wore store-bought suits with pigeon tails, vests, and ties. Some chose to blend fancy and casual clothes, such as brown jeans, a white shirt, white vest, and cutaway coat. But some individuals chose to play down the outfits. One woman recalled that she wore "a dirty work dress with [bare] feet" as a test of her husband-to-be's devotion. If he truly loved her, she reasoned, her wedding attire should not matter to him. One groom admitted that he did not give his bride-to-be a chance to dress up. He appeared at her employer's kitchen on the spur of the moment and took her to the church in their work clothes. The immediacy of the moment was what mattered to him. More important than how the couples dressed was what vows they took at the altar. Women now had to reiterate terms of obedience to their husbands, rather than both husband and wife paying obeisance to masters. The content changed but the patriarchal form was redirected internally within twosomes, outside the sphere of influence of the third flesh.[21]

Ex-slaves remembered these occasions fondly for many years thereafter. They were motivated to formalize their relationships in part by pressure from family members as well as churches, which were rising in number.[22] It was remarkable how quickly most ex-slaves, once denied the legal right to marry, adapted to new precepts from church and state, as most available sources indicate. And yet significant numbers also continued to engage in informal marriage or marriage-like arrangements for decades to come.

Intimate relationships fell along a continuum, though they were not always completely discrete categories that were easy to distinguish in form and function, as was the case during slavery. Couples engaged in "sweethearting," a romantic relationship with some of the benefits of marriage and being single combined. Some couples practiced "taking up," entering into longer-term relationships where the partners lived together and had expectations of exclusivity. Still further along the spectrum was cohabitation, where couples mingled financial resources and responsibilities, shared surnames, and practiced sexual monogamy. Rural inhabitants often had cooperative labor arrangements on Southern plantations. Such situations could be short-term or even long-lived despite their casual start.[23]

Cohabitation could assume the form of legal marriage in every way except actually formalizing their coupling by ceremony or sanctioning it by law. Over time, such partners became "common-law" couples, who were ostensibly recognized in most states—a privilege, like legal marriage, that had been denied to slaves. Couples had novel ways of describing their informal marriages. One woman stated: "I called him 'papa' and he called me 'mama.'" She explained that their commitment was expressed in the private vows they shared: "I told him that if he would take me for his 'bosom wife' that I would not allow any man to come between him and me—that I would not have any thing to do with any other man, and he promised that he would not have any other woman than me."[24]

The resemblance to slave traditions would continue to haunt these relationships. Rarely did critics grant them the same regard as white couples. "Acting married" by whites was treated as homage and respect for the institution. Law and white society counted as legitimate the individual freedom to make private vows even when the legal paradigm dominated. But for ex-slaves, "acting married" was seen as a sign of disrespect, an incapacity and failure to measure up to the standards of normative behavior. The federal government took the lead in asserting a sharp divide between legal and extralegal marriage for ex-slaves in every arena in which it had influence and control, especially through the work of the Freedmen's Bureau and the distribution of pensions to widows of Civil War veterans. African Americans' right to privacy remained under siege. Their domestic lives were not safe from state interventions as judiciaries increasingly cordoned off the private realm of intimate relationships.[25]

The ultimate test of how individuals defined their relationship may have been how they acted within a community of friends, neighbors, and kin, who bestowed or withheld recognition based on what they thought they observed.[26] But one or both spouses could be deliberately vague about the status of their relationship in order to avoid adhering to conventional standards or to retain the option of leaving easily. Ex-slaves continued to use the practice of self-divorce most often to end their relationships, even if they married legally. Legal divorce, where it was allowed, was out of the reach of most couples (because of the financial costs and strict requirements designed to discourage couples) and not deemed necessary. It did not carry the same stigma that was increasingly attached to what was perceived to be a dangerously growing trend of divorce in the later decades of the century. Working-class women, black and otherwise, were less concerned with losing respectability simply because they lived outside marriage as so many did by necessity. Generational differences also played a role in the tendency to marry legally. The older generation, which was comfortable with intimate relationships under the rules of slavery, seemed to be more inclined toward continuing those antebellum traditions than those who came of age after the war. A variety of factors influenced how couples chose to define their relationships, such as their own emotional registers, pressures from family and church, and coercion from the postwar planter elite and the state.

Informal marriages continued, in part, because they had already taken hold and defined relationships or because they were customary patterns that people knew and understood as sufficient. Some couples simply did nothing to formalize their relationships, though it is hard to know if their inaction was deliberate or simply stasis. Some felt strongly that their unions were already solid and had no desire to affirm them through state sanction. Problems within marriages could certainly give couples pause about committing any more of themselves than they already had given. Old patterns formed under duress might even seem optimal once spouses had gained their freedom.

For example, abroad marriages usually meant the consolidation of households after emancipation. But at least on a few occasions, couples decided they liked living separately, though with more frequent visits to maintain their relationships. Some couples who parted after the war found themselves back together again years later as though they had never been separated. The ambiguous beginnings and endings of former times were still relevant in this context, absent hard markers like legalization. In some cases spouses, usually women, kept waiting and hoping for their partners to agree to give their marriages legal recognition. As one woman admitted, her partner kept promising to marry her legally, but twelve children later he still refused, only to eventually leave her for another woman whom he married straight away.[27]

Even some couples starting fresh still chose not to legalize their marriages. One man claimed that he and his wife had "just a home wedding." It was hard to determine from his description whether it was a legal marriage, taking up, or cohabitation. As he explained, he asked her to come live with him as his wife, she agreed, and they began their life together. The reasons that some couples chose informality were not always clear, nor were they necessarily a reflection of their devotion to the relationship. Another man went to great lengths to marry his nominal bride. He ran away from his former owner, who tried to keep him against his will. He rode away on horseback for a hundred miles, turned the horse loose, and walked the rest of the way to be with her. When he reached his beloved, he said, they just agreed to "live together as man and wife."[28]

Couples also faced difficulties in disentangling overlapping relationships in favor of making one of them legal and monogamous, unless death interceded. The challenges of sustaining marriages in wartime became more pronounced afterward. Emma, Clement, and Celestine had complicated and intertwined partnerships. Emma and Clement began a relationship during slavery, when they lived on the same plantation in St. James Parish, Louisiana. Clement was already married to Celestine, a young woman living nearby, when he took up with Emma. Emma's first husband was Reuben, whom she was probably with when she started the relationship with Clement. When Clement left for the army in 1863, Emma was pregnant with their third or fourth child. He returned home in 1866 and immediately went to stay with Emma—for a few weeks. Then he went back to Celestine but discovered that she was living with another man, Willis, so he returned to Emma. He reconnected with Celestine one last time, around 1868 or 1869. Clement confessed to Emma that he had been with Celestine as she lay dying. He stayed up with her all night on her death bed until she took her last breath. Presumably Willis was by her side as well. Clement's relationship with Celestine ended only with her death. From then on he lived with Emma until his own death in the early 1890s.[29]

The decision of whether to formally marry was especially important for widows of Civil War soldiers entitled to pensions. Ironically, the federal government actively discouraged marriage for women who wanted to keep receiving this benefit. It required widows to live alone and discouraged any sign of sexual activity that could be used against them. These women had a direct interest in not legally marrying and keeping their relationships with men discreet, though such constraints could be quite difficult, especially for young women. And yet many hid their relationships with men when questioned by pension agents, refusing to give up informal marital practices.[30]

We have already met Elisabeth Wright, who as a young woman was married to Rufus, and seen her marriage certificate. Their wedding was officiated by the chaplain of Rufus's regiment, Rev. Henry McNeal Turner. After Rufus died during the war, Elisabeth moved back into the home of her stepfather and mother in Norfolk, Virginia. Some of her neighbors claimed that she cohabited with Frank Turner (not related), whom she said was a boarder in her parents' home. No proof could be found that she married Frank. And the reports were mixed as to whether they even had a relationship. Frank was also a former comrade of Rufus's. It was not uncommon for women to take up with a male comrade of their deceased husband's when they stayed near his troop. During Frank's residency at her parent's home, she said that she was away much of the time working. Most neighbors and longtime friends (including attendees at her first wedding) denied that the two had married or lived together as a couple. But a few friends implied that they were more than incidental coresidents.[31] Some people even questioned whether she had ever married Rufus, though her marriage certificate, sent to the U.S. Pension Bureau earlier or in response to this accusation, showed proof of her standing as a widow. This story demonstrates how easily women's records could be besmirched, though in Elisabeth's case she had a bona fide legal document to prove her marriage. Her relationship with Frank remains a mystery. In all likelihood it was no coincidence that they shared the same house. The rules of the bureau made it necessary for her to deny any intimacy with him if she wanted to continue receiving benefits. As a working-class woman earning minimal wages, she could not have easily given up the money from her pension.

It is not surprising that a woman like Elisabeth Turner would form other intimate relationships after the death of her first husband, who died a year after their marriage. Most ex-slaves continued to practice serial monogamy, moving from one relationship to another over the course of their lives. Involuntary separations were no longer the primary motivating factor for multiple relationships. African Americans could now decide for themselves whether to stay married, separate, or divorce. And death, of course, was a constant threat in this period given high mortality rates among African Americans. Elisabeth also demonstrates how individuals might develop different kinds of intimate relationships along the spectrum. In her case, she started with a legal marriage during the Civil War, and then, as a widow, moved on to what was most likely a cohabiting relationship with Frank. The pattern of serial monogamy would continue to be a distinguishing feature of black intimacy through the end of the century.

Bigamous relationships are another pattern of intimacy among ex-slaves that became common after the war was over. Bigamy was a way of exiting one marriage and entering another one when legal divorce was not an easy option. Dissatisfaction with marriages gone awry, long separations, abandonment by either spouse, or perceived failure to fulfill marital obligations could lead to desertion and remarriage. Couples sometimes even negotiated an end to their marriages to their mutual benefit, but without going to court, or, if they did go to court but failed to win legal redress, deciding to go their own way. Desertions and informal separations were far more common than the law allowed. But so was the propensity to marry and remarry, over and over again. Serial monogamy appears to be a standard that cut across race and class, regardless of the legal regime surrounding these acts.[32]

Ex-slaves shared some of the motivations of bigamists unburdened by the legacy of their former status. Bigamy was a sign that marriage was still a porous and flexible institution in which individuals assumed the right to exercise their liberties to enter and exit intimacies despite whatever the laws may have said. Bigamy appeared to be most common among mobile people intermingling on the frontier, in urban areas, or anywhere newcomers could escape community sanction and verification of prior relationships. Bigamy was particularly common among working-class people who refused to abide by idealized Victorian codes of conduct, but it was practiced by middle-class people, too.[33]

Some ex-slaves became bigamists for reasons that were tied to the consequences of their enslavement. The generation of adults who came of age during slavery and married often found themselves caught between two systems after emancipation: one that had deprived them of the legal right to marry and another that imposed legalization on existing relationships after slavery ended. Arbitrary decisions by latent state interests and actions only complicated matters more. The new system was entirely insensitive to the contradictions these changes inflicted on the variety of relationships that slaves were denied, forced into, or chose (with their masters' consent) to assume.[34] Many former slaves refused to abrogate those relationships that masters had breached, even if they remarried. In their own estimations, separation left their marriages still valid.

The atmosphere of the Civil War also encouraged bigamy, as the insecurity of life and the adventure of military service gave men more options for entering and exiting relationships with impunity beyond their home turfs, where their marital status would have been known. In many cases they hid their existing relationships, but in many others they did not, perhaps assuming that the new circumstances would likely sever them from their former ties. More often than not, bigamy was prompted more by the desire to escape detection and the culpability that stood in the way of starting fresh in a new relationship than by the desire to have more than one spouse simultaneously. Soldiers might also assume that they would not either live to see or be able to return to their former families, thus justifying the creation of new lives. Wives left behind might not know that their spouses had met and married other women while away in the army. They considered themselves widows when the soldiers died. But so too did their husbands' wartime wives.[35]

When couples were involuntarily separated under slavery and later reunited, it could be bittersweet when one spouse had moved on to another relationship. Ex-slaves adopted novel ways of negotiating these difficulties when the couples still felt a need to acknowledge, if not to continue, their relationship in some form. One resolution was for the husband to remain with the one wife but provide material support to the other one, like alimony, and give her half of the crop or other products, furniture, and household goods. Another, though not legal, solution was to maintain a relationship with both, in a form of deliberate bigamy—putting them up in the same cabin with twin beds. Slave men who moved about and had wives who lived abroad could have multiple spouses simultaneously and might continue the practice despite formalizing marriages after emancipation. Still others, having nothing to do with former slave relationships, involved actual bigamy, or at least the attempt. Family and community pressure was often brought to bear on these relationships to arrest them before they could fully flourish. But in other situations, bigamists, typically men, faced arrests, fines, and jail time.[36]

Women were rarely charged with bigamy, since they were less mobile and unable to live double lives or get men to agree to the kind of domestic arrangements that would have two men vying to be the head of the same family and household. They were often accused of infidelity, however, which could also lead to prosecution under the law. Legal action could be used as a tactic of retaliation when women left their husbands for other men. Although women could exercise their newfound freedom to leave their spouses, they risked harsh consequences from a bitter spouse. A man could file a complaint against his wife's lover for stealing her affections, as well against the wife for infidelity.[37]

For the first half of the nineteenth century, enforcement of bigamy laws was mostly lax. This would change after the war as government entities stepped in to police the sexual behaviors of the citizenry in diverse ways. Alternative intimate relationships faced greater scrutiny within all American communities in the second part of the century. Laws were passed to strengthen the state's regulation of monogamous marriage and to punish remarriage without divorce. Bigamy became a crime more likely to be punishable as an offense against the state, not simply a violation against one's spouse. This fit within a trend toward "judicial patriarchy," that is, applying laws to protect women from men not living up to their roles as providers and protectors. Marital relationships were scrutinized by the Pension Bureau, eager to ferret out cases of fraud, especially as the laws passed in the last decades of the century expanded the number of women eligible to receive benefits.[38] Many observers saw the legacy of slavery, which African Americans could not escape, as a source of deviance in marital relations, and so they advocated for extra surveillance of ex-slave couples. In some cases African Americans did not know the laws, but in other situations they deliberately ignored and skirted them, preferring to exercise their rights of personal liberty newly obtained or continue established traditions that worked to their advantage.[39]

Being legally married may have looked similar to informal marriage, but it did offer some clear advantages. Without it, it was hard to get a family labor contract (a required agreement between landowners and laborers) in some agricultural districts, and increasingly so as sharecropping was instituted. Being legally married made it easier to gain custody of children from the clutches of white plantation owners seeking to apprentice their labor as though they were orphans. It gave men the legal power to represent their families in labor disputes. And it bolstered the reputation of women asserting their rights as mothers and wives.

Legal marriage imposed certain expectations on freedpeople who accepted its precepts. It instituted gender norms that had been denied to slaves. Marriage gave men property rights in their wives and in their labor, both paid and unpaid. After the Civil War many states passed married women's property laws to give women more control over their property by safeguarding land inherited by widows, allowing women to have more control over the assets they brought into their marriages, and granting them more control over their earnings. But as late as the 1880s, it was still legal in most states for men to control their wives' wages. Legal marriage brought together contracts in marriage and labor under one roof and one authority, ostensibly. Marriage gave women the protection of "cloistering themselves from the generality of men," a safeguard slave women had previously been denied, leaving them vulnerable to sexual assaults and exploitation.[40] The abolition of slavery lifted marriage out of the shadows and heightened its significance. Men would exit slavery to become masters of themselves and their wives, enfranchised with the badges of free men. Women's freedom, however, was transferred from masters to their husbands. Sex differences became embedded in the ideology of separate spheres that shaped the organization of families and households but were not rigidly drawn. Black men gained the benefits of a modified form of coverture, that is, property in their wives. Black women were expected to be wives and wage workers, and the latter was supposed to take precedence. Black men were not paid a family wage to provide a material basis for their authority as heads of households, but they were held legally accountable for the support of their wives and children. They entered the capitalist economy as wage workers at a time when Northern working-class men struggled over this very same issue. The decline of white workingmen's independence meant that many of their women were forced to work for wages because men's wages could not cover them. Even as African-American men were given new authority over their wives, the very meaning of their authority as heads of households was undergoing reform. State legislatures passed laws chipping away at men's power and giving women and children more rights as dependents.[41]

If marriage was a "school of affection," ex-slaves were treated like late bloomers who needed curricular and extracurricular tutelage to bring them up to speed.[42] Marriage had been instrumental in the transformation of industrial capitalist social relations and the making of the working and middle classes. African Americans could not be fully integrated into the political economy without the structure of marriage to inculcate values and behaviors.[43] The federal government was determined to initiate this inculcation as it ventured to make policies securing de jure marriage to usher ex-slaves into civil society and citizenship. Former slaveholders could not be entrusted with this responsibility in the immediate postwar period, though they would be enlisted to take over the federal role in time. Former slaveholding state governments gradually came to see the benefits of offering the carrot of legal marriage, to free itself of further responsibilities for black families and individuals.

The middle-class ideal of marriage that developed over the nineteenth century shifted the focus away from a preoccupation with the transference of property to a relationship built on emotional fulfillment. It was the private union of two individual souls swept up by mysterious forces of love that they could not fully determine or control. It was designed to organize sexual differences for the sustenance of family and to provide a distinction between the domestic sphere and the wider world. Men were to be providers and protectors and to negotiate the outside world while women would preside over matters of the home. Marriage was to be ruled by the heart and with consent; even though men still dominated, they did so with love and empathy, rather than the harshness of patriarchs, taking their wives' happiness into consideration. The practical benefits of marriage were still profoundly important for working-class people who could not afford to be starry-eyed or led by sentiment alone. Survival without the help of at least one other adult and eventually older children was virtually impossible in a rural society. A division of labor, paid and unpaid, ensuring the provision of basic needs like food, shelter, and clothing, was necessary. Consumer goods were still produced mostly on a small scale on people's farms and in their homes. Marriage offered old-age insurance for those who lived long. It ensured that spouses would have each other to lean on, along with the help of their offspring, in their least productive years. Many of these benefits did not require legalization, monogamy, or heterosexual coupling. But the pressures to attach one man to one woman in a lifelong commitment were designed to make it hard for men to escape responsibilities that might imperil the economy as their productivity declined. The legal requirements of marriage still differed state-by-state, but the law played a clearer role in divorce. A person could act married without going to court or church, but only a judge could grant a legal divorce, which gave an individual permission to legally remarry.[44]

Former slaves, like all couples, had expectations for what marriage meant, including shared understandings and gender-based ideas about the roles of husbands and wives. This was true for couples who were legally married and those who claimed each other as husband and wife without formalization. African Americans had to reconcile what marriage meant in the law and according to dominant cultural standards with their own interests, former traditions, and existing arrangements. These expectations were most often articulated in the records available during crises, especially those involving the breakdown between spouses and threats from outside forces. Records indicate that African Americans wanted spouses to be loving, caring, respectful, faithful, loyal, devoted, compatible, compassionate, and supportive in sickness

and in health. They expected each to do their part to keep the peace, to cultivate a shared space of safety and security to guard against outside threats. If
one spouse preceded the other in death, their bond was expected to endure
to the extent that the surviving partner would honor mutual obligations,
such as the care of children, biological and step. Ex-slaves bore additional
burdens that affected their intimate relationships, however. They expected
each spouse to work cooperatively with the other to sustain the household.
They had to establish a united front against menacing outsiders who threatened to impose their wills over the thresholds of their homes. Marriage gave
them license to build the home base to gain control over their own labor,
acquire the benefits of their own exertions, and protect the physical bodies
of kin.[45]

Still, marriage had to be negotiated, especially the internal lines of authority. The marriages of ex-slaves looked and functioned differently when
they had to adjust from living apart to consolidating their households, cohabiting, and sleeping in one bed. Women who had been accustomed to operating with relative independence with husbands living away had to adjust
to men coming home to take charge. Men, too, had to adapt to living with
wives and children full time. The transition could be prickly. Generally
speaking, husbands' roles as heads of households were accepted, though
women retained individual rights, too. Authority was dispersed and shared
according to the practical needs of individual couples. Gender roles were
clearly delineated but also flexible by necessity. Men needed wives as much
as women needed husbands to function in agricultural economies. No one
pattern pertained. But ex-slave families were not patriarchal even if they were
mostly male dominated. Black men's newly acquired rights were outweighed
by obligations and restraints that challenged their ability to fully realize their
household authority. The planter class made some concessions to turn over
the responsibility for subsistence to male heads of households, but they continually rebuffed black men's exercise of unimpeded control over their wives
and children when it ran against their economic and political interests. Men
had to provide for their families during the day by engaging in agricultural or
wage work, and work overtime at night and in the evenings to fish, hunt, and
take care of farm animals that helped to make ends meet. Women had to do
field work or domestic work in addition to shouldering the burdens of child-

care, sewing, gardening, cleaning, and feeding their families, tasks that under slavery were more dispersed throughout plantation communities. Women wanted to take time off for pregnancy and childbirth, which had mostly been denied to them as slaves.[46]

Men spoke on behalf of their families in public, especially with respect to matters related to labor, for which they signed agricultural contracts. They were the ones held accountable when family members failed to satisfy the agreements. But women did not give up all rights over their labor, especially when they worked independently as day workers, mechanics, and domestics without the assistance of men as coworkers. Women took the initiative to handle their own disputes in those instances. They also tended to take on the role of challenging ill-treatment of their children, other kin, and even friends. According to one estimate, they were twice as likely as men to defend families in court cases in some places. Women took strong stands when violence was directed at them regardless of whether they were single or married. They were often their families' fiercest defenders in the Freedmen's Bureau courts, whereas men had more power to directly challenge white control over the cotton crop as heads of households, which probably heightened women's willingness to take issues to court when they had no other recourse available.[47]

The challenges of earning a living in the postwar period had a major impact on how couples conceived of their marital relationships. Both spouses were typically expected to contribute remunerative activities for the family's survival, and when one or both did not, their standing was diminished. Even when women engaged in wage work, they generally expected their husbands to contribute financially to meet their material needs during the marriage and, to some degree, afterward if they split. They did not expect the reverse. As one woman stated about her husband, whom she claimed refused to work and spent all of his time hunting and fishing: "I told him I mar'ed him to take care o' me, not me to take care o' him." His refusal to work for a living in a way that could sustain their household caused a breach. Her husband, however, was less interested in abiding by rules that demanded not only authority but also responsibility for husbands as heads of households.[48]

Men, too, complained if they could not get their wives to work to their satisfaction. Sometimes tensions within the workplace, generally the farm, would boil over into the home. One husband complained that his wife's contentious relationship with the landlord had caused the family to move five different times in one year to please her. Though details are missing, it is likely that this meant she was more confrontational or resistant to the conditions under which they worked. But men most often complained about women's failures around their household chores. These infractions may not have been deal breakers, but they could create tension and lead to conflict about other matters that could eventually lead one spouse or the other to leave.[49] Some men went further than making complaints, to expecting restitution. They asked for a share of their wives' wages if the women left them or refused to follow their dictates about where they should work because they were entitled to control their wages in most states by law. But if they accepted such remuneration, men had to acknowledge their dependence on women's work to get by, which was hardly the mark of patriarchy.[50]

Exclusivity was a baseline expectation for both spouses however much it may have been violated. Women could be especially sensitive when they felt their husbands rejected them, trading them for brighter, shinier objects of affection. One couple's marriage broke down after twenty-three years because, according to the husband, his wife failed to fulfill her wifely duties. The wife listed other reasons: "My husband seem to be so bitter against me and seems to want a younger woman than me but I am not wiling to give him up to no one until I am dead then he can marry who he wil[l]."[51]

In extreme cases conflict could lead to domestic violence. Some men considered it their right as husbands to chastise their wives, verbally and physically, as they deemed fit. Some said so outright. According to long-standing traditions in Anglo-American law, they were correct; so long as they did not cross the line of inflicting permanent damage, courts typically allowed men to moderately "chastise" their wives to command their obedience throughout much of the nineteenth century.[52] Other men were more circumspect in asserting their power. Some were unrepentant when caught and punished. They took whatever opportunities they could, even afterward, to continue to chide their wives—from a distance if necessary, on paper if they had no other choice. Just as breakup letters were a tool of vengeance, letters taking digs at "my once dear wife" could be used to berate an estranged spouse.[53] Some men ran up against women who could fend for themselves. Men could be caught off guard by women who fought back fiercely to defend themselves, though most women did not feel so empowered.

Feminist calls for reform had led to some modifications in popular thinking about wife beating. At midcentury Susan B. Anthony and Elizabeth Cady Stanton had boldly publicized cases of wife beating by white upper-class men. By the 1870s, judges were less likely to be swayed by husbands' claims, though the presumed right to chastisement did not disappear. How the courts dealt with husbands varied considerably, not for the protection of the women, but for the preservation of the right to privacy of the elites. Men like those Anthony and Stanton had outed as wife abusers received less scrutiny as attention shifted to men in the lower orders. This had significant consequences for differential prosecution and punishment of African-American and working-class white men in American courts.

In the aftermath of slavery, couples not only had to negotiate the internal dynamics of their personal relationship in light of their new status and rights, but also to contend with redefining their relationships as parents with children. Most Southern state laws passed in the postwar era that gave legitimacy to ex-slave marriages also recognized the children born in those relationships as legitimate. But this by no means resolved the thorny issues of even how to sort out who the parents were in cases of overlapping and serial relationships, or who deserved custody of children even among agreed-upon parents when marriages broke down. Under slavery, a child could be born to a woman as a product of a relationship that she had with a man on another plantation after being hired out and away from her husband, who was left behind on the plantation. Neither man nor the woman had any legal claims over the child as far as the woman's master was concerned. The situation could cause friction among those individuals and within the community of slaves, but it did not bear on the child's status. Once freedom came, the question then became, Who was the father? The woman's husband or the "sweetheart" who was likely the biological father? Rights and obligations were now attached to that role. In some of these situations both men asserted that they were indeed the father and should be counted as such. How these matters were resolved could also involve the continuing interference of former masters when the children were still minors and their labor was still a value worth fighting for.[54]

Former patriarchal notions that men owned their children and thus were entitled to custody when disputes arose were in decline. The rights of mothers were given more credence. Authorities making decisions about custody adjudicated by courts and the Freedmen's Bureau were most concerned with assigning custody to the parent who could best take care of the child's material needs, so as not to enlarge the pool of dependents unable to survive without aid from government or charity. But various agents also considered how slavery had denied black men legal rights as fathers and amplified women's roles as mothers. Since women carried the lion's share of child care under slavery they were often favored when disputes broke out over custody in the postwar period. State laws that did not give retroactive recognition to slave marriages were used against men seeking custody rights, especially when competing against masters. The stereotypical adage "mama's baby, papa's maybe" showed that men's paternity could always be questioned.[55]

How couples dealt with custody of their children when their marriages broke down provides further insight into the nature of intimate relationships in transition from slavery to freedom. Many couples found amicable solutions to satisfy both spouses, usually involving dividing up the care and responsibilities for their offspring. Mothers might send their sons to live with their fathers when they reached a certain age and both parents felt the male child needed the discipline supplied by a man. When multiple children were involved, they sometimes divided the children along gender, with the girls staying with the mother and the boys going to be with the father. Each parent would continue to have assigned duties for the children in their custody as well as the children living with the other parent. But gender was not a strict dividing line, nor did couples follow even distributions. Many women retained custody of sons and some men gained custody of daughters. Some parents (usually mothers) could have responsibility for multiple children, while the other spouse (usually fathers) took on just a single child. Agreements, however reached, were especially important when children were wage workers as they helped to clarify how the benefits would be distributed. In most states, parents had the right to their children's earnings until a certain age.

Parents had to fight not only against former masters but also against each other, at times, to ensure that they received the desired share of the proceeds of their child's labor. The labor of daughters at home could also be a source of tension, especially when they had younger siblings whom they could help raise. A mother who gained custody of small children but lost custody of an older daughter could see this as a major disadvantage. The other spouse's gain had a direct impact on the mother's ability to earn a living and take care of the younger children.[56]

Arrangements might work for a while and then disintegrate as old issues between the couple resurfaced or new circumstances with the children led one parent to call into question the other's ability to take care of them. Accusations could fly back and forth from the couple's past about infidelity and ill treatment in order to undermine the other's parenting. Some went as far as to seek vengeance by questioning whether they had married in the first place. This accusation especially stung women as the charge could damage their reputations. Suddenly, relationships that had been informal under slavery as a product of coerced labor and the lack of legal rights were used as a weapon against women under freedom. When one man tried to claim that he had never married the mother of his children in a bid to diminish her custody rights, the woman emphasized her desire to be married and challenged his assertions to the contrary. Charlotte Dennis made this retort in claiming rights to her son: "I am rightfully his Guardian—for Hardy Brown & myself were never married—altho I urged him frequently to own me as his wife— which he would not do—after commiting the deed—or act yet having made fair promises before—Still, He—wishes to hold my son—as his lawful Father." Hardy Brown also tried to use the fact that Charlotte had allowed their son to live with him for a few months, until the boy ran back home to her, as a sign that she could not control the child and only he could do so. She refused to accept that she could not control her children and did not concede to the politics of respectability that denigrated her status as a mother raising her children alone: "I would just say that I have done so for 17 years without much trouble & also the other 10—for a longer period with the older ones." She was still raising six children (the others were adults on their own) "& manage them perhaps as well as most mothers—do." She won the custody fight.[57]

Women had special burdens to bear because they were more vulnerable to judgment according to the Victorian sexual mores of the dominant society, which could affect their custody rights. They had to work against a history of stereotypes of black women to gain hearings in public proceedings in which charges about their fitness as mothers were bantered about. Women's character as good and proper mothers centered around two major issues: their work ethic and their sexual propriety. Claiming that a woman lived in "idleness" raised concerns about her productive work habits and her ability to feed her children, but it also led to skepticism about how she supported her family and whether she resorted prostitution. Charges of extramarital affairs could be leveled by either parent against the other, but the label "loose" was lodged against women, gendered in such a way that it caused them particular harm. Single mothers were often put in difficult positions to defend against such charges. A former husband could charge his ex-wife, rightly or wrongly, with living with another man, perhaps the man for whom she had left her husband. By contrast, he could use his own "industrious" and "sober" fitness, his good job, and his remarriage to a "respectable" wife against the mother of their children to gain custody of them. Men could often show that they had new wives, and mothers, on whom they could call to step in to preform the role of mother to make up for what their former wives lacked.[58]

The marriages of ex-slaves were nothing if not improvisational. Slaves had endured a long tenure of intimate relationships that the law refused to recognize. Many went to great lengths to reunite with their spouses and bring their families back together under one roof during Reconstruction while federal troops still occupied the South. The chances were slim for some, but even the few lucky ones who did locate their lost loves often found that the actual reunion could be bittersweet given new intimacies that had been formed since they parted ways. Where the laws of bondage ruled ex-slaves had adapted a broad range of marital practices that had helped them to survive. Many stubbornly refused to give up those traditions even once their legal fortunes were reversed. Others found it difficult to disentangle overlapping ties that had been formed as a product of forced separations and the caprice of bondage. Some continued to practice self-divorce, which could lead to charges of bigamy, by remarrying without proper exits from prior relationships. Fewer (mostly men) deliberately engaged in bigamy to maintain simultaneous marriages. Prosecutions for bigamy increased, interestingly, in this era when the practice became less identified with more affluent classes and more associated with those at the bottom of the class structure, whether black or white. In this way and others, African Americans were disproportionately punished for marital infractions, despite the circumstances they had endured for generations, largely produced by the institution of slavery. The federal government played a large role in shaping policies to ferret out irregular domestic relationships that did not conform to legal marriage. But it also discouraged marriage for Civil War widows who wanted to maintain their status as beneficiaries of pensions that they had earned as a result of their former husbands' service to the nation.

Most ex-slaves chose to enter into a new marital regime by legalizing their former relations or marrying for the first time postwar owing in part to the social and economic benefits it afforded and the trouble it helped them escape. Legal marriage held certain advantages and privileges that informal intimacy did not. It afforded more certain protection for spouses, offspring, and the maintenance of family units, which provided a defensive mechanism previously unavailable to be marshalled against exterior perils. It held out the best hope for economic advancement by allowing couples to pool resources and invest in combined futures.

The gender norms that marriage encouraged proved to be most advantageous for men, however. They acquired power as heads of households, even though the legal capacity of that role was undergoing reform and women's rights were expanding within the law. Women in general gained more rights to their children. They had more protections than ever before against domestic violence. Black men never were fully allowed to inhabit the roles of patriarchs even after slavery ended, however. Black gender roles, comparatively, had to be nimble to accommodate the unconventional functions that women were expected to fulfill as wage earners in order to survive materially and to reinforce racial differences imposed by elites. But while men's power diminished in comparison to earlier times, it was still considerably greater than women's. Women still had more responsibilities for taking care of their children. They were more vulnerable economically and sexually, given the limited place for them in the postwar economy, primarily as wives of farmers and as domestic servants. Men still had more options for how they chose to behave as husbands, fathers, and wage earners. The greatest threat to black marriages and families, however, continued to be external. Landed white elites still controlled the cotton economy and the political system and challenged black men's rights whenever they interfered with whites' interests. Black men and women still had to join forces as they encountered the treacherous terrain of the transition from slavery to freedom. It would remain to be seen how much the legalization of marriage would protect and advance their status as new citizens.

7

"The Most Cruel Wrongs"

Mansfield French, a low-country missionary, was appointed as the supervisor of Missions and Marriage Relations by the Freedmen's Bureau in South Carolina. French became the author of one of the most detailed sets of rules regulating families postwar. His rationale for the rigorous guidelines for reconstructing the intimate affairs of freedpeople was to "correct as far as possible one of the most cruel wrongs inflicted by slavery."[1] The correction was to establish marriage as a permanent, monogamous, exclusive relationship with husbands assuming power and authority for the care of their wives and children. Liberals and conservatives within the federal government, local and state officials, and elite landowners concurred with French's mandate. Over time, they all came to see the value of legally sanctioned marriage in re-creating postwar labor systems and maintaining racial subordination. African Americans needed to regularize their conjugal and familial relations, and the force of law was necessary, not just to help them recognize their rights, but also to compel them to conform.

The federal government played a leading role in this process through the Freedmen's Bureau, which served multiple functions in implementing policies, adjudicating martial conflict, and punishing sexual crimes associated with marriage and nonmarriage during Reconstruction. Agents of the bureau throughout the South were encouraged to set their own rules, like French, to help establish a structure for legal marriage that ex-slaves could adopt and that lawmakers could sanction. They tried to work cooperatively with local and state officials to encourage them to accept the basic principle of marriage equality under the law and to pass the appropriate legislation to extend to ex-slaves rights they had once been denied.

Marriage rules and, more slowly, actual marital laws, were designed not only to inculcate legal monogamous marriage but also to punish various infractions—adultery, bigamy, domestic violence, and desertion. Many of these laws were geared to ensuring that men would live up to their responsibilities as husbands and fathers, and that women would not forsake their duties as wives and mothers, according to middle-class ideals. They leaned more heavily, in theory, toward protecting women, especially against physical abuse, but in practice, draconian and arbitrary punishments often resulted as errant behaviors were disciplined in ways that benefited employers of black labor. Federal backing of this approach encouraged the landowning elites to continue to interfere with African Americans' most intimate relationships to contravene their efforts to create viable independent families and households. Masters-turned-employers were quite selective in their willingness to respect their ex-slaves' newfound citizenship. Labor contracts were especially contested territory, where the line between marital rights and duties and employer rights and obligations had to be redrawn.

Women's labor, in the agricultural economy and in their own newly formed domestic economies, continued to be an area of major dispute and vicious fighting. African Americans had to continually battle for concessions to allow them to reconstruct their families to meet their desires and needs as freedpeople. What they achieved, however, may have been pyrrhic victories in some respects. Although elite landowners conceded to ex-slaves' demands to make their families central to new labor systems, the model of the nuclear family came to dominate with the emergence of sharecropping. By the 1880s, the nuclear family had become the principal labor unit of family farming, taking the place of the antebellum plantation system. Displaced family members and alternative family structures were thrust on to rural peripheries or pushed into urban areas where they could better fend for themselves, limiting the flexibility of family arrangements that had been so crucial to the survival of black people for generations. Widows and single women with children were those most often burdened, whereas single men were still able to find work as day laborers on farms and plantations. By the penultimate decade of the nineteenth century, the right to marry was safe from being re-voked, but securing this civil right came with restrictions.

A broad consensus emerged in the postwar South that the state of black family life needed to be repaired and reversed from its antebellum misfor-tunes. Friends and foes, whites and blacks alike, repeatedly referenced marriage under slavery as being "unknown," very loosely defined, and little regarded by masters and slaves. Ex-slaves entered their new status after emancipation and had to become accustomed to a set of rules about morality that focused on ideas of respectability and sexual propriety. The common perception of ex-slaves was that they accepted out-of-wedlock births as the norm, "took up" frequently with mates, and left each other easily, as enslaved life had left few alternatives. Some observers acknowledged that ex-slaves eagerly embraced the new decree to marry, but many were struck by the reluctance of some to tie the knot. Women were perceived to be more eager than men to take advantage of the formalization of marital bonds because they offered legal protection. Former slaves were also assumed to have multiple spouses simultaneously and extramarital relationships, in addition to marrying many times. Complaints of domestic violence circulated broadly as well, leading some observers to identify it as a racial trait, as though it were a latent gene of African ancestry repressed during slavery and then unleashed after bound labor ceased.[2] It is no wonder that correcting the domestic lives of freed-people became one of the highest priorities of government officials and reli-gious organizations.

Ex-slaves were lectured to, preached at, and repeatedly reminded of the stakes involved in the adoption of legal marriages and settled families. "Your old masters say you cannot take care of yourselves and your families; that if free, you will be a burden to the community; that the government will be compelled to feed and clothe you, and that you will be helpless and depen-dent as children," Isaac Brinckerhoff, a Baptist missionary, told freedpeople on the Sea Islands. The worthiness of the blood that had been shed for emancipation would be judged on how they fared. "The work that you have to do is to *show yourself a man,*" he urged them.[3] By "man" he meant the individual as well as the race as a whole. Ex-slaves needed to be taught the virtues of traditional gender roles, of husbands assuming certain responsibilities as the heads of their families, and of wives assuming the posture of their subordinate helpmeets.

Marriage was presented as the pinnacle of manhood and womanhood. Those who were already in cohabiting relationships were told to immediately legalize their unions and legitimize their children and grandchildren. Those who had multiple spouses were advised to settle on one and to establish permanent conjugality as soon as possible. But younger freedpeople just reaching adulthood were cautioned to wait and prepare themselves to take on these roles. Clinton Fisk, a Freedmen's Bureau official in Tennessee, advised young men: *"Do not be in haste to get married.* Wait until you are at least twenty-one years of age, and until you have a home for your wife. To marry a girl, and have no home to take her to, is foolish. She will soon regret that." Women were likewise warned that they should learn to knit, sew, cook, clean house, garden, and even read and write before looking for the appropriate mate. As slaves they had been denied the opportunity to prove that they could be "true" women, but now they had a chance to rise, gain dignity, and garner respect. Women were warned to take special care of their virtue. "If in your slave life you have been careless of your morals, now that you are free, live as becomes a free Christian woman. Stamp a lie upon the common remark, that colored women are all bad," Fisk urged. Forsake all men, white and black: "Hate them as you hate the devil. You had better hang yourself by the neck until you are dead, than yield to them," Fisk insisted.[4]

Marriage was presented as a partnership, with each spouse complementing the other, acting in unison, in love and companionship, to create happy homes and well-cultivated children. The Bible was invoked to provide proof and verification of the rightness of the traditional hierarchy of husbands as heads and women as helpmeets: "If any provide not for his own, and specially for those of his own house, he hath denied the faith, and is worse than an infidel." Men needed the help of wives who were also industrious, neat, tidy, clean, even tempered, and pretty. Though black women were expected to live up to the virtues of "true" women, they were still expected to do double duty as homemakers and wage workers, expectations that did not apply to white women: "A wife must do her very best to help her husband make a living. She can earn as much money sometimes as he can, and she can save money."[5]

The need for freedpeople to be instructed in dominant gender norms was a common refrain. White men felt compelled to reinforce the importance of male-dominated families and households as they talked to freedmen. Ministers, missionaries, and Republican Party operatives advised black men on how to keep their women in check. "Several speakers have been here who have advised the people to get the women into their proper place—never to tell them anything of their concerns etc., etc.; and the notion of being bigger than woman generally, is just now inflating the conceit of the males to an amazing degree," noted one disapproving female missionary in postwar South Carolina. She mocked what she perceived as foolish mimicry: "Political freedom they are rather shy of, and ignorant of; but domestic freedom—the right, just found, to have their own way in their families and rule their wives that is an inestimable privilege!"[6] Men were called "hen-pecked" when their wives were perceived as overbearing, resisting the authority of white landowners and supervisors and their own "liege lords."[7]

African-American churches were instrumental in encouraging women and men to legally marry and adopt conventional gender roles associated with dominant husbands and subordinate wives. Black ministers and church councils helped adjudicate disputes between couples, curtail assertive wives, punish abusive husbands, and enforce permanence in troubled relationships that would otherwise be severed. Handling disputes within the bounds of churches, family, and community was one thing, but many African Americans, especially the middle class, recoiled from the public ways that couples' disputes were aired before outside authorities, in the courts, on the streets, and in other public spaces.[8] Concerns about propriety and the reputation of the race, not just individual couples, were at stake in how these matters were handled.

And yet very few outside observers were cognizant of the contradictions of both tutoring freedpeople to adopt dominant gender norms and also creating encumbrances that prevented them from achieving the promises of the breadwinner family model. Ex-slaves were forced to break conventional rules of the division of labor in a marriage because women were required to work outside of their homes. It was difficult, and in the context of working at the bottom of agricultural economies, impossible, for black men to function as sole or primary breadwinners. At the same time, black families were judged as failing to live up to normative cultural expectations when wives had to take paid work. Although some agents, such as Austa French, were alert to the racial double standards and sympathetic to the plight of women burdened with the constraints of true womanhood but denied the privileges, most allies would offer only the dispensation that ex-slaves might look forward to better times in the future. But until then the needs of commercial agriculture took precedence.[9]

During Reconstruction, the federal government in the form of the Freedmen's Bureau intensified its role as marriage policymaker for ex-slaves begun during the Civil War. No other group in U.S. history faced such an aggressive campaign to remake its most intimate relationships, to undo not only what the slave states had permitted but what the elite landowner class had required in order to safeguard the preeminence of its property rights. The federal government would do all it could to work cooperatively with its erstwhile combatants in this undoing and remaking. In May 1865, Commissioner O. O. Howard issued Circular 5, urging assistant commissioners throughout the South to fill in the gap wherever local laws failed to marry couples and record them. In most cases the bureau kept records of ceremonies performed by clergy and civil officials and served as officiants themselves. But bureau officials did not see themselves simply as record keepers. Agents functioned as social workers implementing Howard's policies as they deemed useful and necessary. The main approach was to urge and encourage ex-slave couples that were already cohabiting to reconfirm their relationships in marriage. When it came to affirming new relationships, bureau agents did not always simply take the word of couples for granted but adjudicated cases of those they thought might not be appropriate candidates for matrimony. They weighed in further by sanctioning only certain forms of ceremonies and celebrations, preferably without too many festivities.[10]

Under the leadership of Mansfield French, the bureau in South Carolina (which also covered Florida and Georgia) provided the most detailed instructions and rules for couples to meet before they were granted certificates. By August he had established how ex-slaves should settle their entangled intimate relationships and move forward thereafter. He set up rules to reform "the most cruel wrongs" inflicted by slavery founded in the precepts of Christianity. Couples who were marrying for the first time had to be twenty-one (for the men) and eighteen (for the women). Freedmen were told to take a family name and to take charge of their newly reconstituted households. Their shared names became symbolic of a new sovereignty, marked by a familial organization governed by husbands and fathers. The rules established the eligibility of couples wishing to marry, identified appropriate officiants for ceremonies, stipulated methods for dealing with overlapping relationships, spelled out the duties of husbands and wives, and specified appropriate procedures for divorce.[11]

The rules themselves added further complications to ex-slave unions by forcing de facto relationships to be treated retroactively as though they had come under the jurisdiction of the law all along. All monogamous, cohabiting couples were considered married, but they still had to actively reaffirm their relationships by obtaining certificates. Having spoken private vows was insufficient; they now had to be sanctified by ministers or civil authorities. Couples who refused to do so could be forced to separate. The rules established the circumstances for reuniting those partners who had been split apart against their will. If, against the odds, they managed to make their way back to each other after freedom, they would still be required to get permits "from some society or church" before resuming their marriage. Couples who wished to separate were subjected to a number of requisite steps to end their relationships and move on to new ones. They were eligible to remarry new spouses if they presented "satisfactory evidence of either the marriage or divorce of all former companions." Remarriage was permissible to those who had been separated from their spouses for at least three years, as long as there was "no evidence that they were alive; or if alive, that they will ever, probably, be restored to them."

The rules were especially careful about giving priority to parental care of children, above the desires of adult coupling. Men who had more than one wife were told to choose the mother of their children. If a wife returned and a husband did not want to reunite with her (unless he had some moral or legal objection to her), he would be held responsible for supporting her and their children. Men who did not want to reunite with their wives could not remarry until the previous wife died or until she was remarried, unless there was just cause. Men marrying women with children were responsible for taking care of those children until they became adults, even if they were hers and not his.

Divorces were allowed for just two reasons: moral causes (such as fornication and adultery) and "prudential reasons," to dissolve multiple spousal obligations. Religious societies and churches were empowered to decide which couples were eligible for divorce. Couples dissatisfied with the decisions rendered were entitled to an appeals process, by way of a church committee of "five disinterested male persons" set up for this purpose. Women were entitled to alimony—"one half of his real and personal property, and all the household effects"—if the couple divorced because of a moral charge lodged against the man. If the wife had children by him she was entitled to all of his property and custody of the children.[12]

The bureau in South Carolina was unusual in the intensity of its efforts; officials in other areas did not take immediate steps to encourage freedpeople to marry or to help them with the process. Admittedly, the task was daunting, and meager resources and limited personnel typically had to cover large swaths of a region. In Washington, D.C., it was not until April 1866 that Reverend John Kimball was appointed superintendent of marriages and proceeded to promote the contractual bond among ex-slaves. Three months later, Congress passed a law legalizing the marriages of ex-slave couples in the District of Columbia and legitimizing their children. This further motivated Kimball and his agents to traverse the city and surrounding areas to inform freedpeople of the new law, to issue certificates, and to register these relationships.[13]

The Freedmen's Bureau ultimately tried to turn over the responsibilities of marriage-making to localities and the states, to the extent that they could elicit cooperation in the contentious postwar South. They tried to use local courts and guidelines based on state laws that had been previously restricted to white couples until laws could be devised specifically for ex-slaves. Bureau agents looked for partners who would not only acknowledge and honor marital rights but also prosecute marital wrongs. The bureau's first priority was to try to keep couples that were already married from splitting up, using coercion if necessary to achieve that end. Officials lectured couples on proper marital conduct and sent them home to work it out, even when they threatened to do bodily harm if forced back into the marriage. If one spouse wanted to stay married and formalize the relationship and the other did not, the latter could be forced to do so or be prosecuted. Partners who left their spouses were ordered to return to live with them by a certain date or face jail time and fines. Those who committed adultery were especially frowned on. This applied equally to women and to men, though men were most often accused of leaving their spouses. "Taking another man's wife" in some jurisdictions was considered a crime that could result in prison time, where men were sentenced to work on public roads and chain gangs, and fined as well.[14]

While some bureau officials found Southern whites eager to prosecute freedmen and women who failed to live up to proper marital conduct, they also were stonewalled by those officials still resistant to the idea of granting even the right to marry. Many local jurisdictions throughout the South demanded high fees to discourage ex-slaves from marrying or simply refused to give them access to courts or licenses. Although Congress passed the Civil Rights Act of 1866, which granted ex-slaves the right to make contracts of all kinds, including the right to marry, it was up to the states to guarantee this most intimate right.[15]

Former Confederate states debated whether, and in what ways, to grant legality to ex-slave marriages and to legitimize their progeny when they rewrote their constitutions in order to reenter the Union. They passed a series of laws known as the "Black Codes," ostensibly for the purpose of recognizing the citizenship rights of ex-slaves, but in reality attempting to reinstate slavery by another name. Marriage was one of the few positive rights that were recognized in most states, but it was not promulgated without hesitation or resistance. Florida, one of the first state legislatures to convene in the fall of 1865, introduced and postponed the passage of legislation recognizing black marital rights several times before passing it. The committee that framed such legislation viewed it as an allowance of white benevolence. The committee, consisting entirely of former slaveholders, declared that it was the moral duty of white people to correct the immorality of blacks, which they believed was the product of the "only inherent evil" of slavery. The law they introduced to recognize cohabiting couples as legally married was equally a law of enforcement. They believed that slaves would not willingly abide by the standards of proper conjugal relationships without strict compulsion. "Appropriate penalties, the obligations to observe this first law of civilization and morality, chastity and the sanctity of the marriage relation" needed to accompany legal recognition so long denied.[16] Florida passed a law in January 1866, affirming the relationships of cohabiting couples as legitimate. But it required them to appear before designated authorities to take part in a marriage ceremony within nine months of the law's passage. If found cohabiting after the law passed and not married, each could be charged with misdemeanors and upon conviction punished according to the statutes for fornication and adultery. The law was so harsh, however, that critics put the governor and legislature on the defensive. Governor David S. Walker asked the legislature in November 1866 to ease the deadline for registration in order to rebuke "the false and slanderous stories" that were circulating by political foes and watchful observers. Lawmakers agreed to revise the rule by legalizing all cohabiting ex-slave couples the following month.[17]

Many states followed the pattern of affirming existing cohabiting couples, but they still required some formal record-keeping on their part. Mississippi was the first Southern state to act in this way in November 1865. A month later, South Carolina legislators were quite detailed in their stipulations declaring all ex-slaves married based on consent to be legal. They required those with multiple spouses to choose one before April 1866. The laws were consistent with the edicts produced by French and the Freedmen's Bureau. They excluded paupers or public charges from the rights and obligations of marriage. Apprentices could not marry without the permission of their masters. Husbands and wives could not abandon or turn away the other without facing prosecution on misdemeanor charges, fines, or corporal punishment. A husband who was able-bodied and who abandoned his wife could be bound out to labor, with the proceeds directed to maintaining his wife and family—on the basis of "merits and necessities." Similarly, wives could not abandon their husbands and children, though proceeds from their punishment would be given to their children. Abandoned wives were allowed to claim the rights of unmarried women, to contract for service, until their husbands returned.[18]

North Carolina started to take up the issue at its first convention in 1865, but delayed action until the new state legislature met in March 1866. Unlike Mississippi, North Carolina made ex-slave relationships retroactively valid at the start of cohabitation rather than at the time of the postbellum law. It, too, required couples to formally record their marriages with county officials within six months or face prosecution. Each month's delay in complying with the law counted as a separate offense. Breaking the law constituted a misdemeanor crime, but it was left to the discretion of the court to decide how to dole out punishment. Kentucky validated ex-slave marriages in February 1866 retroactively, like North Carolina.[19] Other states (and Congress) passed laws that legitimized cohabiting couples without requiring further registration, such as Virginia (February 1866), Tennessee (May 1866), the District of Columbia (July 1866), Arkansas (December 1866), and Alabama (November 1867). Georgia did so as well in March 1866, though with a slight variation. If couples had multiple spouses they were told to choose one and then register that marriage. Union states like Missouri legitimized marriages in February 1865 before the war ended, though Maryland did not do so until March 1867.[20]

Louisiana and Texas were the laggards on state action. Clearly, the issue of ex-slave marriage was particularly sensitive in those states. It took the seating of Republican-dominated legislatures to act. But even Louisiana Republicans debated the matter for months. African-American delegates introduced resolutions at the Constitutional Convention to legalize ex-slave marriages in late November 1867. But the following February, when the convention concluded its business, no such clause was attached to the constitution. P. B. S. Pinchback, a delegate, took the matter to the Senate after he was elected to the body, which eventually led to legislation passing in November, a year after it had been first brought before the convention. Couples who had lived together for two years previously were required to appear before local officials to record their marriages. The state followed its own antebellum civil tradition that had applied to the marriages of slaves manumitted before the war by retroactively legitimizing these relationships.[21]

In Texas, the Constitutional Convention was not only late to deliberate the issues but also the most resistant to recognizing ex-slave marriage, despite

the urging of the governor as early as 1866. Republicans took up the issue
when they gained control of the legislature in 1869. Freedpeople faced opposition throughout the state from local county clerks, even when they
went with permits in hand from the Freedmen's Bureau. Some clerks began
granting licenses by 1867, but on an inconsistent basis. When the Judiciary
Committee was given the charge to draw up legislation, it rejected the general proposal that had been presented by the larger body, which simply recognized cohabiting couples as married. The committee argued that it was
"both impolitic and unwise" to adopt the suggestion. It worried that it would
sanction licentiousness. Giving legal credence to cohabitation would concede too much tolerance for "an irregular and illegal mode of living." While
the committee acknowledged the conditions that had forced slaves into such
circumstances, it insisted there was another way to repair the damage of their
peculiar past. Rather than licensing cohabitation wholesale, it suggested that
only slaves in lifelong relationships should be affirmed. Only those who
"continued to live together until the death of one of the parties, shall be considered as having been legally married." This language suggested that the legitimacy of ex-slave marriages should be based on their longevity, which
could only be determined at death. Legislators also urged the passage of laws
pertaining to adultery and fornication to apply to ex-slaves in order to punish
marital infractions. The new state constitution of 1869 and a law passed by
the legislature in 1870 finally validated the marriages of ex-slaves who had
cohabited as husband and wife, without further stipulations. Texas was the
last state to do so.[22]

Laws passed by Democratic and Republican legislatures validating marriages of ex-slaves were not the only legal matters that shaped freedpeople's
intimate relationships, however. States such as Texas, Louisiana, and Florida
passed laws mandating that "heads of families" sign contracts promising the
labor of all family members "able to work," meaning women and children,
not just men. And while most African-American families' own views about
household organization followed similar patterns, the matter of legal heads
did not in itself settle how actual relationships were negotiated. Women often

made known that their desires did not always mesh with these expectations, as they frustrated plantation owners' efforts to control them under contracts signed by men. They refuted such agreements on the grounds that their husbands had "no powers to contract" their labor as they were "living free and responsible" like the men.[23] It would be up to the courts to decide the validity of contracts made under these circumstances, but Freedmen's Bureau officials sometimes expressed their skepticism. "My opinion is that a husband cannot contract the services of his wife, (or rather cannot *compel* such services) without her consent," wrote C. W. Pierce, a bureau official. If he did so he would also bear liability for her failures to comply or comport herself appropriately.[24] Men were often held accountable for their wives' behavior, which had been the motivation for making them heads of households in the first place.

Men who failed to comply with their duties as husbands and fathers were also punished under the laws of labor. Vagrancy laws in some states, such as Mississippi, South Carolina, and Texas, penalized those same heads of households who "abandon, neglect, or refuse to aid in the support of their families, and who may be complained of by their families." South Carolina took further steps to circumscribe the home lives of ex-slaves, making it explicit that their dwellings on plantations were not actually their own, but were entirely controlled by plantation proprietors. "Visitors" (anyone not under contract) had to be approved by landowners as well. In Louisiana, visitors could be considered trespassers and subjected to fines of up to $100 or imprisonment for thirty days.[25]

Many states passed laws that counteracted family decisions to limit women's labor in plantation fields to allow them to spend more time taking care of domestic chores and children. Other laws prohibited hunting and fishing in order to limit ex-slaves' ability to earn a living outside of staple-crop production. Poll taxes added extra burdens by forcing families to work for cash or cash crops. Many of the punitive laws passed by Southern legislatures were intercepted and repealed by military commanders and Republican lawmakers once Radicals took over President Johnson's lax Reconstruction plan. But the die had been cast. Plantation owners did all they could to reverse the spirit and the letter of emancipation even in the most intimate of relationships. By 1868 almost all the Freedmen's Bureau operations were withdrawn from Southern states, leaving the states to establish their own laws governing marriage and other aspects of the lives of ex-slaves. In 1872, the bureau was officially dissolved.

Elite landowners continued to see themselves as arbiters of the intimate affairs of ex-slaves in the postwar South during federal occupation and beyond. Former masters assumed the role of tutors, instructing their pupils on appropriate marital behavior and the rule of law. Conflicts between couples became occasions for former slaveholders to intervene. They were most concerned when unresolved issues spilled out of the cabins and onto the cotton fields, thus disrupting the surrounding community or threatening the economic bottom line. Landowners were never more satisfied with the presence of Union troops and the federal government than when they could call upon officials to aid them in their efforts to "scare" the freedpeople and make them "do right." It was one thing for husband and wife to disagree or to fight, but quite another when disputes ended in abrupt departures that left working units shattered or undermined labor contracts already in force. Landowners sometime tried to play their role evenhandedly, instructing both spouses to be reasonable, agreeable, and explaining to them in careful terms the benefits of living together in peace. They urged spouses intent on leaving to work things out, insisting that they could do no better than what they already had in a good spouse. They set out to investigate their workers' character by consulting with the "old servants" to ascertain their reputation among their peers. Who did fellow freedpeople think was to blame in the relationship? Who was "worthy" of being defended? Were their troubles new or long-standing? Neighbors often became self-appointed police, judges, and juries in adjudicating disputes.

They were especially impatient when they perceived women to be unruly and willful and sided with husbands they thought were overpowered by feminine wiles. She "refused to be managed by him" was a common complaint lodged at wives. They judged harshly those wives they considered "object[s] of discord & discomfort" to their husbands and decried those they felt had "no real affection" for their husbands but were financial burdens.[26] Women were seen as materialistic, dictating that their husbands work hard to provide all the comforts their hearts longed for while they sat by indisposed to contribute their own labor.[27] A woman could be accused of stealing, shirking work, quitting in weekly stints, and working "as she pleases."

Marital discord became the pretext for reining in other acts disruptive of plantation discipline. Former masters "pitied" the men and identified with them when their authority was thwarted. One landowner instructed a freedwoman about the new order: "I told her there was a law to govern her as well as me, and that she had to obey her husband in all things." He had clearly learned to take advantage of this new arrangement by turning over at least some of the responsibilities of disciplining female plantation workers to newly endowed household heads.[28] When all else failed, landowners sometimes advised spouses, especially husbands, to leave their errant wives. They promised to help file the appropriate documents and even defray the costs of of divorce when they deemed it best for their own profits.

Women were likely to gain sympathy from landowners when they were abandoned by their husbands, especially when they had young children and were seen as loyal workers. Watt Johnson left his wife, Nancy Roberts, for another woman. He came back for their two oldest children and then apprenticed them to notoriously unscrupulous landowners, leaving Nancy to care for the two youngest children without his help. The couple had a tumultuous history over the course of their twelve-year marriage, punctuated by periodic separations. They each had supporters and detractors when it came to their responsibility for the marital problems. Nancy was deeply distraught and tried to follow the children and work on the same farm. But she suffered from ailments that made it difficult for her to work. She was especially disturbed that Watt gave over her children, binding them out, without her consent. She had an unusual advocate in her former mistress, Clara Garland. Garland wrote to the Freedmen's Bureau: "I would ask in reply what does any mother want with their children? Nancy is a mother & an *injured mother*. If a white mother's children were torn from her at that tender age the community would be in arms at the outrage but as poor Nancy has a dark skin it all passes off well with the parties concerned but I trust that you will take a better view of the case & have justice done the poor afflicted creature."[29] The landowners refused to return Nancy's children even when ordered by the local courts to release them to their mother. They even threatened to shoot her for trying to get them back. Nancy resorted to kidnapping the children as they slipped under the radar of the overseers while picking strawberries one day.[30]

Women were entitled to a hearing if they were subjected to physical abuse. Landowners often used abuse or accusations of abuse as a pretext to advance their own agendas. Former masters claimed that "some of the women receive the lash oftener & more severely now, than they did when they were slaves."[31] Under slavery, masters claimed to prohibit husbands from abusing their wives and had kept "savagery" in check. But once they were freed, landowners asserted, former slaves were prone to brutal behaviors that had remained latent. Landowners' views coincided with the rhetoric around spousal abuse, which was changing in the broader society. Wife beating came to be perceived as a problem of deviant lower-class men with criminal propensities.[32] In the most extreme cases, accusations of wife beating could lead employers to threaten the life of a man. This was the case with Tom Edwards, who was accused of beating his wife. It was no coincidence that Tom was also leader of an armed rebellion on the plantation owned by Nathan B. Forrest, the former Confederate military leader and Ku Klux Klan member, who had a reputation of brutality against African Americans. Forrest shot Edwards to death.[33]

Husbands and wives faced their toughest battles against landowners determined to assert their own interests in labor contracts above the couples' newly endowed marital contracts. The promise of freedom was that former slaves could have unencumbered access to both their labor and their marriage. The right to consent to and benefit from work of their own choosing was at stake. Central to these newly granted rights was the question of which should take precedence: the marriage contract (husband's authority) or the labor contract (employer's authority). The two often came into conflict over the labor of women. Ex-slaves asserted the right to control the labor of their own family members and set priorities for their households. Employers asserted their prerogatives to control labor as they saw fit to meet the needs of the staple-crop economy. Both perspectives had some standing in the law. Ex-slave husbands were entitled to control the labor of their dependent wives and children, keeping the lion's share of the proceeds of their spouses' outside labor and unpaid work at home. Employers were endowed with rights under English common-law traditions that were still being invoked, which allowed them to control workers' time and mandate their obedience. Workers who did not comply could face penalties equaling the sum of their wages under the annual contract.[34]

The nature and extent of women's work generated some of the most fraught clashes. Fights involving fists, guns, and knives often stemmed from the ownership and control of black women's labor power and bodies. Under slavery women were often left to fend for themselves against owners. Men faced imminent danger if they dared interfere. As free people, they refused to abide by the old codes. One husband instructed his wife to stay home after she got into a fight with her employer, who accused her of negligence as a cook just after she had given birth. Whatever work she may have failed to perform to satisfy her employer, it is clear that he was especially perturbed that she had used her recent pregnancy as an "excuse," bringing into the world a child for which he could claim no benefit. The employer was further inflamed by the husband's actions. He told him that "as he had ordered his wife *not* to go to work—he should now order her *to* go to work." The husband did not take kindly to the suggestion and responded that "he'd be G—d— d—d if he would, as he wasn't going to have *his* wife jawed at like a dog."[35]

Husbands took issue with employers who assumed the authority to command their wives to work however they deemed appropriate for their own purposes. One couple got into an extended battle with their employer when he instructed the wife, against the express wishes of the couple, to spin thread late at night. The husband took umbrage when he arrived home at midnight and discovered that his wife was not there. He recalled: "I told her that she was not hired to work night an day for him."[36] But the wife was forced against her will and out of sight of her protective husband. When the husband confronted his employer, the landowner threatened to whip the couple and tried to enlist the wife's parents to side with him. Shotguns were brandished and shots fired by the employer, though no one was hit. The entire family, including the in-laws, were kicked off the farm and denied any portion of the annual wages they had already earned.

Employers increased the workloads of field workers by adding on other chores, like domestic tasks, which they were not hired to do. Ex-slaves chafed at the notion that they should be at their employers' beck and call, as slaves had been. Women tried to invoke their status as wives and the authority of their husbands to get them out of these binds. One woman was told to do a large ironing job after she completed her fieldwork. She responded by saying that she needed to check with her husband first, which infuriated her employer. He beat her over the head for her disobedience and insult. Her husband faced the same punishment when he tried to defend his wife. Both were threatened with death if they dared report the incident to the authorities, but they did so anyway.[37]

The value of women's labor to their own families was often so important that men were willing to step in to do extra jobs to release them so they could work in their own homes. This was the arrangement that one couple made. Friday nights were devoted to shucking corn, which all the women employed on the plantation were expected to do. But since the couple had young children, the husband said he would take her place. The foreman, however, objected to the wife's refusal to do the work herself. The wife spoke back to him, asserting her right to be replaced by her husband. The husband's intervention with the landowner only heightened the tension, and he, too, was cursed at and assaulted. The wife was kicked off the plantation without pay. And so went the whole family.[38] The timing of the retaliation—after the harvest, at paytime—was not a coincidence. Landowners often waited until the work was done to withhold pay and dismiss workers as retribution for earlier conflicts. Sometimes they even manufactured reasons to get rid of parts of families, husbands most often, but also wives, to avoid paying them wages or to reduce the amount they were due.[39]

Nothing annoyed former masters as new employers of ex-slave labor more than workers asserting their freedom to work or coming and going as they pleased. They complained of men's recalcitrance and refusals to adhere to the dictates of landowners, particularly when they chose alternative self-employment. Men were most often prosecuted under the South's notorious "vagrancy" laws for these transgressions. But employers were most irked by women absenting themselves from staple-crop production. In the South's leading agricultural journal, *Debow's Review,* complaints were prolific: "Most of the field labor is now performed by men, the women regarding it as the duty of their husbands to support them in idleness."[40] Ex-slave women were accused of "playing the lady" or acting white. Or, as a Georgia land-owner put it, the men on his plantation worked while their wives did not, as they were accustomed to "pretending to spin—knit or something that really amounts to nothing." Black women were born and bred to be workers, not "idle wives," he asserted. He claimed that this was for their own good. "Both in regard to health & in furtherance of their family wellbeing," it was better for them to continue to work as they had before emancipation. "Their fami-lies could live in better comfort and happiness if only the wives worked too," he argued. He and others feared that the consequences of not doing so would lead women to steal to make up for lost wages. They also worried that "idle" wives set bad examples for the rest of the women in the field. They might foment dissent: "having no employment their brain becomes more or less the Devil's work shop." But the Georgia landowner also admitted the real crux of the matter: "their labor is a very important percent of the entire labor of the South—& if not made available, must affect to some extent—the present crop."[41]

Many historians accepted as an article of faith the so-called withdrawal of women from cotton and other fields in the postwar South. Abundant evi-dence from supporters and detractors of the new order alike seems to sup-port this claim. Women did appear to be, by more objective measures and observations, working less in the fields than they had as slaves. And indeed it was so, but most observers were unable or unwilling to appreciate their mo-tivations. Both women and men reduced the amount of labor they exerted as freedpeople compared with antebellum outputs, and the decline of the labor of women and children was greatest. The violence of the lash could no longer be invoked to command their unrelenting toil. But something more was afoot. Former slaves made conscious decisions about the labor of different family members. Women, especially wives, worked selectively in staple-crop production and spent the rest of their time engaged in unpaid work, taking care of their children, their homes, and their gardens. Reorganizing the pri-ority of women's field labor also had the benefit of helping them avoid the sexual exploitation that was customary under slavery. Critics looked at such choices as the irrational behavior of those not accustomed to the precepts of free labor. African Americans saw it as an assertion of their rights as free people to prioritize the needs of their own household economies. In sum, there was no wholesale withdrawal of women's labor.[42]

Landowners themselves had made the option for women to do intermittent fieldwork less attractive by undervaluing it. They paid women less than men for the same work, especially when they were mothers of young children. Women preferred to trade off time tending to their own domestic duties. Landowners were particularly perturbed by the loss of women's reproductive labor. As slaves they had literally reproduced capital in the bodies of their children as increased chattel. As freedwomen they contributed only productive labor. Their reproductive capacities were now regarded as liabilities, since pregnancy, childbirth, and childcare disrupted the rhythms of commercial agriculture. And it would take years before their children could contribute to the workforce.[43]

Women's domestic labors actually expanded post-emancipation, as work that had been done collectively (such as cooking and childcare) now had to be done within the context of their individual families, and the wife and mother was expected to bear all the costs and burdens. Women worked in the market economy and in their own homes, doing double duty to make ends meet and keep their family afloat amid the unfulfilled promises of a family wage. The designation "idle wives" was yet another racialized marker based on double standards. White yeomen and tenant farming women were not called "idle" for taking care of their homes, and engaged in fieldwork intermittently if at all. Neither were industrial working-class women in the North under the duress of an encroaching wage system that compromised white men's ability to keep their wives at home. While the classical precepts of free labor were being newly implemented in the South, they were under siege in the North. White working-class women were called housewives, entitled to all the benefits and protections that the law of coverture allowed, even as the growth of capitalism threatened traditional livelihoods and made it more difficult for white men in the North to support their families.[44]

Landowners were annoyed with the women, but they also blamed the men. William L. Scott, state legislator in Virginia and landowner, argued that women "are becoming rather disinclined to work for an employer either in the house or in the field, and their husbands have but little control over them as is often the case among more cultivated people."[45] Ex-slave men were perceived to be failed patriarchs, unable to get their wives to submit and follow the postbellum rules of order. Landowners found willing partners in federal agents eager to restore the plantation economy and to keep ex-slaves from becoming dependent on the largesse of others. On the South Carolina side of the Savannah River, a bureau official objected to arrangements in which families were given two acres of land to cultivate, which the wives farmed in place of contracting their labor to the landowner. The official did not think that he had any authority to interfere as long as the husbands could support their wives, but since they had always been accustomed to field labor, he believed that "it is far better to *compel* them if necessary to return to it again." It was for their own good "in order that they may gain a little surplus over their actual expenses." In this case, however, the officer above him in the hierarchy rejected his thinking and rebuffed him: "there can be no coercion used in these cases as the Freed people are entitled to work in their *own* way as long as they choose to do so, and do not become dependent upon the Government."[46]

Landowners often perceived women's recalcitrance over labor issues as individual acts. Sometimes they were. Women, as well as men, had any number of reasons for disagreeing with the way they were treated as emancipated workers and responded accordingly, often spontaneously, to perceived threats, affronts, and violations of their personhood. But women's actions, attitudes, and predispositions were also a product of decisions and priorities that they made in conjunction with their families. Landowners assumed that men could not control their wives because women's actions appeared inconsistent with black male authority, which landowners thought would look more like their own. White Northerners had invested great stock in remaking black masculinity to fit a postslavery world, and even former Confederates had begrudgingly followed suit. Yet despite all that tutelage, black masculinity did not always resemble white masculinity. Couples managed their own negotiations over how power would be shared and divided, however contentious this may have been at times. Even as women appeared to accept men's roles as heads of households, they did not give up all self-determination unconditionally. Men signed and mediated labor contracts on behalf of their families, as employers insisted, but women continued to assert themselves in the workplace and in other arenas, such as the courts, to make wrongs right.

When it became apparent that couples were united and acted in concert or backed up each other, employers became even more angry. The "devil's workshops" in the brains of "idle wives," it turned out, were busy indeed.[47]

These skirmishes over the reconstruction of gender and race relations took place in the context of evolving transformations in the rural economy. The character and structure of black family life were no less central to the operation of the postwar labor system than they had been during slavery. African Americans' first priority after reconstituting and consolidating their kin was to obtain land, the only basis on which their freedom could be secured. As they struggled for land and mostly failed to overcome formidable obstacles, they battled over achieving fair terms of labor in order to maximize control over their families and enhance their livelihoods when forced to work for white landowners.[48]

Marriages and families were deeply affected by how those struggles over labor would be resolved. But it was not self-evident immediately after the war as disparate terms were established to organize black labor. At first, most ex-slaves worked under loosely formed, mostly unwritten contracts. Large numbers of freedpeople were hired as individuals adjoined in collective contracts as gangs, under the supervision of (usually white) overseers. Share wages, payment of a portion of the cotton, tobacco, or rice crop (usually one-third to one-half) prevailed as the form of remuneration in areas where the antebellum economic institutions had been obliterated by war and cash was in short supply. Share wages were a delayed form of compensation subject to proceeds that had yet to be determined by the caprice of nature's harvest, which put ex-slaves in the role of serving as creditors for wealthy elites. This hallmark of postwar Southern agriculture would prove to be enduring: freedpeople shared the risks of planting crops that were incommensurate with the rewards they could or would reap. But ex-slaves objected most to the gang-style organization, in which they were indiscriminately assigned to work in the fields with overseers looking on, very much like slavery. They withheld the labor of some family members from full-time work so that they could balance the low wages with independent economic activities that helped sustain them, such as gardening, fishing, and short-term hire. In most cases, women and younger children were kept out of contracts, while men and older children were put to work. Though selective contracting of family labor was short-lived, these and other measures fueled the complaints about "idle wives" amid labor shortages and gave workers leverage. Landowners moved from large collective contracts to making contracts with "squads" and "companies" when freedpeople refused to agree to sign contracts for the new seasons in 1866 and 1867 without these concessions. These groupings often had at their core one or more families, with other individuals added on. An appointed squad leader from among the freedpeople negotiated the terms of their contracts with employers and organized the productive activities of its members on a daily basis. More and more landowners began to insist on contracting with heads of whole families, though the structure of dispersed ex-slave families was still quite varied at this stage. Employers had resisted transferring power to ex-slave men as husbands and fathers, but they came to appreciate the advantages of doing so.[49]

Amid these struggles over the organization of labor, a distinctive system emerged. Sharecropping started to become prevalent between 1868 and 1876, by most estimates, as squads were replaced with single-family groups. It was distinguished from earlier forms of agricultural production because it signaled the breakdown of the centralized plantation system that had been dominant for centuries under slavery. Land was subdivided into thirty-to-fifty acre plots worked by individual families. In exchange for their labor they received tools and implements, seed, draft animals such as mules and horses, and typically half of the crop at harvest time. They were given credit, in the form of a mortgage on the future of the crop (a crop lien), to purchase any supplies they needed before the harvest. Landowners were forced to surrender centralized control over the production of cotton and other crops, though they continued to dictate what crops could be grown and managed the overall system. Sharecropping was written into the laws of Southern states to impute inferior rights and obligations to croppers and superior rights to landowners and merchants. It was designed to function less like traditional tenant farming and more like wage labor. It was established in the physical layout of plantations, which were rearranged from larger-style slave barracks to multiple single-family dwellings dotting the rural landscape. By 1880 the antebellum plantation was clearly a thing of the past, even if the antebellum landowner class was still largely intact and in command of both capital and labor, and the labor system was no less exploitative.[50]

A distinctive form of family accompanied the sharecropping system and by all accounts also became dominant by 1880: the male-headed nuclear family, with legally married husband, wife, and children. According to the 1870 and 1880 census, the majority of black families in the cotton South were becoming more nuclear in composition with each decade. Nuclear families would first be most prevalent in rural areas, where most African Americans lived. The trend would follow them into cities, but to a lesser extent, as migrant families were even more fragmented. These patterns were directly correlated with events impinging on both rural and urban economies. The family was central to sharecropping in large part because ex-slaves had demanded that it be the cornerstone of whatever postwar labor system was adopted. "Landowners literally were dragged kicking and screaming into the system," one historian argued.[51] Although many factors contributed to the dominance of sharecropping, "the sociology of the family," one economist argues, was perhaps the most important. Under a family-based system it would be the legal responsibility of the family's head to make sure that the work was done, and the labor of everyone under contract was typically required to reach that outcome.[52] In the context of the perceived shortage of labor, sharecropping answered the employers' desires to get women and older children back into the fields. But families still had room to maneuver on a daily basis to determine how to apportion each person's labor, toward field work, domestic work, childcare, elderly care, gardening, and tending to small animals.[53]

Sharecropping grew out of protracted conflicts between former slaves and landowners as each struggled to assert their own interests and needs in the aftermath of plantation slavery. No one could have predicted what the terms of the system that came to prevail would look like. The spoils were by no means shared equally. Employers used the system to their advantage in ways that consigned generations of black agricultural workers to endless debt and oppression that would be codified in the laws. Even though African Americans insisted on family farming, they could not have anticipated how they would be restricted to adherence to one form that would be used to judge the fitness of future generations. African Americans searched for immediate kin, such as spouses and children, most determinedly once emancipated. But they also sought and incorporated extended kin, such as grandparents, siblings, nieces, and nephews. Despite their meager resources, they made room in their tight quarters for those unable to earn a living on their own. Family was the most important source of emotional sustenance and physical survival. Families were not eager to discard the eclectic configurations that had sustained them for generations and continued to be of service as they put the pieces of their lives together. But for employers, particularly cotton landowners, a certain kind of family form was considered most suitable for inculcating stability and encouraging profit-making. Employers used the nuclear family to whittle down labor units to their most efficient figures: married couples and children. Outliers of these relations were either kicked off the land or denied access; alternatively, landowners charged the accounts of the family to cover their presence. Paring down to the individual nuclear family, employers hoped, would force the unit to devote itself exclusively to the production of staple crops and leave little time or spare bodies to engage in other work. The nuclear family functionally preserved laborers on the land year after year, welding them to a system of perpetual debt and exploitation.[54]

The privileging of nuclear families meant that alternative kinship structures and networks were undermined even as the legacy of family disruption and destruction meant that a diversity of forms still prevailed. Recall that Texas and Louisiana actually wrote into their laws that married couples and children were to be hired exclusively. Others did so in practice. Single women and men were pushed off to the margins with unequal prospects for rural work. Unmarried men, typically younger, were often hired as casual agricultural labor, for wages, on a daily or monthly basis. The flexibility sometimes enhanced their bargaining power to earn more than married men. Unmarried or widowed women, especially those with small children, had a much more difficult time finding work on farms, though some did, especially if they had boys old enough to work. Most landowners refused to hire them at all, however. The procreative value of black women had disappeared with freedom in the eyes of white landowners. Women pushed to rural peripheries often migrated to Southern cities to find work as domestics and in other occupations. Thus more unattached women than single men headed to cities.

Marriage rates and family structure varied as a result of the uneven sex ratios that resulted. Though the nuclear family structure came to dominate in cities too, the percentages trailed rural trends.[55]

Despite the legal transformation of slave marriages in the postwar era, slavery's impact on marriage in the South had not been entirely erased.[56] New laws that were designed to be corrective were often punitive toward ex-slaves in ways free white couples never faced. These laws did not simply reverse the absence of legal protection; they often criminalized cohabitation and various marital infractions that failed to conform to the new regime. They diverged significantly from a marital law tradition that had emphasized voluntary practices, to marry or not according to individual predispositions, by making marriage compulsory. No other group was subjected to such scrutiny and directives aimed at ordering their intimate affairs.[57] There was a national trend from the mid-to-late nineteenth century, in response to a perceived "marital crisis," to shore up lifelong monogamy, cut down on bigamy, and deter polygamy. Divorce reform was a double-edged sword as proponents won more state laws favoring legal exits to ease the tensions that encouraged desertions and bigamy. But opponents decried these liberalizations, which they believed led to unprecedented numbers of couples ending their relationships.[58] Still, the racialization of marriage continued to persist in law and in practice.

Congress came closest to removing racial encumbrances in the Civil Rights Act of 1866, which gave African Americans the right to make contracts of all kinds, putting black marriages on the same legal footing of legitimacy and coverture as white unions, with the imprimatur of the nation-state as a guarantor of the fundamental rights of citizenship. Black men were welcomed into the brotherhood of American manhood, entitled to ownership of self, wives, children, and infrangible households.[59] But the actions of the Freedmen's Bureau, nonstate actors, Southern state lawmakers, and elite landowners converged in undermining the spirit and letter of the 1866 act and of marriage as a civil right. Although a "national standard of formal and legal monogamy" gave blacks the equal right to marry, this change was stymied and protracted, and they would continue to be judged by the character of their sexual morality and conjugal ties. And no matter what, marriage could never live up to the hype of saving black people from the grips of poverty or from de facto segregation and disfranchisement that were on the horizon.[60]

In the last three decades of the nineteenth century, white Americans were forced to ponder anew the question of the nature of black people, this time in the context of a post-emancipation world. Given that slavery had been considered a civilizing institution, how, under freedom, would they now become proper citizens? Where did their humanity fit on the scale of mankind? Could they or should they ever be allowed to assimilate among whites? Many white Northerners were eager to push for national reconciliation: "a union of endeavor on the part of those of North and South, of ex-slaveholder and ex-abolitionist alike," as Nathaniel Southgate Shaler, a Harvard scientist and aspiring race expert, advocated.[61] Shaler was speaking of the need to study the "Negro Problem" with fresh insight by shifting the burden from the past sins of slavery to the capacities of the freedmen making their way on their own faculties. The governing fear was that people of African descent would "revert to their ancestral condition," which deeply tainted their sexual ethics and moral compasses. A paradigm shift was called for in order to understand the implications for the formerly enslaved and for the rest of society that would have to accommodate them. Biological determinism was no longer in vogue. Rather than focus on physical differences, as earlier scientists and political thinkers had done since Thomas Jefferson's *Notes on the State of Virginia,* academics shifted to behaviors, on how the Negro governed himself or herself according to a set of normative standards.

New social sciences offered the disciplinary tools such as statistics and surveys that could be used to explain and judge racial inferiority, based on data about criminality, disease, poverty, and intelligence. The character and structure of black family life came under renewed scrutiny within this panoply of tests and measures. The differences between the "two races" were rooted in "the most vital points that part the men who make states from those who cannot rise above savagery," Shaler wrote. "Chief of these is the family, which rests on a certain order of alliance of the sexual instincts with the higher and more human faculties." It was here that ex-slaves would rise or fall: "If the black is weak in these things, he is in so far unfit for an independent place in a civilized state," Shaler insisted. The North would be the new laboratory to view black life and comment on it, as African Americans slowly trickled above the Mason Dixon Line. But white observers would continue to perceive the legacy of blacks' enslavement and Southern rural lives as the major culprit of whatever deficiencies might appear in the urban North. The future of black people would forever be tethered to this past.[62]

The combination of the disposition of ex-slaves, the coercive power of the state, and the actions of the federal government, Christian missionaries, and elite landowners led to a majority of blacks adopting a nuclear family model within a short time after slavery had ended. These competing and allied forces had led to a true achievement: "the most cruel wrongs" had been "corrected as far as possible." And yet "as far as possible" was not good enough. What did that achievement actually entail? African Americans were not attached to a family structure; they were committed to a family sensibility. But share-cropping would shackle them to a particular type of family to the detriment of others. The preponderance of legal marriage and the acceptability of one family form did not and could not forestall Jim Crow, disfranchisement, poverty, and pervasive exploitation. It did not guarantee full citizenship rights. New laws notwithstanding, the validity of slave unions would continue to be questioned in ways that implicated and burdened freedpeople. At century's end, African Americans were still struggling to undo the enduring havoc wreaked on their most intimate affairs.

8

Hopes and Travails at Century's End

I t is nearly thirty years since an emancipated people stood on the threshold of a new era, facing an uncertain future—a legally unmarried race, to be taught the sacredness of the marriage relations," wrote the African-American social activist and writer Frances Ellen Watkins Harper in 1892. On that precipice Harper observed an "ignorant people" who needed to be instructed in "Christian law." She identified "a homeless race" that needed to be instructed on how to make their firesides bulwarks "against sins that degrade the race and vices that demoralize."[1] Leading African Americans took stock of the status of black marriages and families in the final decade of the very long and fraught nineteenth century. W. E. B. Du Bois, scholar and civil rights activist, summarized the consensus view even more bluntly: "Without a doubt the point where the Negro American is furthest behind modern civilization is in his sexual *mores*." The African American, he asserted, is "more primitive, less civilized," and "his family life is less efficient for its onerous social duties, his womanhood less protected." Du Bois saw this situation as an understandable by-product of slavery, but he still worried that these problems could not be easily overcome because they had put blacks far behind Anglo-Saxons on the evolutionary scale of Western civilization. But there were good reasons to be optimistic. However much "the *mores* of the Negro family" still suffered, Du Bois had faith in the hopeful signs embodied in a post-emancipation phenomenon. "The great and most patent fact has been differentiation," he noted, "the emergence from the masses, of successive classes with higher and higher sexual morals."[2] The future looked bright because of growing class stratification.

Harper and Du Bois were the products of this differentiation, which nurtured a small but influential and ambitious group of both formally educated and self-educated African Americans. They were primarily teachers, ministers, intellectuals, entrepreneurs, and journalists, but some were also small proprietors, skilled workers, and common workers able to gain social and economic mobility. They spoke on the lecture circuit, wrote articles and books (fiction and nonfiction), preached in pulpits and classrooms, and gave talks before business groups and at club meetings. Their very existence stood for something remarkable: they were living counterweights to denigrating judgments of the race's intellectual and cultural capacities. Most of them had overcome tremendous odds to achieve personal and professional success presumed to be out of reach for black people. They were eager to use their talents and skills to prove white supremacy wrong by bringing the rest of the race along, correcting its moral deficiencies in order to persuade naysayers of racial equality.

This vibrant, self-appointed leadership class offered critique and scorn of the worse-offs, self-defense and self-help strategies for the race. They organized conferences and created clubs and institutions to address the most pressing concerns of their day, locally, regionally, and nationally. They committed themselves to studying the problems of the race, to implementing plans that would help to correct the difficulties that their studies exposed, and to dislodging the racial antipathy that had become entrenched in the wake of de jure segregation, disfranchisement, lynchings, and the continued exploitation of rural and urban workers. They summoned the newly emergent tools of social science to study every aspect of the material, social, cultural, physical, and economic experiences of African Americans at the turn of the century. The purpose was to expose "the truth" and to use empirical data to make a comprehensive program of self-help and reform. They scrutinized marriage and the family because they considered these areas foundational for everything else they hoped to achieve.[3] As Anna J. Cooper, educator and social activist, argued, "A race is but a total of families. The nation is the aggregate of its homes. As the whole is sum of all its parts, so the character of the parts will determine the characteristics of the whole."[4]

Elite spokespersons rested much hope for racial progress on reforming the individual and group morals reflected in perceived deficiencies in black marriages and families. But African-American patterns were dogged by evolving structural constraints, which grew out of slavery and the systems that replaced it. Late-nineteenth-century sources such as W. E. B. Du Bois's pioneering works offer insight and perspective on these patterns that are critical to reassess in hindsight. But reformers and scholars at the time could not fully account for many details about African-American marital practices and patterns because the evidence simply wasn't available then. We have more quantitative and qualitative sources now, which paint a more complicated picture of black marital trends and family structure that challenge the conventional wisdom of observers from the period. African Americans demonstrated a propensity not only to marry but also to remarry, more often than late-nineteenth-century thinkers assumed. Serial monogamy and varied marital practices had long-standing roots dating back to the capricious conditions of slavery, but they endured after emancipation for reasons that elites did not fully understand or appreciate.

And then there is the law. One of the cruelest ironies of the states' new marriage recognition laws was that they often mired ex-slaves in a system ill-prepared or unwilling to help them in a timely manner. The new legal regime offered many of the protections and benefits that African Americans had long sought, but it could take years of litigation and copious financial resources to resolve matters in court. The status of slave marriage and its effects were still debated at every level of the judiciary, everywhere ex-slaves lived. The contentiousness is evident in criminal cases involving breaches of marital laws such as charges of bigamy and in civil cases concerning inheritance accruing from former slaves. The outcome of seeking legal standing for slave marriages ex post facto was never guaranteed. The descendants of ex-slaves faced a judicial system that could never completely square the reality of antebellum relationships with a retroactive de jure system. No amount of Victorian emulation could save black people from this lasting legacy of bondage.

The marital and familial platitudes that preoccupied the new black elite were reflected in the first major social study of the black family. W. E. B. Du Bois led the study under the auspices of Atlanta University. It was designed to provide concrete data to help usher the race's assimilation into the American mainstream. The summary interpretations and the statistics presented did not always match, however. On the whole, the status of marriage among African Americans was both better off than elites imagined (even judged by their own narrow standards) and more challenged than they had envisaged by the enduring by-products of slavery that emancipation alone could not annihilate.

The publication of the study, *The Negro American Family* (1908), was the product of an annual conference with invited local and national speakers and research undertaken by students under Du Bois's leadership. It relied on both surveys conducted by students visiting the homes of local blacks in Atlanta to observe their daily lives, and data from the 1890 and 1900 U.S. censuses, the most objective statistics available on what those families looked like and how they were faring. It was designed to offer empirical, seemingly objective, evidence to bolster arguments articulated and disseminated by like-minded peers in pulpits, lecture halls, club meetings, pamphlets, newspapers, and journals. The study focused on blacks in cities and rural areas, in the North and the South. And it compared the "conjugal condition" of the black population in the United States, the white native-born population, and foreign-born populations and others in various European countries. Du Bois and his colleagues concluded that "sexual mores" were the primary impediments that stood between black people and racial equality. The proof, he believed, was in the numbers: "In these statistics we have striking evidence of the needs of the Negro American Home. The broken families indicated by the abnormal number of widowed and separated, and the late age of marriage, show sexual irregularity and economic pressure."[5]

The interpretations in *The Negro American Family* were highly influenced by Du Bois's earlier book *The Philadelphia Negro* (1896). The Philadelphia study enabled him to identify and elucidate emergent class stratification, exposing gradients of black life that were largely unknown to the white world. It was here that he conceptualized the idea that a black elite should lead the masses by example and dictate, and that it should represent the capacity of the race for assimilation, which dovetailed with the thinking of other leading intellectuals and reformers. This prior work concluded that morality and family had been despoiled by slavery, and that rectifying them was the key to race progress. Although his findings showed that most black families were overwhelmingly nuclear, even in what he described as the worst sites of urban blight in America, he focused outsized attention on the presumed "pathology" of the minority who did not conform, establishing a tone and a trend for future social scientific work that liberals and conservatives would imbibe and regurgitate for more than a century thereafter. Similarly, the evidence produced in *The Negro American Family* was not entirely consistent with Du Bois's conclusions. Du Bois chose to foreground lax conformity to Victorian morality dating from slavery, which understated the constraints of then-current economic and political conditions that made it difficult for black families to live up to the norms. Du Bois was inconsistent when it came to distancing himself from popular racialist explanations for cultural differences, leading him at times to impugn black people as the primary culprits impeding their own escape from past and present ills.[6]

Du Bois did recognize that economic inequality influenced the conjugal choices of African Americans. Low wages and rising costs led them to postpone marriage to an age that was "dangerously late for a folk in the Negro's present moral development." Oddly, he did not present any data or further explanation showing delayed marriage rates and did not elaborate on the economic roadblocks. Perhaps they were all too obvious to him and his contemporaries. The sex-segregated job market limited possibilities for pairing up because black men were more in demand on farms in the countryside and black women were beckoned to fill posts in the cities, leading especially to disparate urban sex ratios. This much did worry Du Bois. "The predominance of the female element" was particularly troubling as it opened the door for the perpetuation of all kinds of urban vices and "sexual irregularities." Throughout Afro-America, Du Bois found signs of "broken families." He wrote: "These things all go to prove not the disintegration of the Negro family life but the distance which integration has gone and has yet to go."[7]

The statistics in the study told a less alarming story of racial despair in marital trends, however. For the United States as a whole, according to tables in the report, in 1890, 34.8 percent of blacks over age 15 were single, compared with 37 percent of whites; 55 percent of blacks were married compared with 55.4% percent of whites. By 1900, these figures changed only slightly, with more blacks married—58.9 percent compared with 55.9 percent.

Slightly fewer blacks than whites were single: 34.5 percent vs. 35.9 percent. The biggest difference for both decades was the proportion of widows: 9.6 percent and 10.6 percent for blacks and 7.1 percent and 7.5 percent for whites. Within the black population there were gender differences. The marriage rate was close to equal, with slightly more men married. The biggest difference was that there were more single men and more widowed women. None of these figures is highlighted or interpreted in the body of the report, however. These figures do not set off alarm bells about racial difference, which are at best statistically meaningless, though African Americans were marrying at slightly higher rates than whites by 1900.[8]

The data and the interpretations in the report are consistent in highlighting the disproportionate sex ratio among urban blacks. The data for large cities in the South, North, and Midwest (with the exception of Chicago) indicate more black women than men in those populations. But the report offers no explanation for why this was the case. As we have already seen, the political economy of the rural South was tied directly to this phenomenon of cordoning off those who fell outside of nuclear families.[9] This was a trend of significant long-term historical resonance, telegraphing disparate urban job markets that would continue to mount in the twentieth century. But Du Bois was already using the condition of urban blacks as a metonym for the entire race and its potentially dire predicament.

The report also tends to make broader generalizations than the data allow. It assesses "sexual morals" using figures for illegitimacy in Washington, D.C., as reported by hospitals and city physicians. In one set of figures as many as 27 percent of black births in Washington between 1870 and 1900 were illegitimate. While the report noted that the data offered a "very doubtful basis of exact judgment," it seemed more worried about undercounting and underreporting than misleading. How hospitals and physicians made these determinations about legitimacy is left unexamined. Did they ask the mothers giving birth? Did they make assumptions on the basis of whatever criteria they deemed appropriate? Despite the inaccuracies of the figures, the authors spoke confidently that "they point without doubt to wide-spread sexual irregularity." The figures were similar to those used by Frederick Hoffman in his infamous study *Race Traits and Tendencies of the American Negro*. Du Bois used them to articulate a different argument, however. He was more impressed with how they represented stratification, explaining that illegitimacy was a behavior identified with the "undifferentiated mass," not the above-average strivers. Though some within the mass were "decent people," they were "behind civilization by training and instinct."[10]

In the end, Du Bois tried to strike an upbeat note by presenting ample descriptive anecdotes from leading white and black reformers that "there is more female purity, more male continence, and a healthier home life today than ever before." Blacks may have veered too far in excessive sexual activity and loose morality, but the "marriage mores of modern European culture nations" were not perfect either, he wrote. Prostitution, divorce, and childlessness were common among them. "Here the Negro race may teach the world something," he suggested. Working less and resting more, and idealizing motherhood rather than rejecting it, were two areas where blacks excelled. Treating women's virginity too sacredly was ruining white people, he suggested further. African Americans, by contrast, had appetites for sexual pleasure that were healthier and perhaps in the long run more beneficial. "No civilization can long survive which stigmatizes it as essentially nasty and only to be discussed in shamefaced whispers," he concluded. Du Bois understood that African Americans, though often strained by the contradiction and ambivalence of the Victorian era, on some level were representative of the moderns, setting the tone for cultural trends that would later become more customary in the wider society.[11]

Scholars now have access to more detailed and robust demographic data to describe marriage rates and family structure from 1880 to 1900 than what was available to Du Bois and his colleagues when the Atlanta University study was produced. The findings of recent scholars affirm the general picture of the data reported in the study, rather than the authors' textual interpretations or the assertions of those who believed that black respectability was under siege. The current metrics used to assess historic marriage rates include median age at first marriage; marriage age distributions at different age intervals; and the proportion of never-marrieds. African Americans showed a higher propensity to marry than did whites on all these measures. They married at younger ages: the median age for black men was 23, for black women 20, compared with 26 for white men and 22 for white women. Seventy-five percent of black men were married by age 24, black women by age 23, compared with white men by age 29 and white women by 25–26. Fewer blacks fell into the category of never-marrieds (based on those still single past childbearing years at 45–54), with black women having the lowest rates of all. Despite the slightly skewed sex ratios that favored black men in the prime marriage age group (ages 20–24), we would expect black women to have a slightly harder time finding mates, but this was not the case. (The white sex ratio was the reverse, with more white men than women.) To express the marriage data in ways similar to Du Bois's, 60.35 percent of blacks (age 18 and over) were married in 1880, compared with 59.83 percent of whites. And by 1900, that figure was down slightly to 56.17 percent for blacks and 58.75 percent for whites. (See Figures 8.1–8.3.)[12]

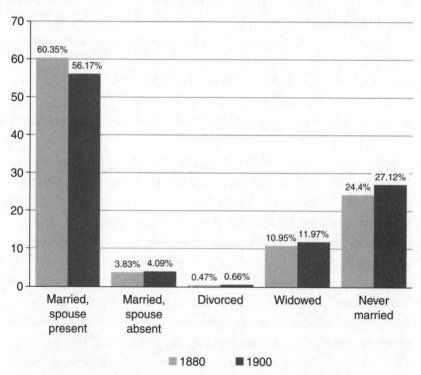

Fig. 8.1   Marital status of blacks, 1880 and 1900. Summary of the 1880 and 1900 census data showing the frequencies of five marital statuses for blacks aged 18 years or older.

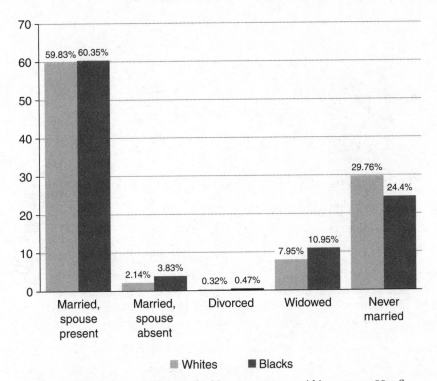

Fig. 8.2   Marital status of blacks and whites, percentages within groups, 1880. Summary of the 1880 census data showing the frequencies of five marital statuses for blacks and whites aged 18 years or older.

Marriage rates tend to run in tandem with larger socioeconomic forces. As goes the economy, so goes marriage. This by no means diminishes the significance of cultural changes, which have been highly consequential as well. But it reflects the strong correlation between marriage patterns and economic events across all historical periods for all racial groups. Thus it should come as no surprise that the prevalence of blacks in the rural South would have a major impact on their embrace of legal marriage at such high rates. Agricultural workers, regardless of race, had the highest marriage rates compared with all occupations. As has been reinforced repeatedly throughout this book, farming was largely a family enterprise that relied on complementary gender systems. Sharecropping, work to which most blacks were limited,

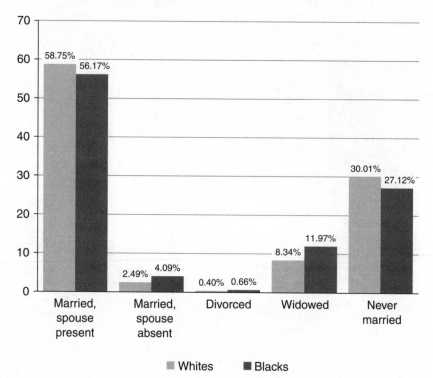

Fig. 8.3   Marital status of blacks and whites, percentages within groups, 1900. Summary of the 1900 census data showing the frequencies of five marital statuses for blacks and whites aged 18 years or older.

especially depended on the labor of all family members to remain a viable system.[13]

Perhaps even more controversial, but closely tied to marriage rates, is the structure of black families and households at the end of the century. Scholars since Du Bois have been preoccupied with discerning the extent to which generations of blacks after emancipation formed nuclear families compared with whites. Historians agree that most black families did constitute two parents, mother and father, with children, though they did so at lower rates than whites. In 1880, married couples (with and without children) led black families at 57.3 percent compared with 67.3 percent of whites. (These rates would go down slightly for both groups by the turn of the century.) Extended families (those with married couples and other kin) constituted 22.5 percent of black families and 19.5 percent of white families. (These rates would go up slightly for both groups by the turn of the century.) Fragmentary families, those with singles living with nonrelatives and female-headed households with children, represented 20.3 percent of black families and 13.2 percent of white families. (These rates would go down slightly for blacks and up slightly for whites by the turn of the century.) Thus there were clear racial differences in every category of family organization and household composition. These differences would be minimal in the nineteenth century compared with later times. With each passing decade after 1900 racial differences would increase, the gap growing ever more widely as the cotton economy collapsed and African Americans migrated to the urban North and West.[14]

The gap between the nearly universal marriage rates, in which blacks outpaced whites, and the more disparate rates in the formation of two-parent families, in which whites overtook blacks, is revealing. It indicates that while African Americans showed strong inclinations to use marriage as a strategy to advance their social and economic survival, they were not always able to translate that into viable households they could sustain. They adopted a much more diverse array of family forms in order to meet the challenges of the still-evolving constraints of racial oppression, just as they had done under slavery. Legal marriage gave them one more option that they did not have as slaves, but it proved to be an insufficient basis for reconstituting their families as free people.

In any case, demographic statistics based on the decennial census cannot tell the whole story of family formation because they do not fully capture the ebb and flow of people's lives, let alone account for the unique history of black conjugality. The disparate racial metrics are suggestive of the differences Du Bois and other elites were trying to capture, however awkward and misinformed their assumptions may have been. They were disturbed most by the signs of "irregularity" they observed, projecting them much farther than warranted as the proclivities of an "infant race." Yet somehow they missed the fact that most black families conformed to the very behaviors that they wanted to indoctrinate (see Figs. 8.4 and 8.5). Nor did they fully comprehend that black family life was even more vulnerable than they surmised. They did not notice or account for the fact that African Americans not only

Fig. 8.4   Jack and Abby. This couple is identified only by their first names. They were former slaves and conceivably had been a couple of long standing. The studio was located in Savannah, Georgia.

married more but also remarried more than whites. Black marriages were often cut short by desertion, separation, divorce, and death—all at higher rates than white unions on average.[15] African Americans were more fluid than whites in responding to these life crises that generated turnover in their private lives. As marriages dissolved, remarriage was yet another tool for reconstituting new familial arrangements. By the end of the nineteenth century, former slaves and their descendants had often engaged in multiple, serial marital relationships, typically a combination of formal marriages and the persistence of informal marriage-like relationships.

No quantitative data on remarriage rates in the late nineteenth century are available because the census did not ask respondents about their prior marital histories until 1910. That census, however, provides significant information that is suggestive when used along with other qualitative data. African Americans remarried more than whites. African Americans were already in risk groups likely to remarry: early age at first marriage, having children in those first marriages, and living on farms where spouses were essential to the

Fig. 8.5 Studio portrait of a young couple. This Virginia couple is depicted with the husband seated and the wife with her hand on his shoulder. If they were descended from slaves, they would have been one or, at most, two generations removed from bondage. By the turn of the century, middle-class couples in appearance, like this one, were more evident in photos.

maintenance of collective production. People who remarried were stimulated by similar circumstances to re-create dual-parent families and restabi-
lize vulnerable relations disrupted by breakups or death, especially during
childbearing years. Men were better off if they married again, especially if
they had children to care for. They needed women's paid and unpaid labor
to contribute to their subsistence. Women with children were also better off
if they remarried, as they were more vulnerable, especially on farms, without
husbands as helpmates. Unattached women were the most marginalized individuals in rural society.[16]

Remarriage rates reveal that different routes could be taken to achieve nuclear families. Households could also contain stepfamilies, with one or both
spouses having children from previous marriages and prior relationships
being raised in blended new units under the same roof. If blacks remarried
more they would have had more of these complex familial arrangements. We
already know that many if not most ex-slaves entering legal marriage for the
first time after the Civil War had also had other marriage-like relationships,
some of which they reconfirmed, others that they started anew, but often
with children from those prior relationships in tow. The conditions of slavery
alone ensured that this trend of stepfamilies and remarriage would not
readily dissipate. The conditions of postwar life were not sufficiently different
to diminish the purposes that these relationships served.

Other qualitative evidence provides more texture and context for understanding the circumstances that led black families to adopt such widely
varying marital and familial forms.[17] The Civil War pension files for widows
of U.S. military veterans reveal strong indications of both the propensity to
marry and to remarry when relationships dissolved and the continuance of
informal marriage. Many if not most widows participated in a combination of
both legal and informal marriages over the course of their lifetimes, as demonstrated by women who married more than once, usually starting before or
during the Civil War and stretching into the late nineteenth century and beyond. In some cases, widows voluntarily gave up their pensions when they remarried rather than risk prosecution for fraud if they tried to keep the benefits
after remarrying. Those who continued to receive benefits covered up their
private lives from the prying eyes of investigators and nosy neighbors or enemies who might turn them in. Exposure could mean loss of a pension or even

prosecution, fines, and jail time. And yet, despite the risks, the widows' files reveal abundant evidence that women did not deprive themselves of the company of men or refuse to form sustained bonds, either legally or informally.

Women who were caught were charged with "adulterous cohabitation or marriage," perjury, filing false claims, and fraud. In some cases, their husbands were prosecuted as well.[18] By some estimates, half of black women on the rolls were subjected to special examinations, compared with only one quarter of whites. Nearly all black women in some localities were subjected to at least one special examination during the time they received benefits. Black women were more closely scrutinized than white women even before the 1882 law that prohibited widows from cohabiting with men. But the federal government also conceded to growing public opinion that marriage was in danger as divorce rates increased and common-law marriage practices persisted doggedly across racial groups. Pension Bureau agents were told to expunge widows discovered to be engaged in "open and notorious adulterous cohabitation" after the deaths of husbands, which they did with renewed intensity. Some agents took liberties to apply the law retroactively anytime during women's widowhood. These attitudes also reflected the tenor of social reform efforts in the 1870s and 1880s aimed at the poor, with increasing emphasis placed on blaming poor people for their own conditions. As more veterans, widows, and minors applied for and received pensions, officials increasingly worried about protecting the nation's coffers from fraudulent claims. African Americans were often singled out in national news reports for criminality and immorality. Special instructions were included for "Colored Claimants" to induce agents to be vigilant.[19]

Government agents kept detailed pension files on hundreds of thousands of veterans and their family members for the purpose of managing the single largest line item (40 percent) of the federal budget by 1890. The pension system was the first large-scale federal social insurance program. But for historians more than a century later, the files provide an unprecedented treasure trove of life histories of mostly working-class people making claims on the basis of entitlement to disbursement in exchange for the service of their husbands, fathers, and sons. Some of the files are quite straightforward, others more complex, depending on the changing circumstances of claimants' lives.[20]

A straightforward approved case looked like this one, exposing the circumstances leading to serial marriages that were common among ex-slaves
and their descendants. Nancy Bass Hearn Thompson was born in 1850. She
married Amaziah Bass in 1863 in Watertown, Tennessee. He enlisted in the
Union Army a year later and died in 1866, leaving her with one child. Nancy
received a pension upon his death but gave it up when she married Smith
Hearn in 1868. Smith died a few years later. She married her third husband,
George W. Thompson, in 1876, and that union lasted until his death in 1920.
At the age of seventy, in financial need no doubt, she applied to have her
pension reinstated, as the widow of her first husband. Nancy, like other widows
whose subsequent marriages ended in divorce or death, was protected by a
1901 law permitting widows who lost their pensions due to remarriage to be
reinstated if they became widowed again.[21]

Women who engaged in serial marriage while they were active on the pension rolls had their own understandings of why they deserved the benefit
regardless of the rules. Their claims were not always easy to sort out, and
their complicated situations made it difficult for bureau agents to assess
whether they fit the regulations, which sometimes worked to the women's
advantage. One woman had a series of marriages: the first by slave custom;
the second, a legalized union, to a soldier who died in the war; and the third
years after his death. She says she had her pension stopped when she
married for the third time but had it resumed when she and her husband
separated. There was no indication of a legal divorce. She was still
married—technically—and thus not eligible for a pension, but she believed
that severing ties with an errant spouse sufficed in ending the marriage. He
"began to drink to excess soon after the marriage, and I ceased to love him
and drove him away from my house," she reported. Her husband's wayward
behavior, she believed, was grounds for her reinstatement on the pension
rolls. She felt she should not be penalized because of his failures. She was
able to strengthen her case to the Pension Bureau by arguing that she later
discovered the marriage had not been legally valid on technical grounds
because the minister who performed it had not paid the required bond. She
won the appeal but was dropped from the pension rolls years later when these
circumstances were questioned anew.[22]

Although most individuals who engaged in serial relationships did so voluntarily when their current relationships ended in divorce or separation, slavery's legacy of involuntary unions and forced separations continued to affect the lives of ex-slaves. The most severe, repeated disruptions from slave sales and the separation of families were evident in what women were called by others or how they identified themselves. Name changes alone could symbolize the treacherous and unstable lives experienced in bondage and after freedom that led to serial relationships. Rebecca, for example, had many surnames over the course of her life, partly the result of multiple slave-ownerships and partly the result of multiple conjugal relationships. She was owned by someone in King William County, Virginia, who sold her to traders in Richmond. Someone in New Orleans bought her, and someone else bought her after that. By the time the war broke out she had four children, born near Greenville, Mississippi, by a man named Henry, though it is not clear that either of them chose to have a relationship. They were paired together after a common sale. Henry died early in the Civil War, and Rebecca did not identify him as a spouse in her pension application. She ended up in Nashville, it appears without her children; perhaps they had been sold away or had died prematurely. Around this time, she called herself by the last name Johnson. Soon after she met and began a relationship with a man with the last name Smith, she called herself Rebecca Smith (Smith was also the name of her last owner). She met and formally married Allen Gathen, a soldier, in 1864. She then became Rebecca Gathen. The regimental chaplain conducted her first legal marriage, which proved short-lived. Her husband died in 1865, whereupon she received a pension as his widow.[23]

Rebecca Gathen may have tried to avoid the risks of losing her monthly stipend as other women did when they remarried. She entered a series of relationships with men with whom she cohabited, short- and long-term, for the rest of her recorded life. When her first legal husband died, she stayed with his troop and shared a tent with another married couple. She took up with Ike Johnson, whom she met at a smallpox hospital, and used his name. They had one son, Gus. Others claimed that Gus's father was Anthony Convington, which she denied. She separated from Johnson, though he died shortly after that in any case. Around 1868, she developed a relationship with

Jim Polk, and they lived together for more than twenty years, during which she called herself Rebecca Polk. Pension Bureau agents opened up an investigation about whether to file criminal charges against her for perjury and filing a false claim. They couldn't prove any legal marriage, but she was dropped from the pension rolls for "open and notorious adultery" with Polk in 1896. Not to be outdone, she appealed, arguing that people of questionable character had falsely testified against her. "I can't see in law or justice where I can be cut off from my lawful pension by the declaration of thieves and murderers or any other unlawful theory the former administrations who[se] efforts were to reduce the pension roll expense," she wrote. She appealed to her status as a deserving woman in need. "Why jump upon widow women and hunt up unlawful testimony against them," she argued, "and make no effort against drunkards, loafers, vagabonds as many of the men drawing pension this day are and no restraint thrown at or around there income from a pension."[24]

Many women who formed a series of domestic partnerships and/or sexual liaisons that were even more casual and not always marriage-like did so for basic economic survival. They often combined wage work with other means of earning money, such as taking in boarders, even when their quarters were spare. But allowing unknown men to share cramped spaces could set off alarm bells among neighbors and pension agents. While boarding transients in their communities was a common way for women to make extra money, the boundaries could be blurred as personal relationships evolved between patrons and clients. When men were spotted hanging on for more than just brief stints, people began to suspect that more was going on than providing food and shelter, especially if there was only one bed in the residence. Pension agents were always interested in prying eyes that claimed to see actual evidence of indiscretions and were willing to go on record saying so. A woman's reputation could be generalized from whatever perceptions "boarding" generated. Assertions might include that "everybody" knew they were sleeping together "same as married people do," or that she "has always had a man" and "wont go two weeks without one." These rumors were hard to quell, even when some of the men testified otherwise: that they slept in the kitchen of a two-room abode; that they paid for room, and sometimes board, or got their meals elsewhere. That they considered the woman always respectable. It all depended on the disposition of the pension agent whether to believe the woman and her supporters' claims or those of her detractors. And of course, those meddlesome neighbors may have been correct.[25]

The pattern of serial monogamy, common-law relationships, and short- and long-term cohabitation evident in these records was a product of customs rooted in Southern slavery and restrictions imposed on the conjugal relationships that could not simply be overturned once slave marriages gained legal recognition and ex-slaves were freely allowed to legally marry. And yet irregular, informal, and repeat marriages were not limited to the Southern population. The pension records of those who lived in the North as free people before the war are also instructive. Free blacks had escaped slavery in the most popular Northern slaveholding states only a few decades ahead of their Southern brethren. They typically entered into protracted periods of indentured servitude, delaying their ability to form and sustain marriages. Most free blacks legally married in the antebellum North, but their ability to do so was challenged by race. That legacy did not disappear easily, any more than it did among those once held in bondage in the former Confederacy.[26]

Serial and informal marriages are evident among African Americans in the North, as they were among many Euro-Americans. This reminds us that statistics indicating conformity to normative standards cannot tell the whole story of marital patterns. Marriage was still a scrappy enterprise, even in mainstream America. Judges throughout the country affirmed the consensus view of the validity of common-law marriage before the Civil War, but late-nineteenth-century reformers worried profoundly about the consequences of irregularity and rising rates of divorce. Marriage was increasingly conceptualized as an institution with public, not just private, interests, which reinforced the calls for greater government oversight.[27]

Congress sponsored a study in 1889, by Carroll D. Wright, the U.S. labor commissioner, to collect national data on marriage and divorce laws in order to assess the state of affairs. Wright discovered that most states did such a bad job of keeping records and requiring licenses that it was hard to draw a precise picture of conjugal patterns. This could not have been news to federal officials, as the familial records of Civil War veterans, based on pension claims, had already revealed national irregularities. Wright's study offered more detailed confirmation and, together with the advocacy of reformers, helped push most states to enact laws to encourage couples to formally wed and obtain licenses. Mississippi instituted one of the strictest laws in 1892 by voiding marriages that did not comply with the new rules. But making informal marriage less appealing and less legally viable did not eliminate common-law practices or judicial sanction entirely. The older view that couples who lived together and acted as "man and wife" should be presumed to be married continued to carry weight. Judges were often loath to invalidate marriages that did not follow exact procedure in a society that still valued the rights to privacy and freedom of action. The strong arm of the state in the nuptial business would be tempered into the twentieth century.[28]

Northern couples also constructed a variety of conjugal relationships over the course of their lives, as partners died and circumstances changed. A woman could be a devout serial bride, with as many as six legal marriages, and as many name changes, stretching from the antebellum era until death after 1900. That was extreme.[29] But many others chose not to legally formalize every single relationship they entered into, meticulously removing themselves from the pension roll with each one and going back on if the marriage dissolved because of death or divorce. As was the case with ex-slaves, Northern blacks engaged in the full range of relationships short of earning the sanction of church or state. In many cases the threat of losing a pension loomed over their decision to skirt the law. When pressed to define their relationships they refused to say that they were married or claimed ignorance about the fact that even cohabiting with men was a violation of pension rules. Or they simply refused to admit to having an intimate relationship with a man, despite evidence to the contrary. "I had my own bed and he had his own bed," one woman noted of her relationship, after years of living with the man, having a child, and using his name. She refused to call him anything other than a "boarder." Her neighbors, however, contradicted her claims by saying they lived as husband and wife. Still, the Civil War widow could insist that the man in question only called her "his old woman"—which was not the same as calling her his wife.[30]

These cases, whether of Northern or Southern origin, are compelling not simply because they provide evidence of the persistence of informal relationships and entangled connections but also because they expose the undercurrent of how and why couples constituted their relationships as they did. Most of these relationships fell into the inescapable category of married or acting married, but many were more casual domestic arrangements formed out of economic and emotional needs. When a spouse died, the surviving partner wanted other companionship. Men and women needed the complementary skills attached to traditional gender roles, which brought money into the household and provided services like cooking, cleaning, and washing clothes. Some retained these relationships without legalizing them, in part, perhaps, because the economic stakes were too high for widows on the roll, but also for reasons that couples always had to negotiate. What was the nature of their relationship and how did they each define it? Did the benefits of state sanction outweigh the costs? These were not always conscious decisions. What started out one way, as a casual encounter, a temporary place to stay, could end up being more meaningful and longer lasting as time passed.[31]

The Pension Bureau tended to look suspiciously on some of these attachments especially when they were formed between younger women and older men, as the population of veterans aged. One woman admitted that she ended up living with a veteran after the unfortunate death of his wife, immediately after the funeral. They lived together for a while but did not marry until close to the time of his own death. Death-bed marriages were especially frowned on. The Pension Bureau considered these women not "deserving" widows but "mercenary" brides.[32]

Although it would be difficult to quantify the frequency of legal remarriage, common-law marriages, and cohabiting relationships, the Civil War widows' pension files are very suggestive. They expose just how complicated relationships of ex-slaves and their descendants continued to be. Serial relationships helped to buttress and to remake marital and familial bonds in response to crises throughout the full span of people's lives. "Until death do us part" was sanctioned in the vows that African Americans could exchange when they tied the knot, unlike what slaves were forced to fudge at the altar. "Until buckra (the white man) part you" was no longer applicable. Many couples, both young and old, were parted only by death. But most faced a range of events and circumstances that made their marriages vulnerable and their ability to keep their vows of permanence problematic to uphold. They faced the challenges that all couples did when trying to merge the proverbial twosomes into one and mediate the conventional gender dynamics of married life. But they also carried extra burdens, unique to the legacy that slavery had wrought and that Jim Crow, disfranchisement, and exploitative labor systems continued to invoke. Du Bois's study and the discourse among black elites more generally did not fully appreciate the constraints they were up against. Elites appeared to take for granted that the laws had been reversed and African Americans' intimate affairs were no longer burdened by legal impediments. What they did not and could not see was that the legal system was tied in Gordian knots. Reversing the lack of legitimacy of slave marriages and the progeny they produced proved far more difficult to achieve than anyone could have foreseen.

God made marriage and the white man continued to make and adjudicate the laws, though African Americans' short-lived suffrage rights during Reconstruction allowed for crucial interventions. Under slavery, Southern law was a potent instrument that contributed to the destruction of slave marriages and families and afforded little protection. After the war, marriage and slavery were no longer completely at odds. Deficient morality was used under slavery as a rationale for not allowing people of African descent to marry, but with emancipation it then became a reason for allowing them to marry and, in some cases, forcing them to do so to guarantee their faithfulness. Paternal legitimacy once denied to slaves was now "restored," at least theoretically in many states, giving children access to inheritance from ex-slave fathers as well as mothers. The marriage rights of former slaves were treated as dormant—denied under bondage, they became available on emancipation. Marriage had been defined as a contract in the antebellum era, which was used to justify why chattel could not marry, as they had no civil rights or civil effects. Ironically, after emancipation marriage was considered not a contract but a status relationship. Stripping marriage of civil liberties meant denying it federal protections, which made it difficult for interracial couples to defend their rights to marry in opposition to increasingly prohibitive state laws. Racial proscriptions were now directed more toward marriages between whites (especially women) and blacks (especially men) than toward unions between intraracial couples.[33]

Still, the marriages of African Americans were not entirely out of the legal wilderness. The framing of postwar state laws legitimizing slave marriages would have consequences that would take decades to fully arbitrate as ex-slaves and their descendants faced the reality that the predicaments produced under the old regime could never be fully reconciled within the new system.

Judges in every slaveholding state, and many others where former slaves lived, had to adjudicate the legal lines of slave marriages and the questions of their effects on matters related to the legitimacy of children, inheritance, property rights, criminal prosecutions of marital violations, and liability. Many of these cases made their way up from municipal and probate courts to the states' highest courts of appeal. Appellate jurists seemed inclined to affirm the marriages of ex-slaves more often than not. This meant affirming cases from lower courts that ruled in this way or reversing those that did not. But there was no guarantee, as there were many instances in which they overruled lower courts that validated slave marriages. These cases demonstrate that marriages formed during slavery were still highly contestable and still unsettled within the law at the turn of the century. The circumstances of the married lives of slaves determined how they would be interpreted retroactively, whether they would be rewarded or punished based on how they measured up to postbellum standards. Even the U.S. Supreme Court ruled in 1875 that slave marriages were not legitimate, in direct disdain of congressional Civil War and postwar legislation; it reverted back to status quo ante when marriages formed under slavery were not legitimate because slaves could not make contracts.[34]

Judges faced a variety of civil and criminal cases that rested on how to regard slaves' marriages. The criminal cases grew out of the conditions that nonlegal recognition produced, putting former slaves in the bind of facing prosecution for arrangements that had once not only been tolerated but also demanded and sanctioned. Appellate judges were especially prone to affirm the prosecution of bigamy cases, most often produced by failure to comply with postwar marital laws. Women and men were sent to prison for bigamy, in some cases because they did not formally divorce their slave spouses or informal partners with whom they had taken up after emancipation before legally marrying as freedpeople. In effect judges upheld the legitimacy of slave marriages in the abstract by using the postwar laws to criminalize slave social relations. African Americans were also prosecuted for marriage-related offenses disproportionately. They were prosecuted for "fornication," with police actually arresting people in bed, sometimes on unconnected charges and then simply adding on fornication or bigamy.[35]

Litigants who were unrelated to slaves often had vested interests in challenging the postwar laws that legitimized slave marriages, in order to reap the material benefits that came through intestate property, claims by creditors, or corporate liability for injury or death. But even former slaves (along with their descendants and other kin) often found themselves at odds in principle with legitimizing slave marriages as they came before bar and bench to represent their economic interests and the legacies for future generations. They often tried to abrogate slave marriages when they worked against them, especially with respect to deciding the division of property. This meant that fights among family members (often including ex-slaves themselves) posed one of the most common challenges to slave marriage legitimacy brought before appellate courts.[36]

A case in Texas summarizes some of the overall problems of a postwar legal regime in which laws passed to bring the marriages of former slaves in line with the marriages of free whites were often used punitively. Lizzie and Alex Davis were married as slaves in 1864 but parted ways in 1876. A couple of years later, Lizzie was charged with committing adultery with London McKnight and prosecuted for violating the state's postwar marriage law, for which she was fined $100. One witness testified to nearly catching the couple in the act when he entered Lizzie's cabin unexpectedly and found them appearing to rise from a pallet on the floor. Given previous rumors, "his mind received the impression that the defendants had been having carnal intercourse." (This gross intrusion of the couple's privacy went unremarked even by the defense counsel.) Another witness claimed that Lizzie had stayed out all night with McKnight, and that on a different occasion she woke up one morning and found the couple sleeping on a lounge. Though Lizzie and Alex were considered married by Texas law, they had done nothing to formalize their relationship and nothing to legally end it. The lower court found that they were considered married, regardless. Thus, Lizzie had committed adultery with London McKnight, based on inferences and suspicions drawn from witnesses. In a rare move by the defense, the lawyers challenged the racial logic of the Texas law's blanket coverage of ex-slave marriages. They challenged the power of the constitutional convention to pass such a law and make all existing cohabiting relationships of former slaves legally binding for life without their consent. It is one of the few cases that offered an explicit critique of how such laws engendered unjust criminalization: "As well might the Convention have said that all white men who are now keeping a mistress shall be considered as married to her." The appeals court, however, had no problem with the interpretation of the law or the power of legislators, but it did find error with witnesses allowed to speculate about sex acts inferred but not actually witnessed. The judgment was reversed and remanded.[37]

The postwar laws in most slaveholding states came under scrutiny in many late-nineteenth-century appellate cases. The courts had to contend with the issue of jurisdiction and the application of laws to those who lived outside of the state at the time they were passed. The rule of recognition or comity, that states should honor the legality of marriage legalized in other states, was not automatically accepted though it was affirmed in most jurisdictions. Could a person's marriage and the legitimacy of their offspring in one state be determined and enforced by another? The supreme court of Florida stated bluntly: "The lex loci rei sitae must prevail and the different States of this Union are foreign countries to each other." The Florida court had no interest in having its cases dictated by a sister state's marriage laws. Rather, this court, and others, preferred to make decisions about slave marriage in which all the relevant parties were residents or former residents of their state, which posed problems for families that dispersed over time and sought fair hearings wherever they landed.[38] Judges wanted to use their discretion as they deemed appropriate, choosing to accept or reject precedents from other jurisdictions.

Some judges disagreed about the intention of lawmakers reflected in postwar laws. In Florida, for example, a judge claimed that the legislature did not intend to validate slave marriages nor legitimize the offspring of such relationships, and in so doing make them eligible to inherit property. This was a problem in states in which postwar laws legitimized existing couples co-habitating at the time the laws were passed, but did not retroactively affirm antebellum marriages.[39] Florida was one of the few states that did not make explicit its intention to legitimize the offspring of slaves. Another judge in the same state criticized the effect of the initial postwar law passed in Florida, which gave ex-slaves nine months to register their unions: it "subjected to prosecution persons who had in good faith consented to the marriage rela-tion at common law and an evil which originated from it was the punishment as criminals of persons who, without any actual intent of committing wrong, had assumed and consented to the marriage relation in good faith." If it had been strictly enforced, he argued, the jails would have been filled with per-sons found in violation of fornication and adultery from "innocent cohabita-tion as husband and wife." But fortunately, the legislature changed the law within three months.[40]

Most cases that pertained to postbellum laws had to do with whether or not couples abided by the letter of the legislation that affirmed ex-slave con-jugal ties. States that required ex-slaves to actively reaffirm their marriages by registering them faced many challenges. Rulings, especially in the immediate postwar years, could be very harsh and contradictory. Could marriages be affirmed without registration? Void if they failed to comply? A Kentucky couple was married according to slave custom in 1850 and cohabitated until the death of the wife in April 1866, a few months after the state passed a law requiring registration. Their marriage was invalid, according to the court. This despite the fact that Kentucky acknowledged slave marriages retroac-tively. But in this instance that proviso did not take effect without active registration.[41] Several years later, in 1870, a different verdict was reached in a similar case. A couple that had been married as slaves were manumitted a decade before the war. They did not legalize their union once freed, though their relationship continued. The husband later left the first wife and remar-ried. The lower court upheld the first slave marriage, despite the absence of registration upon emancipation. The appeals court agreed on this point: "the highest duty which they owed to themselves, their children, and to mo-rality was to consummate and make perfect a union which had hitherto existed only by reason of the consent and approbation of their owners." And yet it considered the first marriage valid and the second one "pretended" because the first wife was still alive at the time of the second marriage and the first couple never legally divorced.[42] These cases demonstrate the inconsistency of the judiciary even within the same state. Laws that were designed to legitimate slave marriages could not be taken for granted. Ex-slaves could be held to the technicalities of registering their unions, even in states where such registration was not required. Still, it was in the interest of the states to validate, rather than overturn, marriages even in past tense. They understood that state legislatures had been especially concerned about the repercussions of not acknowledging antebellum slave marriages for the legitimacy of the slaves' descendants. That would have let black fathers off the hook for taking care of their children. Justices in other states reached similar conclusions, that postwar registration laws were ultimately directory, not mandatory. It was better if ex-slaves formally married. But it was best that the state acknowledge those relationships regardless.[43]

States were not sympathetic to former slaves using the laws strategically to advance certain advantages not intended by lawmakers and contrary to the general purposes of promoting marriage. This did not prevent people from creative attempts to use the laws in whatever ways they wished. African Americans, for example, could use the absence of registration to retroactively void their own nuptials when their relationships soured. Such was the case of one husband after thirty-nine years of marriage and a late change of heart, followed by a remarriage. Or the case of a wife who tried to deny the parental rights of her former husband, who abandoned her after emancipation by arguing that they had not abided by the postwar registration law.[44]

The main problem with automatic laws was that they did not take into account whether the parties affected wished to be considered married under the new legal rules. Individuals or couples could argue that they had never consented to be married under such rules, a core violation of the marriage of free persons. And indeed many did just that, driving up the incidents of divorce in some states. The law did not force people to marry who had not otherwise formed voluntary relations, unlike the old days of slavery. But it did impose a structure on those who were affiliated, acting as though they were married, without the law behind them. That formalization entailed the presumption of a desire for permanence and the need to legally dissolve what the law had bound. Self-divorce was no longer acceptable under these terms, but this did not stop individuals from trying, sometimes leading to prosecution for bigamy if they attempted to remarry. Ex-slaves could and did challenge these laws on the grounds that they were "forced" to marry against their express will. Automatic laws also raised concern about how to discern different forms of marital-like relations. A judge in Tennessee argued that the law was never intended to validate "meretricious cohabitation," for example.[45]

The most numerous cases that judges faced in which slave marriage had to be adjudicated concerned the disposal of property through inheritance, and such cases were consequential beyond the former slaveholding states. Very few Americans in the late nineteenth century had property to pass on to future generations. And only about a quarter of decedents left wills designating how their property should be distributed among their heirs. The predominance of rural societies, illiteracy, and an inchoate legal profession discouraged formalized distribution of assets. Most people died intestate, even when they left behind resources, leaving it up to judges to decide how to apply the rules of succession. African Americans of slave parentage entered into a still-evolving system of inheritance with a distinctly American perspective of republican government moving increasingly in the direction of shedding its British common-law roots, which favored traditions of patrilineal descent, patriarchal control, and the perpetuation of the aristocracy. Over the course of the nineteenth century, laws related to property inheritance underwent significant reform to encourage wider ownership and democratic governance. The most significant transformations were in the expansion of the rights of married women to own and have greater control over property, above the rights of their husbands.[46] But on the whole, men, as husbands and fathers, still maintained their control. How the families of formerly enslaved African descendants fit into this quagmire of property alienation was not so easily discerned.

One set of cases pitted family members of deceased and intestate individuals against creditors and outside interests. In one example the right of children to inherit the property of their father was called into question because they and their parents were former slaves. The case was even more complicated because the father had two sets of children by two mothers. But in this situation, a judge in Alabama ruled that slave marriages were good in common law and thus were "legal natural marriages jure divino," permitted by state and church. They were not "mere adulteries or fornications." If there be any doubt about their status, the results of the Civil War had elevated former slaves to citizens and "their heritable blood was restored, the impediment of slavery which obstructed it before, being thus removed." The offspring of such relationships were thus not bastards and were entitled to be treated as legitimate human beings, and all were eligible to inherit their father's property. This was clearly a case of postwar revisionism, overturning antebellum common-law logic to suggest that the legal effects of slave marriage had only been held in abeyance, waiting to be ratified upon emancipation.[47]

The legalization of the marriages of ex-slaves conferred the right to family membership, to preserve and pass on legacies of their heritage and material resources. But the heart of the matter was that the judiciary (state and federal) was still ambivalent about how to apply the accepted principles of family property distribution when the core issue of slave marriage legitimacy was still not fully settled. Despite postwar laws, the disadvantages of slave marriage had not been fully removed and continued to be litigated. Judges had to determine how to regard multiple serial marriages formed under slavery to decide which if any should take precedence over the others. They had to decide the relationship between first marriages formed under slavery and later marriages formed after freedom. Should children of spouses married under slavery be treated differently from those of couples married under the rules of freedom, for purposes of inheritance? Did former slave parents have any entitlement to the estates of their offspring, who were also slaves? The courts had to determine if the rights of spouses took precedence over those of their stepchildren, who may have been former slaves. Grandchildren made claims on the estates of their elder kin, often involving multiple lines of descent flowing from multiple spouses. The courts had to deal with a morass of collateral heirs as well. Siblings asserted rights to the estates of other siblings, contesting surviving spouses and children. Overwhelmingly, most appellate-level cases involved overlapping and competing family disputes, which meant that some members argued against the validity of slave marriages in order to protect or assert their own economic interests.

The standing of slave marriages would rest in part on how spouses were regarded after the death of one or the other. Given that property was still primarily distributed through paternal lines, this meant that the dower rights of widows were most often challenged. Couples made decisions about their marriage and their relationship to each other in the context of slavery that served to protect their interests back then. But their nimbleness in circumventing the restraints of bondage produced anomalies that would later haunt the reckoning of the status of their relationship, with severe costs to their rights to manage, exchange, preserve, and transfer property. A freeman who purchased his slave wife, but then put her in trust to another (white male guardian) to allow her to remain in the state, made her a nominal slave. In so doing, he challenged the legal status of their marriage. Upon his death, the question would become, could she be considered his widow with dower rights to an estate that had been built upon the earnings and contributions of both spouses? Creditors and reputed kin challenged her rights to the estate on the grounds that she could not be married because of her status as a slave. It would take many decades of litigation, but in this case, the woman was declared the rightful widow and the marriage to her spouse affirmed.[48]

One set of cases involved the problem of overlapping ex-slave widows and the question of which one should be considered the legal wife. Those entangled relationships sometimes occurred during slavery, when a man could have been married to more than one woman at a time. The right of his children from the earlier relationships to share his estate might be challenged on the basis of bigamy by his current wife and widow.[49] Here is one poignant example. A slave couple was legally married in 1866, retroactively recording their 1847 marriage according to the postwar rules of their state. Shortly thereafter, however, the husband decided to abandon his wife and went on to legally marry, he presumed, another woman. Upon his death the courts were forced to determine which woman was the rightful widow. The first wife claimed the right to dower in his lands. The second wife, who had lived with him until his death, also claimed to be his widow. In truth, he had a bigamous relationship with both women during slavery, when he was "in the habit of visiting" the second wife and had a child by her before the presumed official marriage to her in 1866. The courts decided that the second marriage was the "illicit" one. It could not be sanctioned as it was labeled "cohabiting like man and wife," which was not the same as "cohabiting as man and wife."[50]

The widow of the first marriage was legitimate. This was by no means a universal rule. In other cases, second marriages were considered legitimate after first marriages ended by separation, even if against the will of couples. As we have seen, such separations occurred frequently in the context of the Civil War.[51]

Another set of cases involved first marriages as slaves and subsequent marriages after manumission or emancipation. Judges had to decide if the first marriage, by virtue of being first, deserved to take priority over subsequent relationships. A second marriage, however, might be considered a repudiation of the first, in which case the second could be seen as the binding one, especially if it was later ratified after emancipation. The first marriage could be considered "inchoate and imperfect obligations" and thus voidable by either party, again reinforcing antebellum notions that these marriages were not legal. Some judges continued to lean on "proof" that enslaved couples had reaffirmed their marriage vows according to postwar laws in order to recognize them. But first marriages were not always invalidated even if they failed to meet the requirements of postwar registration laws. The U.S. Supreme Court opinion that marriage laws were directory, not compulsory, helped bolster the validity of marriages even absent compliance with registration laws.[52]

Conflicts often evolved around the children of slaves, with one set of children (and their descendants) born of slave marriages pitted against the children of one parent in a marriage formed under freedom. Many cases made their way up the chain of state courts that affirmed the postwar laws declaring that children of slave parents were made legitimate and thus entitled to the appropriate share of their estates. But there were cases, even when slave marriages were supposed to have been recognized retroactively by laws passed in the postwar period, in which the legitimacy was rejected. The imposition of this prerequisite was especially unforgiving when applied to couples who were not able to take advantage of the postwar laws because of the untimely death of one spouse. The children of a Union Army veteran were at a disadvantage in inheriting from their mother who survived the soldier and also had children by another man. The soldier died before he even had the opportunity to register his relationship with his wife, which was used against his children's rights to their mother's property.[53]

The children of enslaved parents were harmed by circumstances that enslaved couples could not control, like forced separations. Robert Church became a wealthy businessman in postwar Memphis, Tennessee. He had married Margaret in Louisiana when both were slaves, and they had a daughter, Laura. The couple was separated against their will, but Robert was able to maintain contact with his daughter. He sent her to Fisk University to be educated. Laura contested his will when he died, claiming to be a legitimate heir. The court instead favored her half-siblings, including Mary Church Terrell, one of the first black women college graduates. Laura could not inherit property from her father's estate because his marriage to her mother was not considered valid.[54]

Inheritance issues adjudicated through the courts were always contentious battles between family members or between family members and outside interests. They were never easy. Questions about the status of slave marriages only amplified the difficulties of these struggles. Postbellum laws sanctioning these relationships presupposed that the legal questions had been resolved. Lawmakers could not have been any more straightforward about their intentions to give standing to past relationships and halt, if not reverse, the disabilities that had previously accrued to them. Matters on the ground were not as straightforward as state legislatures presumed, however. The laws were simplistic compared with the monumental complexity that the absence of legal recognition had wrought upon generations of African Americans. There was no legislative language that could adequately take into account the convoluted scenarios arising out of bondage that would lead to just outcomes for former slaves and their descendants. Lawmakers did not have the vision to foresee what they could not and did not fully comprehend. The cases themselves do not necessarily represent what all ex-slaves experienced. Most never had reason to go to court for civil matters; most were more likely to be summoned for alleged crimes. But they speak powerfully about the lingering effects of slavery on African-American marriages and families. They expose an ambivalent and contradictory judicial system decades after universal emancipation, and they offer insight into what ex-slaves gained and how they continued to suffer.

As African Americans reckoned with the lasting effects of slavery on their marriages and families at the end of the nineteenth century, these relationships were scrutinized from multiple directions, by those who wished to defend and improve them and by others who wished to use them for ideological fodder to demonstrate that black people were not fit to live in freedom in Western civilization. The Progressive era was in its beginning stages, as a generation of reformers emerged to counter the debilitating effects of industrialization and modernization on the lives of ordinary people. African Americans who were a part of this group directed their energies toward the distinctive conditions that their communities faced, especially as they moved from the rural South into urban spaces. Black reformers were also at a disadvantage. Their ability to make demands in the political arena had diminished after Reconstruction ended and the last U.S. troops pulled out, restoring home rule to former Confederate states. The situation steadily grew worse, ending in disenfranchisement by the 1890s. Unable to make progress in electoral politics, they used their social capital on other projects that seemed achievable, leading to a more inward turn toward intraracial matters in the private sphere.[55]

It is no wonder that black middle-class spokespersons spent so much attention on reforming sexual behaviors, marriage, and family organization. It was an established article of faith among reformers at least since abolitionism that the most onerous aspect of slavery was the destruction of black families. Emancipation had signaled the possibilities for profound transformation, but it also presented new concerns. Slavery could no longer be blamed for the social ills that plagued the black community; what mattered now were "those social conditions which he creates for himself," as Eugene Harris, a professor at Fisk University, stated. "It is no longer our misfortune as it was before the war: it is our sin, the wages of which is our excessive number of deaths. Always and everywhere, moral leprosy means physical death." The stakes for mating and marrying according to dominant standards were literally life and death. Black people had only themselves to blame if they could not measure up to dominant standards within their new circumstances.[56]

Harris's language was so fatalistic because he and others were compelled to respond to a rising tide of racialist discourse that hinged on assumptions of African-American sexual incontinence. Reportedly high rates of infant and adult mortality and overall poor health statistics led to scientific studies and Social Darwinist writings that explained these as peculiar "race traits." Black men were bestial, black women insatiable, and their children sexually precocious, according to this logic. At worse, these were inborn traits. At best, they were signs of lower evolutionary stages on the scale of human potential yet to be fully achieved. Hence, the obsessive attention that elites paid to correcting these problems. Collective survival was at stake, and so the century's end saw the emergence of a statistical discourse of black dysfunctionality. Frederick Hoffman, one of the leading pioneers in this field, made this judgment abundantly clear in his pathbreaking book on the Negro Problem using vital statistics to justify his claims: *Race Traits and Tendencies of the American Negro* (1896). "All the facts obtainable which depict truthfully the present physical and moral condition of the colored race, prove that the underlying cause of the excessive mortality and diminishing rate of increase in the population is a low state of sexual morality, wholly unaffected by education," he wrote with confidence.[57] As long as black pathology ran rampant, African Americans could never achieve racial equality no matter how much they tried, he argued. The race was moving backward since slavery, a system under which they were better off. Black reformers constructed a discourse that claimed a history of subjugation could be overcome with training and education. The burden they embraced was to prove that the views of the Hoffmans of the world were erroneous by changing the habits, environments, and behaviors of blacks.

Black marriage, family, and homes became the source of political imaginings of a disenfranchised people. Idealized domesticity offered ways of expressing African Americans' ambitions for belonging to the nation they seemed unable to achieve in any other way. "Marriage constitutes the basis for the home," wrote journalist and civic leader Gertrude Bustill Mossell. "Home is undoubtedly the cornerstone of our beloved Republic. Deep planted in the heart of civilized humanity is the desire for a resting place that may be called by this name, around which may cluster life-long memories." Mary Church Terrell, educator and civil rights activist, agreed wholeheartedly with this sentiment. "It is only through the home that a people can become really good and truly great," she argued. And it was no coincidence that many of these activists were women, rising up and taking on more public leadership roles to meet this goal. The focus on the home enhanced the possibilities for women to expand their role in society, as the primary caretakers of the domestic sphere. They expanded their influence through schools, local clubs, state organizations, and combined efforts through the National Association of Colored Women (NACW), founded in 1896 and led by Terrell, its first president. When Terrell delivered an address two years later to the National American Women's Suffrage Association in Washington, D.C., she emphasized the NACW's focus on home as a sacred domain upon its formation. "Homes, more homes, better homes, purer homes is the text upon which our sermons have been and will be preached," she asserted.[58]

Middle-class reformers focused so intently on the home because it was perceived to be threatened by assault from both within and without. While they could do little to stem the tide of the external political and economic threat, they felt empowered to take on the internal propensities. Some constructed a narrative asserting that things were getting worse. Marriage was in decline, Alexander Crummell, Episcopal priest and educator, argued, noting large numbers of single men and women in cities refusing to tie the knot. Eugene Harris put the onus slightly differently. He argued that there was an "apparent increase of immorality" that was chiefly due to "neglect." Among those who did marry, mothers were forced to work outside of the home, which made them ill-equipped to take care of their children and their domiciles. Men had failed to do their part by not earning enough to uphold their patriarchal breadwinning roles. From yet another perspective, Fannie Barrier Williams, feminist and educator, believed the problem was that the masses of women were not getting the attention they deserved as homemakers: "These women have been left to grope their way unassisted toward a realization of those domestic virtues, moral impulses and standards of family and social life that are the badges of race respectability. They have had no special teachers to instruct them." Like Terrell, she highlighted the work of the club movement, led by the NACW, which was designed for this purpose of correction. She could not have chosen a more appropriate self-description of this leadership class: "It is nothing less than the organized anxiety of women who have become intelligent enough to recognize their own low social condition and strong enough to initiate the forces of reform."[59]

The elite spoke confidently, out of an unrelenting belief in individualism and meritocracy, that black people could will themselves into conforming to normative strictures of marital and family practices and remake themselves as respectable according to the dominant culture. The adoption of middle-class decorum was perceived to be a route to repudiating white supremacist discourse and admittance into full inclusion in the nation-state. With nowhere else to go but home, black people hoped to use domesticity as an emancipatory strategy for uplifting the race (see Fig. 8.6). Changing the behavior of individuals and couples one at a time would lead to personal and group transcendence. Both race women and race men shared in the freedom dreams of idyllic domesticity and patriarchal homes, though feminists advocated an enlarged space for women within the private sphere and public arena. Either way, it put an extra burden on women as exemplars and teachers with unique feminine attributes. Women were eager to accept the mantle of their heightened duties and powers. The idea of marriage long embraced by the white middle class took on an extra urgency for African Americans. Marriage was to be more than a relationship of individual fulfillment or class solidarity and material advancement. It was a partnership of mutual respect and conjugal ardor that could advance the goals of the race. More than anything, it spoke volumes as the ultimate badge of progress and respectability.[60] To make a convincing case for their stance on the marital route to advancement and to disseminate it broadly, the elite turned to the tools of the nascent social sciences. Du Bois's findings in *The Philadelphia Negro* and *The Negro American Family* capture the broader thinking of this group and their optimistic forecasts for how legal, monogamous, Christian marriage was the route out of racial oppression. They put their faith in state structures to prove African Americans' worth. They missed both what black families had already achieved and what they were still up against. Conformity to mainstream norms had not saved elites and middle-class strivers from racist malevolence. Neither could it save the entire race of people.

By 1899, African Americans had literally traveled far and wide in search of lost family members and done all they could to reconstitute their kinship

Dr. Thomas William Burton having the connubial knot tied,
August 3, 1893, to Miss Hattie B. Taylor.

Fig. 8.6 Dr. Thomas William Burton (a former slave) and Hattie B. Taylor Burton of
Springfield, Ohio, are portrayed on their wedding day. Their attire is suggestive of elite
couples adopting ceremonies from the dominant culture by the end of the nineteenth
century. African-American newspapers were filled with notices of such affairs, in which
they described these events and guests in great detail.

ties. Legal marriage provided an important foundation for them to fully access and secure their rights to spouses, children, and the integrity of their households. But induction into this new regime and overturning prior conditions and practices were far more complicated than the preachments of elites would suggest. Under slavery blacks were required to marry outside the law and to have children outside of marriages that were unprotected from the capricious breach of the third flesh. Under freedom, a new regime of respectability was imposed and expected. Despite the implementation of new laws designed to retroactively recognize the legitimacy of black conjugal relations, the laws did not and could not fully comprehend the turmoil they had sanctioned over many generations that emancipation alone could not erase. Slave society had benefited from not allowing slaves to marry, and free society would now punish the reverse, despite the impossibilities of undoing the entanglements it formerly commanded.

Nonetheless, by the turn of the twentieth century, African Americans demonstrated an overwhelming propensity to marry, despite the legacy of slavery that still haunted their relationships. They not only married but also remarried, at rates largely equal to and, in some cases, in excess of whites. They continued to adopt a diverse array of intimate and familial forms that included informal arrangements, many moving from legal marriage to common-law marriage (or the reverse) in serial relationships over the course of their lives. Black marriages have historically looked different from white marriages, owing to the dictates of a society dedicated to white supremacy and a legal system that had regarded them as property for over two centuries. Upon emancipation, the mere injunction to formally marry did not and could not take into consideration the difficulty of reconciling doctrines designed to buttress a slave system with newly implemented laws that were presumed to be race neutral. And yet where African Americans succeeded in overcoming the harsh judgments that had hampered their intimate affairs, their contemporaries failed to notice even as liberal reformers and social scientists were eager to produce such results. What they achieved was remarkable not only because of how much African Americans had to overcome, but also because they gained access to legal marriage as it was undergoing significant transformations, with increasing government oversight.

At the same time, this was a period in which white working-class industrial workers faced some of their toughest trials forming and sustaining families in a period of economic tumult as the manufacturing sector shifted and
expanded. They married at lower rates than ever before, compared with
better-paid middle- and upper-class whites in white-collar and managerial
jobs. Ex-slaves and their descendants were buffered from such wide disparities within race because there was less class stratification. African Americans
were overwhelmingly locked at the bottom of the economy, predominantly in
the rural South. But as the United States industrialized and urbanized even
more after the turn of the century and African Americans moved off the farms
to the North, West, and into cities, they would be hurt by the convergence of
growing racial and class inequalities that would affect their ability to marry
and sustain viable families. The idea that marriage could be an effective liber-
ating strategy that would rescue the race from economic and social ills would
be even harder to sustain in the twentieth century.[61]

Epilogue

Legacies and Challenges

African-American marriage and family have been regarded as intractable problems throughout American history by adversaries and allies alike. There have hardly been moments of reprieve since the Middle Passage. Forms of marital union and family structure were perceived to be vestiges of blacks' African past rather than products of bondage. They were used to help rationalize slavery and have since served as a barometer for judging the fitness of black people for living in a "civilized" society. The path to the American dream and the key to eradicating social and economic inequalities have frequently been tied to how the race measures up to familial standards that are moving targets across the landscape as the nation has been transformed and the history of the family has morphed along the way. But the measurements have never been fairly discerned or based on the material realities of black life in any era, particularly under slavery and the subsequent systems of oppression that took its place after the Civil War. Responsibility for the essential failure has been attributed to African Americans' own inability to conform to white marital patterns that have always differed from their own because of brutal external forces. White families are judged as the standard against which black families are assessed as dysfunctional in comparisons that refuse to account for the conditions that white supremacy created and commanded in order to sustain itself and prosper for centuries.

The history of African-American marriage in the nineteenth century teaches us about a pattern that has been continually replicated with each iteration of the seemingly forward movement toward greater freedom and justice. African-American marriage under slavery and quasi-freedom is a story of twists and turns, of intimate bonds being formed, sustained, broken, and repeatedly reconstituted under the duress of one of the most oppressive institutions invented by human beings and in the aftermath of its destruction. Bondage wreaked utter havoc on black families. Masters did all they could to maintain control over the enslaved, and especially over the profits that accrued from their productive and reproductive labor. African Americans were denied the legal rights to marriage and control over their own children in order to perpetuate their status as laboring bodies and to further the expansion of capital fueling the global market. Property rights in the ownership of chattel took precedence over the integrity of couples' relationships, otherwise slavery could not have been preserved in its particularities. But race, and not just slavery, established the basis for denigrating intimate bonds. African Americans, regardless of status—Northern or Southern, free or slave— faced harsh reprisals from racist ideas and practices that impinged on their relationships.

And yet despite the reign of terror that slavery spawned and no matter how much it altered and disfigured black marriages, it did not and could not annihilate them. African Americans lived and loved and were creative, resourceful, and resilient in building marital forms and kinship ties that functioned for their survival. We should never lose sight of the depth of feelings and affection that undergirded these relationships and the sacrifices that blacks were willing to make for the sake of preserving them. However counterintuitive it may have seemed to abolitionists, free blacks forced into a corner were willing to give up everything, even freedom itself, in order to safeguard their husbands, wives, and children and stay together. Slaveholders eagerly used this sentiment to their own advantage in the hostile 1850s through socalled voluntary slavery. Yet it was the will to prioritize the bonds of affection that outsiders did not honor that motivated this new arrangement. Desperate times led to desperate measures that illuminate the precariousness of the quasi-freedom of a select few before the Civil War.

When the Civil War broke out the pattern of external forces exerting excruciating pressures on expressions of black love would appear to experience its first real rupture. It was a provisional moment of both optimism and peril, of uncertainty and new dictates. The war created a pathway for putting black marriages on new footing, tied to new possibilities for freedom and citizenship generated by blacks' flight from bondage and their willingness to serve the Union Army as military workers and soldiers and in whatever unofficial capacities were allowed. African Americans used the war to preserve the Union, which would advance their own liberation. They forced the Union Army and the federal government to deal with them not just as individuals but as persons embedded in familial networks that may have spanned across geographical boundaries as people fled and moved about during the war. This magnified the far-reaching effects of their service, the benefits, and the costs to all involved.

While under slavery, African Americans were subjected to the will of masters; under new systems of wartime emancipation, those following the foot trails of the Union Army would face new encumbrances from outside interests. Missionaries and abolitionists realized the need to extend marital rights to the enslaved and seized the opportunity to encourage blacks to (re)marry under the flag. The federal government led the way in alliance with these nongovernmental allies to conduct ceremonies for fugitive couples arriving in contraband camps during the war and ex-slaves working in free-labor experiments on confiscated plantations. Though most African Americans were eager to embrace this new opportunity, not all did. This led to a heavy dose of coercion by those who believed they knew best. Many managers of plantation labor and officials of freedmen's villages and contraband camps went so far as to make marriage a requirement for ex-slaves living together under their auspices. Marriage was seen and used as a tool to prepare former slaves for the responsibilities and duties of citizenship. The marital dictates helped inculcate middle-class ideals of domesticity (male-headed households with women and children as dependents) among recently emancipated slaves, in order to structure their personal lives to be consistent with the organization of the republican society they were about to enter.

The federal government's role in marriage-making was unprecedented. By entering the business of regulating black marriages it trespassed on functions previously considered the exclusive prerogative of the states. The government was ambivalent, even if enthusiastic, about promoting marriage so long as it did not conflict with other priorities. Soldiers' wives and children were not always treated with the respect they deserved, as infamous incidents like the violent expulsion from Camp Nelson, Kentucky, revealed in 1864. As black marriages were inducted into the national body politic, the government continued to mark those relationships by race. The federal government left its mark on black familial relationships and formed opinions about them as a national problem that would endure. Debates in Congress about family policies brought forth all the stereotypes of black inferiority from the antebellum era, making them a matter of public record. But some of the ex-slaves' most vociferous liberal defenders refuted many of them for the sake of winning the war, preserving the nation-state, and even safeguarding the integrity of white manly honor.

The practice of marriage under the flag was expanded after universal emancipation and fell under the direction of the Freedmen's Bureau during Reconstruction. The bureau's first goal was to reunite family members who had been separated. Former slaves struggled just to survive, to find food and shelter. But they gave high priority to putting the pieces of shattered family lives back together, either by recommitting (or not) to previously forced unions or establishing their own familial footing as free people. The tensions between marriage as a deeply personal relationship and as a highly regarded public institution became evident as they reunited their families. The bureau encouraged legal marriage for ex-slaves and chided reluctant white Southerners to retroactively recognize those formerly unsanctioned bonds. Most African Americans moved to legalize their existing relationships or enter into their first marriages as legal spouses. But informal domestic arrangements that had of necessity flourished still persisted. Common-law marriage, serial marriage, overlapping relationships, and nonmarried parenting all coexisted, with some individuals moving in and out of different configurations over their lives.

The federal government prevailed upon Southern states to take over the role of sacrilizing former slave marriages, but the latter created cruel contradictions and ironies. Yet another iteration of external forces was imposed on ex-slaves as legislatures passed new laws designed to belatedly recognize black marriages and give legitimacy to the children that resulted from them. Irregular intimate relationships that had been standard, and required, under bondage were now frowned upon and penalized. States used marriage laws not just to grant a new civil right to African Americans but also to punish them for their seeming deviance. Suddenly, marriage did not look as attractive or as self-empowering when legislators and landlords used it to discipline workers by making them conform to inflexible rules. Once reluctant former slaveholders discovered after emancipation that legal marriage was a convenient tool to keep workers in line and to advance the economic interests of white elites. The federal government would continue to play a role, long after the war and Reconstruction, to ferret out and punish intimate arrangements that did not conform to dominant ideals. Compared with white women, black Civil War widows who continued to receive benefits into the twentieth century were subjected to extra scrutiny of their marital and sexual behaviors.

African Americans, especially women, discovered that marriage was a double-edged sword. It was yet another form of bondage, another relationship founded in property rights. This became especially clear in the conception of emancipation in the context of the war. Black men earned their freedom and citizenship as military workers and soldiers, while women gained theirs as wives. The form of marriage that outsiders were eager to inculcate subjected women to stricter submission to men of their own race than they had been previously accustomed to. Once the third flesh had been formally removed from the equation of intimate relationships, former slaves had to renegotiate their marriages anew. Couples faced the contradictions, troubles, and joys of intimacy that all married people contended with, within evolving, but still exigent conditions of freedom. And yet, despite the new rights of coverture, of husband's rights over their wives, black married couples' rights were always subjected to derogation. Those who chose to legalize their marriage understood the trade-offs they made. They carefully weighed the costs and the privileges, though women were more vulnerable to striking out on their own as single women or mothers with children. The perquisites of marriage were not necessarily equally shared, but each sex needed the other to get by in an agricultural economy, leading most to follow the route of lawful wedlock.

The emergence of sharecropping as the dominant organization of agriculture by the 1880s depended on a ready pool of dispossessed workers. Legal marriage and nuclear families had been written into the laws in some states by this time and prescribed by landowners to ensure a steady supply of tenants who could be locked into landlessness. This requirement marginalized other kinds of family formations that ex-slaves had previously drawn on for cultural and economic survival. African Americans valued family but did not idolize a narrow type of it. The insistence on nuclear families, however, scattered those individuals who would have been incorporated into extended kinship networks away from rural areas to find work. Black marriage, once again, had found a purpose in the new economic order to serve external interests that resulted in aiding their own exploitation. Landowners took liberties to interfere in the private affairs of workers when their tensions spilled out beyond their cabins into the fields or threatened the stability of the workforce. So-called marital infractions were used as a pretext, not just to punish relationships gone awry, but also to crush acts of labor resistance designed to improve working conditions and compensation. Meddlesome landowners, not unlike antebellum slave-owners, claimed the authority to assert control over labor contracts above the interests of couples' marriage contracts and their rights to conduct their families as they determined was best for them.

A discourse of respectability, established in the antebellum era, was reinvigorated in the last decade of the century. A small but rising black middle class, self-appointed leaders, looked to reforming marriage and family as a way to prove that blacks were worthy of citizenship and equal rights. The political prospects for making change through electoral politics had dimmed after the achievement of suffrage rights was stripped away. By the 1890s, leaders could only look inward, to the home and to the family, to fulfill any hopes of helping the race measure up. They were put on the defensive by a rising tide of racist thought tied to the social sciences eager to write off black humanity on the basis of perceived moral and sexual infractions. As some scholars have argued, while African Americans have largely identified as heterosexual (a position of privilege in mainstream society), they have not been treated as heteronormative; they have been judged as lagging in the ethics of upstanding citizenship for the straight sexes. Black people's oppression has been explained by the inability to conform to conventional social customs and marital behaviors. But their exploitation has been founded in those very conditions that has made it difficult, and sometimes impossible, to live up to those anticipated norms. Elite African Americans struggled with this tension, to elucidate the constraints, but also to chastise those individuals who failed to rise above the cacophony of opposing forces that transfixed their life prospects and limited their ability to display exemplary marital behaviors.[1]

As the twentieth century opened, blackness would continue to be associated with the perversion of domestic ideals. Meanwhile, critics still showed little regard for or acknowledgment of the vicious structures and practices that have inverted cherished mainstream norms. The harms resulting from centuries of exploitation derived from slavery were monumental for African-American families and did not end with emancipation. African Americans continued to be burdened, as they were at every turning point previously, by external impositions that were out of sync with their lived realities and their own collective values.

And yet, a "fully loaded cost accounting" cannot be boiled down to slavery as the source of very different marital trends that cohered almost a century later. It seems especially perverse that the legacy of slavery would be primarily identified as being carried around in the bodies and culture of black descendants and yet be considered bereft elsewhere in American attitudes and institutions, where it has been presumably purged by the distance of time and progressive social change, as Supreme Court justices have argued. Slaveholders are no longer around to make them culpable, and no one else assumes responsibility for the crimes against humanity upon which the nation prospered and from which many non-slave-owning whites (and later generations) benefitted. Nor should slavery's gravest travesty be seen as the deprivation of patriarchy of male headship or the purported aggressive matriarchal substitutes of female headship, which some inferred from later-twentieth-century familial patterns. The intense focus on the replication of gender norms has made one kind of family (nuclear), one kind of construction of gender (men as superordinate and women as subordinate), worthy of social esteem. This preoccupation with imposing narrow ideologies on a diversity of approaches to intimate relationships has diverted attention away from the factors that have had far greater repercussions for marital trends produced by twentieth-century conditions.[2]

By 1900, marriage was nearly universal for adult African Americans still living in a mostly agricultural society, though there were signs of strain on married couples moving into urban areas or those striving to form new relationships in cities in the North and Midwest. It was in the 1940s, however, that black and white marriage rates began to diverge significantly, and they have grown increasingly different ever since. Not by coincidence, the vast middle class (once taken for granted but now threatened) had its origins in this era. This was the first and only major redistribution of wealth in the century brought on by technological innovations, savings from wartime wages, and the infusion of federal dollars into the economy. For the first time in U.S. history the differences between the earnings of blue-collar and white-collar workers shrank. White marriage rates rose after World War II, thanks in no small part to financial subsidies redistributed through the Selective Service Readjustment Act of 1944, also known as the G.I. Bill of Rights. Between 1944 and 1971 the bill handed ninety-five billion dollars to millions of veterans to buy homes, attend college, start businesses, find jobs—and marry. The bill was designed to give returning veterans the resources to settle into married, civilian life. Men who married received more benefits than those who remained single, to encourage them to transition from the nearly all-male world of the military to civilian family life. The entitlement was ostensibly race-neutral, but black veterans, especially in the South, rarely received due benefits from it because it was managed by state and local agencies that were allowed to discriminate in doling out resources and jobs. Black marriage rates declined as a result of the artificially low racial quotas that constricted employment markets, slowed entry into homeownership, and curtailed educational opportunities. Marriage rates have grown increasingly divergent by race ever since.[3]

All marriages are strongly correlated historically with the health of the economy and the job market, as some sociologists have documented quite convincingly, but the marriages of blacks have suffered even more because they are at the bottom of the economy. In every decade since the 1940s, African Americans have experienced a steady growth of permanent unemployment. It is one thing to face difficulty finding jobs during temporary periods of economic distress. It is quite another to be permanently thrust out of the job market with no prospects for employment in sight. Deindustrialization in the 1960s and 1970s added further insult to injury, ratcheting up racial and class inequities even further. No wonder African Americans did not experience the marriage boom that whites enjoyed in the postwar period. The economic factors have been exacerbated by cultural changes as well, such as the growth of women's employment outside of the home and advances in education. These and other cultural factors have contributed to the overall decline of marriage rates throughout the industrial world, but the economic trends have been most destructive to African Americans.[4]

The Civil Rights Movement generated other important milestones in the history of racial justice and heightened expectations of black meritocracy, of achieving and overcoming racial wrongs. But whatever progress it engendered it could not and did not reverse the pattern of racial disparity in marriage rates at midcentury or since. While civil rights victories enabled the growth of the black middle class, they did more to secure voting rights, desegregation of public accommodations, and expand participation in electoral politics. Economic gains among some African Americans were made in the transition from agricultural and domestic work to industrial jobs. The strongest gains occurred in the public sector, which were fragile and subjected to shifts over the next several decades. But this progress existed alongside a deep well of chronic, permanent unemployment that continued to grow for a significant segment of the most vulnerable, particularly as they moved from the rural South to the industrial North in the era of the world wars.[5] The irony of progress, in fact, may confuse more than it reveals, as detractors use it as a baton for beating down the notion that declines in marital rates or nuclear families could be driven by anything other than individual (or racial) moral dysfunction.

Economic distress has been compounded by and linked to other factors. Heterosexual marriage-making requires roughly even numbers of women and men in the population, but unusual demographic shifts have occurred since the late twentieth century that have threatened the potential for mating. High mortality rates, caused by homicides, heart and respiratory diseases, especially among black men, have lowered their numbers in the pool of marriageable men. In addition, a new variation on an old theme of disfranchisement and unjust imprisonment emerged as the "war on drugs" and mandatory prison laws led to mass incarceration, especially since the 1970s and 1980s, despite the decline of violent crime. More African Americans are under the supervision of the criminal justice system today (probation, parole, jail, or prison) than were enslaved in 1850. This has pushed down marriage rates even further by depriving communities of disproportionate numbers of men in their prime years. Men, and growing numbers of women, are barred, by laws and discriminatory practices, from participating in mainstream economic and political activities that make sustaining marriages while imprisoned and forming them once released difficult at best.[6]

It is an undeniable fact that by 1990 African-American marriage rates were the opposite of where they began in 1900. By the last decade of the twentieth century, most blacks over eighteen (40 percent) were unmarried, whereas the reverse was still true for whites, most of whom (72 percent) were married. Although some policymakers, pundits, and even some scholars wrongly argue that recent patterns of black marriage are the product of slavery, they tend to ignore or minimize the impact of racism on the social, economic, and political conditions that have shaped family formation in the intervening decades long after slavery ended. However much marriage may seem to be simply the by-product of decisions made by individuals to tie or forgo tying the knot, the institutional character of marriage is never more visible than when it is constricted by larger economic, political, and social forces that impact people's ability to think of marriage as materially feasible and emotionally sustainable.[7]

The close connection between economic inequality and the decline of black marriage rates has persisted into the twenty-first century. In 2008, 32 percent of blacks over eighteen were married, compared with 56 percent of whites. But African Americans have also served as the canaries in the coal mine, projecting warnings of ominous situations that await other populations. We have arrived at a moment in time when a few are gaining access to all the accoutrements of citizenship and national belonging and the many appear to be stalling or falling further behind. We see this in how economic inequality is also eroding the prospects for marriage and family formation for working-class and underemployed whites, as it had also done at the end of the nineteenth century during a different period of wide class disparities. Marriage is now perceived to be a privilege of affluence rather than a strategy for survival that working people were able to rely on in the past. It is often considered to be more aspirational than realizable, as something held in high esteem but out of reach by people struggling economically. Marriage is seen as something you do after you have established your material foundation in life, not as a means of building up from it. This problem is further complicated by the fact that many people have outsized expectations of what a spouse should be—not just an equal partner but the perfect soul mate.[8]

And yet, we have also arrived at a historic moment when marriage equality is legally available to all, regardless of sexual orientation, thanks to the U.S. Supreme Court ruling in *Obergefell v. Hodges* in 2015. Still, it is worth remembering that marriage has always been a privilege not even accessible to all straight people. Groups that have been historically deprived of equal marriage rights discover upon achieving them that they need to be supported by economic and social equality in order to truly afford the dignity and the choice intended. Once they gain these rights it becomes more difficult to reject them without incurring disrespect and even anger, further marginalizing unique domestic arrangements that refuse to be (or are unable to be) corralled under the aegis of legal marriage. And marriage equality, of course, is not without its ironies. Members of the LGBTQ (lesbian, gay, bisexual, transsexual, queer) community can now legally wed, yet they are still not fully guaranteed many other basic civil rights that protect against discrimination on the basis of sexual orientation. The achievement of marriage equality, whether in the nineteenth century for African Americans or in the current day for everyone, may ultimately be a Faustian bargain won until and unless our society is committed to providing the commensurate institutional supports that allow people to marry and form healthy, safe, and functioning families of their choosing in a context in which true equality and justice prevail.[9]

ABBREVIATIONS

NOTES

ACKNOWLEDGMENTS

ILLUSTRATION CREDITS

INDEX

Abbreviations

AMA Archives	American Missionary Association Archives, Amistad Research Center, Tulane University
FSSP	Freedmen and Southern Society Project, University of Maryland
NARA	National Archives
Official Records	United States War Department, *The War of the Rebellion: A Compilation of the Official Records of the Union and Confederate Armies*
PAR	Petitions Analysis Records
Pension claim	Civil War Widows' Pension Claims, Records of the Veterans' Administration, Record Group 15, National Archives, Washington, D.C.
RG 105	Records of the Bureau of Refugees, Freedmen, and Abandoned Lands, Record Group 105
SCAHC	South Carolina Archives and History Center
SCHS	South Carolina Historical Society
SHC, UNC	Southern Historical Collection, University of North Carolina
Slavery Petitions Project	The Race and Slavery Petitions Project, University of North Carolina at Greensboro
WPA Narratives	George P. Rawick, ed., *The American Slave: A Composite Biography* (Westport, Conn.: Greenwood Press, 1972)

Notes

Introduction

1. See Annette Gordon-Reed, *The Hemingses of Monticello: An American Family* (New York: W. W. Norton, 2008). Fictional and nonfictional accounts of Jefferson and Hemings have been published for more than two centuries. They are only the most popular representation of the interracial dyad that fascinates Americans. Much of the literature on sexual liaisons and marriage involving blacks and free people during the slavery era focuses on interracial relations. For example, see Peggy Pascoe, *What Comes Naturally: Miscegenation Law and the Making of Race in America* (New York: Oxford University Press, 2010); Joshua Rothman, *Notorious in the Neighborhood: Sex and Families across the Color Line in Virginia, 1787–1861* (Chapel Hill: University of North Carolina Press, 2003); Martha Hodes, *White Women, Black Men: Illicit Sex in the Nineteenth-Century South* (New Haven, Conn.: Yale University Press, 1997); Daniel L. Schafer, *Anna Madgigine Jai Kingsley: African Princess, Florida Slave, Plantation Owner* (Gainesville: University Press of Florida, 2003). Tiya Miles, *Ties That Bind: The Story of an Afro-Cherokee Family in Slavery and Freedom* (Berkeley: University of California Press, 2006), departs from the preoccupation with black/white interracial relations. And for a wider sampling, see Martha Hodes, ed., *Sex, Love, Race: Crossing Boundaries in North American History* (New York: New York University Press, 1999).

2. The marriage certificate of Ellen and Moses and research on the Hunter lineage were provided by Bruce Hunter, the family's historian. The narrative is based on decades of painstaking research in archival records and oral histories. The family history is constantly evolving as we gain access to more data using the latest technology of digitized research, as well as DNA evidence. The biographies detailed here are based on the best available evidence, though some of the information, especially birth dates, is inconsistent in different documents. Documents consulted include U.S. Department of Commerce, Bureau of the Census, Manuscript *Population Schedules, 1830–1870,* Ancestry.com;

Estate of Alexander Hunter, 1864, in Abbeville Estate Papers, South Carolina Department of Archives and History, Columbia, South Carolina; Estate of Charles Simmons, 1822; Estate Papers, 1800–1867 (compliments of Bruce Hunter); General Index to Estate Papers, 1800–1931, South Carolina, Probate Court (Laurens County), Ancestry.com.

3. Vance Creek was originally a part of a white congregation, but it became independent in 1875. Andrew Swilling, a black pastor, became affiliated by 1870 and officiated at the Hunter wedding in 1873. See "Records of the Baptist Church at Vans Creek" (ca. 1869), Office of the Probate Judge, City Hall, Elberton, Georgia. (Compliments of Bruce Hunter.)

4. Quoted in Eugene Genovese, *Roll, Jordan, Roll: The World the Slaves Made* (New York: Random House, 1974), 481.

5. Frances E. Dolan, *Marriage and Violence: The Early Modern Legacy* (Philadelphia: University of Pennsylvania Press, 2009), 3–6.

6. Other scholars who have defined gradations of slaves' (and ex-slaves') intimate and marital relationships include Noralee Frankel, *Freedom's Women: Black Women and Families in Civil War Era Mississippi* (Bloomington: Indiana University Press, 1999); Anthony E. Kaye, *Joining Places: Slaves in the Neighborhoods in the Old South* (Chapel Hill: University of North Carolina Press, 2007); Laura F. Edwards, *Gendered Strife and Confusion: The Political Culture of Reconstruction* (Urbana: University of Illinois Press, 1997); Nancy Bercaw, *Gendered Freedoms: Race, Rights, and the Politics of Household in the Delta, 1861–1875* (Gainesville: University Press of Florida, 2003); Katherine Franke, *Wedlocked: The Perils of Marriage Equality: How African Americans and Gays Mistakenly Thought the Right to Marry Would Set Them Free* (New York: New York University Press, 2015).

7. Nancy Cott, *Public Vows: A History of Marriage and the Nation* (Cambridge, Mass.: Harvard University Press, 2000), 1.

8. Quoted in *Freedom: A Documentary History of Emancipation, 1861–1867*, Series 2, ed. Ira Berlin, Joseph P. Reidy, and Leslie S. Rowland, *The Black Military Experience* (New York: Cambridge University Press, 1982), 672.

9. Hendrik Hartog, *Man and Wife in America: A History* (Cambridge, Mass.: Harvard University Press, 2000); Marilyn Yalom, *A History of the Wife* (New York: HarperCollins, 2000); Michael Grossberg, *Governing the Hearth: Law and the Family in Nineteenth-Century America* (Chapel Hill: University of North Carolina Press, 1985); Cott, *Public Vows;* Mary Beth Norton, *Founding Mothers and Fathers: Gendered Power and the Forming of American Society* (New York: Random House, 1996); Calvin Schermerhorn, *Money over Mastery, Family over Freedom: Slavery in the Antebellum Upper South* (Baltimore, Md.: Johns Hopkins University Press, 2011), 29–40.

10. Kathleen M. Brown, *Good Wives, Nasty Wenches, and Anxious Patriarchs: Gender, Race, and Power in Colonial Virginia* (Chapel Hill: University of North Carolina Press,

1996), 108–120; Jennifer Morgan, *Laboring Women: Reproduction and Gender in New World Slavery* (Philadelphia: University of Pennsylvania Press, 2004).

11. Wendy Warren, *New England Bound: Slavery and Colonization in Early America* (New York: Liveright, 2016), 156.

12. Brown, *Good Wives*, 108–120.

13. Saidiya V. Hartman, *Scenes of Subjection: Terror, Slavery, and Self-Making in Nineteenth-Century America* (New York: Oxford University Press, 1997).

14. Amy Dru Stanley, *From Bondage to Contract: Wage Labor, Marriage, and the Market in the Age of Slave Emancipation* (Cambridge, England: Cambridge University Press, 1998), 24. Also see Stephanie McCurry, *Masters of Small Worlds: Yeoman Households, Gender Relations, and the Political Culture of the Antebellum South Carolina Low Country* (New York: Oxford University Press, 1995), 86–91; Carol Lasser, "Voyeuristic Abolitionism: Sex, Gender, and the Transformation of Antislavery Rhetoric," *Journal of the Early Republic*, 28 (Spring 2008): 83–114.

15. Grossberg, *Governing the Hearth;* Peter W. Bardaglio, *Reconstructing the Household: Families, Sex, and the Law in the Nineteenth Century South* (Chapel Hill: University of North Carolina Press, 1995).

16. See Stanley, *From Bondage to Contract*.

17. Margaret Burnham, "An Impossible Marriage: Slave Law and Family Law," *Law and Inequality*, 5 (1987): 187–225.

18. William Craft, *Running a Thousand Miles for Freedom; or, the Escape of William and Ellen Craft from Slavery* (London: William Tweedie, 1860; reprint ed. Miami: Mnemosyne Publishing Co., 1969), 16.

19. Craft, *Running a Thousand Miles for Freedom*, 27.

20. Ibid., 29.

21. This fact has been lost in most of the scholarship on the black family, which has been preoccupied with long-standing judgments based on comparisons of slaves to elite whites. See Edwards, *Gendered Strife*, 54, 60–64; Bardaglio, *Reconstructing the Household*.

22. See, for example, Herbert G. Gutman, *The Black Family in Slavery and Freedom, 1750–1925* (New York: Vintage, 1977); Brenda Stevenson, *Life in Black and White: Family and Community in the Slave South* (Oxford, England: Oxford University Press, 1970).

23. On gender and slavery, see Jacqueline Jones, " 'My Mother Was Much of a Woman': Black Women, Work, and the Family under Slavery," *Feminist Studies*, 8 (Summer 1982): 235–269; Deborah Gray White, *Ar'n't I a Woman?: Female Slaves in the Plantation South* (New York: Norton Press, 1985); Jacqueline Jones, *Labor of Love, Labor of Sorrow: Black Women, Work, and the Family from Slavery to the Present* (New York: Basic Books, 1985); Elizabeth Fox-Genovese, *Within the Plantation Household: Black and White Women of the Old South* (Chapel Hill: University of North Carolina Press, 1988).

24. Books on the transition to freedom during the Civil War and Reconstruction eras that address marriage include Stanley, *From Bondage to Contract;* Leslie A. Schwalm, *A Hard Fight for We: Women's Transition from Slavery to Freedom in South Carolina* (Urbana: University of Illinois Press, 1997); Frankel, *Freedom's Women;* Edwards, *Gendered Strife;* Ira Berlin and Leslie S. Rowland, eds., *Families and Freedom: A Documentary History of African-American Kinship in the Civil War Era* (New York: The New Press, 1997); Dylan C. Penningroth, *The Claims of Kinfolk: African American Property and Community in the Nineteenth-Century South* (Chapel Hill: University of North Carolina Press, 2002); Bercaw, *Gendered Freedoms;* Kaye, *Joining Places;* Thavolia Glymph, *Out of the House of Bondage: The Transformation of the Plantation Household* (Cambridge, England: Cambridge University Press, 2008); Elizabeth Regosin and Donald Shaffer, eds., *Voices of Emancipation: Understanding Slavery and Reconstruction through the U.S. Pension Bureau Files* (New York: New York University Press, 2008); Mary Farmer-Kaiser, *Freedwomen and the Freemen's Bureau: Race, Gender, and Public Policy in the Age of Emancipation* (New York: Fordham University Press, 2010); Katherine M. Franke, "Becoming a Citizen: Reconstruction Era Regulation of African American Marriages," *Yale Journal of Law and Humanities,* 11 (Summer 1999): 251–308; Franke, *Wedlocked.*

25. Franke, *Wedlocked;* Frankel, *Freedom's Women;* Edwards, *Gendered Strife;* Bercaw, *Gendered Freedoms;* Kaye, *Joining Places;* Farmer-Kaiser, *Freedwomen and the Freemen's Bureau.*

26. Cott, *Public Vows,* 77–104.

27. Literary critics have been especially helpful in thinking about the cultural trends in black marriage: Claudia Tate, *Domestic Allegories of Political Desire: The Black Heroine's Text at the Turn of the Century* (New York: Oxford University Press, 1992); Ann duCille, *The Coupling Convention: Sex, Text, and Tradition in Black Women's Fiction* (New York: Oxford University Press, 1993).

28. W. E. B. Du Bois, ed., *The Negro American Family* (Atlanta, Ga.: Atlanta University Press, 1908); E. Franklin Frazier, *The Negro Family in the United States* (Chicago: University of Chicago Press, 1939). Also see Du Bois, *The Philadelphia Negro* (Philadelphia: University of Pennsylvania, 1899; reprint ed., 1996), which is the starting point for his views on the family.

29. James H. Sweet, "Centering Families in Atlantic Histories," *William and Mary Quarterly,* 70 (April 2013): 251–272; Penningroth, *The Claims of Kinfolk.*

30. See Kenneth M. Stampp, *The Peculiar Institution: Slavery in the Ante-Bellum South* (New York: Vintage Books, 1956); Stanley Elkins, *Slavery: A Problem in American Institutional and Intellectual Life* (New York: University Library, 1963).

31. Daniel Patrick Moynihan, *The Negro Family: The Case for National Action* (Office of Policy Planning and Research, United States Department of Labor, March 1965). For the contemporary response, see Lee Rainwater and William L. Yancey, eds., *The Moynihan*

Report and the Politics of Controversy (Cambridge, Mass.: MIT Press, 1967). For recent debates about Moynihan among mostly sociologists, see Douglass Massey and Robert J. Sampson, eds., *The Moynihan Report Revisited: Lessons and Reflections after Four Decades* (Thousand Oaks, Calif.: Sage Publications, 2009).

32. Gutman, *The Black Family in Slavery and Freedom,* responded most directly to Moynihan. Also see Genovese, *Roll, Jordan, Roll;* Robert William Fogel and Stanley L. Engerman, *Time on the Cross: The Economics of American Negro Slavery* (Boston, Mass.: Little, Brown and Co., 1974); John W. Blassingame, *The Slave Community: Plantation Life in the Antebellum South* (Oxford, England: Oxford University Press, 1979); Walter Allen, "The Search for Applicable Theories of Black Family Life," *Journal of Marriage and the Family,* 40 (1978): 117–129; Niara Sudarkasa, "Interpreting the African Heritage in Afro-American Family Organization," in Harriette Pipes McAdoo, ed., *Black Families* (Thousand Oaks, Calif.: Sage Publications, 1981), 29–48.

33. Angela Davis, "The Black Woman's Role in the Community of Slaves," *The Black Scholar: Journal of Black Studies and Research,* 3 (December 1971): 2–14; White, *Ar'n't I a Woman?;* Jones, *Labor of Love;* Fox-Genovese, *Within the Plantation Household.*

34. See White, *Ar'n't I a Woman?;* and Stevenson, *Life in Black and White.*

35. Historians who deemphasize the dominance of nuclear families include Stevenson, *Life in Black and White*; Allan Kulikoff, *Tobacco and Slaves: The Development of Southern Cultures in the Chesapeake, 1680–1800* (Chapel Hill: University of North Carolina Press, 1986); Ann Patton Malone, *Sweet Chariot: Slave Family and Household Structure in Nineteenth-Century Louisiana* (Chapel Hill: University of North Carolina Press, 1992); Jo Ann Manfra and Robert Dykstra, "Serial Marriage and the Origins of the Black Stepfamily: The Rowanty Evidence," *Journal of American History,* 72 (1985): 18–44; Wilma Dunaway, *The African-American Family in Slavery and Emancipation* (Cambridge, England: Cambridge University Press, 2003); Larry E. Hudson, Jr., *To Have and to Hold: Slave Work and Family Life in Antebellum South Carolina* (Athens, Ga.: University of Georgia Press, 1997); Damian Alan Pargas, *The Quarters and the Fields: Slave Families in the Non-Cotton South* (Gainesville: University Press of Florida, 2010); Penningroth, *The Claims of Kinfolk;* Kaye, *Joining Places.*

36. Some scholars, post-revisionists, have held to arguments of the nuclear family ideal or dominance: Emily West, *Chains of Love: Slave Couples in Antebellum South Carolina* (Urbana: University of Illinois Press, 2004); Orville Burton, *In My Father's House Are Many Mansions: Family and Community in Edgefield County, South Carolina* (Chapel Hill: University of North Carolina Press, 1985); Robert William Fogel, *Without Consent or Contract: The Rise and Fall of American Slavery* (New York: W. W. Norton, 1992); Stephen Crawford, "The Slave Family: A View from the Slave Narratives," in Claudia Goldin and Hugh Rockoff, eds., *Strategic Factors in Nineteenth-Century American Economic History* (Chicago: University of Chicago Press, 1992), 331–350. Also see Daina Berry, *Swing the Sickle for the Harvest Ripe: Gender and Slavery in Antebellum*

Georgia (Urbana: University of Illinois Press, 2007), 69–72, which shows evidence of both diversity and nuclear families in certain counties.

37. See Stevenson, *Life in Black and White;* Malone, *Sweet Chariot;* Manfra and Dykstra, "Serial Marriage and the Origins of the Black Stepfamily"; Dunaway, *The African-American Family in Slavery and Emancipation;* West, *Chains of Love;* Hudson, *To Have and to Hold;* Penningroth, *Claims of Kinfolk;* Kaye, *Joining Places;* Burton, *In My Father's House Are Many Mansions;* Fogel, *Without Consent or Contract;* Crawford, "The Slave Family: A View from the Slave Narratives"; Frankel, *Freedom's Women;* Edwards, *Gendered Strife;* Bercaw, *Gendered Freedoms.*

38. Historians have grappled with black marriage mainly in the context of these controversies about the black family more generally. The topic has been covered mostly as book chapters, though there are a few monographs devoted specifically to slave marriage. The existing literature tends to cover several decades and is typically limited to specific locations. See West, *Chains of Love;* Rebecca J. Fraser, *Courtship and Love among the Enslaved in North Carolina* (Jackson: University of Mississippi Press, 2007); Francis Smith Foster, *'Til Death or Distance Do Us Part: Love and Marriage in African America* (New York: Oxford University Press, 2010).

39. See, for example, Orlando Patterson, *Rituals of Blood: Consequences of Slavery in Two American Centuries* (New York: Basic, Civitas, 1998); Kay S. Hymowitz, *Marriage and Caste in America: Separate and Unequal Families in a Post-Marital Age* (Chicago: Ivan R. Dee, 2006).

1. "Until Distance Do You Part"

1. Henry Box Brown, *Narrative of the Life of Henry Box Brown, Written by Himself* (Manchester, England: Lee and Glynn, 1851), 2, electronic edition, Documenting the American South, University of North Carolina, Chapel Hill.

2. Ibid., 33.

3. Ibid., 46–47.

4. Ira Berlin, *Generations of Captivity: A History of African-American Slaves* (Cambridge, Mass.: Harvard University Press, 2003), 159–244; Walter Johnson, *Soul by Soul: Life inside the Antebellum Slave Market* (Cambridge, Mass.: Harvard University Press, 1999); Michael Tadman, *Speculators and Slaves: Masters, Traders, and Slaves in the Old South* (Madison: University of Wisconsin Press, 1989); Steven Deyle, *Carry Me Back: The Domestic Slave Trade in American Life* (New York: Oxford University Press, 2006); Edward Baptist, *The Half Has Never Been Told: Slavery and the Making of American Capitalism* (New York: Basic Books, 2014); Adam Rothman, *Slave Country: American Expansion and the Origins of the Deep South* (Cambridge, Mass.: Harvard University Press, 2005).

5. On the chattel principle, see Johnson, *Soul by Soul,* 19.

6. Tadman, *Speculators and Slaves;* Johnson, *Soul by Soul;* Berlin, *Generations of Captivity;* Baptist, *The Half Has Never Been Told;* Rothman, *Slave Country.*

7. Ibid.

8. Damian Alan Pargas, *The Quarters and the Fields: Slave Families in the Non-Cotton South* (Gainesville: University Press of Florida, 2011); Calvin Schermerhorn, *Money over Mastery, Family over Freedom: Slavery in the Antebellum Upper South* (Baltimore, Md.: Johns Hopkins University Press, 2011); Tadman, *Speculators and Slaves;* Berlin, *Generations of Captivity,* 190–194, 209–215, 226–230; Johnson, *Soul by Soul,* 33–36, 39–40, 64–65, 122; Marie Jenkins Schwartz, *Born in Bondage: Growing Up Enslaved in the Antebellum South* (Cambridge, Mass.: Harvard University Press, 2000), 156–174; Wilma King, *Stolen Childhood: Slave Youth in Nineteenth-Century America* (Bloomington: Indiana University Press, 2011), 91–114; Heather Andrea Williams, *Help Me to Find My People: The African American Search for Family Lost in Slavery* (Chapel Hill: University of North Carolina Press, 2012), 1–118; Susan Eva O'Donovan, *Becoming Free in the Cotton South* (Cambridge, Mass.: Harvard University Press, 2007); Cheryl Ann Cody, "Sale and Separation: Four Crises for Enslaved Women on the Ball Plantations, 1764–1854," in *Working toward Freedom: Slave Society and Domestic Economy in the American South,* ed. Larry E. Hudson Jr. (Rochester, N.Y.: University of Rochester Press), 119–142; Scott Nesbit, "Scales Intimate and Sprawling: Slavery, Emancipation, and the Geography of Marriage in Virginia," *Southern Spaces* (2011): 1–23; Richard Follet, "Gloomy Melancholy: Sexual Reproduction among Louisiana Slave Women, 1840–1860," in *Women and Slavery: The Modern Atlantic,* vol. 2, ed. Gwyn Campbell, Suzanne Miers, and Joseph C. Miller (Athens: Ohio University Press, 2008), 54–99; Cheryl Ann Cody, "Cycles of Work and Childbearing Seasonality in Women's Lives on Low Country Plantations," in *More Than Chattel: Black Women and Slavery in the Americas,* ed. David Barry Gaspar and Darlene Clark Hine (Indianapolis: University of Indiana Press, 1996), 61–78.

9. Ibid.

10. Ibid.

11. Ibid.

12. Harriet Jacobs, *Incidents in the Life of a Slave Girl* (1861; reprint ed. Dover Publications, 2001), 33.

13. Lunsford Lane, *The Narrative of Lunsford Lane, Formerly of Raleigh, N.C.* (Boston, Mass.: J. G. Torrey, Printer, 1842), 11, electronic edition, Documenting the American South, University of North Carolina, Chapel Hill.

14. Thomas H. Jones, *A Slave for Forty-Three Years, Written by a Friend, as Related to Him by Brother Jones* (Boston, Mass.: Bazin and Chandler, 1862), 30, electronic edition, Documenting the American South, University of North Carolina, Chapel Hill.

15. Also see Benjamin Drew, ed., *North-Side View of Slavery: The Refugee or the Narratives of Fugitive Slaves in Canada. Related by Themselves, with an Account of the*

History and Condition of the Colored Population of Upper Canada (Boston, Mass.: John P. Jewett, 1856), 123; Jessie Sparrow, in George P. Rawick, ed., *The American Slave: A Composite Biography* (Westport, Conn.: Greenwood Press, 1972), South Carolina, vol. 3, pt. 4, 126, hereafter cited as WPA Narratives; Warren Taylor, WPA Narratives, Arkansas, vol. 10, pt. 6, 274; Sarah R. Levering, *Memoirs of Margaret Jane Blake of Baltimore, Maryland* (Philadelphia, Pa.: Press of Innes and Son, 1897), 13; Henry Bibb, *Narrative of the Life and Adventures of Henry Bibb, an American Slave, Written by Himself* (New York: Published by the author, 1849), 38, electronic edition, Documenting the American South, University of North Carolina, Chapel Hill; John W. Blassingame, ed., *Slave Testimony: Two Centuries of Letters, Speeches, Interviews, and Autobiographies* (Baton Rouge: Louisiana State University Press, 1977), 374–375.

16. See Eugene Genovese, "'Our Family, White and Black': Family and Household in the Southern Slaveholders' World View," in *In Joy and Sorrow: Women, Family, and Marriage in the Victorian South, 1830–1900*, ed. Carol Bleser (New York: Oxford University Press, 1991), 69–87; Amy Dru Stanley, *From Bondage to Contract: Wage Labor, Marriage, and the Market in the Age of Slave Emancipation* (Cambridge, England: Cambridge University Press, 1998); Lacy Ford, "Reconfiguring the Old South: 'Solving' the Problem of Slavery, 1787–1838," *Journal of American History,* 95 (June 2008): 95–122; Carol Lasser, "Voyeuristic Abolitionism: Sex, Gender, and the Transformation of Antislavery Rhetoric," *Journal of the Early Republic,* 28 (Spring 2008): 83–114; Michael D. Pierson, "'Slavery Cannot Be Covered Up with Broad Cloth or a Bandanna': The Evolution of White Abolitionist Attacks on the 'Patriarchal Institution,'" *Journal of the Early Republic,* 25 (Fall 2005): 383–415.

17. Lasser, "Voyeuristic Abolitionism"; Pierson, "'Slavery Cannot Be Covered Up with Broad Cloth or a Bandanna.'"

18. Bibb, *Narrative of the Life and Adventures of Henry Bibb,* 192.

19. See the literature on slave marriage: Herbert G. Gutman, *The Black Family in Slavery and Freedom, 1750–1925* (New York: Vintage, 1977); Eugene Genovese, *Roll, Jordan, Roll: The World the Slaves Made* (New York: Pantheon, 1974); John W. Blassingame, *The Slave Community: Plantation Life in the Antebellum South* (Oxford, England: Oxford University Press, 1979); Deborah Gray White, *Ar'n't I a Woman?: Female Slaves in the Plantation South* (New York: Norton Press, 1985); Jacqueline Jones, *Labor of Love, Labor of Sorrow: Black Women, Work, and the Family from Slavery to the Present* (New York: Basic Books, 1985). Also see Elizabeth Fox-Genovese, *Within the Plantation Household: Black and White Women of the Old South* (Chapel Hill: University of North Carolina Press, 1988); Brenda Stevenson, *Life in Black and White: Family and Community in the Slave South* (Oxford, England: Oxford University Press, 1970); Ann Patton Malone, *Sweet Chariot: Slave Family and Household Structure in Nineteenth-Century Louisiana* (Chapel Hill: University of North Carolina Press, 1992); Schwartz, *Born in Bondage,* 177–211; Jo Ann Manfra and Robert Dykstra, "Serial Marriage and the

Origins of the Black Stepfamily: The Rowanty Evidence," *Journal of American History*, 72 (1985): 18–44; Wilma Dunaway, *The African-American Family in Slavery and Emancipation* (Cambridge, England: Cambridge University Press, 2003); Larry E. Hudson, Jr., *To Have and to Hold: Slave Work and Family Life in Antebellum South Carolina* (Athens: University of Georgia Press, 1997); Pargas, *The Quarters and the Fields;* Dylan C. Penningroth, *The Claims of Kinfolk: African American Property and Community in the Nineteenth-Century South* (Chapel Hill: University of North Carolina Press, 2002); Emily West, *Chains of Love: Slave Couples in Antebellum South Carolina* (Urbana: University of Illinois Press, 2004); Rebecca J. Fraser, *Courtship and Love among the Enslaved in North Carolina* (Jackson: University of Mississippi Press, 2007); Francis Smith Foster, *'Til Death or Distance Do Us Part: Love and Marriage in African America* (New York: Oxford University Press, 2010); Williams, *Help Me to Find My People*, 47–88.

20. Several historians have discussed the gradations that slaves used to describe and define their marital relationships, although they do not all agree on where to draw the line between them. My own interpretations are based on the abundant and wide-ranging sources used in researching this book, such as WPA interviews, ex-slave autobiographies, legal cases, and Civil War Widows' Pension Claims. See Noralee Frankel, *Freedom's Women: Black Women and Families in Civil War Era Mississippi* (Bloomington: Indiana University Press, 1999); Anthony E. Kaye, *Joining Places: Slaves in the Neighborhoods in the Old South* (Chapel Hill: University of North Carolina Press, 2007); Laura F. Edwards, *Gendered Strife and Confusion: The Political Culture of Reconstruction* (Urbana: University of Illinois Press, 1997); and Nancy Bercaw, *Gendered Freedoms: Race, Rights, and the Politics of Household in the Delta, 1861–1875* (Gainesville: University Press of Florida, 2003).

21. See especially Kaye, *Joining Places;* Frankel, *Freedom's Women;* Bercaw, *Gendered Freedoms.*

22. Kaye, in *Joining Places* (52–74), tends to draw a sharp line between taking up, living together, and marriage. The latter, he says, were distinguished by ceremonies. My own research shows less clear delineations and more overlap among the categories.

23. Historians of slave marriage have written extensively about forced relationships. I argue here that slaves did not count them as marriage. See Gutman, *The Black Family;* Stevenson, *Family in Black and White;* Manfra and Dykstra, "Serial Marriage and the Origins of the Black Stepfamily"; Dunaway, *The African-American Family in Slavery and Emancipation;* Penningroth, *The Claims of Kinfolk;* Kaye, *Joining Places;* Malone, *Sweet Chariot;* Pargas, *The Quarters and the Fields*, 160–166; Schwartz, *Born in Bondage*, 177–205.

24. Gutman, *The Black Family;* Stevenson, *Family in Black and White;* Manfra and Dykstra, "Serial Marriage and the Origins of the Black Stepfamily"; Dunaway, *The African-American Family in Slavery and Emancipation;* Penningroth, *The Claims of Kinfolk;* Kaye, *Joining Places;* Malone, *Sweet Chariot;* Pargas, *The Quarters and the Fields*, 160–166; Schwartz, *Born in Bondage*, 177–205; Frankel, *Freedom's Women.*

25. Ibid.

26. On trial marriages, see Marshal Butler, WPA Narratives, Georgia, vol. 12, pt. 1, 161; Roberta Manson, WPA Narratives, North Carolina, vol. 15, pt. 2, 103. In a case in Virginia, the slave Jesse Ambler noted that he maintained a Friday-to-Tuesday visiting pattern. He deviated from this plan, however, and ran away with three other slaves and a white man, who was prosecuted for stealing slaves. See the case of the white man, *Blevins's Case,* 5 Grattan 703, December 1848, Virginia, 46 Va. 703, 1848 Va. LEXIS 66.

27. There are examples of women doing the visiting and both husband and wife moving back and forth to see each other, though it was more common for free women married to slave men than for slave women married to slave men. On the latter, see Bethany Veney, *Narrative of Bethany Veney: A Slave Woman* (Worcester, Mass.: Press of Geo. H. Ellis, 1889), 19. On abroad marriages, see West, *Chains of Love;* Fraser, *Courtship and Love;* Gutman, *The Black Family in Slavery and Freedom;* Blassingame, *The Slave Community;* Genovese, *Roll, Jordan, Roll;* Stevenson, *Life in Black and White;* Dunaway, *The African-American Family in Slavery and Emancipation;* Kaye, *Joining Places;* Stephanie Camp, *Closer to Freedom: Enslaved Women and Everyday Resistance in the Plantation South* (Chapel Hill: University of North Carolina Press, 2004), 12–59.

28. Ibid.

29. Jones, *The Experience of Thomas H. Jones,* 5–9; Stroyer, *My Life in the South,* 42–43. On slave economies and subsistence, see Walter Johnson, *River of Dark Dreams: Slavery and Empire in the Cotton Kingdom* (Cambridge, Mass.: The Belknap Press of Harvard University Press, 2013), 178–231; Ira Berlin and Philip D. Morgan, *The Slaves' Economy: Independent Production by Slaves in the Americas* (Portland, Ore.: Frank Cass, 1991); Ira Berlin and Philip D. Morgan, *Cultivation and Culture: Labor and the Shaping of Slave Life in the Americas* (Charlottesville: University Press of Virginia, 1993); Betty Wood, *Women's Work, Men's Work: The Informal Slave Economies of Lowcountry Georgia* (Athens: University of Georgia Press, 1995); Eugene D. Genovese and Elizabeth Fox-Genovese, "The Slave Economies in Political Perspective," *Journal of American History,* 66 (June 1979): 7–23; Hudson, *To Have and to Hold;* Alex Lichtenstein, "'That Disposition to Theft, with Which They Have Been Branded': Moral Economy, Slave Management, and the Law," *Journal of Social History,* 21 (Spring 1988): 413–440; Philip D. Morgan, "Work and Culture: The Task System and the World of Lowcountry Blacks, 1700 to 1800," *William and Mary Quarterly,* 39 (October 1982): 563–599; Penningroth, *The Claims of Kinfolk,* 6–7, 46–79; Pargas, *The Quarters and the Fields,* 112–113.

30. Lane, *Narrative of Lunsford Lane,* 11–14; Brown, *Narrative of the Life of Henry Box Brown,* 37.

31. Jones, *The Experience of Thomas H. Jones,* 34; see Drew, *North-Side View of Slavery,* 79.

32. Nancy Boudry, WPA Narratives, Georgia, vol. 12, pt. 1, 113.

33. See Charles Ball, *Slavery in the United States: A Narrative of the Life and Adventures of Charles Ball* (New York: Published by John S. Taylor, 1837), 18, 263, electronic edition, Documenting the American South, University of North Carolina, Chapel Hill. See also Penningroth, *The Claims of Kinfolk,* 83.

34. William O'Neal, *Life and History of William O'Neal; or, the Man Who Sold His Wife* (St. Louis, Mo.: A. R. Fleming and Co. Printers, 1896), electronic edition, Documenting the American South, University of North Carolina, Chapel Hill, 34–42. For other situations of negotiation, see Lane, *Narrative of Lunsford Lane,* 19–23; Delia to "Master" [Rice Ballard], October 22, 1854, Rice C. Ballard Papers, Southern Historical Collection, University of North Carolina (hereafter SHC, UNC); Langdon Cheves to W[illia]m Jones, August 17, 1822, August 18, 1826, June 7, 1830, June 30, 1830, December 16, 1830, Cheves and Wagner Family Papers, SHC, UNC; Arnold Gragston, WPA Narratives, Florida, vol. 17, 146; P[aul] B. Barringer to Dear Brother [Daniel], August 2, 1849, Barringer Papers, SHC, UNC; Alfred Steele to My Dear Mistress [Mary Steele], November 15, 1835, John Steele Papers, SHC, UNC; Diary December 27 and 29, 1834, 170, 172 (typescript), John Walker Papers, SHC, UNC.

35. See, for example, Brown, *Narrative of the Life of Henry Box Brown,* 2, 37, 41–42; Isaac Williams, *Aunt Sally; or The Cross the Way of Freedom* (Cincinnati, Ohio: American Reform Tract and Book Society, 1858), 56–81; Emily to My dear Mother [Amy Nixon], February 12, 1836; John Little in Drew, *North-Side View of Slavery,* 206; Veney, *Narrative of Bethany Veney,* 19–25. Most of the examples are of men being sold from their wives, but the reverse happened also. See Jones, *The Experience of Thomas H. Jones,* 31–32; Ball, *Narrative of the Life and Adventures of Charles Ball,* 38–39, 70.

36. William Grosse, in Drew, *North-Side View of Slavery,* 84. Also see William Wells Brown, *Narrative of William W. Brown, an American Slave, Written by Himself* (Boston, Mass.: The Anti-Slavery Office, 1847), 84–86, electronic edition, Documenting the American South, University of North Carolina, Chapel Hill, 88.

37. *Samuel Adam, plaintiff in error, v. William H. Adams, defendant in error,* 36 Ga. 236, 1867 Ga. LEXIS 29 (June). Also see *Succession of Walker,* 121 La. 865, 46 So. 890, 1908 La. LEXIS 761; *Watson v. Ellerbe,* 77 S.C. 232, 57 S.E. 855, 1907 S.C. LEXIS 142.

38. Reuben and Betsey Madison, interviewed in 1827 by Abigail Mott, in Blassingame, *Slave Testimony,* 185–186; William Craft, *Running a Thousand Miles for Freedom; or, the Escape of William and Ellen Craft from Slavery* (London: William Tweedie, 1860), 103, electronic edition, Documenting the American South, University of North Carolina, Chapel Hill.

39. *Clement v. Riley,* 33 S.C. 66, 11 S.E. 699, 1890 S.C. LEXIS 126.

40. Civil War Widows' Pension Claims, Records of the Veterans' Administration, Record Group 15, National Archives, Washington, D.C. (hereafter cited as Pension claim with soldier's troop and widow's certificate numbers), Harriet Tisdale, widow of Charles

Tisdale, USCI 35 D, #121 574; Civil War Widows' Pension Claim, Clarissa (aka Claresy) Tisdale, widow of Charles Tisdale, USCI 35 D, #177 811 (note there are many variations of Clarecy's name in the file). See also Civil War Widows' Pension Claim of Ellen Wade in Elizabeth Regosin and Donald Shaffer, eds., *Voices of Emancipation: Understanding Slavery and Reconstruction through the U.S. Pension Bureau Files* (New York: New York University Press, 2008), 172–173.

41. My arguments here are based on synthesis of the diversity of sources used throughout this book.

42. On slave narratives, see William L. Andrews, *To Tell a Free Story: The First Century of Afro-American Autobiography, 1760–1865* (Urbana: University of Illinois Press, 1986); Valerie Smith, *Self-Discovery and Authority in Afro-American Narrative* (Cambridge, Mass.: Harvard University Press, 1987); Jenny Sharpe, *Ghosts of Slavery: A Literary Archaeology of Black Women's Lives* (Minneapolis: University of Minnesota Press, 2003). Also see Alexander G. Weheliye, *Habeas Viscus: Racializing Assemblages, Biopolitics, and Black Feminist Theories of the Human* (Durham, N.C.: Duke University Press, 2014).

43. Ibid.

44. Jones, *A Slave for Forty-Three Years,* 29–30. The sources are extensive; for more, see Charles Ball, *Slavery in the United States,* 30; Mary Raines, WPA Narratives, South Carolina, vol. 3, pt. 4, 2; Camilla Jackson, WPA Narratives, Georgia, vol. 12, pt. 2, 296; Mariah Calloway, WPA Narratives, Georgia, vol. 12, pt. 1, 173; Rev. Noah Davis, *A Narrative of the Life of Rev. Noah Davis, a Colored Man* (Baltimore, Md.: John F. Weishampel, Jr., 1859), 26–27, electronic edition, Documenting the American South, University of North Carolina, Chapel Hill; Laura Sorrell, WPA Narratives, North Carolina, vol. 15, pt. 2, 298; Mandy Hadinct, WPA Narratives, Texas, vol. 4, pt. 2, 104. See also Journal of D. J. Barber, October 2, 1859, 48, Huntington Library, Pasadena, California; Dealla Briscox, WPA Narratives, Georgia, vol. 12, pt. 1, 127; Lindsey Paucette, WPA Narratives, North Carolina, vol. 14, pt. 1, 306; Annie L. Burton, *Memories of Childhood's Slavery Days* (Boston, Mass.: Ross Publishing Co., 1909), 15; Nora Louis Hicks, *Slave Girl Reba and Her Descendants in America* (Jericho, N.Y.: Exposition Press, 1974), 30. On courtship, see West, *Chains of Love;* Fraser, *Courtship and Love among the Enslaved.*

45. Mary J. Bratton, ed., "Fields's Observations: The Slave Narrative of a Nineteenth-Century Virginian," *Virginia Magazine of History and Biography,* 88 (January 1980): 75–93.

46. On urban slavery, see Barbara Jeanne Fields, *Slavery and Freedom on the Middle Ground: Maryland during the Nineteenth Century* (New Haven, Conn.: Yale University Press, 1985); Leslie M. Harris, *In the Shadow of Slavery: African Americans in New York City, 1626–1863* (Chicago: University of Chicago Press, 2003); Richard C. Wade, *Slavery in the Cities: The South, 1820–1860* (New York: Oxford University Press, 1964).

47. Bratton, "Fields's Observations," 89. Also see Davis, *A Narrative of the Life of Rev. Noah Davis*, 82, 88, 89.

48. Hicks, *Slave Girl Reba*, 18, 30.

49. Jacobs, *Incidents in the Life*, 17–26; See also Bibb, *Narrative of the Life and Adventures of Henry Bibb*, 40; H. C. Bruce, *The New Man. Twenty Nine Years a Slave, Twenty Nine Years a Free Man* (York: Anstad and Sons, 1895), 108; Drew, *A North-Side View of Slavery*, 54.

50. Sojourner Truth, *Narrative of Sojourner Truth, a Northern Slave, Emancipated from Bodily Servitude by the State of New York, in 1828* (Boston, Mass.: J. B. Yerrinton and Son, 1850), 35–36; Nell Painter, *Sojourner Truth: A Life, a Symbol* (New York: W. W. Norton, 1996); Margaret Washington, *Sojourner Truth's America* (Urbana: University of Illinois Press, 2009).

51. Annie Huff, WPA Narratives, Georgia, vol. 12, pt. 2, 234; Tempe Pitts, WPA Narratives, North Carolina, vol. 15, pt. 2, 171.

52. Marshall Butler, WPA Narratives, Georgia, vol. 12, pt. 1, 161, 164; Burton, *Memories of Childhood's Slavery Days*, 15; Robert Smalls, interviewed in 1863, in Blassingame, *Slave Testimony*, 374–375.

53. Warren Taylor, WPA Narratives, Arkansas, vol. 10, pt. 6, 274; Marshal Butler, WPA Narratives, Georgia, vol. 12, pt. 1, 161, 164.

54. Craft, *Running a Thousand Miles for Freedom*. Also see Brown, *Narrative of William W. Brown*, 84–86; Bibb, *Narrative of the Life and Adventures of Henry Bibb*, 30.

55. Bibb, *Narrative of the Life and Adventures of Henry Bibb*, 39; Arrie Binns, WPA Narratives, Georgia, vol. 12, pt. 1. See also interview of Sarah Fitzpatrick, in Blassingame, *Slave Testimony*, 639; Willis Coffer, WPA Narratives, Georgia, vol. 12, pt. 1, 207; Mrs. Lou Fergusson, WPA Narratives, Arkansas, vol. 8, pt. 2, 280.

56. On the role of parents, see Schwartz, *Born in Bondage;* King, *Stolen Childhood;* Penningroth, *Claims of Kinfolk*.

57. Veney, *Narrative of Bethany Veney*, 18; Elizabeth Hobbs (Hillsboro, N.C.) to My Dear Mother, April 10, 1938, in Blassingame, *Slave Testimony*, 21.

58. Aunt Virginia Bell, WPA Narratives, Texas, vol. 4, pt. 1, 63; Lucinda Elder, WPA Narratives, Texas, vol. 4, pt. 2, 18; Williams, *Aunt Sally*, 52; Sister L. S. Tibbetts, to Sister [Mrs. Sophia Tibbitts], January 23, 1852, Hiram B. Tibbetts Family Papers, Hill Memorial Library, Louisiana State University; West, *Chains of Love;* Fraser, *Courtship and Love;* Thomas E. Will, "Weddings on Contested Grounds: Slave Marriage in the Antebellum South," *Historian*, 62 (September 1999): 99–118; Genovese, *Roll, Jordan, Roll;* Hudson, *To Have and to Hold*. On the chronology of the evolution of Christianity and religion more generally among slaves, see Michael Gomez, *Exchanging Our Country Marks: The Transformation of African Identities in the Colonial and Antebellum South* (Chapel Hill: University of North Carolina Press, 1998).

59. Jumping the broom is mentioned most frequently in the WPA slave narratives. For a sample of these, see Mary Reynolds, WPA Narratives, Texas, vol. 5, pt. 3, 244; Lina Hunter, WPA Narratives, Georgia, vol. 12, pt. 2, 261; Benjamin Henderson, WPA Narratives, Georgia, vol. 12, pt. 1, 175; George Eason, WPA Narratives, Georgia, vol. 12, pt. 1, 303; Ophelia Whitley, WPA Narratives, North Carolina, vol. 14, pt. 2, 374; James V. Deane, WPA Narratives, Maryland, vol. 16, 7; Bert Mayfield, WPA Narratives, Virginia, vol. 16, 13; Rebecca Hooks, WPA Narratives, Florida, vol. 17, 176; Betty Foreman Chessier, WPA Narratives, Oklahoma, vol. 7, 32; George Taylor, WPA Narratives, Alabama, vol. 6, pt. 1, 372; Will Dill, WPA Narratives, South Carolina, vol. 2, pt. 1, 323; Donaville Broussard, WPA Narratives, Texas, vol. 4, pt. 1, 151; Jeff Calhoun, WPA Narratives, Texas, vol. 4, pt. 1, 189; Cora Armstrong, WPA Narratives, Arkansas, vol. 8, pt. 1, 75; Julie A. White, WPA Narratives, Arkansas, vol. 11, pt. 7, 110. See also Tyler D. Perry, "Married in Slavery Time: Jumping the Broom in Atlantic Perspective," *Journal of Southern History,* 81 (May 2015): 273–312; Patrick O'Neil, "Bosses and Broomsticks: Ritual and Authority in Antebellum Slave Weddings," *Journal of Southern History,* 75 (February 2009): 29–48; Randal D. Day and Daniel Hook, "A Short History of Divorce: Jumping the Broom—and Back Again," *Journal of Divorce,* 10 (1987): 57–73; Blassingame, *Slave Community;* Gutman, *Black Family;* Genovese, *Roll, Jordan, Roll.* For an example of the ritual mentioned in other sources in the antebellum era, see "Slave Marriages Invalid," *Liberator,* June 24, 1859.

60. Cora Armstrong, WPA Narratives, Arkansas, vol. 8, pt. 1, 75; Jeff Calhoun, WPA Narratives, Texas, vol. 4, pt. 1, 189; Mary Reynolds, WPA Narratives, Texas, vol. 5, pt. 3, 244; Tempie Herndon Durham, WPA Narratives, North Carolina, vol. 14, pt. 1, 288.

61. Willis Dukes, WPA Narratives, Florida, vol. 17, 123; Interview of Jennie Hill, in Blassingame, *Slave Testimony,* 591–592.

62. Robert Shepherd, WPA Narratives, Georgia, vol. 13, pt. 3, 261; Jacob Aldrich, WPA Narratives, Texas, vol. 4, pt. 2, 23.

63. Francis Leak Papers, Diary / Plantation Journal, January 24, 1857, 292 (typescript), SHC, UNC. For other examples of Big House weddings or those with contributions of clothing from masters, see Pierce Cody, WPA Narratives, Georgia, vol. 12, pt. 1, 197; Malindy Maxwell, WPA Narratives, Arkansas, vol. 10, pt. 5, 57; Emma L. Howard, WPA Narratives, Alabama, vol. 6, pt. 1, 214; Julia Cole, WPA Narratives, Georgia, vol. 12, pt. 1, 236; Alice Baugh, WPA Narratives, North Carolina, vol. 14, pt. 1, 84; Henry Lewis, WPA Narratives, Texas, vol. 5, pt. 3, 12; Matilda Pugh Daniel, WPA Narratives, Alabama, vol. 6, pt. 1, 103.

64. Charles James McDonald to Dear Cal, December 23, 1854, Farish Carter Family Papers, SHC, UNC. Also see "A Negro Marriage," April 7, 1860, *Macon Telegraph;* Journal of D. J. [Daniel James] Barber, December 5, 1859, 97–105.

65. Julius Nelson, WPA Narratives, North Carolina, vol. 15, pt. 2, 146. For examples of no fanfare or modest celebrations, see Henry Bland, WPA Narratives, Georgia, vol. 12, pt. 1, 83; Julia Bunch, WPA Narratives, Georgia, vol. 12, pt. 1, 158; Gus Feaster, WPA Narra-

tives, South Carolina, vol. 2, pt. 2, 47; Martha Colquitt, WPA Narratives, Georgia, vol. 12, pt. 1, 244. See also Kaye, *Joining Places*, 68–75.

66. Veney, *Narrative of Bethany Veney*, 18, 26; Bibb, *Narrative of the Life and Adventures of Henry Bibb*, 199.

67. Pargas, *The Quarters and the Field*, 145–160. Pargas shows that the numbers were miniscule in lowcountry South Carolina, where coresidential marriage was dominant, and much higher in Northern Virginia, where abroad marriages were the norm. See "Divorces," in *The Colored American*, January 30, 1841, on the impact of extramarital interracial sex on white marriages. On sexual exploitation, see Saidiya V. Hartman, *Scenes of Subjection: Terror, Slavery, and Self-Making in Nineteenth-Century America* (New York: Oxford University Press, 1997); White, *Ar'n't I a Woman?*; Jones, *Labor of Love;* Fox-Genovese, *Within the Plantation Household;* Thelma Jennings, "'Us Colored Women Had to Go through a Plenty': Sexual Exploitation of African-American Slave Women," *Journal of Women's History*, 1 (Winter 1990): 45–74; Thomas A. Foster, "The Sexual Abuse of Black Men under American Slavery," *Journal of the History of Sexuality*, 20 (2011): 445–464; Dianne Miller Sommerville, *Rape and Race in the Nineteenth-Century South* (Chapel Hill: University of North Carolina Press, 2004); Baptist, *The Half Has Never Been Told*, 215–217, 233–244.

68. Henry Watson, *Narrative of Henry Watson, a Fugitive Slave* (Boston, Mass.: Bela Marsh, 1848), 18; William Ward, WPA Narratives, Georgia, vol. 13, pt. 4, 130; Steve Williams, WPA Narratives, Texas, vol. 5, pt. 4, 181; Brown, *Narrative of the Life*, 8; Spencer Barnett, WPA Narratives, Arkansas, vol. 8, pt. 1, 2; Williams, *Aunt Sally*, 50.

69. Silvia King, WPA Narratives, Texas, vol. 4, pt. 2. For clarity, I've normalized the spelling in the quote about Bob. Also see Willie McCullough, WPA Narratives, North Carolina, vol. 15, pt. 2, 78; Bolden Hall, WPA Narratives, Florida, vol. 17, 168; E. B. Holloway, WPA Narratives, Arkansas, vol. 9, pt. 9, 288.

70. Willie McCullough, WPA Narratives, North Carolina, vol. 15, pt. 2, 78; Sam and Louisa Everett, WPA Narratives, Florida, vol. 17, 127; Benjamin Russell, WPA Narratives, South Carolina, vol. 3, pt. 4, 53; Henry Bobbit, WPA Narratives, North Carolina, vol. 14, pt. 1, 123; Carl Hall, WPA Narratives, Kentucky, vol. 16, 34; Charlie Van Dyke, WPA Narratives, Alabama, vol. 6, pt. 1, 399; Thomas Johns, WPA Narratives, Texas, vol. 4, pt. 2, 203; Willie Williams, WPA Narratives, Texas, vol. 5, pt. 4, 189; Robert Barr, WPA Narratives, Arkansas, vol. 8, pt. 1, 122–123; Jacob Manson, WPA Narratives, North Carolina, vol. 15, pt. 2, 97; Henry Clay, WPA Narratives, Georgia, vol. 12, pt. 1, 191. See the literature on breeding: Daina Ramey Berry, *"Swing the Sickle for the Harvest Is Ripe": Gender and Slavery in Antebellum Georgia* (Urbana: University of Illinois Press, 2007), 77–84; Richard G. Lowe and Randolph B. Campbell, "The Slave-Breeding Hypothesis: A Demographic Comment on the 'Buying' and 'Selling' States," *Journal of Southern History*, 42 (August 1976): 401–412; Richard Sutch, "Slave Breeding," *Social Science Working Paper, no. 593* (Pasadena: California Institute of Technology, 1986); Amy Dru Stanley,

"Slave Breeding and Free Love: An Antebellum Argument over Slavery, Capitalism, and Personhood," in *Capitalism Takes Command,* ed. Michael Zakim and Gary Kornblith (Chicago, Ill.: University of Chicago Press, 2012), 119–144.

71. See Penningroth, *Claims of Kinfolk;* Lavinia to Dear Missis, July 1849, Lawton Family Papers, South Caroliniana Library, University of South Carolina, Columbia.

72. "Proceedings of military commission in the case of Moses (colored man), July 29–August 6, 1862, MM-2734, Court-Martial Case Files, ser. 15, Records of the Office of the Judge Advocate General (Army), Record Group 153, National Archives. Copy consulted at the Freedmen and Southern Society Project, University of Maryland, [H-55].

73. Ibid.

74. Ibid.

75. On religion and the church, see Albert J. Raboteau, *Slave Religion: The "Invisible Institution" in the Antebellum South* (New York: Oxford University Press, 1978); John Boles, ed., *Masters and Slaves in the House of the Lord: Race and Religion in the American South, 1740–1870* (Lexington: University Press of Kentucky, 1988); Susan Markey Fickling, "Slave-Conversion in South Carolina, 1830–1860," *Bulletin of the University of South Carolina,* 1924; Janet Cornelius, "Slave Marriages in a Georgia Congregation," in *Class, Conflict, and Consensus: Antebellum Southern Community Studies,* ed. Orville Vernon Burton and Robert C. McMath, Jr. (Westport, Conn.: Greenwood Press, 1982); Janet Duitsman Cornelius, *Slave Missions and the Black Church in the Antebellum South* (Columbia: University of South Carolina Press, 1999).

76. Charles C. Jones, *The Religious Instruction of the Negroes in the United States* (Savannah, Ga.: Thomas Purse, 1842), 132–133, electronic edition, Documenting the American South, University of North Carolina, Chapel Hill. Also see *Proceedings of the Meeting in Charleston, S.C. on the Religious Instruction of the Negroes* (Charleston, S.C.: B. Jenkins, 1845).

77. Jones, *The Religious Instruction of the Negroes in the United States,* 133.

78. Rev. H. N. McTyeire, "Master and Servant," in *Duties of Masters to Servants: Three Premium Essays* (Charleston, S.C.: Southern Baptist Publication Society, 1851), 30, 28; Jones, *Religious Instruction,* 134.

79. For examples, see William Capers, *Catechism for the Use of Methodist Missions* (Charleston, S.C.: John Early, 1853); Richard Ryland, *The Scripture Catechism, for Colored People* (Richmond, Va.: Harold and Murray, 1848); E. T. Winkler, *Notes and Questions for the Oral Instruction of Colored People with Appropriate Texts and Hymns* (Charleston, S.C.: Southern Baptist Publication Society, 1857).

80. Ryland, *Scripture Catechism,* 135.

81. Winkler, *Notes and Questions for the Oral Instruction of Colored People,* 91. See also Ryland, *Scripture Catechism,* 135.

82. Ryland, *Scripture Catechism,* 140.

83. Ibid., 30–31.

84. McTyeire, "Master and Servant," 30–31.

85. Most of the extant church records I've researched are very incomplete and often fragmented. Sometimes individual ministers kept records of marriages performed, rather than the church itself. The best example showing baptisms but not marriages is Church Records, 1841–1861, John P. Margart Church Records, South Carolina Historical Society (hereafter cited SCHS). For others, see Protestant Episcopal Diocese of South Carolina, Philip Gasden Papers and Alexander Glennie Papers, SCHS; Trinity Methodist Episcopal Church Records, SCHS; Edisto Island Presbyterian Church Records, 1837–1901 (black marriages listed beginning in 1865), SCHS; Holy Cross Episcopal Records, 1808–1937, SCHS.

86. See Stanley, *From Bondage to Contract,* 24–25; Genovese, *The World the Slaveholders Made,* 195–202; Ronald G. Walters, "The Erotic South: Civilization and Sexuality in American Abolitionism," *American Quarterly,* 25 (March 1973): 177–201; Kristin Hoganson, "Garrisonian Abolitionists and the Rhetoric of Gender, 1850–1860," *American Quarterly,* 45 (December 1993): 558–595; Michael P. Johnson, "Planters and Patriarchy: Charleston, 1850–1860," *Journal of Southern History,* 46 (February 1980): 45–72.

87. See Gomez, *Exchanging Our Country Marks;* Rabateau, *Slave Religion.*

88. See Minutes of the "Committee on the Colored People," First Baptist Church, Charleston, 1847–1875, South Caroliniana Library. See also other minutes of church committees: Minute book, Antioch Baptist Church, 1830–1895, South Carolina Archives and History Center (hereafter SCAHC); Records of the Barnwell Baptist Church, 1803–1912, SCAHC; Records of the Bethany Baptist Church, 1810–1850, SCAHC; Bethel Baptist Church Records, 1853–1935, SCAHC; Darlington, First Baptist Church Minute Book, 1856–1896, SCAHC; Ebenezer Baptist Church Minute Book, 1823–1860, Florence SC, SCAHC; Elim Baptist Church Minute Book, 1847–1869, Effingham, SC, SCAHC; First Baptist Church, Edgefield, SC, Minutes of 1823–1854, SCAHC.

89. See correspondence between priests, 1830s–1860s, concerning how they should handle slave marriages and some of the dilemmas that separations created regarding remarriage. For example, see Benoit Joseph Eveg De Mandston to (Flaget) Bishop Benedict Joseph, July 17, 1834; Fr. Theodore De Theaux, S.J., to Antoine Blanc, June 3, 1839; Fr. Joseph Giustiniani to Blanc, October 15, 1840; Fr. Joseph Giustiniani to Stephen Rousselon, August 18, 1843; Fr. Charles Dalloz to Antoine Blanc, May 23, 1845 (originals in French) in New Orleans Papers, Notre Dame University Archives.

90. Judith Butler, "Is Kinship Always Already Heterosexual?" *differences: A Journal of Feminist Cultural Studies,* 13 (2002): 25–26.

2. "God Made Marriage, but the White Man Made the Law"

1. Lea VanderVelde and Sandhya Subramanian, "Mrs. Dred Scott," *Yale Law Journal,* 106 (January 1997): 1054. Also see VanderVelde, *Mrs. Dred Scott: A Life on Slavery's*

Frontier (New York: Oxford University Press, 2009). The autobiography is important evidence for interpreting Taliaferro's intentions. He also made similar remarks in a newspaper interview. Other scholars have argued that he gave Harriet to Dred's master, who continued to treat the couple as slaves. See Paul Finkelman, ed., *Dred Scott v. Sandford: A Brief History with Documents* (Boston, Mass.: Bedford / St. Martin's, 1997), 16.

2. Finkelman, *Dred Scott v. Sandford*, 29, 116–117.

3. Several historians of marriage have mentioned this aspect of the case, in the context of discussing the treatment of slave marriages by the courts. The most extended consideration of this aspect of the case is VanderVelde and Subramanian, "Mrs. Dred Scott," 1033–1122. For a general history of the case, see Don E. Fehrenbacher, *The Dred Scott Case: Its Significance in American Law and Politics* (New York: Oxford University Press, 2001).

4. Lawrence Rosen, *Law as Culture: An Introduction* (Princeton, N.J.: Princeton University Press, 2006). See Ariela Gross, "Beyond Black and White: Cultural Approaches to Race and Slavery," *Columbia Law Review*, 101 (April 2001): 640–690; Ariela J. Gross, *Double Character: Slavery and Mastery in the Antebellum Southern Courtroom* (Princeton, N.J.: Princeton University Press, 2000); Thomas D. Morris, *Southern Slavery and the Law* (Chapel Hill: University of North Carolina Press, 1996), 426; Laura F. Edwards, *The People and Their Peace: Legal Culture and the Transformation of Inequality in the Post-Revolutionary South* (Chapel Hill: University of North Carolina Press, 2009).

5. Kathleen M. Brown, *Good Wives, Nasty Wenches, and Anxious Patriarchs: Gender, Race, and Power in Colonial Virginia* (Chapel Hill: University of North Carolina Press, 1996), 108–128.

6. Morris, *Southern Slavery and the Law*, 43–48; Christopher Tomlins, *Freedom Bound*, 455–460; Brown, *Good Wives, Nasty Wenches, and Anxious Patriarchs*; Saidiya V. Hartman, *Scenes of Subjection: Terror, Slavery, and Self-Making in Nineteenth-Century America* (New York: Oxford University Press, 1997); Jennifer Morgan, *Laboring Women: Reproduction and Gender in New World Slavery* (Philadelphia: University of Pennsylvania Press, 2004); Hortense Spillers, "Mama's Baby, Papa's Maybe: An American Grammar Book," *Diacritic*, 17, no. 2 (1987), reprinted in Spillers, *Black, White, and in Color: Essays on American Literature and Culture* (Chicago, Ill.: University of Chicago Press, 2003), 203–229.

7. Margaret Burnham, "An Impossible Marriage: Slave Law and Family Law," *Law and Inequality: A Journal of Theory and Practice*, 5 (July 1987): 218.

8. Spillers, "Mama's Baby," see especially 217, 220, 223; Orlando Patterson, *Slavery and Social Death: A Comparative Study* (Cambridge, Mass.: Harvard University Press, 1982), 5–9, 38; Claude Meillassoux, *The Anthropology of Slavery: The Womb of Iron and Gold*, trans. Alide Dasnois (Chicago, Ill.: University of Chicago Press, 1991). While I share the perspective in these seminal works that slavery made chattel legally kinless, I disagree with some of the conclusions to which this has led. Spillers argues that slaves

were "ungendered" as a result—as does Meillassoux, though his account is based on slavery in Africa. In the United States slaves were engendered in a different way. To suggest that slaves were stripped of gender is to reify the normative category. Gender itself is always cultural, historical, and contingent, marshalled for different uses. For further elaborations of this argument, see, for example, Elsa Barkley Brown, " 'What Has Happened Here' ": The Politics of Difference in Women's History and Feminist Politics," *Feminist Studies*, 18 (Summer 1992): 295–312; Hartman, *Scenes of Subjection*, 94–101.

9. Lorenzo Johnston Greene, *The Negro in Colonial New England* (New York: Columbia University Press, 1942; Atheneum, 1974), 191–195.

10. Ibid., 209; Joel Prentiss Bishop, *Commentaries on the Law of Marriage and Divorce, with the Evidence, Practice, Pleading, and Forms* (Boston, Mass.: Little, Brown and Co., 1881), 156.

11. "Petition for Freedom to Massachusetts Governor Thomas Gage, His Majesty's Council, and the House of Representatives," May 25, 1774, Massachusetts Historical Society, Collections Online, http://www.masshist.org/database/viewer.php?item_id=549; Greene, *Negro in Colonial New England*, 217; Michael Grossberg, *Governing the Hearth: Law and the Family in Nineteenth-Century America* (Chapel Hill: University of North Carolina Press, 1985), 129–130, 350; James Horton and Lois Horton, *In Hope of Liberty: Culture, Community and Protest among Northern Free Blacks, 1700–1860* (New York: Oxford University Press, 1996), 26; Arthur Zilvermsit, *The First Emancipation: The Abolition of Slavery in the North* (Chicago, Ill.: University of Chicago Press, 1967), 8–10, 102.

12. Emphasis in the original document. Opinion of Daniel Dulany, Esquire (December 16, 1767), 1, Thomas Harris Jr. and John McHenry, *Maryland Reports: Being a Series of the Most Important Law Cases, Argued and Determined in the Provincial Court and Court of Appeals of the Then Province of Maryland, from the Year 1700 down to the American Revolution* (New York: L. Riley, 1809), 560; Richard Henry Spencer, "Hon. Daniel Dulany, 1722–1797 (The Younger)," *Maryland Historical Magazine*, 13 (1918): 143–160; Daniel Dulany, Jr., *Biography Series*, Maryland State Archives, online.

13. Opinion of Daniel Dulany, 560–562.

14. Ibid., 559–564. Also note that Maryland passed a law in 1678 that exempted "Negroes, Indians and Molottos" from having to register their marriages or births in county courts. All other "persons" were required to do so. See "Assembly Proceedings, October 1678–November 1678," 76 in *Proceedings and Acts of the General Assembly*, Maryland State Archives, online.

15. On the character of antebellum slave law, see Peter Bardaglio, *Reconstructing the Household: Families, Sex, and the Law in the Nineteenth-Century South* (Chapel Hill: University of North Carolina Press, 1998); Jenny Bourne Wahl, *Bondsman's Burden: An Economic Analysis of the Common Law of Slavery* (Cambridge, England: Cambridge University Press, 2002); Mark Tushnet, *The American Law of Slavery, 1810–1860*

(Princeton, N.J.: Princeton University Press, 1981); Gross, *Double Character;* Morris, *Southern Slavery and the Law;* Eugene Genovese, *Roll, Jordan, Roll: The World the Slaves Made* (New York: Random House, 1974); R. H. Taylor, "Humanizing the Slave Code of North Carolina," *North Carolina Historical Review,* 2 (April 1925): 323–331; William Goodell, *The American Slave Code in Theory and Practice* (New York: American and Foreign Anti-Slavery Society, 1853).

16. Ibid.

17. Hartman, *Scenes of Subjection;* Bardaglio, *Reconstructing the Household;* Wahl, *Bondsman's Burden.*

18. Many historians have talked about the dichotomy of person and property, from various perspectives. See Gross, *Double Character;* Tushnet, *American Law of Slavery;* Wahl, *Bondsman's Burden;* Genovese, *Roll, Jordan, Roll;* Walter Johnson, *Soul by Soul: Life inside the Antebellum Slave Market* (Cambridge, Mass.: Harvard University Press, 1999).

19. See Genovese, *Roll, Jordan, Roll,* 22–23; Andrew Fede, "Legitimized Violent Slave Abuse in the American South, 1619–1865: A Case Study of Law and Social Change in Six Southern States," *American Journal of Legal History,* 29, no. 2 (1985): 93–150.

20. One historian claims that it was in the statutes that the clearest recognition of humanity toward slaves was expressed in the antebellum era. Yet it was here too that the absence of recognition for marital and family rights is starkest. It is striking how often legal scholars and social historians make claims about the "humanity" and "fairness" of slave law and yet the destructive role of the law with respect to marriage and family issues has received far less attention. Some historians have too easily bought into the masters' views of themselves, uncritically accepting the ideology of paternalism as a social fact and guiding motivation in the treatment of slaves. See Morris, *Southern Slavery and the Law,* 436–438; Tushnet, *The American Law of Slavery,* 15. Tushnet relies heavily on Genovese's interpretation of slave law in *Roll, Jordan, Roll.* For others who defend the humanity of the law, see A. E. Keir Nash, "Fairness and Formalism in the Trials of Blacks in the State Supreme Courts of the Old South," *Virginia Law Review,* 56 (1970): 64–100; Nash, "A More Equitable Past? Southern Supreme Courts and the Protection of the Antebellum Negro," *North Carolina Law Review,* 48 (1970): 197–242; Nash, "The Texas Supreme Court and the Trial Rights of Blacks, 1845–1860," *Journal of American History,* 58 (December 1971): 622–642. For those who challenge the humanity thesis, see Margaret Burnham, "An Impossible Marriage: Slave Law and Family Law," *Law and Inequality: A Journal of Theory and Practice,* 5 (July 1987): 187–225; Patricia J. Williams, *The Alchemy of Race and Rights* (Cambridge, Mass.: Harvard University Press, 1991), 219–221; Hartman, *Scenes of Subjection,* 90–98; Thomas D. Russell, "South Carolina's Largest Slave Auctioneering Firm," *Chicago-Kent Law Review,* 68 (1993): 1241–1282; Russell, "Articles Sell Best Singly: The Disruption of Slave Families at Court Sales," *Utah Law Review* (1996), 1161–1209; Leon A. Higginbotham, Jr., *In the Matter of Color: Race and*

the American Legal Process. The Colonial Period (New York: Oxford University Press, 1978).

21. Morris, *Southern Slavery and the Law,* 436–438; Russell, "Articles Sell Best Singly," 171–174. On the Confederacy and reform, see Drew Gilpin Faust, *The Creation of Confederate Nationalism: Ideology and Identity in the Civil War South* (Baton Rouge: Louisiana State University Press, 1989).

22. Harriet Beecher Stowe, *Uncle Tom's Cabin* (1852), was quite effective in making this case for the abolitionist cause in the North.

23. Russell, "South Carolina's Largest Slave Auctioneering Firm," 1241–1282; Russell, "Articles Sell Best Singly," 1161–1209. Quote is from North Carolina Justice Thomas Ruffin, in Russell, "Articles Sell Best Singly," 1178; Gross, *Double Character.* Examples of disputes over estates involving the division of slaves include *Erwin and Others v. Kilpatrick and Others,* 10 N.C. 456, 1825 N.C. LEXIS 37, 3 Hawks 456; *Harris v. Clarissa and Others,* 14 Tenn. 277, 1834 Tenn. LEXIS 66, 6 Yer. 277; *Trotter, adm'r, v. Blocker & Wife, et al.,* 6 Port 269, 1838 Ala. LEXIS 4. On slave trading, see Johnson, *Soul by Soul;* Michael Tadman, *Speculators and Slaves: Masters, Traders, and Slaves in the Old South* (Madison: University of Wisconsin Press, 1989); Steven Deyle, *Carry Me Back: The Domestic Slave Trade in American Life* (New York: Oxford University Press, 2006); Edward Baptist, *The Half Has Never Been Told: Slavery and the Making of American Capitalism* (New York: Basic Books, 2014).

24. Quoted in Herbert G. Gutman, *The Black Family in Slavery and Freedom: 1750–1925* (New York: Random House, 1976), 284. Note that dialect spelling was regularized in the quote.

25. On other ways slaves expressed legal consciousness, see Gross, *Double Character,* 42–45; Francis Foster Smith, *Witnessing Slavery: The Development of Ante-Bellum Slave Narratives* (Madison: University of Wisconsin Press, 1994); Jon-Christian Suggs, *Whispered Consolations: Law and Narrative in African American Life* (Ann Arbor: University of Michigan Press, 2000), 21–32; Edlie L. Wong, *Neither Fugitive nor Free: Atlantic Slavery, Freedom Suits, and the Legal Culture of Travel* (New York: New York University Press, 2009); Christina Accomando, "'The Laws Were Laid Down to Me Anew': Harriet Jacobs and the Reframing of Legal Fictions," *African American Review,* 32 (1998): 229–245. For a more sustained analysis of slaves' legal consciousness elsewhere, see Herman Bennett, *Africans in Colonial Mexico: Absolutism, Christianity, and Afro-Creole Consciousness, 1570–1640* (Bloomington: Indiana University Press, 2003).

26. Margaret Burnham makes the point that the illegality of slave marriages was defined juridically, not in statutes. This is important, though consigned to a footnote. It helps to clarify the ambiguities in the literature, some of which suggest slave marriages were prohibited by law. Burnham, "An Impossible Marriage," 207. On private vs. public law, see Alan Watson, *Slave Law in the Americas* (Athens: University of Georgia Press,

1989), 72; Also see Darlene C. Goring, "The History of Slave Marriage in the United States," *John Marshall Law Review,* 39 (Winter 2006): 299–347.

27. John Spencer Bassett, *Slavery in the State of North Carolina,* ed. Herbert B. Adams (Baltimore, Md.: Johns Hopkins University Press, 1899); Morris, *Southern Slavery and the Law,* 29–30; Gross, *Double Character,* 22–46.

28. Wahl, *Bondsman's Burden,* 22.

29. Most of the cases discussed and cited in this chapter were initially consulted in Helen Tunnicliff Cattarall, ed., *Judicial Cases Concerning American Slavery and the Negro* (Washington, D.C.: Carnegie Institution of Washington, 1926; reprint ed., New York: Negro Universities Press, 1968). I retrieved the full extant records of the cases that I analyze.

30. *North Carolina v. Zadock Roland,* 28 N.C. 241, 1846 N.C. LEXIS 39, 6 Ired. Law 241.

31. *State v. Minos,* 2 Harr. 529 (Del. 1834).

32. Many of these cases will be discussed in this chapter and others. Also see, *Taylor v. Swett,* 3 La. 33, 1831 La. LEXIS 353; *The Inhabitants of Lanesborough v. the Inhabitants of Westfield,* 16 Mass. 74, 1819 Mass. LEXIS 69, Tyng 74.

33. *Frazier v. Spear,* 5 Ky. 385, 1811 Ky. LEXIS 65, 2 Bibb 385.

34. *Overseers of Marbletown v. Overseers of Kingston,* 20 Johns. 1, 1822 N.Y. LEXIS 47; Hendrik Hartog, *Man and Wife in America: A History* (Cambridge, Mass.: Harvard University Press, 2000), 129–130. For other cases in which slave marriages were said to be invalid, see *Jackson, ex dem. The People, v. Lervey,* 5 Cow. 397, 1826 N.Y. LEXIS 199; *The Inhabitants of Andover versus The Inhabitants of Canton,* 13 Mass. 547, 1816 Mass. LEXIS 139, Tyng 547.

35. *Marbletown v. Kingston.*

36. Ibid. But see *Commonwealth ex rel. Johnson, a Negro against Holloway,* 3 Serg. & Rawe 4: 1817, Pa. LEXIS 3. A runaway slave man was charged with fornication and bastardy, in order to collect damages for his child. This contradicts Dulany's argument that slaves could not be charged with such infractions because marriages had no standing. The charge was used as an argument against returning the slave to his master in Maryland.

37. *Commonwealth, ex rel. Susan Stephens v. Clements,* 6 Binney 206, 1814 Pa. LEXIS 1.

38. Ibid.; see also *Hannah Coleman v. The State Missouri,* 14 Mo. 157, 1851 Mo. LEXIS 32. Some of the antebellum treatises that cited Dulany include Jacob D. Wheeler, *A Practical Treatise on the Law of Slavery* (New York: Allan Polock, Jr., 1837), 190; Goodell, *The American Slave Code in Theory and Practice,* 108; George M. Stroud, *A Sketch of the Laws Relating to Slavery in the Several States of the United States of America* (Philadelphia: Kimber and Sharpless, 1827; 2nd ed., 1856), 41; *Thomas R. R. Cobb, An Inquiry into the Law of Negro Slavery in the United States of America: To Which Is Prefixed an Historical Sketch of Slavery* (Philadelphia: T. and J. W. Johnson, 1858), 243.

39. *Girod v. Lewis,* 6 Mart. (o.s.) 559, 1819 La. LEXIS 125. See also *Francis Howard v. Sarah Howard, et al.,* 51 N.C. 235, 1858 N.C. LEXIS 160, 6 Jones N.C. 235; *Hannah Coleman v. State,* 14 Mo. 157 (1851), in John Belton O'Neall, *The Negro Law of South Carolina* (Columbia: Printed by John G. Bowman, 1848), 23, electronic edition, *The Making of Modern Law* (Gale Cengage Learning); Goring, "History of Slave Marriage," 317–318.

40. See *Howard v. Howard;* Grossberg, *Governing the Hearth,* 131.

41. Thomas Jefferson, *Notes on the State of Virginia* (London: Printed for John Stockdale, 1787; 2nd ed.), 231, electronic edition, *Sabin Americana* (Gale Cengage Learning); Cobb, *An Inquiry into the Law of Negro Slavery,* 40, electronic edition, *The Making of Modern Law* (Gale Cengage Learning); Paul Finkelman, "Exploring Southern Legal History," *North Carolina Law Review,* 64 (1985–1986): 97, 113.

42. *Alvany, a free woman of color v. Joseph J. W. Powell, executor of Benjamin Dicken and Others,* 54 N.C. 35, 1853 N.C. LEXIS 44, 1 Jones Eq. 35; *Girod v. Lewis.* Also see the Alabama attorney general's statement in *Smith, a slave, v. State,* 9 Ala. 990, 1846 Ala. LEXIS 209. See Rosen, *Law as Culture,* 65–66, who makes the case that there is nothing "natural" about natural law: "there is only law naturalized."

43. *Howard v. Howard;* Gross, *Double Character,* 5; Burnham, "An Impossible Marriage," 213.

44. See, for example, *Howard v. Howard; State v. Samuel; Coleman v. State.*

45. *Coleman v. State.*

46. *State v. Samuel.* For more on Ruffin's legal views, see Laura F. Edwards, "The Forgotten Legal World of Thomas Ruffin: The Power of Presentism in the History of Slave Law," *North Carolina Law Review,* 87 (March 2009): 856–900.

47. *Malinda and Sarah v. Gardner et al.,* 24 Ala. 719, June 1854, LEXIS 107; *Commonwealth v. Clements;* see also Grossberg, *Governing the Hearth,* 131.

48. See Burnham, "An Impossible Marriage," 211.

49. *Marbletown v. Kingston.* Also see *Commonwealth v. Clements;* Grossberg, *Governing the Hearth,* 349; Woody Holton, "Equality as Unintended Consequence: The Contracts Clause and the Married Women's Property Acts," *Journal of Southern History,* 81 (May 2015): 313–340; Carole Shammas, "Re-Assessing the Married Women's Property Acts," *Journal of Women's History,* 6 (Spring 1994): 9–30; Megan Benson, "*Fisher v. Allen:* The Southern Origins of the Married Women's Property Acts," *Journal of Southern Legal History,* 6 (1998): 97–122; Norma Basch, "The Legal Fiction of Marital Unity in Nineteenth-Century America," *Feminist Studies,* 5 (Summer 1979): 346–366.

50. See Burnham, "An Impossible Marriage," 208–209. For other cases where spousal testimony was allowed, see *William, a Slave, v. State of Georgia,* 33 Ga. 85, 1864 Ga. LEXIS 57; *State v. Jackson, a slave,* 8 La. Ann. 593, 1851 La. LEXIS 292. In the first case, the supreme court of Georgia ruled that slave spouses should not be allowed to testify. The date of this case—1864, toward the end of the Civil War—is much later than the others, however. William, a slave, was convicted of killing his wife, Ann's, alleged lover, George, also

a slave of the same owner. He appealed and won a new trial, arguing that his wife should not have been allowed to testify against him. The appeals court agreed. Also see *Commonwealth v. Clements;* Grossberg, *Governing the Hearth,* 349.

51. *Howard v. Howard; State v. John, a Slave,* 30 N.C. 330, 1848 N.C. LEXIS 81, 8 Ired. Law 330. See Burnham, "An Impossible Marriage," 213–214; Hartog, *Man and Wife,* 228; Hartog, "Lawyering, Husbands' Rights, and 'the Unwritten Law' in Nineteenth-Century America," *Journal of American History,* 84 (June 1997): 67–96. In *Jack, a slave, v. The State,* 26 Tex. 1, 1861 Tex. LEXIS 1, Jack was convicted of killing his wife, Nicey. He appealed on the ground of jury misconduct. After the verdict of guilty was read, one of the jurors said that "he did not think the negro ought to be hanged or punished with death." The case report does not say what the sentence was, but presumably it was death. Nor does it indicate why the juror objected to death, but it could have had something to do with the sentiment that passion killing relating to the discovery of adultery should extenuate the sentence. Jack lost on appeal, however.

52. See the case in which a slave man was convicted of killing his slave wife and sentenced to death: *Baalam, a slave, v. The State,* 17 Ala. 451, 1850 Ala. LEXIS 70.

53. See Wahl, *Bondsman's Burden,* 154. "Crimes of passion" were tolerated among whites, who were shown leniency for murdering in cases of adultery and instances where it was deemed appropriate for husbands to chastise their wives, for example.

54. *Alfred (a slave) v. The State of Mississippi,* 37 Miss. 296, 1859 Miss. LEXIS 19. Also see *State v. David, a Slave,* 49 N.C. 353, 1857 N.C. LEXIS 95, 4 Jones Law 353; and Burnham, "An Impossible Marriage," 214.

55. There is a broad literature on customary rights and slavery. Legal scholars have increasingly argued that we should distinguish the text of laws from their applications, and that the latter gave disenfranchised people more room to maneuver, especially at the local level. This is true in many instances, but as I argue here, marriage was of a different kind. Mere local recognition could not suffice in giving slave marriages the security that they lacked. See Edwards, *The People and Their Peace;* Gross, *Double Character;* Johnson, *Soul by Soul;* Martha S. Jones, "Leave of Court: African American Claims-Making in the Era of *Dred Scott v. Sandford,*" in *Contested Democracy: Freedom, Race, and Power in American History,* ed. Manisha Sinha and Penny Von Eschen (New York: Columbia University Press, 2012), 54–74. Others have downplayed the particular character of slave marriage and how legal disabilities may have caused harm. Mark Tushnet minimizes the law's impact by reducing its role to not providing "mechanisms of ceremonial marriages," while not acknowledging the destructive role of the law and the construction of slave marriages outside its norms. See Tushnet, *The American Law of Slavery,* 15. On the general concept of comity, see Hartog, *Man and Wife,* 269–275; Joanna L. Grossman, "Resurrecting Comity: Revisiting the Problem of Non-Uniform Marriage Laws," *Oregon Law Review,* 84 (June 2005): 433–488; Joel Prentiss Bishop, *Commentaries on the Law of Marriage and Divorce, and Evidence in Matrimonial Suits* (Boston, Mass.: Little, Brown

and Company, 1852), 107–108, 111–113, 116, 538, 613. This issue would resurface later in the century, as I discuss in later chapters.

56. Tomlins, *Freedom Bound,* 508.

57. Tapping Reeve, *The Law of Baron and Femme, of Parent and Child, Guardian and Ward, Master and Servant, and of the Powers of the Courts of Chancery,* ed. Lucius E. Chittenden (New York, 1846), 188, 340, electronic edition, *The Making of Modern Law* (Gale Cengage Learning). This treatise has been used by some scholars to suggest that Northern states were significantly more liberal toward slave marriages than Southern states. Reeve said that in Connecticut slaves were emancipated upon marriage, but he did not cite actual cases to substantiate this claim. I could not find evidence in which this legal reasoning held any weight. See VanderVelde and Subramanian, "Mrs. Dred Scott," 1104–1106.

58. *Claudius F. Le Grand v. Nicholas Darnall,* 27 U.S. 664, 7 L. Ed. 555, 1829 U.S. LEXIS 427; VanderVelde and Subramanian, "Mrs. Dred Scott," 1100.

59. VanderVelde and Subramanian, "Mrs. Dred Scott," 1033–1122. My analysis here is a summary of the points made in this article about the Scotts's marriage. While I agree with the persuasive argument they make about how Harriet's residency would have made a stronger case for the lawyers to push for the couple's freedom, I disagree that this can be tied to Northern states having more liberal views about slave marriage. The authors suggest that the North and South differed in how they approached the tensions between slavery and marriage, which favored emancipation. The article leans heavily on Tapping Reeve to make this case, but he argues on principle, not on actual cases of slaves obtaining their freedom upon marriage.

60. Finkelman, *Dred Scott v. Sandford,* 116–117.

61. Quotes from Marriage ceremony, November 14, 1832, recorded November 23, 1832, vol. 1, p. 199, 1838, Marriage Records, St. Louis City Hall.

62. See Harrison Anthony Trexler, *Slavery in Missouri* (Baltimore, Md.: Johns Hopkins University Press, 1914), 85–90, 125–133; Diana Williams, "'They Call It Marriage': The Interracial Louisiana Family and the Making of American Legitimacy" (PhD diss., Harvard University, 2007), 1–87. Williams notes Spanish priests' "registering" slave marriages in the late eighteenth century. There were conflicts in Louisiana between the Crown and civil officials regarding marriage policies and practices.

63. Bennett, *Africans in Colonial Mexico;* James H. Sweet, *Recreating Africa: Culture, Kinship and Religion in the African-Portuguese World, 1441–1770* (Chapel Hill: University of North Carolina Press, 2003); Sandra Lauderdale Graham, *Caetana Says No: Women's Stories from a Brazilian Slave Society* (Cambridge, England: Cambridge University Press, 2002); Barbara Bush, S*lave Women in Caribbean Society: 1650–1838* (Bloomington: Indiana University Press, 1990); David Geggus, "Slave and Free Colored Women in Saint Domingue," in *More Than Chattel: Black Women and Slavery in the Americas,* ed. David Barry Gaspar and Darlene Clark Hine (Bloomington: Indiana University Press, 1996);

Verena Martinez-Alier, *Marriage, Class and Colour in Nineteenth-Century Cuba: A Study of Racial Attitudes and Sexual Values in a Slave Society* (Ann Arbor: University of Michigan Press; 2nd ed., 1989). For older debates about the comparative mildness of different slave regimes in Latin America versus elsewhere, see Frank Tannenbaum, *Slave and Citizen* (New York: Albert A. Knopf, 1946).

3. More Than Manumission

1. *Seaborn C. Bryan (plaintiff in error) v. Hugh Walton, adm., defendant Supreme Court of Georgia,* 14 Ga. 185, 1853 Ga. LEXIS 210.

2. On interracial relationships, see Peggy Pascoe, *What Comes Naturally: Miscegenation Law and the Making of Race in America* (New York: Oxford University Press, 2010); Joshua Rothman, *Notorious in the Neighborhood: Sex and Families across the Color Line in Virginia, 1787–1861* (Chapel Hill: University of North Carolina Press, 2003); Martha Hodes, *White Women, Black Men: Illicit Sex in the Nineteenth-Century South* (New Haven, Conn.: Yale University Press, 1997).

3. See Joanne Pope Melish, *Disowning Slavery: Gradual Emancipation and 'Race' in New England, 1780–1860* (Ithaca, N.Y.: Cornell University Press, 1998); Leslie M. Harris, *In the Shadow of Slavery: African Americans in New York City, 1626–1863* (Chicago, Ill.: University of Chicago Press, 2003); Erica Armstrong Dunbar, *A Fragile Freedom: African American Women and Emancipation in the Antebellum City* (New Haven, Conn.: Yale University Press, 2008); James O. Horton and Lois Horton, *In Hope of Liberty: Culture, Community and Protest among Northern Free Blacks, 1700–1860* (New York: Oxford University Press, 1997); Martha S. Jones, "Time, Space, and Jurisdiction in Atlantic World Slavery: The Volunbrun Household in Gradual Emancipation New York," *Law and History Review,* 29 (November 2011): 1031–1060; Gary B. Nash and Jean R. Soderlund, *Freedom by Degrees: Emancipation in Pennsylvania and Its Aftermath* (New York: Oxford University Press, 1991), 179–180; Gary Nash, *Forging Freedom: The Formation of Philadelphia's Black Community, 1720–1840* (Cambridge, Mass.: Harvard University Press, 1988), 163; Clare A. Lyons, *Sex among the Rabble: An Intimate History of Gender and Power in the Age of Revolution, Philadelphia, 1730–1830* (Chapel Hill: University of North Carolina Press, 2006), 217–218; Theodore Hershberg, "Free Blacks in Antebellum Philadelphia: A Study of Ex-Slaves, Freeborn, and Socioeconomic Decline," *Journal of Social History,* 5 (Winter 1971–72): 183–209.

4. Ibid.

5. Brenda Stephenson, *Life in Black and White: Family and Community in the Slave South* (Oxford, England: Oxford University Press, 1997); Emily West, *Family or Freedom: People of Color in the Antebellum South* (Lexington: University Press of Kentucky, 2012); Wilma King, *The Essence of Liberty: Free Black Women during the Slave Era* (Columbia: University of Missouri Press, 2006); E. Franklin Frazier, *The Free Negro Family* (New

York: Arno, 1968); David Barry Gaspar and Darlene Clark Hine, eds., *Beyond Bondage: Free Women of Color in the Americas* (Urbana: University of Illinois Press, 2004); Michael P. Johnson and James L. Roark, *Black Masters: A Free Family of Color in the Old South* (New York: W. W. Norton, 1984); Amrita Chakrabarti Myers, *Forging Freedom: Black Women and the Pursuit of Liberty in Antebellum Charleston* (Chapel Hill: The University of North Carolina Press, 2011); Suzanne Lebsock, *The Free Women of Petersburg: Status and Culture in a Southern Town, 1784–1860* (New York: W. W. Norton, 1984); Jane H. Pease and William H. Pease, *Ladies, Women, and Wenches: Choice and Constraint in Antebellum Charleston and Boston* (Chapel Hill: University of North Carolina Press, 1990); Michael P. Johnson and James L. Roark, "Strategies of Survival: Free Negro Families and the Problem of Slavery," in *In Joy and in Sorrow: Women, Family, and Marriage in the Victorian South, 1830–1900,* ed. Carol Bleser (New York: Oxford University Press, 1991), 88–102; Whittington B. Johnson, "Free African American Women in Savannah, 1800–1860," *Georgia Historical Quarterly,* 76 (Summer 1992): 260–283; Ira Berlin, *Slaves without Masters: The Free Negro in the Antebellum South* (New York: New Press, 1974); Carter G. Woodson, *Free Negro Heads of Families in the United States in 1830 together with a Brief Treatment of the Free Negro* (Washington, D.C.: The Association for the Study of Negro Life and History, 1925).

6. Ibid.; A. P. Upshur et al., Northampton County, to Virginia Legislature, 1831, Petitions Analysis Records [hereafter cited as PAR] #11683101, Loren Schweninger, ed., *The Southern Debate over Slavery,* vol. 1: *Petitions to Southern Legislatures, 1778–1864* (Urbana: University of Illinois Press, 2001), 128–131.

7. West, *Family or Freedom;* Stephenson, *Life in Black and White;* Charles S. Sydnor, "The Free Negro in Mississippi before the Civil War, *American Historical Review,* 32 (July 1927): 769–788; Berlin, *Slaves without Masters;* Adele Logan Alexander, *Ambiguous Lives: Free Women of Color in Rural Georgia, 1789–1879* (Fayetteville: The University of Arkansas Press, 1991); Loren Schweninger, "The Fragile Nature of Freedom: Free Women of Color in the U.S. South," in *Beyond Bondage: Free Women of Color in the Americas,* ed. David Barry Gaspar and Darlene Clark Hine (Urbana: University of Illinois Press, 2004), 106–124.

8. There is very little literature written specifically about mixed-status marriages. The exceptions are Terri L. Snyder, "Marriage on the Margins: Free Wives, Enslaved Husbands, and the Law in Early Virginia," *Law and History Review,* 30 (February 2012): 141–171; and Michelle McKinley, " 'Such Unsightly Unions Could Never Result in Holy Matrimony': Mixed-Status Marriages in Seventeenth-Century Colonial Lima," *Yale Journal of Law and the Humanities,* 22 (Spring 2010): 217–255. Also see Paul Lokken, "Marriage as Slave Emancipation in Seventeenth-Century Rural Guatemala," *Americas,* 58 (October 2001): 175–200. They are discussed briefly in the literature on free blacks. See, for example, Schweninger, "The Fragile Nature of Freedom," 108; King, *The Essence of Liberty,* 56–57; West, *Family or Freedom;* Myers, *Forging Freedom;* Orville Vernon Burton,

In My Father's House Are Many Mansions: Family and Community in Edgefield, South Carolina (Chapel Hill: University of North Carolina Press, 1985), 217; Dunbar, *A Fragile Freedom*, 31–32. Also see how families were split apart by those who successfully ran away to the North, leaving behind enslaved family members. See Sydney Nathans, *To Free a Family: The Journey of Mary Walker* (Cambridge, Mass.: Harvard University Press, 2012).

9. Snyder, "Marriage on the Margins," 141–171; see Criminal Actions Concerning Slaves and Free Persons of Color, Craven County Records, North Carolina State Archives; *North Carolina v. Zadock Roland*, 28 N.C. 241, 1846 N.C. LEXIS 39, 6 Ired. Law 241; John Hope Franklin, *The Free Negro in North Carolina, 1790–1830* (Chapel Hill: University of North Carolina Press, 1943; 1995); Guion Griffis Johnson, *Antebellum North Carolina: A Social History* (Chapel Hill: University of North Carolina Press, 1937); Louisiana Code Noir (1724), Article VI, http://www.blackpast.org/primary/louisianas-code-noir-1724#sthash.46yN92L6.dpuf; *A Digest of the Civil Laws Now in Force in the Territory of Orleans* (New Orleans: Bradford and Anderson, 1808) (aka Louisiana Civil Code), Book 1, Title IV, Chapter II, Article 8, http://digestof1808.law.lsu.edu/?uid=11&tid=9&ver=en#11; Emily Clark, *The Strange History of the American Quadroon: Free Women of Color in the Revolutionary Atlantic World* (Chapel Hill: University of North Carolina Press, 2013), 87–88; Diana Williams, " 'They Call It Marriage': The Interracial Louisiana Family and the Making of American Legitimacy" (PhD diss., Harvard University, 2007), 1–88; and West, *Family or Freedom*, 33.

10. Snyder, "Marriage on the Margins," 141–171; Schweninger, "The Fragile Nature of Freedom," 108; King, *The Essence of Liberty*, 56–57; West, *Family or Freedom;* Myers, *Forging Freedom;* Burton, *In My Father's House Are Many Mansions;* Dunbar, *A Fragile Freedom*, 31–32.

11. Petition of William Lewis to the Senate and House of Representatives of Alabama, 1839, PAR #10183901, Schweninger, *The Southern Debate over Slavery*, 168–169. See, for example, *Overseers of Morris v. Overseers of Warren*, 26 N.J.L. 312, 1857 N.J. Sup. Ct. LEXIS 29.

12. Ibid.; Petition of John Winston to the Virginia General Assembly, December 11, 1820, PAR #11682001, Schweninger, *The Southern Debate over Slavery*, 63–64.

13. Petition of Stephen Lytle to the Tennessee General Assembly, ca. 1832, PAR #11483320, Schweninger, *The Southern Debate over Slavery*, 139–142.

14. Petition of Henry Ash, to the Honorable General Assembly of the State of North Carolina, 1894, PAR #11280404, The Race and Slavery Petitions Project, University of North Carolina at Greensboro, Proquest.com, *Race, Slavery and Free Blacks* [hereafter cited as *Slavery Petitions Project*], Series 1, *Petitions to Southern Legislatures, 1777–1867*.

15. Petition of Jeremiah Gill, to the Senate and House of Representative of the State of Mississippi in General Assembly convened, 1830, PAR #11083005, Schweninger, *The Southern Debate over Slavery*, 122–124. Bill was drafted but did not become law.

16. For example, see Petition of Lewis Evans, et al. To The Honorable, the Legislative Council and House of Representative of the Mississippi Territory in General Assembly convened, PAR #11801601, Proquest.com, *Slavery Petitions Project,* Series 1, *Petitions to Southern Legislatures.*

17. Petition of Sally Dabney to the General Assembly, December 20, 1834, Richmond City, PAR #11683414, Schweninger, *The Southern Debate over Slavery,* 151–152.

18. Petition of Samuel K. Jennings, To the honorable the Speaker and Members of the House of Delegates, of Commonwealth of Virginia [on behalf of Will, a Slave], PAR #11681518, Proquest.com, *Slavery Petitions Project,* Series 1, *Petitions to Southern Legislatures.*

19. Petition of Ned Hyman and Elizabeth Hagans to the North Carolina General Assembly, November 23, 1833, PAR #11283305, Schweninger, *The Southern Debate over Slavery,* 147–148.

20. Petition of Henry Lewis, To the General Assembly of Virginia, December 1833, PAR #11683309, Proquest.com, *Slavery Petitions Project,* Series 1, *Petitions to Southern Legislatures.* Also see related PAR #116833214.

21. See, for example, *Fambro v. Gantt,* 12 Ala. 298, 1847 Ala. LEXIS 278.

22. *William T. Lemmond & AL. v. Richard Peoples & Al.,* 41 N.C. 137, August 1849. See Luther Porter Jackson, *Free Negro Property Holders in Virginia, 1830–1860* (1942), 203, note 6 on a deed of loan made by a slave-owner to the free spouse of his slave woman.

23. See, for example, Anonymous, "A law case [*Miss Dunlap v. Peggy Thomas*]," *The New-York Magazine and General Repository of Useful Knowledge,* July 1814, 162–166; *Commonwealth, ex rel. Susan Stephens v. Clements,* 6 Binney 206, 1814 Pa. LEXIS 1.

24. *Kyler and wife v. Dunlap,* 57 Ky. 561, Ky. LEXIS 67, 18 B. Mon. 561.

25. *The Inhabitants of Hallowell v. the Inhabitants of Gardiner,* 1 Me. 93, 1820 Me. LEXIS 18.

26. Ibid.

27. Ibid.; *The Overseers of the Poor of the Town of Marbletown v. the Overseers of the Poor of the Town of Kingston,* 20 Johns. 1, 1822 N.Y. LEXIS 47. See John Wood Sweet, *Bodies Politic: Negotiating Race in the American North, 1730–1830* (Baltimore, Md.: Johns Hopkins University Press, 2003), 149, 154.

28. *Brewer v. Harris,* 46 Va. 285, 1848 Va. LEXIS 47, 5 Gratt. 285.

29. *Hannah Coleman v. The State Missouri,* 14 Mo. 157, 1851 Mo. LEXIS 32.

30. Ibid.

31. *Thomassin v. Raphael's Executor,* 11 La. 128, 1837 La. LEXIS 77.

32. *Holmes v. Holmes,* 6 La. 463, 1834 WL 681, 26 Am. Dec. 482.

33. Pascoe, *What Comes Naturally,* 25; *Code of Mississippi, being an Analytical Compilation of the Public and General Statues of the Territory and State* (1848), 492, electronic edition, *The Making of Modern Law* (Gale Cengage Learning).

34. *Bryan v. Walton.*

35. R. F. Akin, guar. of Susan Ranghill, plaintiff in error v. John W. Anderson, guar. Of Margaret Williams, defendant in error. 19 Ga. 229, 1856 Ga. LEXIS 163.

36. Ibid. This case prefigures postbellum inheritance disputes in which family members squared off in court, often contesting the legitimacy of each other's relationships, which will be discussed in a subsequent chapter.

37. See examples in Alexander, *Ambiguous Lives*, 56, 60, 89, 155. Some of these couples took steps immediately after the Civil War to remarry, under the auspices of laws passed in Georgia and legislatures in former slaveholding states making all black marriages legitimate. This phenomenon of free blacks' remarrying has not been noted by other scholars.

38. According to one historian, marriages between free people doubled between 1810 and 1819 and 1820 and 1829. Despite the emergence of the stereotype of the New Orleans "quadroon" engaging in illicit sex with white men, marriage was actually the most common pattern that free people of color preferred in this era. See Clark, *American Quadroon*, 71–96, 123–124.

39. This was affirmed in *Ex Pare Louisa Merry, Supreme Court of Texas*, 26 Tex. 23, 1861 Tex. LEXIS 3.

40. *Brewer v. Harris*.

41. *Frank and Lucy v. Denham*, 15 Ky. 330, 1824 Ky. LEXIS 102, 5 Litt. 330; Louisiana, *A Digest of the Civil Laws* (1808); *Thomassin v. Raphael*.

42. *Stover v. Boswell's Heir et al.*, 33 Ky. 232, 1835 Ky. LEXIS 80, 3 Dana 232; *Kyler v. Dunlap*.

43. *Barkshire v. The State*, 7 Ind. 309, 1856 Ind. LEXIS 274, May 26, 1856.

44. See Melish, *Disowning Slavery*, 129; Ruth Wallis Herndon, *Unwelcome Americans: Living on the Margins in Early New England* (Philadelphia: University of Pennsylvania Press, 2001). For examples of cases, see *Town of Castleton v. Town of Clarendon*, Brayt. 181, 1820 WL 967 (Vermont); *Overseers of the Town of Guilderland v. Overseers of the Town of Knox*, 5 Cow. 363, 1826 N.Y. LEXIS 191.

45. Carole Shammas, *A History of Household Government in America* (Charlottesville: University of Virginia Press, 2002), 173–174. See also Steven Ruggles, "The Origins of African-American Family Structure," *American Sociological Review*, 59 (February 1994): 143–144, 230–242; Lebsock, *Free Women of Petersburg;* Horton and Horton, *In Hope of Liberty;* Stevenson, *Life in Black and White;* Dunbar, *A Fragile Freedom;* King, *The Essence of Liberty*. It is worth noting here that the number of female-headed households would fall after the Civil War for the black population as a whole and would not reach its antebellum level again until after 1950. See data in Shammas, *A History of Household Government in America*.

46. "A Stray Husband," *New York Daily Tribune*, March 12, 1850.

47. William Wells Brown, "To the Public," *Liberator*, July 12, 1850.

48. *Liberator*, July 12, 1850.

49. Loren Schweninger, *Families in Crisis in the Old South: Divorce, Slavery, and the Law* (Chapel Hill: University of North Carolina Press, 2014), ix–xv, 1–16; Hendrik Hartog, *Man and Wife in America: A History* (Cambridge, Mass.: Harvard University Press, 2000); Stevenson, *Life in Black and White,* 140–158, 229, 233, 256; Norma Basch, *Framing American Divorce: From the Revolutionary Generation to the Victorians* (Berkeley: University of California Press, 1999).

50. Schweninger, *Families in Crisis in the Old South,* ix–xv, 119–124.

51. Ibid., 18–28, 44–52, 67–70; Stevenson, *Life in Black and White,* 140–158, 229, 233, 256; Jane Turner Censer, " 'Smilling through Her Tears': Ante-Bellum Southern Women and Divorce," *American Journal of Legal History,* 25 (January 1981): 24–47.

52. Schweninger, *Families in Crisis in the Old South,* 77–78. Schweninger claims that most of the free people of color who filed for divorce were property owners. But very few of the extant petitions mention property that the litigants either wanted to claim, divide, or prevent from being distributed.

53. Petition of Jane Davis [Mount Edmunds] against William Edmunds, To the Honorable Judge of the Fifteenth Judicial District of the State of Louisiana holding Court in and for the Parish of St Landry, February 1847 to June 1849, PAR #20884719, Proquest .com, *Slavery Petitions Project,* Series II, *Petitions to Southern County Courts, Part F;* Petition of Jane Davis [Mount Edmunds] against William Edmunds, To the Honorable Judge of the Fifteenth Judicial District of the State of Louisiana holding Court in and for the Parish of St Landry, May 1850–May 1851, PAR #20885023, Proquest.com, *Slavery Petitions Project,* Series II, *Petitions to Southern County Courts, Part F.* See also Petition of Ann Mather Bienville against St. Luke Bienville, To the Hon. the Judge of the third Judicial district Court in and for the parish of East Baton Rouge State of Louisiana, February 1836–June 1843, PAR #20883605, Proquest.com, *Slavery Petitions Project,* Series II, *Petitions to Southern County Courts, Part F;* Elizabeth Walden Armistead against Joseph Armistead, To the Hon. Thos. S Gholson, Judge of the Circuit Court of Petersburg, February–April 1860, PAR #21686023, Proquest.com, *Slavery Petitions Project,* Series II, *Petitions to Southern County Courts, Part C;* Elizabeth Walden Armistead against Joseph Armistead, To the Hon. Thos. S Gholson, Judge of the Circuit Court of Petersburg, April–May 1860, PAR #21686007, Proquest.com, *Slavery Petitions Project,* Series II, *Petitions to Southern County Courts, Part C.*

54. Petition of Jane Milton against Elisha Milton, To the Honorable the Judge of County of Guilford Superior Court, North Carolina, January 1856–1858, PAR #21285624, Proquest.com, *Slavery Petitions Project,* Series II, *Petitions to Southern County Courts, Part D.*

55. See, for example, Marie Seraphine Llorens Metoyer against Auguste D'Orestan Metoyer, To the Hon. Judge of the Sixteenth Judicial District of the State of Louisiana, sitting in and for the Parish of Natchitoches, November 1850–September 1851, PAR

#20885018, Proquest.com, *Slavery Petitions Project*, Series II, *Petitions to Southern County Courts, Part F.*

56. See, for example, Genevieve Sabal Menard [Sabale] against Lion Menard, To the Honorable James Pitot Judge of the Parish Court for the Parish and City of N. Orleans, December 28, 1819, PAR #20881933, Proquest.com, *Slavery Petitions Project*, Series II, *Petitions to Southern County Courts, Part F*; Elizabeth Walden Armistead against Joseph Armistead, To the Hon. Thos. S Gholson, Judge of the Circuit Court of Petersburg, February–April 1860, PAR #21686023, Proquest.com, *Slavery Petitions Project*, Series II, *Petitions to Southern County Courts, Part C;* Elizabeth Walden Armistead against Joseph Armistead, To the Hon. Thos. S Gholson, Judge of the Circuit Court of Petersburg, April–May 1860, PAR #21686007, Proquest.com, *Slavery Petitions Project*, Series II, *Petitions to Southern County Courts, Part C.*

57. Petition of George Conley against Josephine Helms Conley, To the Honorable Seth J. W. Luckey, one of the judges of the Circuit Courts of Tennessee sitting in and for the county of Washington of said State, June 1852, PAR #21485229, Proquest.com, *Slavery Petitions Project*, Series II, *Petitions to Southern County Courts, Part E.*

58. Petition of John Taylor against Nancy Berry Taylor, To the Hon. Thos. S Gholson, Judge of the Circuit Court of Petersburg, October 1859, PAR #2168590, Proquest.com, *Slavery Petitions Project*, Series II, *Petitions to Southern County Courts, Part C.*

59. Petition of Jean Baptiste Guillory against Marguerite Carabaillo Guillory, to the Honorable the Judge of the 5th District court western circuit division of the state of Louisiana sitting in and for the parish of Saint Landry, May–June 1829, PAR #20882913, Proquest.com, *Slavery Petitions Project*, Series II, *Petitions to Southern County Courts, Part F;* Petition of Cornelius Jackson against Sarah Briggs Jackson, To the Honorable the Judge of the Circuit Court of the City of Petersburg sitting in chancery, PAR #21686308, Proquest.com, *Slavery Petitions Project*, Series II, *Petitions to Southern County Courts, Part C.*

60. See, for example, Petition of Watkins Jones against Arena Thomas Jones, To the Honorable John W. Nash, Judge of the Circuit Court for the City of Petersburg, in Chancery Sitting, March–May 1852, PAR #21685230, Proquest.com, *Slavery Petitions Project*, Series II, *Petitions to Southern County Courts, Part C.*

61. West, *Family or Freedom*, 21–53. Also see Edlie L. Wong, *Neither Fugitive nor Free: Atlantic Slavery, Freedom Suits, and the Legal Culture of Travel* (New York: New York University Press, 2009); Thomas D. Morris, *Southern Slavery and the Law* (Chapel Hill: University of North Carolina Press, 1996), 31–36.

62. Petition of Joe Bird, To the Hon Senate and House of Representatives of the State of Mississippi, 1859, PAR #11085916, Proquest.com, *Slavery Petitions Project*, Series 1, *Petitions to Southern Legislatures.*

63. Petition of C. A. Featherston, To the Honorable General Assembly of the State of North Carolina, Gaston County, November 1862, PAR #11286203, Proquest.com, *Slavery*

Petitions Project, Series 1, *Petitions to Southern Legislatures.* Petitions for voluntary slavery are too numerous to list. For other examples beyond the ones discussed in this chapter involving spouses, see Petition of Walker Fitch, To the Honorable General Assembly of the State of Virginia, Augusta County, January 7, 1861, PAR #11686102, Proquest.com, *Slavery Petitions Project,* Series 1, *Petitions to Southern Legislatures;* Petition of Wilson Melton and John W. Sproles, To the Legislature of Mississippi, Holmes County, 1859, PAR #11085915, Proquest.com, *Slavery Petitions Project,* Series 1, *Petitions to Southern Legislatures.* See Petition of Lucinda, King of George County to Virginia Legislature, 1813, in Schweninger, *The Southern Debate over Slavery,* 49–50. See other examples on 236, 246–247.

64. Petition of Percy Ann Martin, To the Honorable General Assembly of the State of North Carolina, Davidson, NC, January 1863, PAR #11286301, Proquest.com, *Slavery Petitions Project,* Series 1, *Petitions to Southern Legislature.*

65. A. H. Kemper et al., To the General Assembly of Virginia, January 1836, Culpepper County, PAR #11683609, Proquest.com, *Slavery Petitions Project,* Series 1, *Petitions to Southern Legislatures;* Wong, *Neither Fugitive nor Free.*

66. West, *Family or Freedom;* Berlin, *Slaves without Masters;* Woodson, *Free Negro Heads of Families in the United States,* iii.

67. West, *Family or Freedom,* 101.

68. Petition of Emmarilla Jeffries, To the Hon Senate and House of Representatives of the State of Mississippi, 1860 January 19, PAR #11086010, Proquest.com, *Slavery Petitions Project,* Series 1, *Petitions to Southern Legislatures;* West, *Family or Freedom,* 79–98.

69. West, *Family or Freedom,* 79–98.

70. See Petition Lucy Andrews to the Senate and the House of Representatives of South Carolina, 1858, Lancaster Parish, PAR #11385806, in Schweninger, *The Southern Debate over Slavery,* 233–234; Petition of Lucy Andrews to the Senate and the House of Representatives of South Carolina, November 1861, PAR #11386101, Proquest.com, *Slavery Petitions Project,* Series 1, *Petitions to Southern Legislatures;* Petition of Lucy Andrews to the Senate and the House of Representatives of South Carolina, November 1863, Lancaster Parish, PAR #11386302, Proquest.com, *Slavery Petitions Project,* Series 1, *Petitions to Southern Legislatures;* West, *Family or Freedom,* 99–101; Schweninger, "The Fragile Nature of Freedom," 112–113. It is curious that Andrews had a white mother but appeared to be treated as a black woman. Her white parentage may have been why her appeal to be enslaved was rejected, although she had the endorsement of many white residents. Also see Julie Saville, *The Work of Reconstruction: From Slave to Wage Laborer in South Carolina, 1860–1870* (New York: Cambridge University Press, 1996), 102–110, on the distinctive experiences of up-country South Carolina during slavery and the Civil War and their impact on families.

4. Marriage "under the Flag"

1. Affidavit of Hannibal Sibley, January 11, 1893, Civil War Pension Claim of Solomon Sibley, in Elizabeth A. Regosin and Donald R. Shaffer, eds., *Voices of Emancipation: Understanding Slavery, the Civil War, and Reconstruction through the U.S. Pension Bureau* (New York: New York University Press, 2008), 131; excerpt from the Affidavit of Lucinda Sibley, January 11, 1893, Civil War Pension Claim of Solomon Sibley, in Regosin and Shaffer, *Voices of Emancipation,* 131. For Solomon Sibley's military records, see "Compiled Military Service Records of Volunteer Union Soldiers Who Served the U.S. Colored Troops," 63rd US Colored Infantry, Co. G, Civil War Service Records, Union Records, Colored Troops, Fold3.com.

2. The phrase is found in Civil War documents such as widows' pension files and the writings of chaplains and officers. For example, see Deposition of Emma Frederick, June 2, 1899, Civil War Pension Claim of Clement Frederick, in Regosin and Shaffer, *Voices of Emancipation,* 180. Also see Noralee Frankel, *Freedom's Women: Black Women and Families in Civil War Era Mississippi* (Bloomington: Indiana University Press, 1999), 41, 79; Keith P. Wilson, *Campfires of Freedom: The Camp Life of Black Soldiers during the Civil War* (Kent, Ohio: Kent State University Press, 2002), 176; Anthony E. Kaye, *Joining Places: Slaves in the Neighborhoods in the Old South* (Chapel Hill: University of North Carolina Press, 2007), 198–199; Nancy Bercaw, *Gendered Freedoms: Race, Rights, and the Politics of Household in the Delta, 1861–1875* (Gainesville: University Press of Florida, 2003), 76.

3. See Robert Francis Engs, *Freedom's First Generation: Black Hampton, Virginia, 1861–1890* (Philadelphia: University of Pennsylvania Press, 1979), 18–20, 187–188; Edward Pierce, "The Contrabands of Fortress Monroe," *Atlantic Monthly,* 8 (November 1861): 627; Lynda J. Morgan, *Emancipation in the Virginia Tobacco Belt, 1850–1870* (Athens: University of Georgia Press, 1992), 117; Adam Goodheart, *1861: The Civil War Awakening* (New York: Knopf, 2011). Mallory married in 1889.

4. Benjamin Butler to Simon Cameron, July 30, 1861, letter excerpt quoted in *Freedom: A Documentary History of Emancipation, 1861–1867,* Series 1, vol. 1, ed. Ira Berlin, Barbara Fields, Thavolia Glymph, Joseph P. Reidy, and Leslie Rowland, *The Destruction of Slavery* (Cambridge, England: Cambridge University Press, 1985), note 75.

5. "Letter from Fortress Monroe, in the *Independent,*" reprinted in *Anti-Slavery Standard,* 28 (September 1861).

6. See cartoon widely circulated in the North: "The (Fort) Monroe Doctrine," Library of Congress Prints and Photographs Division, Washington, D.C., http://www.loc.gov/pictures/resource/cph.3a36574/.

7. Pierce, "The Contrabands of Fortress Monroe," 628.

8. John Eaton, "Answers to Interrogatories," April 29, 1863, in Ira Berlin and Leslie S. Rowland, eds., *Families and Freedom: A Documentary History of African-American Kinship in the Civil War Era* (New York: New Press, 1997), 157.

9. Lockwood to American Missionary Association, September 16, 1861, in *American Missionary,* 5 (October 1861): 249–250. See Herbert G. Gutman, *The Black Family in Slavery and Freedom, 1750–1925* (New York: Vintage, 1977), 412.

10. Lockwood to American Missionary Association, September 16, 1861, in *American Missionary,* 5 (October 1861): 249–250.

11. Ibid.

12. Rev. Lockwood, "The Virginia Freedmen: Their Moral and Intellectual Improvement," September 23, 1861, published in *American Missionary,* 5 (November 1861): 256–257; names listed in "Freedmen's Bureau Marriage Certificates Records, 1861–1869," http://www.rootsweb.ancestry.com/~vaggsv/freemens_records.htm.

13. T. W. Conway, "Marrying on Roanoke Island," *Anti-slavery Standard,* October 25, 1862; "Sabbath-Day Exercises," *Anti-slavery Standard,* September 28, 1861; Gutman, *The Black Family,* 412–413; Bureau of Refugees, Freedmen and Abandoned Lands Record Group 105.2, Records of the Commissioners Office, 1861–1872, Textual Records: Freedmen's marriage certificates, 1861–69, http://freedmensbureau.com/virginia/gloucester.htm; http://www.rootsweb.ancestry.com/~vaggsv/freemens_records.htm.

14. Harriet Jacobs to J. Sella Martin, April 13, 1863, Jean Fagan Yellin, Joseph M. Thomas, Kate Culkin, and Scott Korb, eds., *Harriet Jacobs Family Papers,* vol. 2 (Chapel Hill: University of North Carolina Press, 2008), 471, 478, 480.

15. "Journal of Miss Susan Walker, March 3d to June 6th, 1862," *Quarterly Publication of the Historical and Philosophical Society of Ohio,* 7 (January–March 1912): 32.

16. Letter from Lucy Chase, January 29, 1863, in Henry L. Swint, ed., *Dear Ones at Home: Letters from Contraband Camps* (Nashville, Tenn.: Vanderbilt University Press, 1966), 37.

17. Report from Miss L[ucinda] Humphrey, Camp Fiske, Tennessee, August 20, 1863, in *American Missionary,* 7 (October 1863), 235–236.

18. On Confederate patrols, see Berlin et al., *The Destruction of Slavery,* 106; David Williams, *I Freed Myself: African American Self-Emancipation in the Civil War Era* (New York: Cambridge University Press, 2014), 61–65.

19. Report from Miss L[ucinda] Humphrey. She also noted that seventy-five couples were married the same day by Chaplain Kingsbury at the island camp nearby.

20. *Freedom: A Documentary History of Emancipation, 1861–1867,* Series 1, vol. 2, ed. Ira Berlin, Steven F. Miller, Joseph P. Reidy, and Leslie S. Rowland, *The Wartime Genesis of Free Labor: The Upper South* (Cambridge, England: Cambridge University Press, 1993), 94–98.

21. Harriet Jacobs Report, May 7, 1863, in Second Report of a Committee of the Representatives of New York Yearly meeting of Friends Upon the Condition and Wants of Colored Refugees 1863, 12–13.

22. Letter from Lucy Chase, July 1, 1864, Swint, *Dear Ones at Home,* 123–124.

23. Letter from Lucy Chase, March 4, 1863, Swint, *Dear Ones at Home,* 53–54.

24. Letter from Lucy Chase, January 29, 1863, Swint, *Dear Ones at Home,* 33–34.

25. Letter from Lucy Chase, July 1, 1864, Swint, *Dear Ones at Home,* 121.

26. Willie Lee Rose, *Rehearsal for Reconstruction: The Port Royal Experiment* (Oxford, England: Oxford University Press, 1964; reprint University of Georgia Press, 1999), 236.

27. Excerpts from Chaplain John Eaton, Jr., to Lt. Col. Jno. A. Rawlins, April 29, 1863, in *Freedom: A Documentary History of Emancipation, 1861–1867,* Series 1, vol. 3, ed. Ira Berlin, Thavolia Glymph, Steven F. Miller, Joseph P. Reidy, Leslie S. Rowland, and Julie Saville, *The Wartime Genesis of Free Labor: The Lower South* (Cambridge, England: Cambridge University Press, 1990), 695.

28. Rules and Regulations for Leasing Abandoned Plantations and Employing Freedmen, January 7, 1864, in Berlin et al., *Wartime Genesis of Free Labor: The Lower South,* 774–779; Colonel H. Lieb to Lieut. Col. H. C. Rodgers, September 13, 1864, in Berlin et al., *Wartime Genesis of Free Labor: The Lower South,* 845. Also see Berlin et al., *Wartime Genesis of Free Labor: The Lower South,* 642; *Freedom: A Documentary History of Emancipation, 1861–1867,* Series 2, ed. Ira Berlin, Joseph P. Reidy, and Leslie S. Rowland, *The Black Military Experience* (Cambridge, England: Cambridge University Press, 1982), note, 712.

29. Chaplain A. B. Randall to Brig. Gen. L. Thomas, February 28, 1865, in Berlin et al., *Black Military Experience,* 712; Chaplain C. W. Buckley to Lt. Austin R. Mills, February 1, 1865, in Berlin et al., *Black Military Experience,* 623–624.

30. Simon Cameron to Maj. Gen. Butler, May 30, 1861, in Berlin et al., *The Destruction of Slavery,* 72–73; Berlin et al., *Wartime Genesis of Free Labor: The Upper South,* 86–87; Ira Berlin, Barbara J. Fields, Steven F. Miller, Joseph P. Reidy, and Leslie S. Rowland, eds., *Slaves No More: Three Essays on Emancipation and the Civil War* (Cambridge, England: Cambridge University Press, 1992), 94; Saidiya V. Hartman, *Scenes of Subjection: Terror, Slavery, and Self-Making in Nineteenth-Century America* (New York: Oxford University Press, 1997), 152–161.

31. Berlin et al., *Wartime Genesis of Free Labor: The Upper South,* 86–87.

32. Lockwood to AMA, September 10, 1861, in *American Missionary,* 5 (October 1861): 245.

33. Pierce, "The Contrabands of Fortress Monroe," 633; Berlin et al., *The Destruction of Slavery,* 59–63; Engs, *Freedom's First Generation,* 27.

34. *American Missionary,* 5 (November 1861): 259.

35. See Berlin et al., *Wartime Genesis of Free Labor: The Upper South,* 168–174, 694.

36. *American Missionary,* 5 (November 1861): 259.

37. Lewis Lockwood to AMA, January 4, 1862, Document #H1-4348, microfilm, American Missionary Association Archives, Amistad Research Center, Tulane University (hereafter AMA Archives). This letter was also published in *American Missionary,* February 1862, 32. Berlin et al., *Wartime Genesis of Free Labor: The Upper South,* 89.

38. Berlin et al., *Wartime Genesis of Free Labor: The Upper South,* 89.

39. Berlin et al., *Wartime Genesis of Free Labor: The Upper South*, 88; *American Missionary*, 6 (February 1862): 30.

40. Sergt. Edwd Thomas et al. to Hon. E. M. Stanton, November 28, 1864, in Berlin et al., *Wartime Genesis of Free Labor: The Upper South*, 353–354, 30, 87–88, 111, 314–321; Berlin, et al., *Slaves No More*, 116–117.

41. American Freedmen's Inquiry Commission, "Preliminary Report Touching on the Condition and Management of Emancipated Refugees Made to the Secretary of War," (June 30, 1863), 4, in United States War Department, *The War of the Rebellion: A Compilation of the Official Records of the Union and Confederate Armies*, Series 3, vol. 3. For a perspective that acknowledges but downplays the amount of federal relief and Northern aid that poor whites received, see Stephen V. Ash, "Poor Whites in the Occupied South, 1861–1865," *Journal of Southern History*, 57 (February, 1991): 39–62.

42. Berlin et al., *Wartime Genesis of Free Labor: The Upper South*, 91–92; Berlin et al., *Wartime Genesis of Free Labor: The Lower South*, 628.

43. American Freedmen's Inquiry Commission, "Preliminary Report," 14–15.

44. Berlin, et al., *Slaves No More*, 182.

45. Lewis Lockwood to AMA, March 15, 1862, Document #H1-4398, AMA Archives; Lewis Lockwood to AMA, March 18, 1862, Document #H1-4400, AMA Archives.

46. See Armstead L. Robinson, " 'Worser dan Jeff Davis': The Coming of Free Labor during the Civil War, 1861–1865," in Thavolia Glymph and John James Kushma, eds., *Essays on the Postbellum Southern Economy* (College Station, Tex.: TAMU Press, 1985), 15; Berlin et al., *Wartime Genesis of Free Labor: The Upper South*, and *Wartime Genesis of Free Labor, Lower South*. See, for example, excerpts from the testimony of Alonzo Jackson, March 17, 1873, in Berlin et al., *The Destruction of Slavery*, 813–818.

47. Rose, *Rehearsal for Reconstruction;* Julie Saville, *The Work of Reconstruction: From Slave to Wage Laborer in South Carolina, 1860–1870* (Cambridge, England: Cambridge University Press, 1996).

48. See Bercaw, *Gendered Freedoms;* Armstead Robinson, *Bitter Fruits of Bondage: The Demise of Slavery and the Collapse of the Confederacy, 1861–1865* (Charlottesville: University of Virginia Press, 2005). In the Mississippi Valley, for example, ex-slaves had the distinction of enjoying emancipation for an entire year before federal occupation. Slaves freed themselves as planters fled after the Vicksburg campaign in the spring of 1862. They took charge of the land and chose to plant and harvest cotton. Again, Northern prewar assumptions made no room for such knowledge and skills among the slaves. Union officers were especially surprised by the slaves' effective system of marketing cotton. They selected a few men to negotiate the price and sale of cotton with nearby military camps and then divided the money they earned by family. When the federal government took over and introduced the "free-labor" system that leached all the profits to outside capitalists and former masters, Delta ex-slaves became just as loath to growing cotton as South Carolinians.

49. Rose, *Rehearsal for Reconstruction, 223;* Armstead Robinson, "'Worser dan Jeff Davis'"; Berlin, et al., *Slaves No More,* 134, 155–156; Eric Foner, *Free Soil, Free Labor, Free Men: The Ideology of the Republican Party before the Civil War* (New York: Oxford University Press, 1970).

50. American Freedmen's Inquiry Commission, "Preliminary Report," 6.

51. See Rose, *Rehearsal for Reconstruction;* Bercaw, *Gendered Freedoms;* Frankel, *Freedom's Women.*

52. The paintings are at the Metropolitan Museum of Art: http://www.metmuseum .org/collections/search-the-collections/13345. See Aaron Carico, "The Free Plantation: Slavery's Institution in America, 1865–1910" (PhD diss., Yale University, 2012).

53. Thavolia Glymph, "'This Species of Property': Female Slave Contrabands in the Civil War," in Edward D. C. Campbell, Jr., and Kym S. Rice, eds., *A Woman's War: Southern Women, Civil War, and the Confederate Legacy* (Richmond, Va.: The Museum of the Confederacy, 1996); Stephanie McCurry, "War, Gender, and Emancipation in the Civil War South," in William A. Blair and Fisher Younger, eds., *Lincoln's Proclamation: Emancipation Reconsidered* (Chapel Hill: University of North Carolina Press, 2009); Frankel, *Freedom's Women,* 23–24; Crystal Feimster, "General Benjamin Butler and the Threat of Sexual Violence during the American Civil War," *Daedalus* (Spring 2009): 126–134; Kim Murphy, *I Had Rather Die: Rape in the Civil War* (Batesville, Va.: Coachlight Press, 2014); Kate Masur, "A Rare Phenomenon of Philological Vegetation: The Word 'Contraband' and the Meanings of Emancipation in the United States," *Journal of American History,* 93 (March 2007): 1050–1084; Louis Gerteis, *From Contraband to Freedman: Federal Policy toward Southern Blacks, 1861–1865* (Westport, Conn.: Greenwood Press, 1973).

54. Benj. F. Butler to Lieutenant Genl. Scott, May 27,1861, in Berlin et al., *Black Military Experience,* 728; Berlin et al., *Destruction of Slavery,* 70–72; Glymph, "'This Species of Property.'"

55. Lincoln letter to War Department, April 16, 1863 (in reply to letter from Maj. Gen. S. A. Hurlbut, March 27, 1863), in Berlin et al., *The Destruction of Slavery,* 306. Note that the facsimile of the document here identifies the document date as August 15, 1863: http://www.armchairgeneral.com/forums/showthread.php?p=1665340.

56. Harriet Jacobs to William Lloyd Garrison, August 1862, in Yellin et al., *Harriet Jacobs Family Papers,* 402.

57. Lewis Lockwood to AMA, March 15, 1862, Document #H1-4398, AMA Archives; Glymph, "'This Species of Property'"; Glymph, "Du Bois's Black Reconstruction and Slave Women's War for Freedom," *South Atlantic Quarterly,* 112 (Summer 2013): 498–501.

58. Susie King Taylor, *Reminiscences of My Life in Camp with the 33rd United States Colored Troops* (1902), vi, 67–68, electronic edition, Documenting the American South, University of North Carolina, Chapel Hill.

59. Quoted in Berlin et al., *Wartime Genesis of Free Labor: The Lower South*, 501.

60. Edward L. Pierce to Hon. Salmon Chase, February 3, 1862, in Berlin et al., *Wartime Genesis of Free Labor: The Lower South*, 144.

61. See Berlin et al., *Slaves No More*, 103; Glymph, " 'This Species of Property,' " 61.

62. Edward Pierce, "The Freedmen at Port Royal," *Atlantic Monthly*, 12 (September 1863): 309.

63. See Hartman, *Scenes of Subjection*, 152–157.

64. George T. Converse to Capt. S. W. Cozzens, April 6, 1864, in Berlin et al., *Wartime Genesis of Free Labor: The Lower South*, note, 536.

65. Jno. C. M. Conner to S. W. Cozzens, September 29, 1863, in Berlin et al., *Wartime Genesis of Free Labor: The Lower South*, notes, 469.

66. Austa M. French, *Slavery in South Carolina and the Ex-Slaves, or, the Port Royal Mission* (New York: W. M. French, 1862), 105–106, 112–114.

67. See Nancy Cott, *Bonds of Womanhood: "Woman's Sphere" in New England, 1780–1835* (New Haven, Conn.: Yale University Press, 1977); Barbara Leslie Epstein, *The Politics of Domesticity: Women, Evangelism, and Temperance in Nineteenth-Century America* (Middletown, Conn.: Wesleyan University Press, 1981).

68. John Eaton and Ethel Osgood Mason, *Grant, Lincoln, and the Freedmen: Reminiscences of the Civil War* (New York: Longmans, Green, and Co., 1907), 217; quote from Philbrick in Rose, *Rehearsal for Reconstruction*, 298, 303–314; quote from Wisconsin group in Gerteis, *From Contraband to Freedman*, 145; American Freedmen's Inquiry Commission, "Preliminary Report," 40. Also see Bercaw, *Gendered Freedoms*, 34–38; Frankel, *Freedom's Women*, 51.

69. Carole Pateman, *The Sexual Contract* (Stanford, Calif.: Stanford University Press, 1988), 116–242; Nancy Fraser and Linda Gordon, "Contract vs. Charity: Why Is There No Social Citizenship in the United States?" *Socialist Review*, 22 (1992): 45–68. To be sure, this was more ideal than reality even for many white wage earners. See Lawrence B. Glickman, *A Living Wage: American Workers and the Making of Consumer Society* (Ithaca, N.Y.: Cornell University Press, 2015).

70. On black soldiers, family, and gender issues, see Jim Cullen, " 'I's a Man Now': Gender and African American Men," in Catherine Clinton and Nina Silber, eds., *Divided Houses: Gender and the Civil War* (New York: Oxford University Press, 1992); Donald R. Shaffer, *After Glory: The Struggles of Black Civil War Veterans* (Lawrence: University Press of Kansas, 2004), 97–118; Richard M. Reid, *Freedom for Themselves: North Carolina's Black Soldiers in the Civil War Era* (Chapel Hill: University of North Carolina Press, 2008), 215–253; Wilson, *Campfires of Freedom*, 176–209.

71. Pension claim of Ellen Young, widow of Roger Young, USCI 33, Co. H, #123524; Pension claim of Julia Lafond, widow of Louis Lafond, USCI 73, Co. C, #177335. See also Louis Lafond, "Compiled Military Service Records of Volunteer Union Soldiers Who Served the U.S. Colored Troops," Civil War Service Records, Union Records,

Colored Troops, Fold3.com; Pension claim of Mary Ann Lewis, widow of James Lewis, USCI 34, Co. H, #148952.

72. Deposition of Alfred Ward, in Regosin and Shaffer, *Voices of Emancipation*, 52; Pension claim of Elizabeth Wilson, widow of Charles H. Wilson, USCI 22, Co. I, #67745; Pension claim of Francis S. E. Wilkinson, widow of Charles Wilkinson, USCI 22, Co. I, #257397.

73. See, for example, Pension laim of Talitha (Lithia) Taft, widow of Gray Payton (aka Gray Taft), USCI 36, Co. D #361760, and Pension claim of Ann Greenwood Payton, widow of Gray Payton (aka Gray Taft), USCI 36, Co. D, #89262; Pension claim of Harriet A. Brown, widow of Moses Brown, USCI 4, Co. I, #113624. See Shaffer, *After Glory;* Cullen, "'I's a Man Now'"; Reid, *Freedom for Themselves.*

74. See Drew Gilpin Faust, *This Republic of Suffering: Death and the American Civil War* (New York: Vintage, 2008).

75. Pension claim of Rebecca Gathen, widow of Allen Gathen, USCI 42, Co. H, #78541. Also see Shadrack Holland, USCI 42, Co. H, "Compiled Military Service Records of Volunteer Union Soldiers Who Served the U.S. Colored Troops," Civil War Service Records, Union Records, Colored Troops, Fold3.com; and Allen Williams, USCI 42, Co. H, "Compiled Military Service Records of Volunteer Union Soldiers Who Served the U.S. Colored Troops," Civil War Service Records, Union Records, Colored Troops, Fold3.com.

76. Pension claim of Elisabeth Wright, widow of Rufus Wright, USCI 1, Co. D, #152132. For later document, see Berlin et al., *Families and Freedom*, 165–167. For similar cases, see Pension claim of Mary Robinson, widow of Jeffrey Robinson, USCI 33, Co. D, #128564; Pension claim of Rosetta Beasley, widow of Spencer Beasley, USCI 36, Co. C, #117790.

77. Pension claim of Charlotte Capehart, widow of Caesar Banks, USCI 35, Co. D, #15783; Pension claim of Mary Bennett, widow of John Bennett, USCI 108, Co. C, #131045.

78. Chaplain Jas. Peet to Brig. Gen'l. L. Thomas, September 30, 1864, in Berlin et al., *Black Military Experience,* 604; Chaplain A. B. Randall to Brig. Gen. L. Thomas, February 28, 1865, in Berlin et al., *Black Military Experience,* 712.

79. Genl. Orders No. 41, Head Quarters 60th U.S. Cold Inft., February 3, 1865, in Berlin et al., *Black Military Experience,* 709; Wilson, *Campfires of Freedom,*176–209.

80. Brig. Genl. Wm. A. Pike to Maj. Genl. Rosecrans, February 23, 1864, in Berlin et al., *Black Military Experience,* 245–246; Lt. A. A. Rice to Col, March 31, 1864, in Berlin et al., *Wartime Genesis of Free Labor: The Upper South,* 600; Justice to Maj. Gen. N. Banks, April 3, 1863, in Berlin et al., *Wartime Genesis of Free Labor: The Lower South,* 432–434.

81. Private Aaron Oates to Hon. Ed. M. Stanton, January 26, 1865, in Berlin et al., *Black Military Experience,* 692–693. Also see [Private Spotswood Rice] to My Children, [September 3, 1864], in Berlin et al., *Black Military Experience,* 689.

82. Richard D. Sears, *Camp Nelson, Kentucky: A Civil War History* (Lexington: University Press of Kentucky, 2002).

83. Brig. Genl. Speed S. Fry to Brig. Genl. S. G. Burbridge, July 5, 1864, in Berlin et al., *Wartime Genesis of Free Labor: The Upper South*, 671–673.

84. Affidavit of John Higgins, November 28, 1864, in Berlin et al., *Wartime Genesis of Free Labor: The Upper South*, 687.

85. Affidavit of John Burnside, December 15, 1864, in Berlin et al., *Black Military Experience*, 687–688.

86. Berlin et al., *Wartime Genesis of Free Labor: The Upper South*, 680–686.

87. Affidavit of Abisha Scofield, December 16, 1864, in Berlin et al., *Black Military Experience*, 716.

88. American Freedmen's Inquiry Commission, "Preliminary Report," 20.

89. Letter from Lucy Chase, April 1, 1863, in *Dear Ones at Home*, 59–60; Glymph, " 'This Species of Property.' " See literature on sexual citizenship, including Bryan S. Turner, "Citizenship, Reproduction and the State: International Marriage and Human Rights," *Citizenship Studies*, 12 (February 2008): 45–54; James Burk, "The Citizen Soldier and Democratic Societies: A Comparative Analysis of America's Revolutionary and Civil Wars," *Citizenship Studies*, vol. 4, no. 2 (2000): 149–165; Mimi Sheller, *Citizenship from Below: Erotic Agency and Caribbean Freedom* (Durham, N.C.: Duke University Press, 2012); Ursula Vogel, "Marriage and the Boundaries of Citizenship," in Bart van Steenbergen, ed., *The Condition of Citizenship* (London: Sage Publications, 1994).

90. Judith Butler, "Is Kinship Always Already Heterosexual?" *difference: A Journal of Feminist Cultural Studies*, 13 (2002): 23.

91. See Shiller, *Citizenship from Below*.

5. A Civil War over Marriage

1. Ira Berlin, Barbara J. Fields, Steven F. Miller, Joseph P. Reidy, and Leslie S. Rowland, eds., *Slaves No More: Three Essays on Emancipation and the Civil War* (Cambridge, England: Cambridge University Press, 1992), 192–193; Eric Foner, *The Fiery Trial: Abraham Lincoln and American Slavery* (New York: W. W. Norton, 2010), 214; Heather C. Richardson, *Greatest Nation of the Earth: Republican Economic Policies during the Civil War* (Cambridge, Mass.: Harvard University Press, 1997), 211–227.

2. United States, *Statutes at Large, Treaties, and Proclamations of the United States of America*, vol. 12 (Boston, 1863), 597–600.

3. Thirty-seventh Congress, 2nd session, *Congressional Globe*, July 11, 1862, 3235, 3249, 3251.

4. Thirty-seventh Congress, 2nd session, *Congressional Globe*, July 16, 1862, 3341, 3343.

5. Thirty-seventh Congress, 2nd session, *Congressional Globe,* July 16, 1862, 3341, 3343, 3348.

6. Thirty-seventh Congress, 2nd session, *Congressional Globe,* July 11, 1862, 3234, 3228, 3231.

7. Thirty-seventh Congress, 2nd session, *Congressional Globe,* July 16, 1862, 3249, 3339.

8. James Oakes, *Freedom National: The Destruction of Slavery in the United States, 1861–1865* (New York: W. W. Norton, 2010), 360–361.

9. Berlin et al., *Slaves No More.*

10. See Oakes, *Freedom National,* 360, 386. Oakes acknowledges that the law "introduced a patriarchal criterion for emancipation." He sees it as compensation for the gender distinction made in emancipation policy. He claims that it was intended to expand rather than restrict emancipation. But it did both. It created a major disability for women and restricted their route to emancipation and to citizenship. See Thavolia Glymph, "Rose's War and the Gendered Politics of a Slave Insurgency in the Civil War," *Journal of the Civil War Era,* 3 (December 2013): 517–521; Glymph, "Du Bois's Black Reconstruction and Slave Women's War for Freedom," *South Atlantic Quarterly,* 112 (Summer 2013): 494–498.

11. On the implications of gender and emancipation, see Glymph, "Rose's War," 501–532; Glymph, "Du Bois's Black Reconstruction," 489–505; Stephanie McCurry, "War, Gender, and Emancipation in the Civil War South," in William A. Blair and Karen Fisher Younger, eds., *Lincoln's Proclamation: Emancipation Reconsidered* (Chapel Hill: University of North Carolina Press, 2009), 120–150; Amy Dru Stanley, "Instead of Waiting for the Thirteenth Amendment: The War Power, Slave Marriage, and Inviolate Human Rights," *American Historical Review,* 115 (June 2010): 732–765; Nancy D. Bercaw, *Gendered Freedoms: Race, Rights, and the Politics of Household in the Delta, 1861–1875* (Gainesville: University Press of Florida, 2003); Leslie A. Schwalm, *A Hard Fight for We: Women's Transition to Freedom in South Carolina* (Urbana: University of Illinois Press, 1997); Noralee Frankel, *Freedom's Women: Black Women and Families in Civil War Era Mississippi* (Bloomington: Indiana University Press, 1999).

12. For another poignant example, see Martha to My Dear Husband [Richard Glover], December 30, 1863, in Ira Berlin and Leslie S. Rowland, eds., *Families and Freedom: A Documentary History of African-American Kinship in the Civil War Era* (New York: New Press, 1997), 97.

13. Historians have rarely analyzed the debates leading up to the passage of this legislation. For exceptions, see Mary Frances Berry, *Military Necessity and Civil Rights Policy: Black Citizenship and the Constitution, 1861–1868* (Fort Washington, N.Y.: Kinnikat Press, 1977), 79–82; and for the most detailed treatment, see Stanley, "Instead of Waiting for the Thirteenth Amendment," 732–765. Also see Nancy Cott, *Public Vows: A History*

of Marriage and the Nation (Cambridge, Mass.: Harvard University Press, 2000), 76, 80–84.

14. Thirty-eighth Congress, 1st Session, *Congressional Globe,* January 27, 1864, 362; *Congressional Globe,* January 28, 396.

15. Thirty-eighth Congress, 1st Session, *Congressional Globe,* February 2, 1864, 438.

16. Thirty-eighth Congress, 2nd Session, *Congressional Globe,* December 19, 1864, 64; Thirty-eighth Congress, 2nd Session, *Congressional Globe,* January 7, 1865, 114; Thirty-eighth Congress, 1st Session, *Congressional Globe,* March 18, 1864, 1179, 1181–1182.

17. Thirty-eighth Congress, 1st Session, *Congressional Globe,* March 18, 1864, 1176–1177. See also the original letters: Capt. A. J. Hubbard to Brig. Genl. Pile, February 6, 1864, 687–688, in *Freedom: A Documentary History of Emancipation, 1861–1867,* Series 2, ed. Ira Berlin, Joseph P. Reidy, and Leslie S. Rowland, *The Black Military Experience* (Cambridge, England: Cambridge University Press, 1982); Brig. Genl. Wm. A. Pile to Maj. O. D. Greene, February 11, 1864, enclosing 1st Lieut. William P. Denning to Brig. Genl. Pile, February 1, 1864, 242–243, in Berlin et al., *Black Military Experience.*

18. Ann to My Dear Husband, January 19, 1864, 686–687, in Berlin et al., *Black Military Experience;* Thirty-eighth Congress, 1st Session, *Congressional Globe,* March 18, 1864, 1177. See original letter: Brig. Genl. Wm. A. Pile to Maj. Genl. Rosecrans, February 23, 1864, 245–246, in Berlin et al., *Black Military Experience.* Also see Martha to My Dear Husband [Richard Glover], 244, in Berlin et al., *Black Military Experience.*

19. These letters are contained within the archives of the Freedmen's Bureau. They can be cross-referenced with the excerpts that appear in the *Congressional Globe,* as I have done here.

20. Thirty-eighth Congress, 1st Session, *Congressional Globe,* March 18, 1864, 1177. Almost the exact same letter was written to Congressman Henry T. Blow. See Brig. Genl. Wm. A. Pile to Hon. Henry T. Blow, February 26, 1864, in Berlin et al., *Black Military Experience,* 248–249; Stanley, "Instead of Waiting for the Thirteenth Amendment," 732–765.

21. Thirty-eighth Congress, 1st Session, *Congressional Globe,* March 22, 1864, 1229.

22. Thirty-eighth Congress, 1st Session, *Congressional Globe,* March 21, 1864, 1212; Thirty-eighth Congress, 2nd Session, *Congressional Globe,* January 9, 1865, 160.

23. Thirty-eighth Congress, 2nd Session, *Congressional Globe,* January 9, 1865, 160. Also see Richardson, *Greatest Nation on Earth,* 229.

24. Benjamin Quarles, *The Negro in the Civil War* (Boston, Mass.: Little, Brown and Co., 1953; reprint 1969), 200–202; Berlin et al., *Slaves No More,* 214–215.

25. Thirty-eighth Congress, 1st Session, *Congressional Globe,* February 13, 1864, 638, 640.

26. Thirty-eighth Congress, 1st Session, *Congressional Globe,* February 13, 1864, 639.

27. Thirty-eighth Congress, 1st Session, *Congressional Globe,* February 13, 1864, 639–640.

28. Thirty-eighth Congress, 1st Session, *Congressional Globe,* February 13, 1864, 639.

29. A. Lincoln to Hon. Charles Sumner, May 19, 1864, facsimile in Roy P. Basler, "And for His Widow and His Orphan," *Quarterly Journal of the Library of Congress,* 27 (October 1970): 290.

30. Thirty-eighth Congress, 1st Session, *Congressional Globe,* June 2, 1864, 265, June 25, 1864, 3233, and July 2, 1864, 3514, 3534; Basler, "And for His Widow and His Orphan," 290–294.

31. See Megan J. McClintock, "The Impact of the Civil War on Nineteenth-Century Marriages," in Paul Cimbala and Randall M. Miller, eds., *Union Soldiers and the Northern Home Front: Wartime Experiences, Postwar Adjustments* (New York: Fordham University Press, 2002), 395–416; McClintock, "Civil War Pensions and the Reconstruction of Union Families," *Journal of American History* (September 1996): 473–476.

32. Thirty-eighth Congress, 2nd Session, *Congressional Globe,* January 10, 1865, 161.

33. Ibid., 166.

34. Thirty-eighth Congress, 2nd Session, *Congressional Globe,* February 22, 1865, 1003.

35. Figures from *New York Times,* March 13, 1865. Also see Herbert G. Gutman, *The Black Family in Slavery and Freedom, 1750–1925* (New York: Vintage, 1977), 375; *Freedom: A Documentary History of Emancipation, 1861–1867,* Series 1, vol. 2, ed. Ira Berlin, Steven F. Miller, Joseph P. Reidy, and Leslie S. Rowland, *Wartime Genesis of Free Labor: The Upper South* (Cambridge, England: Cambridge University Press, 1993), 625–638.

36. Thomas James, *Life of Rev. Thomas James, by Himself* (Rochester, N.Y.: Post Express Printing Company, 1886), 19, electronic edition, Documenting the American South, University of North Carolina, Chapel Hill; Berlin et al., *Slaves No More,* 70, 73, 206–207; Gutman, *Black Family,* 375–378; *New York Times,* March 13, 1865; John McAuley Palmer, *Personal Recollections of John M. Palmer: The Story of an Earnest Life* (Cincinnati, Ohio: R. Clarke Co., 1901), 233, 234, 237–239; Bvt. Col. W. H. Sidwell to Capt. J. Bates Dickson, May 17, 1865, 601, in *Freedom: A Documentary History of Emancipation, 1861–1867,* Series I, vol. 1, ed. Ira Berlin, Barbara Fields, Thavolia Glymph, Joseph P. Reidy, and Leslie Rowland, *The Destruction of Slavery* (Cambridge, England: Cambridge University Press, 1985); *New York Times,* March 13, 1865.

37. Stanley, "Instead of Waiting for the Thirteenth Amendment," 732–765.

38. *Pastoral Letter from the Bishops of the Protestant Episcopal Church to the Clergy and Laity of the Church in the Confederate States of America, Delivered before the General Council, in St. Paul's Church, Augusta, Saturday, Nov. 22d, 1862* (Augusta, Ga.: Steam Power Press Chronicle and Sentinel, 1862), 11, electronic edition, Documenting the American South, University of North Carolina, Chapel Hill.

39. Gerardo Gurza-Lavalle, "Slavery Reform in Virginia, 1816–1865" (PhD diss., University of North Carolina, Chapel Hill, 2008), 225–228; Eugene Genovese, *A Consuming Fire: The Fall of the Confederacy in the Mind of the White Christian South* (Athens: Uni-

versity of Georgia Press, 1998), 22–23, 51–60; Drew Faust, *The Creation of Confederate Nationalism: Ideology and Identity in the Civil War South* (Baton Rouge: Louisiana State University Press, 1989), 78; Kimberly R. Kellison, "Toward Humanitarian Ends? Protestants and Slave Reform in South Carolina, 1830–1865," *South Carolina Historical Magazine,* 103 (July 2002): 210–225.

40. James Adair Lyon, "Slavery, and the Duties Growing out of the Relation," *Southern Presbyterian Review,* 16 (July 1863): 25, 29, 31.

41. Lyon, "Slavery, and the Duties Growing out of the Relation," 31, 35, 36.

42. Gurza-Lavalle, "Slavery Reform in Virginia," 228–239.

43. "A Slave Marriage Law," *Southern Presbyterian Review,* 16 (October 1863): 145, 146, 147.

44. Ibid., 149, 157.

45. Ibid., 154–155.

46. Ibid., 157.

47. Ibid., 153.

48. Ibid., 152.

49. Ibid., 148.

50. Ibid., 151.

51. Ibid., 160.

52. See Stephanie McCurry, *Confederate Reckoning: Power and Politics in the Civil War South* (Cambridge, Mass.: Harvard University Press, 2010), 315–357.

53. P[atrick] R. Cleburne et al., to Commanding General, The Corps, Division, Brigade, and Regimental Commanders of the Army of Tennessee [William H. T. Walker], January 2, 1864, in United States War Department, *The War of the Rebellion: A Compilation of the Official Records of the Union and Confederate Armies,* series 1, vol. 52, pt. 2, 586–587 [hereafter cited as *Official Records*]; McCurry, *Confederate Reckoning,* 324–357.

54. Cleburne to Walker, 587–588.

55. McCurry, *Confederate Reckoning,* 322–325.

56. Ibid., 325–327.

57. Cleburne to Walker, 588–592.

58. Davis to General W. H. T. Walker, January 13, 1864, *Official Records,* 596.

59. Anderson to Lieut. Gen. L. Polk, January 14, 1864, *Official Records,* 599.

60. See McCurry, *Confederate Reckoning,* 330–357; Bruce Levine, *Confederate Emancipation: Southern Plans to Free and Arm Slaves during the Civil War* (Oxford, England: Oxford University Press, 2007), 27–29.

6. Reconstructing Intimacies

1. Ira Berlin and Leslie S. Rowland, eds., *Families and Freedom: A Documentary History of African-American Kinship in the Civil War Era* (New York: New Press, 1997),

173, 176. Also see Herbert G. Gutman, *The Black Family in Slavery and Freedom, 1750–1925* (New York: Vintage, 1977), 424–425.

2. Chery? Williams to Nardy? Williams, June 1866, W-136 1866, Registered Letters Received, ser. 3379, TN Asst. Comr., Records of the Bureau of Refugees, Freedmen, and Abandoned Lands, Record Group 105 (hereafter cited as RG 105), National Archives (hereafter cited as NARA) [FSSP A-6357]. Copies of National Archives documents consulted at the Freedmen and Southern Society Project, University of Maryland, are hereafter cited in brackets as FSSP, followed by the project's file number. (Note that the names are difficult to decipher in the original records.)

3. Dorothy Sterling, ed., *We Are Your Sisters: Black Women in the Nineteenth Century* (New York: W. W. Norton, 1984), 312–313; Frances Smith Foster, ed., *Love and Marriage in Early African America* (Boston, Mass.: Northeastern University Press, 2008), 293–296; Heather Andrea Williams, *Help Me to Find My People: The African American Search for Family Lost in Slavery* (Chapel Hill: University of North Carolina Press, 2012).

4. A. Murdock to Col. Thomas, 17 July 1865, in *Freedom: A Documentary History of Emancipation, 1861–1867,* Series 3, vol. 1, ed. Steven Hahn, Steven F. Miller, Susan E. O'Donovan, John C. Rodrigue, and Leslie S. Rowland, *Land and Labor, 1865* (Chapel Hill: University of North Carolina Press, 2008), 513–514; Chapn. Isaac Cross to Col. Jno. Eaton, June 13,1865, in *Freedom: A Documentary History of Emancipation, 1861–1867,* Series 1, vol. 2, ed. Ira Berlin, Steven F. Miller, Joseph P. Reidy, and Leslie S. Rowland, *Wartime Genesis of Free Labor: The Upper South* (Cambridge, England: Cambridge University Press, 1993), 541–542; Affidavit of Jacob Giles, September 12, 1865, in *Freedom: A Documentary History of Emancipation, 1861–1867,* Series 1, vol. 1, ed. Ira Berlin, Barbara Fields, Thavolia Glymph, Joseph P. Reidy, and Leslie Rowland, *The Destruction of Slavery* (Cambridge, England: Cambridge University Press, 1986), 387; Joshua S. Clarke to Col. John Eaton, [Sept? 1865], Berlin et al., *The Destruction of Slavery,* 388–389.

5. Sergeant Alex Shaw to Mr. E. M. Stanton, November 19, 1865, in *Freedom: A Documentary History of Emancipation, 1861–1867,* Series 2, ed. Ira Berlin, Joseph P. Reidy, and Leslie S. Rowland, *The Black Military Experience* (Cambridge, England: Cambridge University Press, 1982), 776; Sergeant Alex Shaw to Mr. E. M. Stanton, February 8, 1866, in Berlin et al., *Black Military Experience,* 776; A. A. Shaw to hon. E. M. Stanton, November 12, 1866, in Berlin et al., *Black Military Experience,* 776.

6. Unsigned to Sir, Dec. 1865, in Berlin et al., *Black Military Experience,* 725–727; Sergt. Richard Estheredge and Wm. Benson to Genl. Howard [May or June 1865], in Berlin et al., *Black Military Experience,* 729. See also Berlin et al., *Black Military Experience,* 727–728.

7. Nancy Cott, *Public Vows: A History of Marriage and the Nation* (Cambridge, Mass.: Harvard University Press, 2000); Laura F. Edwards, *Gendered Strife and Confusion: The Political Culture of Reconstruction* (Urbana: University of Illinois Press, 1997); Nancy Bercaw, *Gendered Freedoms: Race, Rights, and the Politics of Household in the*

Delta, 1861–1875 (Gainesville: University Press of Florida, 2003); Katherine Franke, *Wedlocked: The Perils of Marriage Equality: How African Americans and Gays Mistakenly Thought the Right to Marry Would Set Them Free* (New York: New York University Press, 2015); Hendrik Hartog, *Man and Wife in America: A History* (Cambridge, Mass.: Harvard University Press, 2000); Michael Grossberg, *Governing the Hearth: Law and the Family in Nineteenth-Century America* (Chapel Hill: University of North Carolina Press, 1985); Karen Lystra, *Searching the Heart: Women, Men and Romantic Love in Nineteenth-Century America* (New York: Oxford University Press, 1992); Peter W. Bardaglio, *Reconstructing the Household: Families, Sex, and the Law in the Nineteenth-Century South* (Chapel Hill: University of North Carolina Press, 1995).

8. Lystra, *Searching the Heart,* 12–27.

9. Fanny Smart to Adam Smart, February 13, 1866, in Sterling, *We Are Your Sisters,* 316–317; also see Lawrence Levine, *Been in the Storm So Long: The Aftermath of Slavery* (New York: Vintage, 1980), 234.

10. Lystra, *Searching the Heart,* 28–55.

11. Elizabeth A. Regosin and Donald R. Shaffer, eds., *Voices of Emancipation: Understanding Slavery, the Civil War, and Reconstruction through the U.S. Pension Bureau* (New York: New York University Press, 2008), 2–6; Beverly Schwartzberg, " 'Lots of Them Did That': Desertion, Bigamy, and Marital Fluidity in Late-Nineteenth-Century America," *Journal of Social History,* 37 (April 2004): 573–600.

12. Regosin and Shaffer, *Voices of Emancipation;* Schwartzberg, " 'Lots of Them Did That,' " 573–600.

13. Mary Farmer-Kaiser, *Freedwomen and the Freemen's Bureau: Race, Gender, and Public Policy in the Age of Emancipation* (New York: Fordham University Press, 2010), 141–166; Bercaw, *Gendered Freedoms;* Noralee Frankel, *Freedom's Women: Black Women and Families in Civil War Era Mississippi* (Bloomington: Indiana University Press, 1999); Edwards, *Gendered Strife and Confusion;* Leslie A. Schwalm, *A Hard Fight for We: Women's Transition from Slavery to Freedom in South Carolina* (Urbana: University of Illinois Press, 1997); Herbert G. Gutman, *The Black Family in Slavery and Freedom, 1750–1925* (New York: Vintage, 1977); Franke, *Wedlocked,* 69–84, 126–142.

14. Regosin and Shaffer, *Voices of Emancipation,* 172–177. See also Franklin Shelton to Mr. Hutchinson, 15 May 1866, Letters Received, ser. 3690, Columbia TX Subasst. Comr., RG 105, NARA [FSSP A-3380].

15. Lucy Skipwith to "My Dear Master," December 7, 1865, in Sterling, *We Are Your Sisters,* 310; "Letters of George Skipwith," http://nationalhumanitiescenter.org/pds/maai /enslavement/text4/skipwith.pdf; Randall M. Miller, ed., *Dear Master: Letters of a Slave Family* (Ithaca, N.Y.: Cornell University Press, 1978), 194.

16. Mary Lacey to Col. W. W. Rogers, November 17, 1866; and Affidavit of James Lacey, November 28, 1866, in *Freedom: A Documentary History of Emancipation, 1861–1867,* Series 3, vol. 2, ed. René Hayden, Anthony E. Kaye, Kate Masur, Steven F. Miller,

Susan E. O'Donovan, Leslie S. Rowland, and Stephen A. West, *Land and Labor, 1866–1867* (Chapel Hill: University of North Carolina Press, 2013), 837–838.

17. W C Hebener to Grandma, 20 Jan. 1865, W. C. Hebener to Miss Maggie, 5 July 1865, and William Hebener to the Provost Marshal, 9 Aug. 1865, #18 1865, Registered Letters Received, ser. 4239, Richmond VA Supt., RG 105, NARA [FSSP A-8297].

18. W C Hebener to Grandma.

19. Ibid.; Affidavit of Mariah Logston, 17 Oct 1866, L-170 1866, Letters Received, ser. 1068, KY Asst. Comr., RG 105, NARA [FSSP A-4283].

20. Henry D. Jenkins, WPA Narratives, South Carolina, vol. 3, pt. 3, 24.

21. Ed MCCree, WPA Narratives, Georgia, vol. 13, pt. 3, 64; Aunt Silvia Witherspoon, WPA Narratives, Alabama, vol. 6, pt. 2, 430. Also see Hannah Crasson, WPA Narratives, North Carolina, vol. 14, pt. 1, 189; Rachel Adams, WPA Narratives, Georgia, vol. 12, pt. 1, 8; Susan Castle, WPA Narratives, Georgia, vol. 12, pt. 1, 18; Alec Bostwick, WPA Narratives, Georgia, vol. 12, pt. 1, 111; Sophie D. Bell, WPA Narratives, Arkansas, vol. 8, pt. 1, 139; Georgia Johnson, WPA Narratives, Georgia, vol. 12, pt. 2, 334; James Bolton, WPA Narratives, Georgia, vol. 12, pt. 1, 103; Harriet Jones, WPA Narratives, Texas, vol. 4, pt. 2, 235.

22. See, for example, Ruby Lorraine Radford, WPA Narratives, Georgia, vol. 13, pt. 4, 320.

23. See, for example, Pension claim of Lydia Smith, widow of William Grant, USCI 33, Co. C, #118450; Pension claim of Susan Johnson Pyatt, widow of John Johnson, USCI 21, Co. D, #169265. Note that these categories of intimate relationships can be overlapping and confusing in the records, and historians have offered no completely consistent definitions of them. I've based my definitions on the broad range of documents I've examined that implicitly and explicitly reveal them. See Bercaw, *Gendered Freedoms,* 106–110, 147–151; Frankel, *Freedom's Women,* 80–90, 100; Schwalm, *A Hard Fight for We,* 243–248.

24. Regosin and Shaffer, *Voices of Emancipation,* 179–186.

25. On common-law marriages, see the following: Ariela R. Dubler, "Wifely Behavior: A Legal History of Acting Married," *Columbia Law Review,* 100 (May 2000): 957–2000; Ariela Gross, "Governing through Contract: Common Law Marriage in the Nineteenth Century," *Yale Law Journal,* 107 (1998): 1885–1920; Sara L. Zeigler, "Wifely Duties: Marriage, Labor, and the Common Law in Nineteenth-Century America," *Social Science History,* 20 (Spring 1996): 64–96; Norma Basch, "Marriage and Domestic Relations," in *Cambridge History of Law in America,* ed. Michael Grossberg and Christopher Tomlins, vol. 2 (Cambridge, England: Cambridge University Press, 2008); Ellen Kandoian, "Cohabitation, Common Law Marriage, and the Possibility of a Shared Moral Life," *Georgetown Law Journal,* 75 (1986–1987). On informal marriages, see Cott, *Public Vows*; Hartog, *Man and Wife;* Karl N. Llewellyn, "Behind the Law of Divorce: I," *Columbia Law Review,* 32 (December 1932): 1281–1308; Schwartzberg, "'Lots of Them Did That,'" 573–600; Barry A.

Crouch, "The 'Chords of Love': Legalizing Black Marital and Family Rights in Postwar Texas," *Journal of Negro History,* 39 (1994): 334–335; Bercaw, *Gendered Freedoms;* Frankel, *Freedom's Women;* Edwards, *Gendered Strife and Confusion;* Schwalm, *A Hard Fight for We;* Franke, *Wedlocked,* 63–92.

26. On community standing, see Cott, *Public Vows;* Bercaw, *Gendered Freedoms;* Frankel, *Freedom's Women;* Edwards, *Gendered Strife and Confusion;* Schwalm, *A Hard Fight for We;* Dylan C. Penningroth, *The Claims of Kinfolk: African American Property and Community in the Nineteenth-Century South* (Chapel Hill: University of North Carolina Press, 2002).

27. Regosin and Shaffer, *Voices of Emancipation,* 156–162; Adeline Willis, WPA Narratives, Georgia, vol. 13, pt. 4, 166; Matilda Miller, WPA Narratives, Arkansas, vol. 10, pt. 5, 91; Melvin Smith, WPA Narratives, Georgia, vol. 13, pt. 3, 293; Interview of Sarah Fitzpatrick, 1938, Alabama, in John W. Blassingame, ed., *Slave Testimony: Two Centuries of Letters, Speeches, Interviews, and Autobiographies* (Baton Rouge: Louisiana State University Press, 1977), 639–655.

28. Eli Coleman, WPA Narratives, Texas, vol. 4, pt. 1, 238–239; Toby Jones, WPA Narratives, Texas, vol. 4, pt. 2, 251.

29. Regosin and Shaffer, *Voices of Emancipation,* 179–186.

30. Megan J. McClintock, "Binding Up the Nation's Wounds: Nationalism, Civil War Pension, and American Families, 1861–1890" (PhD diss., Rutgers University, 1994); McClintock, "Civil War Pensions and the Reconstruction of Union Families," *Journal of American History,* 83 (September 1996): 456–480; Brandi Clay Brimmer, "All Her Rights and Privileges: African-American Women and the Politics of Civil War Widows' Pensions" (PhD diss., University of California, Los Angeles, 2006); Brimmer, "Black Women's Politics, Narratives of Sexual Immorality, and Pension Bureaucracy in Mary Lee's North Carolina Neighborhood," *Journal of Southern History,* 80 (November 2014): 827; Elizabeth Regosin, *Freedom's Promise: Ex-Slave Families and Citizenship in the Age of Emancipation* (Charlottesville: University of Virginia Press, 2002); Regosin and Shaffer, *Voices of Emancipation;* Michelle A. Krowl, " 'Her Just Dues': Civil War Pensions of African American Women in Virginia," in Janet L. Coryell, ed., *Negotiating Boundaries of Southern Womanhood: Dealing with the Powers That Be* (Columbia: University of Missouri Press, 2000), 48–70; Sven E. Wilson, "Prejudice and Policy: Racial Discrimination in the Union Army Disability Pension System, 1865–1906," *American Journal of Public Health,* 100 (February 2010): 2–11; Frankel, *Freedom's Women,* 87; Franke, *Wedlocked,* 69–84.

31. Pension claim of Elisabeth Wright, widow of Rufus Wright, USCI 1, Co. G, #152132.

32. Timothy J. Gilfoyle, "The Hearts of Nineteenth-Century Men: Bigamy and Working-Class Marriage in New York City, 1800–1890," *Prospects,* 19 (October 1994): 135–160; Schwartzberg, " 'Lots of Them Did That,' " 573–600; Cott, *Public Vows;* Hartog,

Man and Wife; Llewellyn, "Behind the Law of Divorce: I," 1281–1308; Franke, *Wedlocked,* 131–140, 164–170.

33. Gilfoyle, "The Hearts of Nineteenth-Century Men," 135–160.

34. See Pension claim of Lucy Findley Boles, widow of Booker Boles, USCI 56, Co. E, #109996.

35. Pension claim of Talitha (Lithia) Taft, widow of Gray Payton (aka Gray Taft), USCI 36, Co. D, #361760; Pension claim of Ann Greenwood Payton, widow of Gray Payton (aka Gray Taft), USCI 36, Co. D, #89262.

36. *David Brown vs. Elinor & Emma Brown,* 2 Nov. 1865, Affidavits and Papers Relating to Complaints, ser. 1017, Savannah GA Subasst. Comr., RG 105, NARA [FSSP A-5780]; WPA Narratives, Georgia, vol. 12, pt. 2, 268–271; Lina Hunter, WPA Narratives, Georgia, vol. 12, pt. 2, 268; Jos. McWhorter to Maj. Knox, 19 April 1867, and Jos. McWhorter to Maj. Knox, 28 April 1867, Unregistered Letters Received, ser. 721, Athens GA Subasst. Comr., RG 105, NARA [FSSP A-5719]; Affidavit of Sarah Oliver, 16 May 1867, vol. 121, p. 226, Letters Sent, ser. 697, Albany GA Agent, RG 105, NARA [FSSP A-5545].

37. *Flakes Bulletin* (Galveston, TX), September 8, 1865: *James Hall v. Mary Hall.* The charges were brought a bit prematurely in this case, as the state of Texas had not passed laws regarding ex-slave marriages to place them in sync with laws applied to free white people. The judge dismissed the case and the husband lost his wife.

38. Gilfoyle, "The Hearts of Nineteenth-Century Men."

39. Bercaw, *Gendered Freedoms,* 164–172; Gutman, *The Black Family,* 86; Complaint of Anderson Meriwether, 26 April 1867, vol. 174, p. 30, Register of Complaints, ser. 723, Athens GA Subasst. Comr., RG 105, NARA [FSSP A-5721].

40. Carole Shammas, *A History of Household Government in America* (Charlottesville: University of Virginia Press, 2002), 8; Joyce W. Warren, *Women, Money, and the Law: Nineteenth-Century Fiction, Gender, and the Courts* (Iowa City: University of Iowa Press, 2009); Joan Hoff-Wilson, *Law, Gender, and Injustice: A Legal History of U.S. Women* (New York: New York University Press, 1991).

41. Amy Dru Stanley, "Marriage, Property, Class," in Nancy Hewitt, ed., *A Companion to American Women's History* (Malden, Mass.: Blackwell Publishers, 2008), 193–205; Amy Dru Stanley, *From Bondage to Contract: Wage Labor, Marriage, and the Market in the Age of Slave Emancipation* (Cambridge, England: Cambridge University Press, 1998), 1–59, 138–174; Cott, *Public Vows;* Christine Stansell, *City of Women: Sex and Class in New York, 1789–1860* (New York: Albert A. Knopf, 1982); Lawrence Glickman, *American Workers and the Making of Consumer Society* (Ithaca, N.Y.: Cornell University Press, 1999).

42. Cott, *Public Vows,* 19.

43. Stanley, "Marriage, Property, Class"; Stanley, *From Bondage to Contract;* Cott, *Public Vows.*

44. Lystra, *Searching the Heart;* Hartog, *Man and Wife;* Llewellyn, "Behind the Law of Divorce: I," 1281–1308; Grossberg, *Governing the Hearth;* Cott, *Public Vows.*

45. The character of expectations such as these can be found in the following documents, among others: Affidavit of Allen Robinson, 15 Aug. 1866, filed with Catherine Robinson to Bvt. Brig. Gen'l O. Brown, 26 July 1866, Letters Received, ser. 4192, Petersburg VA Supt., RG 105, NARA [FSSP A-7998]; *Edward Smith vs. Harriet Smith,* 1 May 1867, vol. 506, Proceedings of Freedmen's Court, ser. 4352, Yorktown VA Asst. Subasst. Comr., RG 105, NARA [FSSP A-8373]; *Thomas Carey vs. Nancy Carey,* 1 May 1867, vol. 506, Proceedings of Freedmen's Court, ser. 4352, Yorktown VA Asst. Subasst. Comr., RG 105, NARA [FSSP A-8373]; J. C. DeGress, "To all whom it may concern," 3 Dec. 1866, vol. 100, p. 367, Letters Sent, ser. 3716, Houston TX Subasst. Comr., RG 105, NARA [FSSP A-3414].

46. Bercaw, *Gendered Freedoms;* Frankel, *Freedom's Women,* 79–122.

47. Bercaw, *Gendered Freedoms,* 147–154.

48. Interview of Sarah Fitzpatrick, 1938, in Blassingame, *Slave Testimony,* 639–655. Also see Capt Fred. Mosebach to Capt. N. S. Hill, 8 May 1866, vol. 222, p. 17, Letters Sent and Endorsements Sent and Received, ser. 832, Columbus GA Subasst. Comr., RG 105, NARA [FSSP A-5622]. See Bercaw, *Gendered Freedoms,* 110–118.

49. Underwood for Ned Nuffer to Maj. Pierce; 30 Nov. 1866, Letters Received, ser. 80, Demopolis AL Supt., RG 105, NARA [FSSP A-2138]; Petition of Clary Rosser, [July? 1866], unsigned statement, [July? 1866], and Clary Rosser to Lutenant Foot, [July? 1866], all enclosed in Bvt. Col. A. G. Bready to Lt. John M. Foote, 30 July 1866, Letters Received, ser. 2666, Halifax NC Asst. Supt., RG 105, NARA [FSSP A-924].

50. See Bercaw, *Gendered Freedoms,* 110–118.

51. Petition of Clary Rosser.

52. See, for example, L A Hildreth to Agt of Freedmens Bureau, May 25, 1866, in Hayden et al., *Land and Labor, 1866–1867,* 610. See also Frankel, *Freedom's Women,* 106–107, 127, 155, which indicates that 5 percent of the complaints filed by Mississippi freedmen with the Freedmen's Bureau were related to domestic violence; Reva B. Siegel, "'The Rule of Love': Wife Beating as Prerogative and Privacy," *Yale Law Journal,* 105, no. 8 (June 1996): 2117–2207.

53. Charles Reddick to "my once dear wife," 18 Sept [1866], filed with Bvt. Maj. Jno. J. Knox to subassistant commissioner at Charleston, SC, 8 Apr. 1867, Unregistered Letters Received, ser. 721, Athens GA Subasst. Comr., RG 105, NARA [FSSP A-5718].

54. See, for example, Petition in case of *Lewis Dale vs. David J. Dickinson,* [27 May 1866], Affidavits & Petitions of Freedmen and White Citizens, ser. 653, GA Asst. Comr., RG 105, NARA [FSSP A-5163]. In this case the man who was the sweetheart claimed to be the father and had acted in that capacity during the girl's life. He contested custody over the master's rights to the child. The mother had been sold away and her husband did not come forward to claim custody. Rebecca J. Scott, "The Battle over the

Child: Child Apprenticeship and the Freedmen's Bureau in North Carolina," in N. Ray Hiner and Joseph M. Hawes, eds., *Growing up in American: Children in Historical Perspective* (Urbana: University of Illinois Press, 1985), 193–207; Karin L. Zipf, "Reconstructing 'Free Woman': African-American Women, Apprenticeship, and Custody Rights during Reconstruction," *Journal of Women's History*, 12 (Spring 2000) 8–3; Farmer-Kaiser, *Freedwomen and the Freemen's Bureau.*

55. Frankel, *Freedom's Women*, 123–145; Farmer-Kaiser, *Freedwomen and the Freedmen's Bureau.*

56. 2nd Lt Ira D. McClary to Capt William H. Sterling, 21 Feb. 1867, in Hayden et al., *Land and Labor, 1866–1867*, 633–634, 634–369; Affidavit of Charlotte Dennis, March 1867, TX; *Maria Kiddoo vs. Isaac Kiddoo* (alias Isaac Runnells), 24 June 1867, vol. 238, pp. 12–15, Register of Complaints, ser. 859, Cuthbert GA Agent, RG 105, NARA [FSSP A-5558]; Sharlotte Paris to the Federal authorities, 18 Oct. 1866, in Hayden et al., *Land and Labor, 1866–1867*, 625–626; A. B. Clark to Capt. W. F. White, 25 May 1867, Letters Received, ser. 973, Newton GA Agent, RG 105, NARA [FSSP A-5600].

57. Affidavit of Charlotte Dennis, March 18, 1867, in Hayden et al., *Land and Labor, 1866–1867*, 635–636; Two letters from Charlotte Dennis to General Dennis, March 28 & May 18, 1867, Hayden et al., *Land and Labor, 1866–1867*, 636–639; Charlotte Dennis to General Griffin, May 18, 1867, Hayden et al., *Land and Labor, 1866–1867*, 637–639.

58. 2nd Lt Ira D. McClary to Capt William H. Sterling, February 21, 1867, in Hayden et al., *Land and Labor, 1866–1867*, 633–634; Affidavit of Charlotte Dennis; Affidavit of Peter G. Graham, 2 Mar. 1867, Miscellaneous Records, ser. 2851, Salisbury NC Supt., RG 105, NARA [FSSP A-997].

7. "The Most Cruel Wrongs"

1. General Orders No. 8, "Marriage Rules," August 11, 1865, Headquarters Assistant Commissioner, Bureau of Refugees, Freedmen, and Abandoned Lands, South Carolina, Georgia, and Florida, in 39th Congress, 1st Session, serial vol. 1256, House Ex. Doc. No. 70, "Report of Commissioners of Freedmen's Bureau," March 1866, 108–111.

2. Frances Butler Leigh, *Ten Years on a Georgia Plantation since the War* (London: R. Bentley and Son, 1883), 165–167; Isaac Brinckerhoff, *Advice to Freedmen*, rev. ed. (New York: American Tract Society, 1865), 27–28; Whitelaw Reid, *After the War: A Southern Tour: May 1, 1865, to May 1, 1866* (Cincinnati, Ohio: Moore, Wilstach and Baldwin, 1866), 95, 106–107, 109, 126, 538–539; John Richard Dennett, *The South as It Is: 1865–1866* (Tuscaloosa: University of Alabama Press, 1965), 164; Sidney Andrews, *The South since the War: As Shown by Fourteen Weeks of Travel and Observation in Georgia and the Carolinas* (Boston, Mass.: Ticknor and Fields, 1866), 178–179; Edward King, *The Great South; A Record of Journeys in Louisiana, Texas, the Indian Territory, Missouri, Arkansas, Mississippi, Alabama, Georgia, Florida, South Carolina, North Carolina, Kentucky, Tennessee,*

Virginia, West Virginia, and Maryland (Hartford, Conn.: American Publishing Co., 1875), 430, 779–780, 782; Testimony of William J. Minor, Smith-Brady Commission, April 25, 1865, in *Freedom: A Documentary History of Emancipation, 1861–1867,* Series 1, vol. 3, ed. Ira Berlin, Thavolia Glymph, Steven F. Miller, Joseph P. Reidy, Leslie S. Rowland, and Julie Saville, *Wartime Genesis of Free Labor: The Lower South* (Cambridge, England: Cambridge University Press, 1990), 599–607.

3. Brinckerhoff, *Advice to Freedmen,* 10, 13. Also see Clinton B. Fisk, *Plain Counsels for Freedmen: In Sixteen Brief Lectures* (Boston, Mass.: American Tract Society, 1866), 31; Saidiya Hartman, *Scenes of Subjection: Terror, Slavery, and Self-Making in Nineteenth-Century America* (New York: Oxford University Press, 1997), 130–161.

4. Fisk, *Plain Counsels,* 23, 26–27.

5. Ibid., 32, 34; Brinckerhoff, *Advice to Freedmen,* 29.

6. Laura Matilda Towne, *Letters and Diary of Laura M. Towne Written from the Sea Islands of South Carolina, 1862–1884,* ed. Rupert Sargent Holland (Cambridge, Mass.: Riverside Press, 1912), 183.

7. 1st Lt. Edwin Lyon to Brv't. Brig. Gen'l. O. Brown, 31 May 1866, Narrative Reports of Conditions of Bureau Affairs, ser. 3802, VA Asst. Comr., RG 105, NARA [FSSP A-7435]. For related documents, see *Freedom: A Documentary History of Emancipation, 1861–1867,* Series 3, vol. 2, ed. René Hayden, Anthony E. Kaye, Kate Masur, Steven F. Miller, Susan E. O'Donovan, Leslie S. Rowland, and Stephen A. West, *Land and Labor, 1866–1867* (Chapel Hill: University of North Carolina Press, 2013), 415–420.

8. See, for example, Letter From Samuel Smith, *Savannah Tribune,* April 18, 1876; Dylan Penningroth, *The Claims of Kinfolk: African American Property and Community in the Nineteenth-Century South* (Chapel Hill: University of North Carolina Press, 2003); Elizabeth Pleck, "Wife Beating in Nineteenth-Century America," *Victimology,* 4 (1970): 60–74; Noralee Frankel, *Freedom's Women: Black Women and Families in Civil War Era Mississippi* (Bloomington: Indiana University Press, 1999). See articles in the *Christian Recorder* inculcating conventional ideas about marriage: December 26, 1868; July 3, 1873; August 14, 1873; May 13, 1875; and January 24, 1878.

9. Austa M. French, *Slavery in South Carolina and the Ex-Slaves, or, The Port Royal Mission* (New York: W. M. French, 1862), 165; Brinckerhoff, *Advice to Freedmen,* 29.

10. Policies and practices of the Freedmen's Bureau, as well as state and local governments, are based on the following sources: U.S. Senate, "Laws in Relation to Freedmen," Senate Ex. Doc. 6, 39th Congress, 2nd session, serial vol. 1276 (January 1867); U.S. House of Representatives, "Report of the Commissioners of the Freedmen's Bureau," Exec. Doc. No. 70, 39th Congress, 1st session, serial vol. 1256 (March 1866); Elaine C. Everly, "Marriage Registers of Freedmen," *Prologue,* 5 (Fall 1973): 150–154; Reginald Washington, "Sealing the Sacred Bonds of Holy Matrimony: Freedmen's Bureau Marriage Records," *Prologue,* 37 (Spring 2005): 58–65; John Wallace, *Carpet-bag Rule in Florida: The Inside Workings of the Reconstruction of Civil Government* (Jacksonville, Fla.: Da Costa

Printing, 1888), 33; William Watson Davis, *The Civil War and Reconstruction in Florida* (New York: Columbia University Press, 1913); Frankel, *Freedom's Women;* Herbert G. Gutman, *The Black Family in Slavery and Freedom, 1750–1925* (New York: Vintage, 1977); Katherine M. Franke, "Becoming Citizen: Reconstruction Era Regulation of African American Marriages," *Yale Journal of Law and the Humanities,* 11 (1999): 251–309; Nancy Cott, *Public Vows: A History of Marriage and the Nation* (Cambridge, Mass.: Harvard University Press, 2001); Darlene C. Goring, "The History of Slave Marriage in the United States," *John Marshall Law Review,* 39 (2006): 299–347; Barry A. Crouch, "The 'Chords of Love': Legalizing Black Marital and Family Rights in Postwar Texas," *Journal of Negro History,* 39 (1994): 334–351; "Virginia's Legitimization Act of 1866," *Virginia Magazine of History and Biography,* 86 (July 1978): 339–344; Laura Edwards, *Gendered Strife and Confusion: The Political Culture of Reconstruction* (Urbana: University of Illinois Press, 1997); Leslie A. Schwalm, *"A Hard Fight For We": Women's Transition from Slavery to Freedom in South Carolina* (Urbana: University of Illinois Press, 1997), 19–44; Nancy Bercaw, *Gendered Freedoms: Race, Rights, and the Politics of Household in the Delta, 1861–1875* (Gainesville: University Press of Florida, 2003); Barnetta McGhee White, *Somebody Knows My Name: Marriages of Freed People in North Carolina County by County* (Athens, Ga.: Iberian Publishing, 1995); Donald G. Nieman, *To Set the Law in Motion: The Freedmen's Bureau and the Legal Rights of Blacks, 1865–1868* (Millwood, N.Y.: KTO Press, 1979).

    11. U.S. Senate, "Laws in Relation to Freedmen," 208; Schwalm, *A Hard Fight For We,* 241; Everly, "Marriage Registers," 152–153.

    12. General Orders No. 8, "Marriage Rules," August 11, 1865, in "Report of the Commissioners of the Freedmen's Bureau," 108–111.

    13. Everly, "Marriage Registers of Freedmen," 153; Goring, "The History of Slave Marriage," 337.

    14. *Edward Smith vs. Harriet Smith,* 1 May 1867, vol. 506, Proceedings of Freedmen's Court, ser. 4352, Yorktown VA Asst. Subasst. Comr., RG 105, NARA [FSSP A-8373]; *Thomas Carey vs. Nancy Carey,* 1 May 1867, vol. 506, Proceedings of Freedmen's Court, ser. 4352, Yorktown VA Asst. Subasst. Comr., RG 105, NARA [FSSP A-8373]; William Sullivan to Lieut. T. H. Ward, 13 Dec. 1865, Unregistered Letters Received, ser. 3522, Memphis TN Supt., RG 105, NARA [FSSP A-6520]; John C. Dickson to Genl Davis Tillson, April 28, 1866, in *Freedom: A Documentary History of Emancipation, 1861–1867,* Series 3, vol. 2, ed. René Hayden et al., *Land and Labor, 1866–1867* (Chapel Hill: University of North Carolina Press, 2013), 604–605; Testimony in *United States vs. Collins Epps,* n.d., and decision by DeWitt Brown, 25 May 1867, Letters Received, ser. 3786, Wharton TX Subasst. Comr., RG 105, NARA [FSSP A-3459]; N. Gallaher to Capt W W Deane, 10 May 1866, Warrenton, GA; L A Hildreth to Agt of Freedmens Bureau, May 25, 1866, in Hayden et al., *Land and Labor, 1866–1867,* 610; Katherine Franke, *Wedlocked: The Perils*

of Marriage Equality: How African Americans and Gays Mistakenly Thought the Right to Marry Would Set Them Free (New York: New York University Press, 2015).

15. Cott, *Public Vows*, 88, 94–96, 99–102; Eric Foner, *Reconstruction: America's Unfinished Revolution: 1863–1877* (New York: Harper and Row, 1988), 243–246; Peggy Cooper Davis, *Neglected Stories: The Constitution and Family Values* (New York: Hill and Wang, 1997), 50.

16. Florida, *Journal of Proceedings of the Convention of Florida, Begun and Held at the Capital of the State, at Tallahassee, Wednesday, October 25th, A.D. 1865;* Wallace, *Carpet-bag Rule in Florida*, 33; Also see Davis, *The Civil War and Reconstruction in Florida*, 416.

17. Florida, *Journal of the House of the Representatives of the General Assembly of the State of Florida*, 2nd Sess., 14th Gen. Ass. (Tallahassee, Fla.: Dyke and Sparhawk, 1866), 19, on November 14, 1866; Wallace, *Carpet-bag Rule in Florida*, 33; Davis, *Civil War and Reconstruction in Florida*, 416; Circular no. 9, Freedmen's Bureau, Tallahassee, FL, November 15, 1866 (issued by T. W. Osborn), in "Report of the Commissioners of the Freedmen's Bureau," 86–87; Darlene Goring, "The History of Slave Marriage," 333–334.

18. U.S. Senate, "Laws in Relation to Freedmen," 208; *The Statute at Large of South Carolina Vol. XII containing the Acts from December 1861 to December 1866. An Act to Establish and Regulate the Domestic Relations of Persons of Color and to Amend the Law in Relation to Paupers and Vagrancy Act No. 4733. General Assembly, 19 December 1865* (Columbia, S.C.: Republican Printing Corp., 1875): 269–285; Schwalm, *A Hard Fight for We*, 241–242.

19. U.S. Senate, "Laws in Relation to Freedmen," 198, 182; Washington, "Sealing the Sacred Bonds of Holy Matrimony"; Goring, "The History of Slave Marriage," 318, 323; Edwards, *Gendered Strife*, 32; White, *Somebody Knows My Name*, xiv–xv.

20. U.S. Senate, "Laws in Relation to Freedmen," 162–163, 168, 179–180, 221, 227–228; Alabama, Constitutional Convention (1867), *Official Journal of the Constitutional Convention of the State of Alabama, Held in the City of Montgomery, Commencing on Tuesday, November 5th;* "Virginia's Legitimization Act of 1866, " 339–344; Goring, "History of Slave Marriage," 316, 320, 337.

21. Louisiana, *Official Journal of the Proceedings of the Convention, for Framing a Constitution for the State of Louisiana* (New Orleans, La.: J. B. Roudanez and Co., 1867–1868), 16, 48, 106, 192, 206–207; *Acts Passed by the General Assembly of the State of Louisiana* (New Orleans, La.: A. L. Lee, 1868), 278–279; Charles Vincent, "Negro Leadership and Programs in the Louisiana Constitutional Convention of 1868," *Louisiana History,* 10 (Autumn 1969): 346–349.

22. Texas, *Journal of the Reconstruction Convention: Which Met at Austin, Texas, June 1, A.D., 1868,* vol. 1 (Austin, Texas: Tracy, Siemering and Co., Printers, 1870), 240, 751–752, 767; Ocie Speer, *A Treatise on the Law of Marital Rights in Texas* (Rochester,

N.Y.: The Lawyers Co-Operative Publishing Co., 1916), 8; Crouch, "The 'Chords of Love,'" 334–351; Bercaw, *Gendered Freedoms*, 164.

23. J. L. Thorp to Lieut. John Tyler, 30 April 1867, Narrative Reports of Operations from Subordinate Officers, ser. 242, AR Asst. Comr., RG 105, NARA [FSSP A-2486]; Circular no. 9, Freedmen's Bureau, Tallahassee, FL, November 15, 1866 (issued by T. W. Osborn, Col. and Asst commissioner, BRFAL, FL) in "Report of the Commissioners of the Freedmen's Bureau," 86–87; "Laws in Relation to Freedmen," 182, 223.

24. C W Pierce to S L Bennett, May 25, 1866, in Hayden et al., *Land and Labor, 1866–1867*, 609.

25. U.S. Senate, "Laws in Relation to Freedmen," 182, 223, 226; *The Statute at Large of South Carolina*, 269–285; Texas Constitutional Convention, *Journal of the Reconstruction Convention*, 1868, 226; Theodore Brantner Wilson, *The Black Codes of the South* (Tuscaloosa: University of Alabama Press, 1965), 61–80.

26. W. W. Dugger to Major Pierce, n.d. [1866], Letters Received, ser. 80, Demopolis AL Supt., RG 105, NARA [FSSP A-2141].

27. Joel Mathews to Brig. Genl Davis Tillson, December 6, 1865, *Freedom: A Documentary History of Emancipation, 1861–1867*, Series 3, vol. 1, ed. Steven Hahn, Steven F. Miller, Susan E. O'Donovan, John C. Rodrigue, and Leslie S. Rowland, *Land and Labor, 1865* (Chapel Hill: University of North Carolina Press, 2008), 859–861.

28. F. R. Robert to Col. Howard, 31 Aug. 1867, Letters Received, ser. 700, Albany GA Agent, RG 105, NARA [FSSP A-5551]; Thoˢ H. Anderson to the Provost Marshall [*sic*], 27 March 1866, Unregistered Letters Received, ser. 3067, Anderson Court House SC Acting Subasst. Comr., RG 105, NARA [FSSP A-7220].

29. Clara Garland to Provost Marshall Louisa C. House, April 15, 1867, in Hayden et al., *Land and Labor, 1866–1867*, 598–600.

30. Clara Garland to Maj Hopkins, May 17, 1867, and May 23, 1867, in Hayden et al., *Land and Labor, 1866–1867*, 601–603.

31. Joel Mathews to Davis Tillson.

32. Pleck, "Wife Beating in Nineteenth-Century America," 60–74; Reva B. Siegel, "'The Rule of Love': Wife Beating as Prerogative and Privacy," *Yale Law Journal*, 105, no. 8 (June 1996): 2117–2207.

33. Lieut. Geo. W. Corliss to Lieut Stuart Eldridge, April 9, 1866, in Hayden et al., *Land and Labor, 1866–1867*, 409–412. On threats see, for example, L A Hildreth to Agt of Freedmens Bureau, May 25, 1866, in Hayden et al., *Land and Labor, 1866–1867*, 610.

34. On marriage and labor contracts, see Cott, *Public Vows*, 80–82; Amy Dru Stanley, *From Bondage to Contract: Wage Labor, Marriage, and the Market in the Age of Slave Emancipation* (Cambridge, England: Cambridge University Press, 1998), 1–59, 138–174; Sara L. Zeigler, "Wifely Duties: Marriage, Labor, and the Common Law in Nineteenth-Century America," *Social Science History*, 20 (Spring 1996): 64–96; Norma Basch, "Marriage and Domestic Relations," in Michael Grossberg and Christopher Tomlins,

eds., *Cambridge History of Law in America*, vol. 2 (Cambridge, England: Cambridge University Press, 2008). See Hahn et al., *Land and Labor, 1865*, 311; Bercaw, *Gendered Freedoms*, ch. 6.

35. Beaton Smith to Lt. McDougall, September 5, 1866, Aiken, SC, in Hayden et al., *Land and Labor, 1866–1867*, 619–620.

36. Affidavit of Buck Dean, Rome, Ga., September 8, 1866, in Hayden et al., *Land and Labor, 1866–1867*, 622.

37. Affidavit of Sam Brown and affidavit of Christiana, July 16, 1866, in Hayden et al., *Land and Labor, 1866–1867*, 431–432.

38. S. Crawford to Brv^t Maj. Genl Tilson, 22 Sept. 1866, enclosing testimony in the case of Ephraim Smith vs. Miss Mary Lizzie Lamkin, 22 Sept. 1866, Unregistered Letters Received, ser. 632, GA Asst. Comr., RG 105, NARA [FSSP A-5352]. Other examples of couples disputes: Geo P Ellis to Maj. C W Pierce, July 31, 1866, in Hayden et al., *Land and Labor, 1866–1867*, 618–619.

39. See, for example, Capt. C. A. de la Mesa to Brv't. Maj. Gen'l Tillson, July 13, 1866, in Hayden et al., *Land and Labor, 1866–1867*, 616–617.

40. *DeBow's Review* (June 1866): 659.

41. M. C. Fulton to Brig. Genl Davis Tilson, April 17, 1866, in Hayden et al., *Land and Labor, 1866–1867*, 594–595. Also see M. Wells to Major Willauer, July 3, 1866, in Hayden et al., *Land and Labor, 1866–1867*, 613; Andrews, *The South since the War*, 187; Mary Farmer-Kaiser, *Freedwomen and the Freemen's Bureau: Race, Gender, and Public Policy in the Age of Emancipation* (New York: Fordham University Press, 2010), 66–67, 74, 81–84; Thavolia Glymph, *Out of the House of Bondage: The Transformation of the Plantation Household* (Cambridge, England: Cambridge University Press, 2008), 146–147, 210–214; Hartman, *Scenes of Subjection*, 126–130, 136, 143, 146, 156.

42. Historians who have supported the argument that women withdrew from the fields include Vernon Wharton, *Negro in Mississippi: 1865–1890* (New York: Harper and Row, 1947; rev. 1966), 118; Peter Kolchin, *First Freedom: The Responses of Alabama's Blacks to Emancipation and Reconstruction* (Westport, Conn.: Greenwood Press, 1972), 62–63; Jerrell Shofner, *Nor Is It over Yet: Florida in the Era of Reconstruction, 1863–1877* (Gainesville: University Press of Florida, 1974), 125; Joe Gray Taylor, *Louisiana Reconstructed, 1863–1877* (Baton Rouge: Louisiana State University Press, 1974), 326–327; C. Peter Ripley, *Slaves and Freedmen in Civil War Louisiana* (Baton Rouge: Louisiana State University Press, 1976); Roger L. Ranson and Richard Sutch, *One Kind of Freedom: The Economic Consequences of Emancipation* (Cambridge, England: Cambridge University Press, 1977; 2nd ed., 2001), 44–45, 55; Leon F. Litwack, *Been in the Storm So Long: The Aftermath of Slavery* (New York: Random House, 1979), 244–245, 341, 393, 434; Gerald David Jaynes, *Branches without Roots: Genesis of the Black Working Class in the American South, 1862–1882* (New York: Oxford University Press, 1986), 230–232; Jonathan M. Weiner, *Origins of the New South: Alabama, 1860–1865* (Baton Rouge: Louisiana State

University Press, 1981), 47; Jacqueline Jones, *Labor of Love, Labor of Sorrow: Black Women, Work, and the Family from Slavery to the Present* (New York: Basic Books, 1985), 58–60. Those who have taken a more critical perspective include Schwalm, *A Hard Fight For We*, 205–207, 211–214, 234–235, 268, 272–273; Frankel, *Freedom's Women*, 56–78; Hahn et al., *Land and Labor, 1865*, 42–43, 502–503; Hayden et al., *Land and Labor, 1866–1867*, 556–562; Farmer-Kaiser, *Freedwomen and the Freemen's Bureau*, 51, 64–66, 67–68, 84–86; Bercaw, *Gendered Freedoms*, 121–128, 185–186; Steven Hahn, *A Nation under Our Feet: Black Political Struggles in the Rural South, from Slavery to the Great Migration* (Cambridge, Mass.: The Belknap Press of Harvard University Press, 2003), 171, 172.

43. Hahn et al., *Land and Labor, 1865*, 38–43, 62, 500–504, 921; Hayden et al., *Land and Labor, 1866–1867*, 37–39, 556–562. Other examples of complaints can be found in Charles Nordhoff, *The Cotton States in the Spring and Summer of 1875* (New York: Burt Franklin, 1876), 72; *Hunt's Merchants Magazine and Commercial Review*, 61 (October 1869): 271.

44. Stanley, *From Bondage to Contract*, 138–174; Stephanie McCurry, *Masters of Small Worlds: Yeoman Households, Gender Relations, and the Political Culture of the Antebellum South Carolina Low Country* (New York: Oxford University Press, 1995).

45. W^m L Scott to Lieut. Edwin Lyon, 18 May 1866, Narrative Reports of Conditions of Bureau Affairs, ser. 3802, VA Asst. Comr., RG 105, NARA [FSSP A-7435].

46. Lieut. O. T. Lemen to Major H. W. Smith, March 29, 1866, in Hayden et al., *Land and Labor, 1866–1867*, 590–591.

47. See Bercaw, *Gendered Freedoms*, 147–157; Elsa Barkley Brown, "Negotiating and Transforming the Public Sphere: African American Political Life in the Transition from Slavery to Freedom," *Public Culture*, 7 (Fall 1994): 107–146.

48. On conflicts over the distribution of land, see Hahn et al., *Land and Labor, 1865*, 392–413; Hahn, *A Nation under Our Feet*, 135–159; Julie Saville, *The Work of Reconstruction: Slave to Wage Laborer in South Carolina, 1860–1870* (Cambridge, England: Cambridge University Press, 1996); Hayden et al., *Land and Labor, 1866–1867*, 211–225.

49. Hayden et al., *Land and Labor, 1866–1867*, 28–46, 361–385, 553–569; Jaynes, *Branches without Roots*, 158–190; Ira Berlin and Leslie S. Rowland, eds., *Families and Freedom: A Documentary History of African-American Kinship in the Civil War Era* (New York: New Press, 1997); Hahn, *A Nation under Our Feet*, 163–185.

50. Ransom and Sutch, *One Kind of Freedom;* Jaynes, *Branches without Roots;* Ronald L. F. Davis, *Good and Faithful Labor: From Slavery to Sharecropping in the Natchez District, 1868–1890* (Westport, Conn.: Praeger, 1982); Weiner, *Origins of the New South;* Gavin Wright, *Old South New South: Revolutions in the Southern Economy since the Civil War* (Baton Rouge: Louisiana State University Press, 1986); Edward Royce, *The Origins of Southern Sharecropping* (Philadelphia: Temple University Press, 1993); Foner, *Reconstruction*, 171–174, 404–409; Saville, *The Work of Reconstruction*, 125–127;

Ralph Shlomowitz, "The Origins of Southern Sharecropping," *Agricultural History,* 53 (July 1979): 557–575; Martin Ruef, *Between Slavery and Capitalism: The Legacy of Emancipation in the American South* (Princeton, N.J.: Princeton University Press, 2014); Hahn et al., *Land and Labor, 1865,* 32–38, 60–70, 311–331; Hayden et al., *Land and Labor, 1866–1867,* 28–46, 361–385, 553–569.

51. Ibid.; Jones, *Labor of Love,* 62, 84, 333–336; Gutman, *Black Family,* chs. 9, 10, and 443–447; Carole Shammas, *A History of Household Governance in America* (Charlottesville: University of Virginia Press, 2002), 174, 177–178; Steven Ruggles, "The Origins of African-American Family Structure," *American Sociological Review,* 59 (February 1994): 136–151; Bercaw, *Gendered Freedoms,* 121–128; "Inside the Negro Cabins," *Harper's Weekly,* November 13, 1880; [David C. Barrow], "A Georgia Plantation," *Scribner's Monthly,* 21 (March 1881): 830–836. Quote from Davis, *Good and Faithful Labor,* 190.

52. Jaynes, *Branches without Roots,* 190.

53. Ibid., 187–190, 230–232; Bercaw, *Gendered Freedoms,* 124–128, 147–151; Jones, *Labor of Love,* 80–109; Frankel, *Freedom's Women,* 70–78.

54. Ibid.

55. Ibid.; Hayden et al., *Land and Labor, 1866–1867,* 370–373; Susan O'Donovan, *Becoming Free in the Cotton South* (Cambridge, Mass.: Harvard University Press, 2007); Wright, *Old South New South;* Tera W. Hunter, *To Joy My Freedom: Southern Black Women's Lives and Labors after the Civil War* (Cambridge, Mass.: Harvard University Press, 1997); Jones, *Labor of Love,* 113.

56. Nancy Cott argues that postwar laws pushed aside regional differences, bringing the South in line with the rest of the nation (*Public Vows,* 103). Peter Bardaglio argues that regional differences in domestic governance continued; see Peter Bardaglio, *Reconstructing the Household: Families, Sex, and the Law in the Nineteenth-Century South* (Chapel Hill: University of North Carolina Press, 1998), 227.

57. On marriage laws being directory, see Ariela Gross, "Governing through Contract: Common Law Marriage in the Nineteenth Century," *Yale Law Journal,* 107 (1998): 1885–1920; Michael Grossberg, *Governing the Hearth: Law and the Family in Nineteenth-Century America* (Chapel Hill: University of North Carolina Press, 1985).

58. Basch, "Marriage and Domestic Relations"; Timothy J. Gilfoyle, "The Hearts of Nineteenth-Century Men: Bigamy and Working-Class Marriage in New York City, 1800–1890," *Prospects,* 19 (October 1994): 135–160; Cott, *Public Vows;* Grossberg, *Governing the Hearth;* Shammas, *A History of Household Governance;* Bardaglio, *Reconstructing the Household.*

59. Stanley, *From Bondage to Contract,* 55–59; Cott, *Public Vows,* 90–94.

60. Quotes from Cott, *Public Vows,* 103–104.

61. Nathan S. Shaler, "The Future of the Negro in the Southern States," *Popular Science Monthly,* 57 (June 1900): 153; Khalil Gibran Muhammad, *Condemnation of Blackness:*

Race, Crime, and the Making of Modern Urban America (Cambridge, Mass.: Harvard University Press, 2010), 15–34.

62. Shaler, "The Negro Problem," *Atlantic Monthly,* 54 (November 1884): 702; Muhammad, *Condemnation of Blackness,* 15–34; Stanley, *From Bondage to Contract,* 138–174.

8. Hopes and Travails at Century's End

1. Frances Harper, "Enlightened Motherhood: An Address: by Mrs. Frances E. W. Harper; before the Brooklyn Literary Society," November 15, 1892, 1, Daniel P. Murray Collection, Library of Congress.

2. W. E. B. Du Bois, ed., *The Negro American Family: Report of a Social Study Made Principally by the College Classes of 1909 and 1910* (Atlanta, Ga.: Atlanta University Press, 1908), 37.

3. See Michele Mitchell, *Righteous Propagation: African Americans and the Politics of Racial Destiny after Reconstruction* (Chapel Hill: University of North Carolina Press, 2004); Kevin Gaines, *Uplifting the Race: Black Leadership, Politics, and Culture in the Twentieth Century* (Chapel Hill: University of North Carolina Press, 1996); Khalil Gibran Muhammad, *The Condemnation of Blackness: Race, Crime, and the Making of Modern Urban America* (Cambridge, Mass.: Harvard University Press, 2010); Hazel Carby, *Reconstructing Womanhood: The Emergence of the Afro-American Woman Novelist* (New York: Oxford University Press, 1987); Claudia Tate, *Domestic Allegories of Political Desire: The Black Heroine's Text at the Turn of the Century* (New York: Oxford University Press, 1992); Evelyn Brooks Higginbotham, *Righteous Discontent: The Women's Movement in The Black Baptist Church, 1880–1920* (Cambridge, Mass.: Harvard University Press, 1993); Stephanie J. Shaw, *What a Woman Ought to Be and to Do: Black Professional Women Workers during the Jim Crow Era* (Chicago, Ill.: University of Chicago Press, 2010); Deborah Gray White, *Too Heavy a Load: Black Women in Defense of Themselves, 1894–1994* (New York: W. W. Norton, 1999); Stephanie J. Shaw, "Black Club Women and the Creation of the National Association of Colored Women," *Journal of Women's History,* 3, no. 2 (1991): 11–25; Tera W. Hunter, *To 'Joy My Freedom: Southern Black Women's Lives and Labors after the Civil War* (Cambridge, Mass.: Harvard University Press, 1997).

4. Anna J. Cooper, *A Voice from the South: By a Black Woman of the South* (Xenia, Ohio: The Aldine Printing House, 1892), 29.

5. Du Bois, *Negro American Family,* 31, 37. See Muhammad, *Condemnation of Blackness,* 20–25, 31–32; Elliott M. Rudwick, "W. E. B. Du Bois and the Atlanta University Studies on the Negro," *Journal of Negro Education* (1957): 466–476; James B. Stewart, "Back to Basics: The Significance of Du Bois's and Frazier's Contributions for Contemporary Research on Black Families," in Harold E. Cheatham and James B.

Steward, eds., *Black Families: Interdisciplinary Perspectives* (New Brunswick, N.J.: Transaction Publishers, 1990); Melinda Chateauvert, "Framing Sexual Citizenship: Reconsidering the Discourse on African American Families," *Journal of African American History,* 93 (Spring 2008): 198–222; Susan Gilman and Alys Eve Weinbaum, eds., *Next to the Color Line: Gender, Sexuality, and W. E. B. Du Bois* (Minneapolis: University of Minnesota Press, 2007), see especially article by Vilashini Cooppan, "Move on Down the Line: Domestic Science, Transnational Politics, and Gendered Allegory in Du Bois," 48–55.

6. David Levering Lewis, *W. E. B. Du Bois: Biography of a Race,* vol. 1 (New York: Macmillan, 1994), 209–210, 222–223, 378–379; Muhammad, *Condemnation of Blackness.* I make the point that the *Philadelphia Negro* also took liberties with sociological interpretations of black marriage patterns that were not based on the statistical evidence presented in the study. See Tera W. Hunter, "'The "Brotherly Love" for which This City Is Proverbial Should Extend to All': Working-Class Women in Philadelphia and Atlanta in the 1890s," in *W. E. B. Du Bois, Race, and the City: "The Philadelphia Negro" and Its Legacy,* ed. Michael B. Katz and Thomas J. Sugrue (Philadelphia: University of Pennsylvania Press, 1998), 130.

7. Du Bois, *Negro American Family,* 36, 31.

8. Ibid., see Tables, 27.

9. See Hunter, *To Joy My Freedom;* Susan E. O'Donovan, *Becoming Free in the Cotton South* (Cambridge, Mass.: Harvard University Press, 2009); Jacqueline Jones, *Labor of Love, Labor of Sorrow: Black Women, Work, and the Family, from Slavery to the Present* (New York: Basic Books, 2009).

10. Du Bois, *Negro American Family,* 37–41; Frederick Hoffman, *Race Traits and Tendencies of the American Negro* (New York: Macmillan, 1896).

11. Du Bois, *Negro American Family,* 38; Hoffman, *Race Traits,* 236–237; Muhammad, *Condemnation of Blackness,* 49–53, 42. See Saidiya Hartman, *Wayward Lives, Beautiful Experiments* (forthcoming). James B. Stewart argues that Du Bois saw African Americans exhibiting traits the rest of the society might soon follow regarding how they adapted to economic conditions in an industrial society. See Stewart, "Back to Basics."

12. Data used from Catherine A. Fitch and Steven Ruggles, "Historical Trends in Marriage Formation," in Linda Waite et al., eds., *Ties That Bind: Perspectives on Marriage and Cohabitation* (New York: de Gruyter, 2000), 59–88; Steven Ruggles and Catherine Fitch, "Trends in African-American Marriage Patterns," n.d., Minnesota Population Center (Data collection funded by the National Science Foundation and the National Institutes of Health); and Michael R. Haines, "The Long-Term Marriage Patterns in the United States from Colonial Times to the Present," *History of the Family: An International Quarterly,* 1 (1996): 5–39. Other sources show the same trend lines: Jones, *Labor of Love;* Stewart Tolnay, *The Bottom Rung: African American Family Life on Southern Farms* (Urbana: University of Illinois Press, 1999); Deidre Bloome and Christopher Muller, "Tenancy

and African American Marriage in the Postbellum South," *Demography,* published online July 30, 2015, 1-22; Orville Vernon, *In My Father's House Are Many Mansions: Family and Community in Edgefield, South Carolina* (Chapel Hill: University of North Carolina Press, 1987). The numbers cited are estimates taken from the charts in Ruggles and Fitch. According to Haines's data, white women had fewer never-marrieds in 1880, whereas black women had the fewest in 1890 and 1900. Also see *New York Times,* February 3, 1890, article which noted that black marriage rates were higher than white marriage rates in Georgia.

13. See Jones, *Labor of Love,* 333-342, which provides data on twenty-seven cotton counties in the South, showing very high marriage rates among African Americans. Also see Tolnay, *Bottom Rung,* which provides data showing that blacks in the rural South married more than whites; and Burton, *In My Father's House Are Many Mansions.* Fitch and Ruggles make the most convincing case for the historical correlation between economics and marriage across centuries. Also see Andrew J. Cherlin, *Labor's Love Lost: The Rise and Fall of the Working-Class Family in America* (New York: Russell Sage Foundation, 2014). This idea is rejected by many conservatives who see moral values as playing a predominant role in marriage rates.

14. Data cited here taken from Steven Ruggles, "The Origins of African-American Family Structure," *American Sociological Review,* 59 (February 1994): 136-151. See Table 1, 138. His findings are generally consistent with S. Philip Morgan et al., "Racial Differences in Household and Family Structure at the Turn of the Century," *American Journal of Sociology,* 98 (January 1993): 799-828. Others deemphasize racial differences; see Tolnay, *Bottom Rung;* Burton, *In My Father's House Are Many Mansions;* Jones, *Labor of Love;* Herbert G. Gutman, *The Black Family in Slavery and Freedom, 1750-1925* (New York: Vintage, 1977). African Americans in the rural South tended to adopt nuclear family forms more often than those in the urban South or the North, but in each case they did so less often than whites. See Morgan et al. above.

15. See Dylan Penningroth, "African American Divorce in Virginia and Washington, D.C., 1865-1930," *Journal of Family History,* 33 (January 2008): 1-15; Steven Ruggles, "The Rise of Divorce and Separation in the United States, 1880-1990," *Demography,* 34 (November 1997): 455-466.

16. This is an important area of historical inquiry that not many scholars have explored. The exceptions are Jo Ann Manfra and Robert R. Dykstra, "Serial Marriage and the Origins of the Black Stepfamily: The Rowanty Evidence," *Journal of American History,* 72 (June 1985); Cheryl Elman and Andrew S. London, "Influence of Remarriage on the Racial Differences in Mother-Only Families in 1910," *Demography,* 38 (May 2001): 283-297; Elman and London, "Sociohistorical and Demographic Perspectives on U.S. Remarriage in 1910," *Social Science History,* 26 (2002): 199-241. Other scholars who have studied the 1910 census concur that remarriage rates for blacks were striking. See S. Philip Morgan et al., "Racial Differences in Household and Family Structure at the Turn

of the Century," *American Journal of Sociology* (January 1993): 799–828; Samuel Preston, Suet Lim, and S. Philip Morgan, "African-American Marriage in 1910: Beneath the Surface of Census Data," *Demography,* 29 (February 1992). See O'Donovan, *Becoming Free,* on marginalized rural women; and Jones, *Labor of Love.*

17. Also note that the WPA slave narratives show patterns of serial monogamy and also persistence of informal marital practices that had originated in slavery. The number of ex-slaves who married only once, for forty or even fifty years, was striking. In many cases, first marriages were as very young slaves, aged thirteen to fifteen, which were followed by subsequent marriages, usually after the death of a spouse. Paul Escott estimates based on samples from oral histories that 69 percent of former slaves were married once, 20 percent married twice, 11 percent married three times, and 2 percent married more than four times. The ex-slaves reported that death overwhelmingly was the cause of breakups, and relatively few reported separation, divorce, or desertion. These numbers seem low compared with those in other studies. See Paul D. Escott, *Slavery Remembered: A Record of Twentieth-Century Slave Narratives* (Chapel Hill: University of North Carolina Press, 1979), 198, 169–171. For examples of slave marriages lasting more than forty years, see Benny Dillard, WPA Narratives, Georgia, vol. 12, pt. 1, 297–298; Laura Bell, WPA Narratives, North Carolina, vol. 14, pt. 1, 101–102; Henry Rogers, WPA Narratives, Georgia, vol. 13, pt. 3, 227. For marriages lasting more than fifty years, see Ike Derricotte, WPA Narratives, Georgia, vol. 12, pt. 1, 279–280; Lucy Ann Dunn, age ninety, WPA Narratives, North Carolina, vol. 14, pt. 1, 281–282; Barbara Haywood, WPA Narratives, North Carolina, vol. 14, pt, 1, 386–388, 387; Tanner Spikes, WPA Narratives, North Carolina, vol. 15, pt. 2, 310–311; Georgia Telfair, WPA Narratives, Georgia, vol. 13, GA, pt. 4; Joseph Samuel Badgett, WPA Narratives, Arkansas, vol. 8, pt. 1, 81. For examples of slaves married at very young ages, see Neal Upson, WPA Narratives, North Carolina, vol. 14, pt. 4, 69–70; Nancy Smith, WPA Narratives, Georgia, vol. 13, pt. 3, 312–315; Alice Bradley, WPA Narratives, Georgia, vol. 12, pt. 1, 120; Jasper Battle, WPA Narratives, Georgia, vol. 12, pt. 1, 62–70; Julia Banks, WPA Narratives, Texas, vol. 4, pt. 1, 99–105; Betty Powers, WPA Narratives, Texas, vol. 5, pt. 3, 191–192; Charles Green Dortsch, WPA Narratives, Arkansas, vol. 8, pt. 2, 176–178; Alice Johnson, WPA Narratives, Arkansas, vol. 9, pt. 4, 62. For some examples of second marriages, see Tom Mills, WPA Narratives, Texas, vol. 5, pt. 3, 91–100; Ellen Cragin, WPA Narratives, Arkansas, vol. 8, pt. 2, 47–48; Elmira Hall, WPA Narratives, Arkansas, vol. 8, pt. 3, 254–255; Mary Jones, WPA Narratives, Arkansas, vol. 9, pt. 4, 159–162. For some examples of those married three times or more, see Mary Anngady, WPA Narratives, North Carolina, vol. 14, 1, 36–37; Susan Ross, WPA Narratives, Texas, vol. 5, pt. 3, 257–261; Beatrice Black, WPA Narratives, Arkansas, vol. 8, pt. 1, 166–167; Charlie Vaden, WPA Narratives, Arkansas, vol. 11, pt. 7, 1.

18. See, for example, Pension claim of Emily Caldwell, widow of Nathan Caldwell, USCI 107, Co. B, #136523; Pension claim of Violet Carr, widow of Green Carr, USCI 42, Co. F, #1776643.

19. See Elizabeth A. Regosin and Donald R. Shaffer, eds., *Voices of Emancipation: Understanding Slavery, the Civil War, and Reconstruction through the U.S. Pension Bureau* (New York: New York University Press, 2008), 3–4; Noralee Frankel, *Freedom's Women: Black Women and Families in Civil War Era Mississippi* (Bloomington: Indiana University Press, 1999); Megan J. McClintock, "Binding Up the Nation's Wounds: Nationalism, Civil War Pension, and American Families, 1861–1890" (PhD diss., Rutgers University, 1994); McClintock, "Civil War Pensions and the Reconstruction of Union Families," *Journal of American History* (1996): 456–480; Brandi Clay Brimmer, "All Her Rights and Privileges: African-American Women and the Politics of Civil War Widows' Pensions" (PhD diss., University of California, Los Angeles, 2006); Brimmer, "Black Women's Politics, Narratives of Sexual Immorality, and Pension Bureaucracy in Mary Lee's North Carolina Neighborhood," *Journal of Southern History*, 80 (November 2014): 827; Elizabeth Regosin, *Freedom's Promise: Ex-Slave Families and Citizenship in the Age of Emancipation* (Charlottesville: University of Virginia Press, 2002); Michelle A. Krowl, "'Her Just Dues': Civil War Pensions of African American Women in Virginia," in Janet L. Coryell, ed., *Negotiating Boundaries of Southern Womanhood: Dealing with the Powers That Be* (Columbia: University of Missouri Press, 2000), 48–70; Sven E. Wilson, "Prejudice and Policy: Racial Discrimination in the Union Army Disability Pension System, 1865–1906," *American Journal of Public Health*, 100 (February 2010): 2–11.

20. Historians have tended to use the pension files to explore the history of the Civil War and Reconstruction era but not the late nineteenth century or later. In this book I discuss the files over the course of the claimants' eligibility to highlight the evolution of their intimate relationships and what they had faced by the turn of the century.

21. Pension claim of Nancy Thompson formerly Bass, widow of Amaziah Bass, USCI 40, Co. G, #97906. The records indicate that the request for reinstatement was under review but did not report the findings. See also Pension claim of Helen M. Smith Freeman, widow of Joseph R. Smith, USCI 8, Co. B, #48030; Pension claim of Mary Robinson, widow of Jeffery Robinson, USCI 33, Co. D, #129564. See McClintock, "Binding Up the Nation's Wounds."

22. Pension claim of Rosetta Beasley, widow of Spencer Beasley, USCI 36, Co. C, #117790. Quote from Rosetta's affidavit, April 6, 1901. Spencer also had married at least once before Rosetta. A woman named Sabra Nicholls tried to claim a pension as his widow. It appears that they were married in 1859, before he took up with Rosetta. Nicholls also was legally remarried by 1868. See also Pension claim of Charlotte Capehart, widow of Caesar Banks, USCI 35, Co. D, #157 383. Charlotte married two times by slave custom, beginning in 1854 to Isaac Sawyer and then to Caesar Banks, her soldier-husband sometime before his enlistment. After his death she legally married David Holloway in 1866, and stayed married until his death in 1872. Then she was married to Austin Capehart from 1875 until his death in 1887. Her pension was dropped as a result of her remarriage.

23. Pension claim of Rebecca Gathen, widow of Allen Gathen, USCI 42, Co. H, #78541.

24. Ibid. Quote is from the affidavit taken November 26, 1897.

25. Pension claim of Mary Bennett, widow of John Bennett, USCI 108, Co. C, #131045; Affidavit of Pointer, May 4 and 18, 1901; Affidavit by Boyd, May 6, 1901.

26. See Jane E. Dabel, *A Respectable Woman: The Public Roles of African American Women in 19th-Century New York* (New York: New York University Press, 2008), 41–58.

27. Schwartzberg, "Grass Widows"; McClintock, "Binding Up the Nation's Wounds"; Nancy Cott, *Public Vows: A History of Marriage and the Nation* (Cambridge, Mass.: Harvard University Press, 2001); Hendrik Hartog, *Man and Wife in America: A History* (Cambridge, Mass.: Harvard University Press, 2000); Michael Grossberg, *Governing the Hearth: Law and Family in Nineteenth Century America* (Chapel Hill: University of North Carolina Press, 1985); Peter Bardaglio, *Reconstructing the Household: Families, Sex, and the Law in the Nineteenth-Century South* (Chapel Hill: University of North Carolina Press, 1996); Timothy J. Gilfoyle, "The Hearts of Nineteenth-Century Men: Bigamy and Working-Class Marriage in New York City, 1800–1890," *Prospects*, 19 (October 1994): 135–160; Carole Shammas, *A History of Household Governance in America* (Charlottesville: University of Virginia Press, 2002); Norma Basch, "Marriage and Domestic Relations," in Michael Grossberg and Christopher Tomlins, eds., *Cambridge History of Law in America*, vol. 2 (Cambridge, England: Cambridge University Press, 2008).

28. Grossberg, *Governing the Hearth*, 64–102; Hartog, *Man and Wife*; Cott, *Public Vows*; Schwartzberg, "Grass Widows," 214–271; McClintock, "Binding Up the Nation's Wounds"; Carroll D. Wright, *A Report on Marriage and Divorce in the United States, 1867–1886* (Washington, D.C.: Government Printing Office, 1891).

29. Pension claim of Sarah C. Slinger Hart, widow of Milton H. Slinger, USCI 56, Co. C, #121524.

30. Pension claim of Frances Water, widow of Samuel Waters, USCI 8, Co. C, #42438, quotes from affidavit of Frances, May 4, 1884. See also Pension claim of Lizzie L Johnson, widow of Charles H Johnson, USCI 54, Co. F, # 50151.

31. Pension claim of Emma Louisa Cook, widow of Albert Cooke, USCI 41, Co. I, #96604.

32. McClintock, "Binding Up the Nation's Wounds," 245–247.

33. Peggy Pascoe, *What Comes Naturally: Miscegenation Law and the Making of Race in America* (New York: Oxford University Press, 2009), 30–45, 62–67; Adrienne D. Davis, "The Private Law of Race and Sex: An Antebellum Perspective," *Stanford Law Review* (January 1999): 221–288.

34. *Hall v. United States, United States v. Roach*, 92 U.S. 27, 23 L. Ed. 597, 1875 U.S. LEXIS 1721, 2 Otto 27; Grossberg, *Governing the Hearth*, 133–136. The case pitted former slaveholders against former slaves in ascertaining ownership of proceeds from

cotton seized by the U.S. Army. See also editorial on the adjudication of slave marriages, *New York Times,* December 2, 1888.

35. Examples of these sexual infractions can be found in multiple sources. See Georgia State Penitentiary Clemency Files (compliments of Sarah Haley), Applications for Clemency, Executive Department Papers, Georgia Department of Archives and History, Morrow, Ga. See files for Mary Stewart, 1887, prosecuted for bigamy; Clara Johnson, 1903, arrested for vagrancy, also charged with fornication. See Sarah Haley, *No Mercy Here: Gender, Punishment, and the Making of Jim Crow Modernity* (Chapel Hill: University of North Carolina Press, 2016). See reports on criminalization in the *New York Times,* February 25, 1884, April 1, 1885. See also Mary Frances Berry, "Judging Morality: Sexual Behavior and Legal Consequences in the Late Nineteenth-Century South," *Journal of American History,* 78 (December 1991): 835–856; Katherine Franke, *Wedlocked: The Perils of Marriage Equality: How African Americans and Gays Mistakenly Thought the Right to Marry Would Set Them Free* (New York: New York University Press, 2015).

36. Dylan Penningroth is writing a book that explores law and everyday life among black Southerners in the late nineteenth and early twentieth century. He is uncovering many examples in which African Americans conflicted with each other in legal cases brought to local courts, over family land and church business, for example.

37. *L. McKnight and Lizzie Davis v. The State,* 6 Tex. Ct. App. 158, 1879 Tex. Crim. App. LEXIS 74.

38. *Mark Williams for Use of John Wallace, Appellant, vs. Adolphus Kimball, Appellee,* 35 Fla. 49, 16 So. 783, 1895 Fla. LEXIS 136. See also *Clifton Anderson and Julie Ann Fox vs. William Smith,* 2 Mackey 275, 1883 U.S. App. LEXIS 2597; *Wallace v. Godfrey et al.,* 42 F. 812, 1890 U.S. App. LEXIS 2244; *Jennings v. Webb.,* 8 App. D.C. 43, 1896 U.S. App. LEXIS 3147. On comity, see Hartog, *Man and Wife,* 269–275; Joanna L. Grossman, "Resurrecting Comity: Revisiting the Problem of Non-Uniform Marriage Laws," *Oregon Law Review,* 84 (June 2005): 433–488; Joel Prentiss Bishop, *Commentaries on the Law of Marriage and Divorce, and Evidence in Matrimonial Suits* (Boston, Mass.: Little, Brown and Company, 1852), 107–108, 111–113, 116, 538, 613.

39. *Louis Adams, J. C. Greeley and Samuel Gauze, Plaintiffs in Error, vs. Page Sneed, Nancy Ross Allen, Lucien Ross, Margaret Ross Bronson and Violet Ross, a Minor, by her next friend, Lucien Ross, Defendants in Error,* 41 Fla. 15, 25 So. 893, 1899 Fla. LEXIS 148.

40. *Sarah and Bethel Daniel and Bernice Sams, Appellants, vs. Mollie Sams, Appellee,* 17 Fla. 487, 1880 Fla. LEXIS 12.

41. *Estill vs. Rogers,* 64 Ky. 62, 1866 Ky. LEXIS 86, 1 Bush 62. See also *Stewart, &c., of color, vs. Munchandler, &c.,* 65 Ky. 278, 1867 Ky. LEXIS 74, 2 Bush 278.

42. *Jane Ewing v. Elizabeth Bibb, &c.,* 70 Ky. 654, 1870 Ky. LEXIS 147, 7 Bush 654. Note that the case ultimately rested on other considerations. Though the second marriage was invalid, the second wife won on appeal to keep the estate of her husband because the property in contention was actually paid for by her and not him. The point

is the arguments made about marriage within the context of this case. See also *Whitesides, &c. v. Allen, guardian, &c.,* 74 Ky. 23, 1874 Ky. LEXIS 4, 11 Bush 23.

43. *State v. Johnson Adam and Hagar Reeves,* 65 N.C. 537, 1871 N.C. LEXIS 165, *State v. Albert Whitford,* 86 N.C. 636, 1882 N.C. LEXIS 26; *Alice and William Cumby v. Charlotte and Jack Henderson,* 6 Tex. Civ. App. 519, 25 S.W. 673, 1894 Tex. App. LEXIS 32. See also U.S Supreme Court case *Meister vs. Moore,* 96 U.S. 76, 24 L. Ed. 826, 1877 U.S. LEXIS 1628, 6 Otto 76.

44. *State v. Allen Melton,* 120 N.C. 591, 26 S.E. 933, 1897 N.C. LEXIS 138; *Mary Allen v. Charles Allen,* 71 Ky. 490, 1871 Ky LEXIS 88, 8 Bush 490.

45. See, for example, *Francis v. Francis,* 72 Va. 283, 1879 Va. LEXIS 4, 31 Gratt. 283. See also Penningroth, "African American Divorce in Virginia and Washington, D.C., 1865–1930"; *Washington V. Washington,* 69 Ala. 281, 1881 Ala. LEXIS 109; *McConico v. The State,* 49 Ala. 6, 1873 Ala. LEXIS 56; *Solomon McReynolds vs. The State,* 45 Tenn. 18, 1867 Tenn. LEXIS 87, 5 Cold. 18; *Scoggins vs. The State,* 32 Ark. 205, 1877 Ark. LEXIS 40; *Brown v. Cheatham et al.,* 91 Tenn. 97, 17 S.W. 1033, 1893.

46. Carole Shammas, Marylynn Salmon, and Michel Dahlin, *Inheritance in America from Colonial Times to the Present* (New Brunswick, N.J.: Rutgers University Press, 1987), 3, 15–17, 23, 32–39, 63–67, 83–86, 99; Davis, "Private Law of Race and Sex."

47. *Stikes, Administrator, v. Swanson,* 44 Ala. 633, 1870 Ala. LEXIS 115. See also *Dowd and wife v. Hurley, &c.,* 78 Ky. 26, 1880 Ky. LEXIS 7; Succession of Henry Pearce, 30 La. Ann. 1168, 1878 La. LEXIS 317; Davis, "Private Law of Race and Sex."

48. *Tempe Downs v. James C. Allen et al.,* 78 Tenn. 652, 1882 WL 4197 (Tenn.).

49. *David Jones, Frances Jones and others vs. Henry Jones,* 45 Md. 144, 1876 Md. LEXIS 88. This case is also related to *Frances Jones, Administratrix of Andrew D. Jones, deceased, vs. George W. Jones, Joshua A. Jones, Sarah Ann Robinson, and others,* 36 Md. 447, 1872 Md. LEXIS 90. In this case, the nieces and nephews of Andrew Jones won a portion of their uncle's estate.

50. *Washington v. Washington,* 69 Ala. 281, 1881 Ala. LEXIS 109. See also *Francis v. Francis,* 72 Va. 283, 1879 Va. LEXIS 4, 31 Gratt. 283. In this case the first marriage was affirmed because the husband left the first wife for another woman and tried to disown the relationship. The couple cohabited as free people in the slavery era.

51. *Johnson's Heirs v. Raphael. In re Raphael,* 117 La. 967, 42 So. 470, 1906 La. LEXIS 804. Also see *McDowell v. Sapp,* 39 Ohio St. 558, 1883 Ohio LEXIS 410. In this case, a slave man ran away to Canada and remarried; his second marriage was considered legal and legitimate.

52. *Mariah Butler et al. v. John H. Butler et al.,* 161 Ill. 451, 44 N.E. 203, 1896 Ill. LEXIS 1628. See also *Roberson v. McCauley,* 61 S.C. 411, 39 S.E. 570, 1901 S.C. LEXIS 168; *Succession of Washington. Opposition of Washington et al.,* 153 La. 1047, 97 So. 35, 1923 La. LEXIS 1868; *Sarah and Bethel Daniel and Bernice Sams, Appellants, vs. Mollie Sams, Appellee,* 17 Fla. 487, 1880 Fla. LEXIS 12; *Alice and William Cumby v. Charlotte*

and Jack Henderson, 6 Tex. Civ. App. 519, 25 S.W. 673, 1894 Tex. App. LEXIS 32. In the case of *Jane Ewing v. Elizabeth Bibb, &c.,* 70 Ky. 654, 1870 Ky. LEXIS 147, 7 Bush 654, the first slave marriage was validated but the widow (second slave marriage) ended up winning over the children of the first on the grounds that property in the estate was purchased with Jane's money, not her husband's.

53. *Wallace v. Godfrey et al.,* 42 F. 812, 1890 U.S. App. LEXIS 2244; *Martha Diggs vs. William H. A. Wormley, Trustee, et al.,* 1 Tuck. & Cl. 477, 1893 U.S. App. LEXIS 3084; *Jennings v. Webb,* 8 App. D.C. 43, 1896 U.S. App. LEXIS 3147; *Succession of Walker,* 121 La. 865, 46 So. 890, 1908 La. LEXIS 761.

54. *Napier v. Church et al.,* 132 Tenn. 111, 177 S.W. 56, 1915 Tenn. LEXIS 5, 5 Thompson 111. Thanks to Beverly Bond for sharing documents related to this case. There are numerous cases involving the offspring of slaves. See *Silas Middleton v. John W. Middleton,* 221 Ill. 623, 77 N.E. 1123, 1906 Ill. LEXIS 274; *Heirs of Moses Speese, Appellees, v. Estate of Jeremiah Shores, Appellant,* 81 Neb. 593, 116 N.W. 493, 1908 Neb. LEXIS 167. Other cases involve collateral kin challenging widows. Brothers and sisters (and their children) of intestate individuals or those with estates often challenged the legitimacy of their siblings' slave marriages in order to claim a portion of their estate. In some cases siblings won at least a share of an inheritance. In other cases widows did. Collateral kin also challenged lineal kin, nieces and nephews against the children of the decedents, on the grounds that the decedent's marriage was not legitimate. See, for example, *Jennie Erwin v. William Nolan et al., Appellants,* 280 Mo. 401, 217 S.W. 837, 1920 Mo. LEXIS 200; *Auguste and Joseph Pierre v. Auguste Fontenette et als.,* 25 La. Ann. 617, 1873 La. LEXIS 266. See *Cantelou v. Doe, ex. Dem. Hood,* 56 Ala 519, 1876 Ala. LEXIS 580; *Whitesides, &c. v. Allen, guardian, &c.,* 74 Ky. 23, 1874 Ky LEXIS 4, 11 Bush 23; *Scott v. Raub,* 88 Va. 721, 14 S.E. 178, 1892 Va. LEXIS 24.

55. On Progressives and race, see Gaines, *Uplifting the Race;* Mitchell, *Righteous Propagation;* Noralee Frankel and Nancy S. Dye, eds., *Gender, Class, Race, and Reform in the Progressive Era* (Lexington: University Press of Kentucky, 1991); Muhammad, *Condemnation of Blackness.*

56. Thomas N. Chase, ed., *Social and Physical Condition of Negroes in Cities* (Atlanta, Ga.: Atlanta University Press 1897), 26–27.

57. Muhammad, *Condemnation of Blackness,* 7, 35–87; Hoffman, *Race Traits,* vol. 11, nos. 1–3, 207.

58. Mrs. N[athan]. F. Mossell, *The Work of the Afro-American Woman* (Philadelphia: G. S. Ferguson, 1894; 2nd ed., 1908), 115–116; Mary Church Terrell, "The Progress of Colored Woman," an address delivered before the National American Women's Suffrage Association at the Columbia Theater, Washington, D.C., February 18, 1898, on the occasion of its fiftieth anniversary (Washington, D.C.: Smith Brothers, Printers [1898]), 10, 15. Also see Harper, "Enlightened Motherhood," 2; Tate, *Domestic Allegories of Political Desire.*

59. Alexander Crummell, "Marriage a Duty," in *Tracts for the Negro Race* (Washington, D.C., 1880), electronic edition, Hathi Trust, Digital Library; Eugene Harris, "The Physical Condition of the Race; Whether Dependent upon Social Conditions or Environment," in *Social and Physical Condition of Negroes in Cities,* ed. W. E. B. Du Bois (Atlanta, Ga.: Atlanta University Press, 1897), 28, 33–34; Fannie Barrier Williams, "The Club Movement among Colored Women," 1900, reprinted in Sidonie Smith, *Before They Could Vote: American Women's Autobiographical Writing, 1819–1919* (Madison: University of Wisconsin Press, 2006), 282–284; Mary Jo Deegan, ed., *The New Woman of Color: The Collected Writings of Fannie Barrier Williams, 1893–1918* (Dekalb: Northern Illinois University Press, 2002).

60. See Gaines, *Uplifting the Race;* Mitchell, *Righteous Propagation;* Higginbotham, *Righteous Discontent;* Willard B. Gatewood, *Aristocrats of Color: The Black Elite, 1880–1920* (Fayetteville: University of Arkansas Press, 1990); Robin D. G. Kelley, *Freedom Dreams: The Black Radical Imagination* (New York: Beacon Press, 2002).

61. Cherlin, *Labor's Love Lost,* 1–59. The book does not take into account whether or how rural America was affected by the class inequalities in marriage rates, as it examines only urban and industrial populations.

Epilogue

1. See Roderick A. Ferguson, *Aberrations in Black: Toward a Queer of Color Critique* (Minneapolis: University of Minnesota Press, 2004); Candice Jenkins, *Private Lives, Proper Relations: Regulating Black Intimacy* (Minneapolis: University of Minnesota Press, 2007); Christina Sharpe, *Monstrous Intimacies: Making Post-Slavery Subjects* (Durham, N.C.: Duke University Press, 2010); Michael Warner, *The Trouble with Normal: Sex, Politics, and the Ethics of Queer Life* (New York: Free Press, 1999); Melinda Chateauvert, "Framing Sexual Citizenship: Reconsidering the Discourse on African American Families," *Journal of African American History,* 93 (Spring 2008): 198–222.

2. See arguments made by U.S. Supreme Court justices in the voting rights case *Shelby County, Alabama v. Eric H. Holder, Jr., Attorney General,* 133 S. Ct. 2612 (2013). The quoted phrase is taken from Nell Irvin Painter, "Soul Murder and Slavery: Toward a Fully Loaded Cost Accounting," 15–39, Painter, *Southern History across the Color Line* (Chapel Hill: University of North Carolina Press, 2002). On narrow conceptions of family structure, see Daniel Patrick Moynihan, *The Negro Family: The Case for National Action* (Office of Policy Planning and Research, United States Department of Labor, March 1965). For recent debates about Moynihan among sociologists who mostly affirm his overall arguments, see Douglass Massey and Robert J. Sampson, eds., *The Moynihan Report Revisited: Lessons and Reflections after Four Decades* (Thousand Oaks, Calif.: Sage Publications, 2009); Orlando Patterson, *Rituals of Blood: Consequences of Slavery in Two American Centuries* (Washington, D.C.: Civitas / CounterPoint, 1998); Kay S.

Hymowitz, *Marriage and Caste in America: Separate and Unequal Families in a Post-Marital Age* (Chicago, Ill.: Ivan R. Dee, Publisher, 2006). For critiques, see William P. Ryan, *Blaming the Victim* (New York: Vintage, 1972; revised 1976); Susan D. Greenbaum, *Blaming the Poor: The Long Shadow of the Moynihan Report on Cruel Images about Poverty* (New Brunswick, N.J.: Rutgers University Press, 2015).

3. See Margot Canaday, "Heterosexuality as a Legal Regime," in *The Cambridge History of Law in America,* vol. 3, ed. Michael Grossberg and Christopher Tomlins, *The Twentieth Century and After (1920–)* (Cambridge, England: Cambridge University Press, 2008), 456–458; David H. Onkst, " 'First a Negro . . . Incidentally a Veteran': Black World War Two Veterans and the G.I. Bill of Rights in the Deep South, 1944–1948," *Journal of Social History,* 31 (Spring 1998): 517–543; Catherine Fitch and Steven Ruggles, "Historical Trends in Marriage Formation," in *Ties That Bind: Perspectives on Marriage and Cohabitation,* ed. Linda Waite and Christine Bachrach (New York: Aldine de Gruyter, 2000), 59–88; M. Belinda Tucker and Claudia Mitchell-Kernan, eds., *The Decline in Marriage among African Americans: Causes, Consequences, and Policy Implications* (New York: Russell Sage Foundation, 1995); William A. Darity, Jr., and Samuel L. Myers, Jr., "Family Structure and the Marginalization of Black Men: Policy Implications," in Tucker and Mitchell-Kernan, *Decline in Marriage,* 263–308; Andrew J. Cherlin, *Labor's Love Lost: The Rise and Fall of the Working-Class Family in America* (New York: Russell Sage Foundation, 2014); Michael B. Katz, Mark J. Stern, and Jamie J. Fader, "The New African American Inequality," *Journal of American History,* 92 (June 2005): 75–108; Michael B. Katz, ed., *The "Underclass" Debate: Views from History* (Princeton, N.J.: Princeton University Press, 1993).

4. Fitch and Ruggles, "Historical Trends in Marriage Formation," Waite and Bachrach, eds., *Ties That Bind;* Tucker and Mitchell-Kernan, *The Decline in Marriage Among African Americans;* Darity and Myers, "Family Structure and the Marginalization of Black Men: Policy Implications"; Cherlin, *Labor's Love Lost;* Katz et al., "The New African American Inequality"; Katz, *The "Underclass" Debate.*

5. Katz et al., "The New African American Inequality."

6. Michelle Alexander, *The New Jim Crow: Mass Incarceration in the Age of Colorblindness* (New York: New Press, 2010), 6–7, 175, 271n7; Bruce Western, *Punishment and Inequality in America* (New York: Russell Sage, 2006); "1.5 Million Missing Black Men," *New York Times,* April 20, 2015.

7. "The Decline of Marriage and Rise of New Families," Pew Research Center, Washington, D.C., November 18, 2010, 9, http://www.pewsocialtrends.org/2010/11/18/the-decline-of-marriage-and-rise-of-new-families/. On cultural explanations and ties to slavery, see Patterson, *Rituals of Blood;* and Hymowitz, *Marriage and Caste in America.* For my response to similar arguments in the political discourse, see "Putting an Antebellum Myth to Rest," *New York Times,* August 2, 2011.

8. "The Decline of Marriage and Rise of New Families," 9; Andrew J. Cherlin, "Demographic Trends in the United States: A Review of Research in the 2000s," *Journal of Marriage and Family,* 72 (June 2010): 403–419; Cherlin, *Labor's Lost Love;* Charles Murray, *Coming Apart: The State of White America, 1960–2010* (New York: Crown Forum, 2012); Kathryn Edin and Maria Kefalas, *Promises I Can Keep: Why Poor Women Put Motherhood before Marriage* (Berkeley: University of California Press, 2005); Stephanie Coontz, *Marriage, a History: How Love Conquered Marriage* (New York: Penguin Books, 2006).

9. Katherine Franke, *Wedlocked: The Perils of Marriage Equality* (New York: New York University Press, 2015); Warner, *The Trouble with Normal;* Melissa Murray, "Marriage as Punishment," *Columbia Law Review,* 112 (January 2012): 101–168; Timothy Stewart-Winter, "The Price of Gay Marriage," *New York Times,* June 26, 2015; Aderson Bellegarde François, "To Go into Battle with Space and Time: Emancipated Slave Marriage, Interracial Marriage, and Same-Sex Marriage," *Journal of Gender, Race & Justice,* 13 (Fall 2009): 105–151.

Acknowledgments

The research for this book began while I was consulting documents from the Freedmen's Bureau in the files of the Freedmen and Southern Society Project at the University of Maryland. I was in the final stages of doing research for my book *To 'Joy My Freedom: Southern Black Women's Lives and Labors after the Civil War* as I was drawn to documents unraveling the resourceful ways in which recently freedpeople articulated their understandings of marriage and family. I culled these documents and incorporated a few in the book, but I knew then that I could not fully capture their richness there. I put the bulk of the materials that I collected aside, thinking I might write an article on marriage during the era of Reconstruction. But I eventually felt compelled to write a fuller portrayal of African American married lives than an article focused on a limited time frame could contain.

Therefore, my first thanks go to the editors of the Freedmen's Project for allowing me access to their unpublished records, but especially for the monumental contributions of their published multivolume documentary histories. These documentary histories have enabled me and so many other scholars to study the transition from slavery to freedom and to hear the formidable voices of enslaved and formerly enslaved people. Without their work, writing this book would have been far more difficult and far more impoverished of sources that only a collective research enterprise of many scholars working over decades could amass and publish. Leslie Rowland, the director of the project, provided critical editorial guidance in using the documents and keen insight about the historical context in conversations we had every time we met. Joseph Reidy and Steven Miller, who were on staff at times of my visits, were both very helpful in guiding me through the project's voluminous files.

I have accumulated more debts to many other people and institutions in researching and writing this book than I can fully account for here as this project unfolded over many years. Librarians and archivists provided significant support as I navigated manuscript collections and materials at the following institutions: Albert and Shirley Small Special Collections Library, University of Virginia; American Antiquarian Society; Amistad Research Center, Tulane University; Briscoe Center for American History, University of Texas, Austin; David M. Rubenstein Rare Book and Manuscript Library, Duke University; Fisk University Special Collections and Archives; Hill Memorial Library, Louisiana State University; Historical Society of Pennsylvania; Houghton Library at Harvard University; The Huntington Library; The Library Company of Philadelphia; Library of Congress; National Archives; Maryland State Archives; Missouri Historical Society; Moorland-Spingarn Research Center, Howard University; Schomburg Center for Research in Black Culture; Senator John Heinz History Center; South Carolina Department of Archives and History Center; South Carolina Historical Society; South Caroliniana Library, University of South Carolina, Columbia; Southern Historical Collection, Wilson Library, University of North Carolina, Chapel Hill; St. Louis City Hall; University of Notre Dame Archives; and Virginia State Library.

This book would not have been possible without the generous financial support of grants for leave time, travel, and other research-related expenses. I received a Rockefeller Foundation Humanities Fellowship from the Center for Research on Women, University of Memphis, and a Mary I. Bunting Institute Fellowship from the Radcliffe Institute for Advanced Study at Harvard University. At the University of Memphis, I was fortunate to have a close-knit circle of scholars: Beverly Bond, Andrea Simpson, Sharon Monteith, and Dennis Laumann. At the Radcliffe Institute, I enjoyed a feast of collegiality that has yet to be matched and continues to nourish me from Vincent Brown, Geraldine Brooks, Tony Horwitz, Stacy Kline, Vyvyane Loh, Claudia Olivetti, and, especially, Susan Terrio, Eva Troutt Powell, Salem Mekuria, and Betty Shamieh (my "sisters").

Most of the funding for this book came from my home institutions. I began the study while I was a faculty member at Carnegie Mellon University (CMU) and completed it after moving to Princeton University. At CMU, I had the support of chairs of the History Department, Steven Schlossman and Joe William Trotter. The Center for Africanamerican Urban Studies and the Economy (CAUSE), which Trotter directed and I served as the associate director of, also provided important resources. I was surrounded by scholars at CMU who were important to my community there: Edda Fields-Black, Kathy Newman, Stephanie Batiste, Susan Williams McElroy, Kiron Skinner, Caroline Acker, Wendy Goldman, Donna Harsch, Katherine Lynch, Scott Sandage, John Soluri, and Ayanah Moor.

At Princeton, my department chairs in History and African American Studies also provided enthusiastic support for my work: Jeremy Adelman, Bill Jordan, Valerie Smith, and Eddie Glaude. David Dobkin, the dean of the faculty who hired me, deserves my thanks as well. Colleagues throughout the university, especially Dirk Hartog, Sean Wilentz, Keith Wailoo, Emily Thompson, Regina Kunzel, Joshua Guild, Alison Isenberg, Wendy Belcher, Stacey Sinclair, Wallace Best, Daphne Brooks, Noliwe Rooks, Judith Weisenfeld, Carol Stack, and Mitchell Duneier, have been crucial interlocutors and fellow travelers. I have benefited from the affiliation of a fabulous group of postdoctoral fellows over the years in African American Studies whose conversations about their work and mine have been fruitful and inspiring: Sarah Haley, Carina Ray, Emmanuel Raymundo, Salamishah Tillet, Aaron Carico, Lyndon Gill, Jordan Camp, Jarvis McInnis, and Courtney Bryan. I had the honor of co-teaching a course with Bob Moses while he was our distinguished visiting fellow. We had a running two-person weekly seminar of our own as we prepped for our class, which gave me extended benefits of his wisdom.

Staff members at both CMU and Princeton have also provided support to make my professional life and research much easier: Nancy Aronson, April Peters, Dionne Worthy, Judith Hanson, Debora Macy, Brooke Fitzgerald, Carla Zimowsk, and Barbara Gershen. I have benefited from working with talented undergraduate and graduate students. Some provided crucial work as research assistants: Rebecca Kluchin, Kate Chilton, Terrence Johnson,

Wyliena Guan, Max Cuneo-Grant, Jennifer Jones, Keisha Blain, and Anne Kerth. Others energized me in our chats about our shared scholarly interests as their own projects blossomed: Jessie Ramie, Chris Florio, Alix Lerner, and Justene Hill. Students in my History of African American Families course allowed me to think out loud about the longue durée of the topics covered in this book and more.

Colleagues (and public audiences) pushed me to develop many ideas as I presented them in lectures and seminars at the following institutions: Africana Studies Program, George Washington University; Chabraja Center for Historical Studies and Center for African American History, Northwestern University; Institute on Ethnicity, Culture, and the Modern Experience, Rutgers University, Newark; School of Humanities, Ramapo College of New Jersey; College of Arts and Sciences and the Center for African, Black and Caribbean Studies, Adelphi University; Department of History and African, African American, and Diaspora Studies Program, University of North Carolina, Chapel Hill; Global History Institute, Georgetown University; Department of Feminist Studies, University of California, Santa Barbara; Rothermere American Institute, Oxford University; University of Connecticut Law School; Department of History, Purdue University; Franklin College of Arts and Sciences, Departments of History and African-American Studies, University of Georgia; Gender and Women's Studies Program and the Center for the Comparative Study of Race and Ethnicity, Connecticut College; Thomas Jefferson Foundation, Monticello, Virginia; Carter G. Woodson Institute, University of Virginia; Departments of American Studies and History, Notre Dame University; Department of History, University of California, Santa Cruz; Department of African and African-American Studies, Northwestern University; Department of History, Social History and the City Program, Cleveland State University; Center for African and African-American Studies, University of Texas, Austin; Department of History, University of Connecticut, Storrs; and Department of History, Duquesne University.

The people who have had the most direct impact on this book read chapters or the entire manuscript and gave me sharp and generous feedback at pivotal moments: Tony Horwitz, Sharon Dolovitch, David Sharpstein, Dylan Penningroth, Matt Karp, Jennifer Morgan, Dirk Hartog, Daniel Rodgers, Keith Wailoo, Cheryl Hicks, Kate Masur, and Nancy Cott. Some endured more rough drafts than anyone should be subjected to: Saidiya Hartman, Ula Taylor, and Donna Tatro. I could not have survived the ordeal of writing without them. The two anonymous readers for the press offered insightful comments that helped me make crucial final revisions of the manuscript.

Other colleagues and friends have provided support that took a variety of forms over the years: Deborah McDowell, Crystal Feimster, Kali Gross, (the late) Earnest Obadele-Starks, Darlene Clark Hine, Dana Frank, Diana Williams, and Eileen Boris. I am grateful to friends who fired me up at the start of every summer in our annual writers' retreat at Martha's Vineyard: Elsa Barkley Brown, Sharon Harley, and Julie Saville. My college "roomies" give me something to look forward to every year knowing that I will be rejuvenated by their company: Valerie Mosley, Rhonda Holmes, Kimberly Henderson, Stephanie Pinder-Amaker, and Royce A. Warrick. Other friends provided places to stay during research trips, cooked meals, went on excursions, played tennis, and created other (semi) raucous distractions: Jerma Jackson, Saidiya Hartman, Daphne Brooks, Valerie Smith, Robin D. G. Kelley, Lisa Gay Hamilton, Richard Pierce, Ula Taylor, Edda Fields-Black, the Highland Park tennis community in Pittsburgh, Gloria Hill, LaWade Garris, Terri Collier Snowden, Janette Webster, Dianne Johnson, Lisa Levenstein, Amy Campbell, Janis Runkle, Donna Tatro, and Ronald Rose. John Burns and Sandra Yarock provided key support as well.

I am grateful to the staff at Harvard University Press. Joyce Seltzer, my editor for the second time, helped me to envision writing this book; her close readings and incisive comments helped me to bring it to fruition. I could not have asked for a better copy editor than Christine Thorsteinsson, whose perceptive and judicious editing improved my prose.

And last, but not least, I thank my family for always being there. Cousin Bruce Hunter's research on the Hunter family tree and our conversations over the years about history have been indispensable. My siblings, in-laws, and nephews (their wives and children) keep me grounded: Alaric and Iris Hunter; Teretta and John King; Antwain, Armand, and Jessica Hunter; Alaric II and Angela Hunter; and Auriel Hunter. Being around my goddaughters Amanda Diamond and Kasia Hartman Miller brings me joy and keeps me on my toes. The little ones who this book is dedicated to: Anaya, Alaric III,

Armand II, and Avery, give me hope for the future. To those who have been there from the start, I am forever grateful: my aunt Hilda Harper Hutto; my dad, Willie James Hunter; and, in memory of my mother, Inell Harper Hunter, whose works on earth have left an indelible imprint and whose spirit lives on in us all. And to the ancestors I never knew, may their suffering and their sacrifices not be in vain.

Illustration Credits

I.1 Elbert County Marriage Book. Compliments of Bruce Hunter.

I.2 © Tera W. Hunter.

1.1 Timothy H. O'Sullivan (1840–1882), photographer. 1862. Civil War Photograph Collection, Library of Congress Prints and Photographs Division, Washington, D.C. (LC-DIG-ppmsc-00057)

1.2 Mary A. (shton) Livermore (1820–1905). *The Story of My Life: Or, The Sunshine and Shadow of Seventy Years . . . Superbly Illustrated with One Hundred and Twenty Engravings from Designs by Eminent Artists, Made Expressly for this Book* (Hartford, Conn.: A. D. Worthington & Co., Publishers, 1899) Figure 62, p. 257. Reproduction courtesy of Jean Blackwell Hutson Research and Reference Division, Schomburg Center for Research in Black Culture, The New York Public Library, Astor, Lenox and Tilden Foundations. (Image ID: 1232877)

1.3 Mary A.(shton) Livermore (1820–1905). *The Story of My Life: Or, The Sunshine and Shadow of Seventy Years . . . Superbly Illustrated with One Hundred and Twenty Engravings from Designs by Eminent Artists, Made Expressly for this Book* (Hartford, Conn.: A. D. Worthington & Co., Publishers, 1899), Figure 63, p. 258. Reproduction courtesy of Jean Blackwell Hutson Research and Reference Division, Schomburg Center for Research in Black Culture, The New York Public Library, Astor, Lenox and Tilden Foundations. (Image ID: 1232878)

2.1 *Frank Leslie's Illustrated Newspaper.* June 27, 1857. Library of Congress Prints and Photographs Division, Washington, D.C. (LC-USZ62-79305)

4.1 James F. Gibson (b. 1828), photographer. May 14, 1862. Library of Congress Prints and Photographs Division, Washington, D.C. (LC-DIG-cwpb-01005)

4.2 Thomas Waterman Wood (1823–1903), artist. 1865. Gift of Charles Stewart Smith, 1884. The Metropolitan Museum of Art, New York. (Accession Number: 84.12a)

4.3 Thomas Waterman Wood (1823–1903), artist. 1866. Gift of Charles Stewart Smith, 1884. The Metropolitan Museum of Art, New York. (Accession Number: 84.12b)

4.4 Thomas Waterman Wood (1823–1903), artist. 1866. Gift of Charles Stewart Smith, 1884. The Metropolitan Museum of Art, New York. (Accession Number: 84.12c)

4.5 Letters and Orders Received, Series 4180, Norfolk Virginia Assistant Subassistant Commissioner, Bureau of Refugees, Freedmen, and Abandoned Lands, Record Group 105, National Archives and Records Administration, Washington, D.C.

6.1 c. 1863–1865. Liljenquist Family Collection of Civil War Photographs, Library of Congress Prints and Photographs Division, Washington, D.C. (LC-DIG-ppmsca-36454)

6.2 c. 1861–1865. Detroit Institute of Arts / Founders Society Purchase, DeRoy Photographic Acquisition Endowment Fund and Coville Photographic Fund / Bridgeman Images

6.3 c. 1865. Randolph Linsly Simpson African-American Collection, Beinecke Rare Book & Manuscript Library, Yale University. (Image ID: 1032293)

6.4 Alfred Randolph Waud (1828–1891), artist. 1866. *Harper's Weekly*, V. 10, No. 496 (June 30, 1866), p. 412 (top). Library of Congress Prints and Photographs Division, Washington, D.C. (LC-USZ62-138383)

8.1 Census data from IPUMS-USA, University of Minnesota, www.ipums.org. Steven Ruggles, Katie Genadek, Ronald Goeken, Josiah Grover, and Matthew Sobek. Integrated Public Use Microdata Series: Version 6.0 [Machine-readable database]. Minneapolis: University of Minnesota, 2015. Data extracted and charts prepared from IPUMS and STATA by Donna Tatro with assistance from Ofira Schwartz-Soicher, Princeton University. Graph compiled by the author.

8.2 Census data from IPUMS-USA, University of Minnesota, www.ipums.org. Steven Ruggles, Katie Genadek, Ronald Goeken, Josiah Grover, and Matthew Sobek. Integrated Public Use Microdata Series: Version 6.0 [Machine-readable database]. Minneapolis: University of Minnesota, 2015. Data extracted and charts prepared from IPUMS and STATA by Donna Tatro with assistance from Ofira Schwartz-Soicher, Princeton University. Graph compiled by the author.

8.3 Census data from IPUMS-USA, University of Minnesota, www.ipums.org. Steven Ruggles, Katie Genadek, Ronald Goeken, Josiah Grover, and Matthew Sobek. Integrated Public Use Microdata Series: Version 6.0 [Machine-readable database]. Minneapolis: University of Minnesota, 2015. Data extracted and charts prepared from IPUMS and STATA by Donna Tatro with assistance from Ofira Schwartz-Soicher, Princeton University. Graph compiled by the author.

8.4 O. Pierre Havens (1838–1912), photographer. [ca. 1868–1900]. Robert N. Dennis Collection of Stereoscopic Views, The Miriam and Ira D. Wallach Division of Art, Prints and Photographs. The New York Public Library. (Image ID: G92F136_047ZF)

8.5 The Carbon Studio, Norfolk, Virginia, photographer. ca. 1900. Cabinet Card Collection, Schomburg Center for Research in Black Culture, Photographs and Prints Division. The New York Public Library. (Image ID: 31SCCAB)

8.6 Thomas William Burton (b. 1860). *What Experience Has Taught Me: An Autobiography of Thomas William Burton* (Cincinnati: Press of Jennings and Graham, ca. 1910). *Documenting the American South*, North American Slave Narratives Collection, First-Person Narratives of the American South Collection. Courtesy of the University of North Carolina at Chapel Hill Library.

Index